Between Jesus and the Market

BETWEEN JESUS AND

The Emotions That Matter in Right-Wing America

THE MARKET

LINDA KINTZ

DUKE UNIVERSITY PRESS   *Durham & London 1997*

CONTENTS

INTRODUCTION

We should read the Bible one more time. — Julia Kristeva

If life has always been to some extent incoherent, the question is precisely whether and how one manufactures lines between the fragments. — Lawrence Grossberg

Perhaps Money, in America, is a force so extreme as to become a religious force, a confusing deity, which demands either idolatry or a spiritual education. — Eva Hoffman

I turn on my answering machine and hear a very familiar voice. It's that of an older woman — soft, gentle, caring, almost shy, not at all groomed or practiced at leaving messages. She sounds very much like my well-loved grandmother, her voice showing her age as well as her sincerity, its tone the same as if she were telling about a meeting to help a local family in need. Instead she reminds me to come to a meeting of the Oregon Citizens Alliance on Thursday night at the Irving Grange, where Lon Mabon is to speak about a ballot initiative to ban gays from constitutional protection. This is the voice that troubles my critical analysis more than any other, far more than Lon Mabon's or Pat Robertson's, for while I am repelled by her involvement in this activism, something else happens to me as I listen. The tone and timbre of her voice, its immediate familiarity, speaks to me before her words do. Bringing me in too close, the voice won't let me keep my distance because its intimate familiarity — even though I have never met her — breaks down my defenses and tempts me to forget the content of her message. Though I think of that message as hateful, she doesn't sound at all the way I expect hate to sound.

   A different kind of problem is raised by another woman, whom I also cannot keep safely other, for she too troubles my stereotypes of the conservative woman. Here is a description of Bay Buchanan, who, along with Phyllis Schlafly, headed Patrick Buchanan's presidential campaign:

> "There's one presidential campaign in either party that has a woman in charge — and that's Pat Buchanan's," declares the woman in charge, Angela "Bay" Buchanan, sister, adviser and field general of the man whose family, faith and country campaign seem thoroughly inhospitable to women like, well, herself. She's a divorced woman raising her three young sons on her own (their pictures are the only softening touches in her office). She has a more-than-full-time job, nothing new for her, and her combative intensity rivals her brother's. If anything, this hyperefficient operative seems more like an exemplar of mainline feminism than the far right's idea of the traditional woman.
>
> She has put her political skills at the service of a nasty nativism. But she cannot be dismissed as a victim of false consciousness. She is a modern traditional woman. If that seems paradoxical, it is a paradox that is more and more a common fact of American life. It makes liberals uneasy. It doesn't seem to bother her brother at all.[1]

The activism of these two women, the motherly, sweet one and the antifeminist modern traditional one, has helped move American political discourse far to the right in the last decade, for it is only with women's help that the public-policy concerns of conservative economic theory and its attacks on government have been so powerfully collapsed into people's feelings about the family, or at least their own families. That collapse has also paradoxically helped establish a symbolic framework that returns manliness to the center of culture and brings the traditional morality of fundamentalist religion together with the fundamentalism of the market, the belief that the workings of the market provide the template of reality.

Yet though I am tempted to condescend to the woman whose voice is so familiar, or to rage at Bay Buchanan for being so good at what she does, many observers of contemporary politics have more simply just ignored them, in part because they have stereotypically underestimated the political import of issues that were historically, even if mistakenly, associated primarily with women: emotions, religion, and the family. And though many people were unprepared for the contemporary conservative resurgence, it was predictable to anyone who had observed with real curiosity, rather than ironic condescension, what conservative religious women were doing. The fact that their interests and activism were either trivialized or ignored, however, actually worked to their advantage, giving them a cover of invisibility for a wide range of effective organizing, which recalls the invisibility that descended over fundamentalists and evangelicals after the Scopes trial of 1925. At the time, secular observers presumed that their influence had been contained once and for all, only to discover that they had simply gone into hibernation to build up very effective church communities, grassroots organizations, and national networks, the results of which we see all around us.

Curiously, even after recognizing how far to the right conservative religious activism has moved politics in the last decade, many observers still ignore traditionalist women, an oversight that now takes the form of accepting at face value claims that the gender gap in electoral polls proves once and for all that conservatism does not appeal to women. But this prediction should give us pause. As one of the rising young stars of conservatism, Kellyanne Fitzpatrick, argues, many angry white females are in the process of making themselves heard: "There are women right above the poverty level but lower than middle-class who absolutely resent the welfare system because they believe it sucks up their tax dollars and goes to people who don't do what they do . . . go to work. The only thing they know about affirmative action is that in their minds it has cost their brother, father, son, boyfriend, or husband a promotion."[2] Though it's hard for many people to understand how women could be attracted to traditionalist conservatism, given its history of masculine privilege and its opposition to the social safety net, reproductive rights, and the ERA, this attraction becomes more comprehensible if it is assessed from the perspective of its own adherents, not simply from the outside.

Working through texts that are not often read by liberals and progressives (not that they are kept secret — they have just not been given much critical attention), this book will discuss both religious and secular traditionalist conservatism, which depend on a similar narrow interpretation of natural law, such as that articulated by Antonin Scalia or Robert Bork. First, it shows how traditionalist conservatism appeals to many women because it promises them community, a legitimate if contradictory sense of female agency, and the security of responsible male behavior. The book then follows the way this appeal to women is related to other messages to men through a discussion of the Christian men's movement, which counters feminist messages to women by reconstructing manhood as tender but virile and in the process remasculinizing Christ to reclaim religion from its association with women. Next, the book links these religious texts to the work of several secular conservative proponents of the free-market economy, both domestic and global. Here many of the tenets familiar from religious conservatism help shape market fundamentalism by sacrificing certain groups to the purity of the market while displacing attacks on workers, people of color, gays, and lesbians into the abstractions of economic theory. Finally, the book investigates the passions aroused by attempts to reconstruct manliness in relation to the legacy of Vietnam, the militarization of popular culture, and the totalizing conspiracy theories of a member of the far-right fringe. It ends with the relation between cultural anxieties about masculinity and the story of a young girl's pro-life activism. Though the traditionalist conservatives I discuss here are by no means homogeneous — and on one level, most would adamantly and justifiably disapprove of being associated in this way — on another level, they are linked by a passionate symbolic cohesion. It is the complexity and resonance of that cohesion that is the focus of this study.

The texts discussed here are part of a revisionary reconstruction of the role of the emotions in political life, possibly the most important achievement of the Right's culture wars, which have been waged to disengage passion from the popular culture of the sixties and associate it with the popular culture of traditional morality. While it was long apparent that the success of politicians like Ronald Reagan was in large part due to their ability to arouse emotional responses, nuanced discussions of the relation between politics and the emotions have often remained locked within a number of inadequate analytic frameworks. One of these frameworks associates emotional matters primarily with women, overlooking the emotional resonance of regional identifications and differences. Another underestimates the emotional resonance of charismatic Christianity for both men and women. And a last one, the feminist analysis of the hierarchy in Western philosophy that privileges masculine rationality over feminine emotion, is often inadequately historicized. While that hierarchy has certainly influenced the way that the emotions have been trivialized, at another level, men have powerfully drawn on emotions in their own interests, in the media construction of a cultural imaginary, as well as in the emotions of masculinity in relation to patriotism, property, the frontier, and guns.

That feminist critique, however, helped make visible another binary that hinders analyses of traditionalist conservatism by implying that rationality can be analyzed separately from irrationality, which has usually been associated with the emotions. This misses the most important point in a discussion of political identity of any kind, whether religious or secular, left or right: the fact that politics are not only about abstract reasoning or economic interests but also about belief, which combines the rational and the irrational, the conscious and the unconscious, thought and feelings, the abstract and the physical. Because traditionalist conservatives have understood this fact far better than many of their critics, the videotapes and books examined here can show the psychic and social frameworks in which two things come together: rational convictions (the kinds of reasons one can explain according to some logical framework) and social fantasy (the historically specific social imaginary of a culture that is for the most part unconscious and unremarked), which is more often simply "felt." Jacqueline Rose describes this psychic framework as a combination of convictions that "hover somewhere between an articulable belief" and the emotional and symbolic fantasy "in which collective self-imaginings take shape."[3]

It is the relation between articulable convictions and the collective self-imaginings of society, particularly in terms of popular culture, which needs to be defined much more broadly to include a wide range of publishing and media, not simply Hollywood and mainstream television. Academics and others who feel justifiably threatened by traditionalist conservatism are often unable to understand its appeal because we are not used to understanding beliefs that are not expressed according to our own scholarly expectations. By dismissing arguments that are not articulated in the terms with which we are familiar, we overlook the very places where politics come to matter most: at the deepest levels of the unconscious, in our bodies, through faith, and in relation to the emotions. Belief and politics are rational, and they are not.

Because of this doubleness, the book is organized according to a dialectic that will repeat itself over and over in these texts: the relation between a rich complexity of beliefs, on the one hand, and the reductive clarity available from a structure of vaguely symmetrical layers, on the other. Here a wide variety of groups can retain many of their differences while they are loosely joined under the umbrella of a remarkably clear and comprehensible cosmology, in which certain things can be changed on earth even if the general hierarchy or order cannot, because, like fate, the natural order is beyond the range of human effort; it is in the hands of God. This is a cosmology built on a narrow interpretation of natural law, in which the only natural form of sexual activity occurs within the monogamous traditional family, where gender differences and heterosexuality are absolute. These are fundamental elements of a universal moral order, its truths absolute, not relative or situational, with ethical behavior based at the deepest level on the Ten Commandments. God's "driver's manual" for human behavior. As this book will show, this is argued not only by religious conservatives, but by secular figures who have framed the policy language of free-market conservatism advocated by Newt Gingrich and the Republicans elected in 1994.

Though there are many permutations to this belief in both secular and religious conservatism, its claims to clarity rest on a structure that was already a part of American mythology and might be visualized as a closed set of concentric circles stacked one on top of the other and ascending heavenward: God, property, womb, family, church, free market, nation, global mission, God. Their symmetrical relation is glued together both by the symbolic figuration of the proper woman and by her activism, though the contradictions that risk unsettling this symmetry are obvious. Equally obvious, however, is the difficulty of trying to convince those who believe in this structure that such contradictions really matter, for attempts to do so rarely address the moral and emotional universe of its adherents. Understanding the things that matter in this moral universe is easier if the reader is exposed to their emotional appeal and the needs they address.

This leads to a concept that is very important to this study: resonance. In its general acoustical sense, resonance is defined as the intensification and prolongation of sound produced by sympathetic vibration. In the context of this study, resonance refers to the intensification of political passion in which people with very different interests are linked together by feelings aroused and organized to saturate the most public, even global, issues. Resonance is the almost ineffable element that constantly threatens to collapse church into state when politics are made (traditional) family-like: "In the beginning God created the family," in the words of Texas congressman Tom DeLay.[4] Here the traditional family takes precedence over both the individual right of privacy and the individual freewheeling capitalist, while it provides a metaphoric resolution of the inherent tensions between cultural traditionalism and economic dynamism. These are resolved, as Allen Hunter argues, in a "systematically gendered view of the world. . . . The organic unity of the family resolves male egoism and female selflessness into a smoothly functioning expression of divine intent."[5]

In this conservative cosmology, resonance is created by familiarization, which the culture wars are all about, really. In fierce opposition to the influence of feminism, traditionalist conservatism has reconstructed the primacy of a narrow definition of moral culture and the family so that it is the mother's responsibility to train children in familiarity. That is, her intimate training of them can repress critical distance. By so doing, it grounds a political system in things that are already familiar, excluding difference from the earliest moments of child rearing. Children are raised to feel and experience their own sensuality, their own bodies, in very particular ways, and to look for and find others whose feelings, values, and identities are intimately familiar to them. While the most basic element in this construction of familiarity is the definition of woman primarily as mother and man as father and head of the family, its corollary is the claim that anyone outside the traditional family is illegitimate, in the legal, historical, and metaphysical sense of the word. It is here that the rational arguments of familiarization are made to work in the very matter of the body, where they will resonate.

David W. Murray shows how the religious and secular lessons of intimate familiarity come together at the highest levels of public policy in his article "Poor Suffering Bastards: An Anthropologist Looks at Illegitimacy," in *Policy Review,* the journal of the Heritage Foundation. This is the powerful corporate-funded think tank that conducted initiation sessions for the newly elected freshman Republicans in 1994 and published a 570-page candidate-education guide called *Issues '96* as a primer for conservative candidates in the 1996 elections. The Heritage Foundation has also been instrumental in providing public-policy language for such things as welfare reform, immigration policy, and tax reform. As Murray writes,

> Legitimacy is nothing more nor less than the orderly transfer of social meaning across the generations. . . . Remember that children are the ultimate illegal aliens. They are undocumented immigrants to our world, who must be socialized and invested with identity, a culture, and an estate. By conferring legitimacy, marriage keeps this process from becoming chaos.[6]

The power of familiarization can be seen in the way this thoroughly public discourse already presumes what it advocates, as Murray draws on the familiarity of those whose moral universe begins with the traditional family. Its resonance, like my memory of my grandmother, is so deep as to be in most ways inarticulable and readily available for displacement onto political issues if a politics is able to frame its rhetoric in the right way.

Resonance and familiarity are sealed by linking the passions for what matters in the family to national identity, and for many, the Declaration of Independence functions as the nation's statement of faith, which immediately engages church and family with the nation whose founding is described as having been inspired by God. A single sentence in the Declaration fuses the sacred and the political, bringing the intimate experience of the family and everyday life, national political passions, property, and eternal values together with resounding poetic impact, sealed by a flag: "We hold these truths to be self-evident, that all men are created equal, that they are endowed by their Creator with certain unalienable Rights, that among these are Life, Liberty and the pursuit of Happiness." The quasi-sacred nature of this form of populism, which is elicited by the phrase "We, the people," now underlies the claim that human rights are defined by a narrow interpretation of natural law and the traditional family: those rights are "unalienable," those meanings "self-evident." As Peter Marshall Sr. told the Christian Coalition convention in the fall of 1995, "America is God's project . . . the only nation in the world deliberately founded on the Bible" and dedicated to Jesus Christ by the Pilgrims. Because the nation is now threatened by the greatest crisis it has ever faced, "national revival and restoration of Biblical principles in every area of life" must be the goal of Christian activists. We have, says Marshall, "no King but King Jesus."[7]

Adding to the resonance of traditionalist conservatism, both religious and secular, is the apocalyptic narrative, whose influence on the myths of American history is not new. The features of the apocalyptic narrative are easy to recognize when they are taken to their limit in stories of purifying, cleansing fire and violence, such as Hal Lindsey's apocalyptic nuclear vision in *The Late Great Planet Earth* or David Koresh's predictions. But in a broader and less obvious way, the apocalyptic narrative also organizes other stories traditionalist conservatism tells about itself, for its meaning is dependent on a clear beginning, represented by Creation, and a clear ending, or the guarantee of an escape from death or nonbeing: "If we know where we came from and where we're going, it is not that difficult to know what we should be doing in the interim," as an orthodox Jewish rabbi, Daniel Lapin, tells the Christian Coalition, of which he is a leading member.[8]

The generic apocalyptic narrative includes an eschatology, a discourse about the events that will lead up to the last days. Michael O'Leary argues that apocalyptic narratives share certain characteristics: a sense of history as a divinely predetermined totality, a sense of pessimism about the present and the conviction of an imminent crisis, and a belief in the judgment of evil and the triumph of good.[9] They also imply the eventual triumph of a transcendent theological meaning which provides a rhetorical solution to the problem of evil on both a rational and a mythical level. And as Elaine Pagels argues, "The faith that Christ has conquered Satan assures Christians that in their own struggles the stakes are eternal, and victory is certain. Those who participate in this cosmic drama cannot lose."[10]

O'Leary also sorts his archive of apocalyptic narratives into the dramatic genres of tragedy and comedy. Tragic ones take the form of apocalyptic scenarios, like those of Lindsey or Koresh, which are characterized by ominous predictions of a violent, catastrophic end of the world at Armageddon for which the only reaction is prayer and waiting. Comic narratives, which are not humorous but utopian, in the sense that they imply a closure based on reconciliation and redemption, include the postmillenialist interpretation now held by people like Pat Robertson. Robertson's pragmatic theological shift to a less cataclysmic version of the apocalyptic narrative was related to his campaign for the presidency and his more recent attempts to set the nation's political agenda. Robertson's modernized apocalyptic interpretation, sanitized for public discourse by Ralph Reed Jr., holds that Christ can return only if born-again Christians prepare the conditions for the Second Coming rather than simply waiting to be raptured out of harm's way. As Robertson said to members of the Coalition, drawing on the resonance that joins the religious and the political, "The tide is turning and the victory is coming in sight for the things we believe in."[11] The subtext here, of course, is provided by Robertson's less publicized statements, in which he continues to warn of an apocalyptic end if conservative religious believers do not determine the course of American politics.[12]

The power of apocalyptic and millennial narratives on both left and right (religious, environmental, revolutionary) also depends on fear, and because fear is undependable, it must be sustained, O'Leary argues. As an example, Jeane Kirkpatrick shows how to keep fear alive on a global scale, as she takes the familiar conservative support of militarization and reconfigures it in a post–Cold War world. Earlier this century, she argues, every outbreak of violence came as a surprise, orchestrated by new men who had previously been unknown to the political class. Now, in a world that is still just as full of invisible danger, we must be constantly on guard: "No one knows where, why, when it will come."[13]

One last feature of this structure of clarity is the insistence that language is inherently simple, transparent, and clear, because it is at bottom linked to the natural order of the cosmos. In this view, true words or metaphors, such as "woman," "man," "nation," "family," are those that match God's natural order, because his inerrant natural law precedes all interpretation. It is not hard to see how this concept of the inerrant, self-evident, unalienable link between language and the natural order can be called on to ground the social contract in the symmetrical structure of homologies described earlier: one kind of family, community, market, nation, global mission, and so on.[14] Within this powerful structure, America was named by the Founding Fathers, whose religious intentions and discernment produced a political document that almost miraculously came to match the unalienable truths of God's natural law.

The clarity of traditional conservatism is thus paradoxically increased by its strategic but passionate vagueness. And such passionate vagueness finds a powerful match with media culture, in which "clarity" can be achieved through simplification and emotion, as can the simple logic of profit and the bottom line. Differences come together within an emotional resonance under the umbrella of a relatively simple political framework. They are then crucially mediated by the passionate simplifications of secular figures such as Rush Limbaugh or religious figures such as Pat Robertson and Paul Weyrich, with their extensive media networks. Such movements produce highly coherent meanings; however, the point of this study is to describe that coherence in a way that avoids claiming that it is conspiratorial. For it works much more loosely — and powerfully — by means of the resonance made possible both by its clarity and by its ability to recognize the libertarian insistence on (certain familiar kinds of) individual differences.

Traditionalist conservative culture's attempt to link the public to the private and reconstruct manhood rests uneasily not simply on the mother but upon the *tie* between mother and child. And as we already know and will see again, a woman's insistence on control of her own body threatens not only the conservative social contract, but the liberal one as well. The aim of this discussion will be to allow a variety of texts and videotapes to elaborate the stakes of the culture wars of contemporary traditionalist conservatism, stakes described with concision by Julia Kristeva: "Where life and discourse come together, that is where the destiny of subjectivity is caught up in the claims of civilization. Today, the pill and the Pope know this indeed."[15]

ii.

In bringing together these very different kinds of issues, this book traces various layers of the symmetrical framework of family, nation, and God. Chapter 1, "Sacred Intimacy," includes a discussion of three books by women, Beverly LaHaye's *Desires of a Woman's Heart,* Connie Marshner's *Can Motherhood Survive? A Christian Looks at Social Parenting,* and Linda Weber's *Mom: You're Incredible!* to follow their antifeminist reconstruction of motherhood as a heroic choice for women as proper mothers. This revalorization of women's work is in part a reaction by many conservative women to the misogyny of secular culture and its contempt for women and mothers. This revalorization also shows how important women's involvement in child care is to teaching the lessons of familiarity and sacred intimacy.

Chapter 2, "The Heart of the Matter," broadens that description of women's work through Lawrence Grossberg's description of conservative popular culture's role in moving the center of American politics far to the right. What he calls the "contemporary national popular" depends on the conservative reconstruction of "mattering" in reaction to the popular culture of the 1960s and sexual liberation. This is followed by a discussion of a book of marriage advice by Tim and Beverly LaHaye, *The Act of Marriage,* which articulates the intimacy of the sexual body through the concept of the heart, which joins head and body together in a sensual, organic, sacred body. That body and its absolute sexual difference are defined by natural law grounded in a reading of the Bible based on inerrancy, which structures a world whose contours are determined by daily personal and group Bible readings, citations, and study. The chapter also includes short discussions of a videotape on abstinence for teenagers, *Wait for Me;* the second *Gay Agenda* videotape, which focuses on anti-discrimination curricula in public education; and a videotape from the Christian Coalition's School Board Training Seminar.

Chapter 3, "Kitchen Table Politics: The Folking of America," is a discussion of the effects of the proper mother's influence in the public sphere when she takes on an activist role. The texts include a training manual for prayer chapter leaders in Concerned Women for America; a videotape from the Christian Coalition Leadership School Video Training Series in which Rebecca Hagelin teaches women and men how to be media spokespersons; a videotaped speech in which Kay Coles James, a national

leader of conservative women and an African American, situates her conservatism within the context of the African American church in the South
and its traditions of storytelling and oratory; and several pamphlets by
Star Parker, the founder of an organization that teaches Christian entrepreneurship in South Central Los Angeles. The chapter then turns to
two members of the Oregon Citizens Alliance, Loretta Neet and Kathy
Phelps, in order to follow the logics of constitutional activism and property rights, which also rely on an absolutist definition of the family. It
concludes with an important link between religious activism and secular
politics: Elizabeth Dole's speech to the Christian Coalition in 1994. Dole
describes her own very passionate relationship to her southern Christian
grandmother and to her religion, but she does so in a place that allows
that personal witness to become an instrument to be used by one of the
most powerful political organizations in America. Thus the stage upon
which she speaks her intimate and personal story helps turn that sacred
intimacy into traditionalist conservative public policy. And finally, this
chapter shows the significance of women's work in producing homogeneous communities of the same kind of people, a phenomenon that also
manifests itself in the growth of gated communities, the abandonment of
cities as people move to the suburbs and small towns, as the successful
secede from their public responsibilities.

Chapter 4, "Tender Warriors," is a detailed discussion of a book by a
man active in the Christian men's movement, Stu Weber, entitled *Tender
Warrior: God's Intention for a Man*. Weber, who served in the Green Berets
in Vietnam and then founded a large evangelical church in the suburbs of
Portland, Oregon, draws on popular discourses of military friendship and
television westerns to teach Christian men how to develop a sense of
intimacy, both in their families and with their male friends. This is an
intimacy that reclaims virile "tenderness" from effeminate "softness,"
while it also reclaims Christ himself from effeminacy and pacifism and
turns him back into a manly and militant peacemaker with a sword. The
discussion also draws on a collection of essays published by the Promise
Keepers, the rapidly growing evangelical Christian men's organization
founded by Bill McCartney, the former football coach at the University of
Colorado and one of the leaders of that state's anti-gay-rights movement.
The sense of a dynamic, explosive revival on the part of the men's movement is partially enabled by the revisionary reading of the apocalyptic
narrative that gives Christians a sacred duty to engage in political activism
and bring about the return of Christ.

Chapter 5, "Postmodern Hunters and Gatherers," discusses a book that functions as a pivot between the sacred masculinity of Christian warriors and the secular, free-market version of that masculinity, the two linked by a "sexual constitution" guaranteed by natural law and the Bible. That book is George Gilder's *Men and Marriage,* formerly titled *Sexual Suicide.* In it he describes absolute sexual difference in terms of the archaic nature of men as hunters, women as nurturers, and then shows how the Industrial Revolution and capitalism, now generically seen as the source of universal values, must culturally reconstruct the nuclear family and masculine privilege on which they depend. Gilder, like Newt Gingrich and Margaret Thatcher, finds inspiration in the discipline and hard work of the middle class in the last century, and George Mosse's concept of respectability, which brought together nation and class in the eighteenth and nineteenth centuries, helps show the reasons for his nostalgia. By drawing on "moments of eternity" reflected by patriotism, religion, and nature, the middle class countered the frightening effects of the social and technological revolutions it had itself instigated. The consequence of respectability, argues Mosse, a historian of the roots of European fascism, was the exclusion of the tolerance of difference.

Chapter 6, "Riding the Entrepreneurial Frontier," is a reading of several chapters by Newt Gingrich, George Gilder, and Arianna Huffington in Gingrich's college textbook, *Readings in Renewing American Civilization.* It also includes a discussion of Rush Limbaugh's *See, I Told You So* and his "Why Liberals Fear Me," published in the Heritage Foundation's *Policy Review.* This chapter shows how the story of dynamic trickle-down economics, as espoused by Gingrich, Gilder, Huffington, and Limbaugh, is told according to a familiar American narrative, Frederick Jackson Turner's thesis that American identity depends on the existence of a frontier. It also links the question of sexual performance raised by Gilder in his discussion of masculine sexuality to economic performance as the basic unit of the creation of wealth and to a concept of a frontier whose organic resources are ideas and capital. The discussion of Limbaugh shows how he draws on the skepticism of the postmodern audience in order to use the resources of postmodernity in reconstructing a place of absolute truth, a media performance guaranteed by the logic of the market. Huffington's contribution brings the exhilarated affluent immigrant's view of American possibility together with a passionate, free-flying combination of New Age and Christian religion as she translates the Twelve Steps of Alcoholics Anonymous directly into the call for a capitalist recovery and revival.

Chapter 7, "God's Intentions for the Multinational Corporation: See-ing Reality True," includes a reading of two books by Michael Novak, of the American Enterprise Institute: *Toward a Theology of the Corporation* and *This Hemisphere of Liberty.* Novak is a conservative Catholic scholar who brings together biblical advice about poverty and the admonition to create wealth in a revisionary reading of the corporation as the key to the unique nature of American democracy, arguing that it must be exported, especially to Latin America and Eastern Europe. Claiming that econo-mists have not yet understood the way Christ revolutionized the concept of political economy, he develops a theoretical basis to explain that con-cept by arguing that corporations have been created in the image of God. This match is made clear by the fact that the essence of God is creation, which, in the creation of wealth, is also the essence of the corporation. The fundamental export, in Novak's view, is a cultural one: the export of reality, of the truth of the universal nature of democratic capitalism. The chapter also includes a short discussion of the graduate catalog of Pat Robertson's Regent University to show the direct relationship between economics and missionary training, evangelical belief and training in law, and missionary training and the most sophisticated media facilities and resources.

The closing chapter, "Warriors and Babies," shows how the clear, abso-lutist apocalyptic narrative is brought together with a certain interpreta-tion of the U.S. Constitution, establishing an exact match between the legal requirements for human rights, on the one hand, and the moral and sexual requirements of a narrowly conceived version of natural law, on the other. The Constitution is thus interpreted in legal and sexual terms at one and the same time, the two terms to be kept together by force, if necessary. In showing the impact of traumatized masculinity on that in-terpretation, this chapter turns to the effects of Vietnam on concepts of warrior masculinity. After a discussion of Robert Timberg's *The Night-ingale's Song,* I follow James William Gibson's study, *Warrior Dreams,* in which he traces the influence of Vietnam on the paramilitarization of popular culture reflected in Hollywood movies, the founding of *Soldier of Fortune* magazine, the popularity of war games, and the explosive market in imported guns. He also shows how that paramilitarization has influ-enced recreation, in the form of paint-ball games, which have also legiti-mated the intimate link between masculine identity and guns in both paramilitary popular culture and conspiracy theories. That is followed by a reading of a book by an extremist religious writer and conspiracy theorist, Texe Marrs. His book *Big Sister Is Watching You* provides literal clarity in a perfectly symmetrical logic in which it is not only Jews who control the world but women — in particular, aggressive women coded as lesbians. This linkage between the Jew and the Dyke produces a terrifyingly monstrous and omnipotent She/He who controls the new world order.

The final chapter also includes a brief discussion of a training workshop given by Randall Terry to a militia group, the U.S. Taxpayers Party. The leader of that group, Matthew Trewhella, also the head of the Missionaries to the Pre-Born, teaches a lesson about the construction of intimacy in which he advises his audience about the intimate training of their own children in terms of the sacred mandate to learn to use guns. This lesson then brings the book back to the questions of women and intimacy with which it began, in the discussion of a book called *Gianna,* the story of a seventeen-year-old girl who survived her mother's botched attempt to abort her and who now speaks at pro-life rallies all over the country. While the biography reveals the very moving intimacy and naïveté of a young girl, as well as her deep personal sense of the moral duty to save unborn children, it is also juxtaposed to the exploitation of that message by groups like Human Life International, headed by Father Paul Marx and linked to far-right extremist groups. Gianna also embodies the postmodern deconstructed subject — she did, after all, survive her own abortion and was not really born, in the conventional sense, a literal subject-in-process. My discussion of Gianna will thus see her as the embodiment of the violent battle over the undecidability of naming — of America, the fetus, the woman, and, perhaps most dangerously, the man. Her story and the stages upon which she has told it show how fraught this intensely personal and violently public question of abortion is and how it inspires violent attempts to enforce an absolutist sexual and legal Constitution, which establishes the most rigid version of natural law as the foundation of the state. And finally, Gianna's story will bring me back to the message on my answering machine where public and private have become fused. This study of resonance, of the saturation of the most wide-ranging political issues with intimate emotions, will begin and end with the motherly voice.

ONE

Sacred Intimacy

Our world is reeling from the ravages of feminist rebellion against
God and God-given authorities. — Beverly LaHaye

We learn identity letter by letter. — Gayatri Spivak

The remarkably clear yet thoroughly contradictory framework of mother,
family, property, nation, and God links together a wide variety of groups
and discourses, sealed by the resonance of a very particular form of familiarity. This chapter deals with the most important element in that familiarity: the belief that the fundamental definition of a woman is her identity as a nurturant mother. In postmodernity, because women are able to
do all kinds of other things, too, such a belief has to be learned, and
somebody has to teach it. Though conservative women have been involved in the more obvious political activities of monitoring school
boards, circulating initiative petitions, distributing voters' guides to support political candidates, and running for office, their most important
political contribution may well be their role in the construction of feelings
of sacred intimacy. The deepest, most inarticulable feelings are those
learned prior to the entry into language by means of the caregiving of
mothers. That intimate caregiving begins to structure what, at birth, is
primarily an unformed mixture of drives and the earliest forms of psychic
identity. It will be into these networks of physical and psychical organization that language will later be inscribed.

The contradictions that might otherwise trouble this symmetrical
structure can seem irrelevant, because familiarity has neutralized them
through *affect,* through the strong emotions and feelings that are experienced as enigmatic and inarticulable. These are the kinds of feelings that

are most deeply ordered prior to the child's learning to speak; this cultural ordering might be referred to by the term Julia Kristeva uses, the "semiotic level of culture." The enigmatic nature of feelings, the fact that they are considered to be unreadable, has a long history, which means that we are far less able to analyze and understand feelings than we are to differentiate among complex abstract systems of thought. In some ways, as we try to understand contemporary American culture, we find that the critical theories we are using have yet to be adequately historicized to fit an American context. The charismatic religions and regional cultural differences of the American South, Midwest, and West have never fit comfortably into a European model that saw reason to be opposed to feeling in a binary that privileged the unemotional, supposedly objective perspective. Similarly, the American relationship to property has a very different emotional resonance than does the European one, which originated in a culture in which the ownership of land was related to aristocracy. In part because of secular analyses that have too often coded feeling and spirituality as irrational and feminized, religious conservatism and its understanding of media have been able to appropriate feeling in the interests of masculine privilege in a way that often leaves their secular critics unable to understand quite what happened. Part of what happened is that absolutist Christianity has situated meaning in the heart of Christ rather than the head of Man, continuing a rhetorical tradition that has long been a part of American religious discourse.

In following lessons about that heart and its influence on what matters, I begin with a discussion of *Desires of a Woman's Heart,* a book by Beverly LaHaye, who founded Concerned Women for America in 1979 in reaction to NOW's claim to speak for American women, an important event in what conservative women saw as the disruption of the true American story. CWA has long claimed to have six hundred thousand members, though exact numbers are hard to come by. LaHaye's book is a kind of informal textbook designed for use in the prayer chapters that are the grassroots units of CWA's structure. As in many books of this kind, produced by Christian publishing houses and designed for group use, at the end of each chapter is a set of questions for reflection and discussion, extending the personal space of prayer and biblical discernment out to the influence of a larger community of believers. The groundwork is also laid for everyday life's homogeneity and sameness, as loving familiarity is made available to others but only *so long as* they are converted to its terms.[1]

LaHaye's contribution to the pedagogy of familiarity begins with basic terminology as she divides women into two groups: true women and radical feminists. Here feminists, increasingly marginalized as radical and extremist, are described as women who want to exclude all gender difference in order to be just like men; who want to shrug off all authority whatsoever; who want to jettison all family responsibilities in their careerism; who hate men; who are responsible for "rampant individualism"; who insist on abortion on demand; who have misled men into thinking they should not respect women; who have destroyed all civility and courtesy in public life; who have become so masculine in their appearance that few men are attracted to them; who, because of their selfishness, want only self-advancement; who have caused sexual harassment because they insisted on sexual liberation; who confuse the roles of men and women; and whose victory will rob us of "all love, compassion, gentleness, and warmth in all of our relationships." (73) The cultural disintegration that must be addressed and remedied will thus have been brought about because of a central problem: the confusion of gender identities that should be kept absolutely separate. It is this confusion that causes homosexuality, divorce, sexual abuse, promiscuity, social awkwardness, emotional distress, and suicide. It has also led directly to a much larger national crisis of identity, for just as individuals require a firm, stable identity based on absolute gender differences legitimated by God, so too does the nation. Unless they are grounded in God's inerrant Word, both nation and individual are left with a void at the center of their identities, and, like Ralph Reed, LaHaye draws on Pascal to describe this void: "Before we knew Christ, we were not complete. We had a God-shaped vacuum within our souls."[2]

This version of feminism will be unrecognizable to most feminists. Yet to understand its appeal, and to assess why this appeal to many women seems stronger than that of feminism, it is important to follow LaHaye's text on her own terms, for if pointing out empirical errors worked, then all the time and effort taken by feminists to do just that would have succeeded. Something else engages the women who are LaHaye's audience. First of all, and most obvious to someone, like me, from a small town in the Bible Belt of West Texas, is the familiarity, even the ordinariness, to my eyes, of LaHaye's middle-class appearance; the respectable, fashionable though not flashy, style of dress; and the soft, gentle tone of voice, her sweetness. It may be, as the Republican pollster Frank Lunz has always known, that the place to assess the popular sense of "America," now that technology has reduced the dominance of urban culture, is in a small town, an imaginative space too many academics seem unable to enter.

The demographics of this appeal are both representational and regional, for this kind of niceness and respectability link the small towns in the West, Midwest, and South to the mythologized nonspace of the suburbs. The West, in particular California, where Beverly and Tim LaHaye helped found the Moral Majority and where the campaign to elect Ronald Reagan president originated, has helped shape the rise of radical conservatism. Richard White, in an aptly titled history, *"It's Your Misfortune and None of My Own": A New History of the American West,* traces the West's influence on national politics after World War II.[3] In particular, political parties in the West long ago became less important than the marketing of candidates, as single-issue politics of the initiative and referendum process were linked to the politics of personality and anticommunism. Trademarks of western politics, they became trademarks of national politics in general. In addition, the trend toward political campaigns run by public-relations firms originated after the war with the involvement of Campaigns Incorporated of California, which hired itself out to interest groups rather than to political parties. In the mass-marketing and advertising strategies of such campaigns, candidates began to tailor themselves according to marketing strategies rather than political positions: "Again, the West created what would be a national pattern." (576)

California's weak political party system also allowed for the growth of the power of lobbyists. Though prior to the 1950s westerners strongly supported the New Deal, by 1960 the liberal majority had dissipated. In contrast to northerners and southerners, westerners were already more focused on individual opportunities and less interested in a government that could mediate between social groups or provide services individuals could not provide for themselves. And importantly, as we will see in chapters 4, 5, and 6 on the continuing influence of Frederick Jackson Turner's frontier mythology, "although couched in terms of frontier self-reliance and older western self-images, western individualism in its most recent form is very much the product of an urban, prosperous, middle-class West whose very existence was the result of federal programs and policies." (576) White describes the rise of the New Right in the West as a "coalition of resentments" against the federal government, against moral laxity, against the social justice and cultural movements of the 1960s, and against immigrants, in particular after the Immigration Act of 1965, which changed the ethnic mix of immigrants by dropping the system of national quotas. While earlier immigration had been largely European, this change led to an increase in immigrants from Mexico, the Philippines, Taiwan, Hong Kong, Korea, and India. The results of that change could be seen most clearly in western cities.

But the feature of westernization of most significance for popular conservatism and popular culture is what White calls "plain folks Americanism." This is an identity that, while often racist, was also influenced by other factors, such as the populist and libertarian traditions of the West and South and Pentecostalism, with its strong beliefs in traditional values, personal responsibility, and the work ethic. Though earlier populist attacks on those who did not work had been focused on elites, those attacks shifted in the sixties to an attack on the minority poor and radical whites. These traditions joined the sensual and spiritual traditions of fundamentalist and evangelical religions, whose importance in Southern California Nancy Ammerman traces, to the emotional traditions of country and western music:

> Both western religious fundamentalism and country and western music had their strongest roots in Texas and Oklahoma and among the California migrants from those states. Plain folks Americanism spread easily to working-class whites who were neither migrants from the rural West nor Protestants. They, too, shared the strong anticommunism of the rural emigrants and were sensitive to accusations of communist influence. What had once been a despised regional culture became an expression first of white working-class culture and then of a larger political movement, the New Right. (601)

The way such plain folks Americanism gets translated into the entrepreneurial terms and popular culture of people who are neither western nor Pentecostal nor working class nor lovers of country music will occupy several later chapters. Though in that earlier period, plain folks Americanism was hostile to minority and feminist activism, it nevertheless drew on a similar postmodern language of equality, special status, and identity politics to describe itself in terms of self-discipline and hard work. As such, it offered a sense of group pride and special status for the ordinary folks considered to be the real core of society. Plain folks Americanism was thus linked to "invented, borrowed, and inherited traditions" to allow ordinary people, mostly white, to claim their status as real Americans. Ronald Reagan's election as governor of California, in White's analysis, was made possible by tapping the roots of this Americanism, taking advantage of the construction of a pure center threatened by objects of fear and disgust: "He had found the necessary enemies. Reagan had made urban demonstrators, striking farm workers, black rioters, radical students, criminals, and wasteful bureaucrats from Johnson's War on Poverty his targets. He lined them up like ducks in a shooting gallery. Each time he shot, he won big political prizes." (603)

Another characteristic of the West that will be important to this study is the way attacks on government and postmodernity were made in terms of a West that never existed:

> Those Californians who most ardently believed in these "traditional" values were often themselves newcomers to the state. The New Right sank its strongest roots among the modern immigrants to the West who came not as a part of groups or to seek utopian ends but for individual advancement. These were the residents of the suburbs, particularly the suburbs of southern California, which were the fastest-growing and most rapidly changing section of the United States in the 1960's. Southern California was a land of migrants who were not particularly Western in origin. . . . It would have been difficult to find a less likely site for a defense of traditional values.
>
> But the rapidity of change in southern California was, in fact, the point. The New Right prospered in southern California because the pace of change was frenetic. In southern California, except when race was concerned, boundaries seemed permeable. Ethnic and religious division mattered less than elsewhere. People were mobile; community ties were weak; and the aspirations that brought migrants to the regions were overwhelmingly individualistic and material, not much different in fact than those that had prompted the gold rush more than a century earlier. Spectacular success always seemed possible, and that made failure all the more demeaning. There was no failure as bitter as western failure.
>
> The California New Right wanted it both ways. They wanted the opportunity for material success unhampered by government controls, but they wanted government to halt social change and return society to an imagined past. (606)

And it was not only the Right that was influenced by the West. The suburban white middle class also produced radicals, hippies, New Agers, who, like the radical conservatives and libertarians, viewed social problems in individual terms.[4]

Ronald Reagan's significance to the rise of the New Right also had to do with his persona as both actor and corporate representative, his beliefs perhaps as much about expediency as about deep belief in traditional values, White argues. Such utilitarianism and the performative abilities it depends on currently define Newt Gingrich's political performances. And the very concept of utilitarianism will be central to many later New Right discussions of culture. Reagan tapped deeply into the West's resentment of the East, even though the East was no longer Wall Street but Washington and even though his support came, in fact, from an informal "millionaires' club" of Southern California businessmen. Reagan's success was also directly linked to the growth in the 1970s of religious broadcasting and the evangelical revival of the 1970s; 50 million adult Americans were reported to have had born-again conversion experiences in 1976, one of those being Ronald Reagan.

Tim LaHaye, then of San Diego, was a member of the original board of the Moral Majority, formed after meetings with Richard Viguerie, Paul Weyrich, Ed McAteer, and Howard Phillips in hopes of splitting the Catholic vote within the Democratic Party by forming a visibly Christian organization. LaHaye was also in charge of registering evangelical Christian voters for the Reagan-Bush reelection committee in 1984, having already established the American Coalition for Traditional Values (ACTV), funded primarily by television ministries. According to Sara Diamond, LaHaye traded his religious organizational support for appointments in the Reagan administration drawn from a talent bank of born-again Christians available for government service.[5] Many of the institutional structures of the New Right were developed during the days of the Contra counterinsurgency in Nicaragua when government support for the Contras was illegal. The formation of intricate networks of both religious and secular groups to provide them with nongovernmental funding and support provided a training ground for the sophisticated electronic and direct-mail capabilities and networks that have since propelled religious conservatism into such prominence.

The significance of the economic and political power of the West has joined that of the South, which also has much to do with the influence of women like Beverly LaHaye, whose motherly activism links conservative women of the suburban West to the women of a southernized GOP. The 1994 congressional elections saw all but one of the new leaders of the

Republican Congress elected from states that were once part of the Con-
federacy: the South also elected mostly Republican governors.[6] Michael
Lind traces that southern shift to the 1960s campaigns and southern
strategies of Barry Goldwater and Richard Nixon, who were aided by
George Wallace in essentially turning the Republican Party into a white
man's party. As Goldwater said in 1961 in Atlanta, "We're not going to get
the negro vote as a block in 1964 and 1968, so we ought to go hunting
where the ducks are" (quoted in Lind 23), a strategy that has held ever
since. Reagan's later attacks on welfare queens, Larry McCarthy's Willy
Horton ads, and David Frumm's advice to focus on affirmative action are
different versions of the same strategy. On top of that older structure,
however, the Christian Coalition is now attempting to legitimate itself as
the religious heir to the Civil Rights movement by equating the responsibility of Christians to oppose abortion with earlier Christian moral
opposition to slavery. At the 1995 Road to Victory conference in Washington, D.C., Ralph Reed distributed Christian Coalition pledge cards
based on the pledge drafted by Martin Luther King Jr. for the Southern
Christian Leadership Convention; that same convention featured many
African American speakers and preachers on its program, and of all the
speakers, both African American and white, Alan Keyes was by far the
most enthusiastically received.

That revisionary reading of the Civil Rights movement attempts to
counter Goldwater's opposition in 1964 to federal civil-rights legislation.
His presidential bid shattered the influence of the older northeastern
Republicans as it empowered a new conservative coalition from the
South, Southwest, and West; carrying only six states in that election, five
of Goldwater's victories were in the South. The defeat of George Bush
was in part a result of his cultural association with northeastern conservatism. The influence of the South is also strongly reflected in contemporary media demagoguery, which also has a southern lineage, Lind argues,
in particular in the funding of radio and television broadcasts and networks by H. L. Hunt, the Dallas oilman who in the 1950s founded Facts
Forum, which dealt with radical conservative themes, such as the threat to
national sovereignty by the UN, the conspiracies of socialists and wealthy
Jews, the corruption of mainline religion, and the evils of homosexuality.
Hunt also subsidized the Campus Crusade for Christ and Life Line,
which spread conspiracy theories and attacks on Kennedy and Johnson.
In 1982, his son Nelson Bunker Hunt, whose views were similar to those
of the John Birch Society and who contributed to the Wallace campaign,

raised $350,000 for the National Conservative Political Action Committee. The Hunts helped preside, says Lind, "at the marriage of the far right and the Republican Party." (27)

Citing the political scientist V. O. Key Jr., Lind suggests that southern political influence has been determined far more by wealthy southerners, whom he refers to as southern Bourbons, than by those who might be stereotyped as "poor white trash," or angry white rednecks. But it is the revalorized symbolism of the ordinary American that now provides two simultaneous, but contradictory, identifications. On the one hand, the legitimate mistrust of the state on the part of many ordinary people finds expression in the populist language of plain folks Americanism. On the other hand, corporations are able to efface their wealth and power by fitting their own wish to be free of state regulations and taxes into the same terms. The result is a kind of Transparent American Subject, in which resentment of the government on the part of the lower middle class is represented in the same terms as resentment of the government on the part of multinational corporations. The belief in a Transparent American Subject thus includes the claim that there is no class system in the U.S. Here the wealthy can come together with the not-so-wealthy in a symbolic identification as plain folks Americans rebelling against the federal government, the cultural elite, immigrants, people of color, and, further to the right, Jews. Newt Gingrich is an example of what such transparency hides. Though he was not raised in the South, he strategically moved to a district in Cobb County, Georgia, which he thought he could win, though he almost lost his last two races. Because the district also happens to be the home of Lockheed and other defense corporations, it is the largest recipient of federal funding in the country. Gingrich, in a simple utilitarian way, links southern cultural and economic conservatism to multinational corporate interests, both of which then oppose the federal government.

Lind argues that in the South, the Bourbons have long manipulated racism to retain control of economics and politics in a form of conservatism that prefers low taxes and low services, unlike an earlier northern model of conservatism. The 1978 Kemp-Roth tax-cut legislation, based on supply-side economics, resulted in enormous deficits and, like contemporary attempts to turn governing functions over to the states, was heavily influenced by southern conservatism, even though there are any number of legitimate reasons to reconsider the tax structure and to support efforts to limit a bureaucracy that often runs on its own steam rather than democratically.[7] But part of the resistance to taxes also has to do with what Lind calls a "rigid, quasi-religious expression of the Jacksonian political culture of the Southern and Western United States." (23) That expression, however, is often not simply quasi-religious, but directly religious, as balancing the federal budget is made analogous to caring for one's family, part of a divine mandate. Similarly, Lind argues, contemporary attacks on government interference in the economy have replaced northern Whig-Republican economic nationalism that favored public investment in infrastructure and high wages. A political economy that favors weak unions and low labor costs was common to the South after the Civil War as part of an attempt to attract northern manufacturing. The promise of cheap labor costs and low taxes, however, was also accompanied by a crumbling infrastructure and underfunded public schools.

Anti-intellectualism, too, was long a part of the southern legacy, still evidenced by the visibility of southerners like Jesse Helms who lead attacks on funding of the arts, now the official position of the Christian Coalition. In spite of the fact that school reform aims at the very real deficiencies of underfunded public schools, such reform efforts also provide cover for attacks on secular humanism and for the support of vouchers and school choice. Though its chief beneficiaries "would be Southern Protestant evangelical bible schools, which, incidentally, would have almost exclusively white student bodies" (26), the school-choice movement has become increasingly strong in some minority communities as well. The history of the school-choice movement also has to take into account the fact that it was in the Civil Rights period that public schools were sometimes closed by state legislatures rather than allowed to integrate; only the federal judiciary had the power to interfere with such attempts.

And the southern ideal of a homogeneous community of people who are alike, an ideal that has always had to ignore all evidence to the contrary, in particular in relation to miscegenation, continues to influence the radical conservative political agenda.[8] The national political agenda has now come to resemble that of the southern Bourbons in other ways as well. In both Old and New South, upper-class and working-class whites were united against lowland black majorities. The most important geographic division was that between the Bourbon-dominated tidewater areas that were heavily black and the middling-to-poor white up-country of the Piedmont, or the areas of the Blue Ridge and Appalachian Mountains. Lind argues that national political strategies now draw on alliances that repeat this pattern. A "brown belt" of urban areas on both coasts and in the lowland areas like Florida, Texas, and the South, made up of concentrations of the wealthy and minorities, both African Americans and immigrants, is juxtaposed to the uplands, the Rocky Mountain and northern interior states which have relatively few minorities and less extreme income disparities. And the brown belt populations are themselves divided in two, into "minority-dominated inner cities and homogeneous white suburban and exurban rings" (28), from which there is also a white exodus to upland regions and an increasing abandonment of the inner cities. This "national Bourbon" division, Lind suggests, produces a dangerous alliance between "wealthy, outnumbered suburban whites in majority-nonwhite coastal states like California, Texas and Florida [and] middling whites in the Rocky Mountain and Plains states." (28) The political power of the uplands is exaggerated by the fact that political representation in the Senate gives low-population, culturally homogeneous states the same representation as high-population states with greater diversity.

Such a view of the South, of course, makes it appear far more homogeneous than it is, but recognizing its contours might help keep its racial outline visible, particularly as religious conservatives counter charges of racism by drawing conservative minorities into an alliance united in opposition to a different set of scapegoats: gays, feminists, welfare mothers, and immigrants. As Lind, who like me is a former Texan, says,

> Attacking Southern political culture is not anti-Southern — enlightened Southerners have been doing it for centuries. . . . Resisting the Southernization of America is a political task principled Southerners and Northerners should be able to agree upon. If they fail, George Wallace's boast may yet prove to be a prophecy: "Alabama has not joined the nation, the nation has joined Alabama!" (29)

But it will have joined it in a highly sophisticated form that attacks postmodernity by means of the most sophisticated use of grassroots organizing and media, modeling itself on the Civil Rights movement, the biblical foundations of America, and the revolutionaries of Valley Forge. This is the postmodern South.

ii.

Such a detour through the West and South may help read the niceness that marks Beverly LaHaye's appearance. If the conservative influences of the South and West are to be countered, their appeal has to be understood, for they also address very legitimate concerns, and sometimes niceness is simply niceness. Yet the reaction to videotapes of LaHaye by audiences made up of what could be called cultural elites, even the most progressive ones who would presumably benefit from understanding her appeal, is very revealing. A curious thing happens on such occasions. A condescension takes over in which both men and women feel free to mock her appearance and tone of voice, and this is usually as much about a blindness to gender, regional, religious, and class differences in American culture as it is about a legitimate disagreement with her absolutist beliefs. A simple example from popular culture helps make this point. In a segment of the sitcom *Wings,* one of the characters searches for an insult to hurl at Crystal Bernard's character, Helen, who speaks with a southern accent. When she finally comes up with the appropriate insult, referring to Helen's "trailer-park accent," she ends up collapsing Helen's regional identity into the codings of class and poor white trash, expressing contempt for all of them. By doing so, she has excluded a wide range of people from her categories of acceptability and fallen squarely into the trap of insulting plain folks Americans.

Any analysis of the definitions of normality on the part of radical conservatism will have to keep in mind what that sitcom incident has to say about a different kind of presupposition: that normal people are hip and urban, and if they do not come from the Northeast or Hollywood, their intellectual formation does. Such reactions to LaHaye and women like her no doubt helped make religious conservatism's early successes relatively invisible to progressive analysts and journalists, who either overlooked or trivialized the very people whose activism helped bring them about.

That invisibility played right into the hands of people like LaHaye and Phyllis Schlafly, who heard the contempt for region, religion, and especially housewives and mothers that goes along with this trivialization. And paradoxically, the niceness, even sweetness, that is so marked in terms of region and class as to be susceptible to mockery, is in other contexts unmarked. White, middle-class niceness becomes the invisible norm of respectability, a term to be discussed more fully in a later chapter. It is a norm whose requirements of conformity become evident when it is contrasted to ethnic differences, often described with adjectives like "pushy" or "aggressive." That plain folks American coding produces a powerful symbolic image, especially in political races where the other candidate is clearly marked in terms of some other identity. Niceness, of course, is not enforced for conservative white men, much of whose conduct seems to establish sixth-grade rudeness instead as the model of adult male behavior.

To understand LaHaye's offer of solace and comfort to women who have felt either humiliated or enraged by being dismissed, it helps to try to imagine ourselves into her argument, to see how the need for solace and, at times, retribution sets the stage for women's involvement in what many people see to be a politics of hatred. Imagining ourselves into LaHaye's argument also helps illuminate how important women's involvement is in redefining in terms of a very legitimate concern for one's family what might otherwise look like phobia. For many conservative women sincerely believe that they are not acting out of racist or homophobic intentions, even though in a postmodern mass-mediated society, the politics of hatred are not so much about intentions as they are about effects. The violent and hateful effects of niceness have proven to be no less harmful to many people than if they *had* been intended. As a result, a number of questions need to be asked about niceness and familiarity. What kind of powerful rhetoric can call itself love without recognizing that its effects are the same as if it called itself hatred? What powerful, intimate feelings ground the deeply sensual, spiritual, and moral values that, from the perspective of those outside the circle of familiarity, are terrifying? And in following LaHaye, I have to keep reminding myself not to describe her as other, overlooking the fact that in more ways than I want to admit, she is very much like me.

LaHaye begins *Desires of a Woman's Heart* by strategically drawing on themes from secular popular culture in order to recode them. Among these themes is the popular discussion of self-esteem. She understands very well what creates the need to talk about self-esteem: the sense of insecurity and fright on the part of many women who face a culture changing before their eyes. Their children are far better able to adapt to postmodernity and the information age than they are, even though those children face a future in which finding a job can look more like a gamble than a certainty. Self-esteem is part of "our craving for significance," LaHaye's term for our need to find meaning, but the question she and other Christians ask is not, Who am I? but, Whose am I? (25)[9] There is a remarkable turn here as the emotional appeal of her argument becomes more and more obvious. Unlike other angry, judgmental texts, her version of Christianity returns again and again, through the relay of her own image as a loving mother, to an image of a loving and gentle father. Her belief is thus enveloped in the requirement that there be an actual anthropomorphic figuration of a sheltering and loving God who seems to be the opposite of the forbidding Father who has been deconstructed by cultural theorists. He is, rather, the attentive father we wish ours had been, the perfect father there to comfort and care for us, to assure us that life really is ultimately fair, and to provide a deep, personal sense of being loved: "Our almighty Creator longs to communicate with us and share his desires for our lives." (27)[10] The rhetorical strategy she uses to express this longing for the missing good father of her youth (and ours) is based on folk traditions of storytelling now encoded within a version of biblical revelation that is immediately and emotionally accessible and reassuring:

> We need to wake up to the truth about self-esteem. Our worth is not found in what we do or what we own or what we accomplish. Our worth is found in the simple fact that we are God's creation. We are worth more than the earth, trees, animals, and all the rest of creation because God sent his Son to redeem us. God created us and he loves us. Our worth is inestimable. As God's creation, we are conceived and born with great worth, for God does not create worthless lives. . . . If you ever have cause to doubt your own worth, consider the great price God paid to redeem you! (24)

He gave up his own *child* for us, and in this postmodern context, in which people are struggling to keep families intact, this is the most moving, powerful sacrifice one could imagine. And as we will see later, the child proves to be the key to the reconstruction and legitimation of sacred gender and the kind of politics that collapses family, religion, and patriotism into the same highly sensual configuration. Christianity is here translated directly into the terms of one's own intimate experiences in the family, or at least one's own *desired* experiences within the family. Obviously, read from the direction of financial or intellectual security, this passage sounds egocentric and anthropomorphic, yet one has to imagine its impact from the perspective of a single mother whose children are threatened by violence and drugs in the inner city, a mother in an unemployed mill worker's family in the Northwest, or a bored suburban mother at home. Yet not all radical Christians are suffering, of course. Many are affluent suburbanites who flooded the offices of the *Washington Post* with calls, letters, and faxes after being referred to as "poor, uneducated, and easy to lead."[11] But this *solace* for the financially, emotionally, even physically insecure, a solace translated into the terms of a parent and the child who longs for parental love and security, is located in precisely the same place as in the dangerous *certainty* of self-righteousness that shows up in the behavior of many of those who are "saved." The sensual indistinguishability between these two poles, especially when it is pulled into the machinery of a utilitarian national political movement, provides the most dangerous linkage possible between the popular, the populist, and fundamentalist certainty.

It is here, in the worth of each person as a unique and beloved creature of God, that the opposition to abortion is also located, for every conception partakes of this unique worthiness and is guaranteed, as well, as we have seen, by an absolutist reading of the Declaration of Independence. This frame allows LaHaye to offer antifeminism as solace to women who feel exhausted and desperate because they cannot keep up with the competitive world supposedly introduced by feminism, a world in which women who have felt humiliated by the more general historical contempt for women now feel even less secure because they are unable to keep up, not just with men, but with other women: "I don't have to buy into the feminist agenda and 'be all I can be' in order to feel that I'm a worthy individual. . . . God has freed me from the performance trap and I can let him tell me how he wants to work in my life." (26)

But women trying to find some sense of self-worth do not need to denigrate men, says LaHaye: "Some men have embraced the serious misconception that all women are to submit to all men. Nothing could be further from the truth. Yes, husbands are to lead their wives and male pastors are to lead churches, but no, men are not to lead women!" (56) The distinction here is a puzzling and uneasy one, referred to as traditionalist in opposition to an emerging evangelical feminism, such as that of Rebecca Merrill Groothuis, who argues in a far more scholarly way than does LaHaye that a hermeneutic reading of the Bible shows that masculine headship can be understood in terms of historical and institutional, not divine, mandates. This more flexible view of heterosexual masculinity and femininity, however, does not translate into flexibility on homosexuality. Groothuis's feminism works very handily to steer these feminist evangelical women into the same homophobic politics.[12]

LaHaye, however, condemns even that much feminism and constructs a rationale for women's special identity by redefining their secondariness. Echoing the discourse of Christian women reformers of the turn of the century, she describes heroic Christian women as a "mighty army of women armed with the power of prayer" (81), while reminding us, as feminists also have, that the press has always ignored women's work, especially that of religious women, even though "the number of women actively involved in church work has always outnumbered men." These women were not trapped housewives but intelligent, dedicated, and hardworking leaders who were devoted to helping others, not to working for self-fulfillment. Contemporary biblical heroines "need not be intimidated by the intellectual class that arrogantly parades itself as the judge and final arbiter over the Word of God." (87)

LaHaye then takes the time to acknowledge those single women who may be members of church communities: "Single women are uniquely endowed with the opportunity to seek and serve Christ without distractions" (108), although "it is natural for women to desire marriage, because God created women with such a desire." (106) In softening the harshness of the fate of single women within a community that defines normality in terms of the traditional family, LaHaye again provides solace to soothe that emptiness: "When a women meets Christ, she has met her Savior and the lover of her soul. He completes her with an eternal love." (106)[13]

Christ is not only the kind and gentle father and the model of the perfect lover; he is also the perfect friend: "How awesome is our opportunity to be friends with God, the almighty Creator of all!" (48) He loves us unconditionally and will tell us the truth if we let him: "When we show God that we earnestly desire him and his gifts, he fills us with treasures of unspeakable worth and incomparable value. These treasures come in many forms; one very big one is the perfection of our character. And when we delight ourselves in the Lord, he will give us the desires of our hearts." (106) This personal and specific yet paradoxically highly orthodox relationship provides steadying emotional and spiritual guidance and an absolute conviction that one can make contact with truth that is not judgmental and angry but consoling and loving. This is a remarkable relationship, and perhaps the closest one can come to an analogy is the aesthetic process. An artist works according to a conviction that with enough discernment, she will arrive at the truth even if it is a truth she cannot fully explain. When it is complete, when its forms have been discerned aesthetically, she simply knows that it is organically "true." Similarly, the way people talk about their loved ones takes on the characteristics of a truth so ineffable it cannot be completely articulated, yet it is all the more powerful, truer, precisely because of that.

The aesthetic dimensions of this personal relationship with Christ are also evident in the style of LaHaye's descriptions, which are far closer to oral narratives or poetic language than to most philosophical or theological discourse. Living inside this religious framework means living inside a world of textual quotations and references to biblical passages, interpretations and reinterpretations among a community of believers who know all the same stories and all the same passages. There is also a comforting physical, tactile sense to all this, as well-thumbed Bibles become the reservoir of sensual memories, most often linked to family and church and to periods of mourning and of loss, as well as of joy and birth. This kind of interpretation, with its powerful layering of experience, memory, remembering, rewriting, might also be analyzed the way Freud reads and interprets dreams as the scaffolding of an architecture of signifying relationships: heterogeneous emotional and physical histories, chronological and atemporal meanings, the inseparability of mental and physical processes, the interwoven layerings of the unconscious and of conscious thought, of sign and referent. To imagine that pointing out the contradictions in a dream or in a work of art will convince the dreamer or the artist that there is an error is just as unrealistic as imagining that such an argument will convince someone so deeply immersed in and moved by this religious structure.

What has to be criticized, however, is the utilitarian use of this absolutist religious structure and the claim that it could ever result in democratic, inclusive public policy, for any legitimate participant would also have to live inside this Book. That is, their interpretation of the world is literally checked against the Bible, whose narrow interpretation is reinforced by the immediate community. Its Borges-like labyrinth seems to have no outside; the most ordinary, everyday experience can become the occasion for a citation that elicits a nod of familiarity from others also steeped in a world whose very contours are always already biblical and framed within an apocalyptic narrative. The recognition of that citation also retranslates that biblical passage into a new site-specific relevance and so renews it, making it a part of an ongoing life.

The fact that one is so immersed in daily prayer sessions and study gives believers a world always already biblically written, as the Bible becomes the Book of the World. The Bible in this sense provides the frame, or the Symbolic order, that grounds both belief and the body. And because of the intimate training of the body by the mother, it is also part of the semiotic, Kristeva's term for the most basic relationship between cultural meaning and the physiological nature of the body.[14] While postmodern theorists have teased this structuration out of Western metaphysics as if it were hidden and covert, here it is resolutely made overt. In fact, it is required. The framework within which subjectivity and body come to be recognized and felt, the place where, as LaHaye says, God writes "His Word on the tablets of our hearts," is located not so much in the head as in the heart. This structure draws on a long American rhetorical tradition of the jeremiad as well as on the history of enthusiasm and Puritanism in American literature.[15] This is a heart written by the sensuous collapse of the legal tablets of God into the very intimacy of the body and family relationships.

This deeply personal structure can be grounded only in heterosexual marriage in which the man is head. "'Haven't you read,' Jesus once asked his disciples, 'that at the beginning the Creator made them male and female'" (111), a version of Creation that also established woman's secondariness: "Eve came into existence from something already created; in other words, she was an extension, or part of, man." (115) Though God created man, he fashioned woman, perhaps taking greater care with her, even though "she was designed to complement the man, not replace him." (115) And it is in this insistent, repetitive response to feminism that LaHaye makes her stand: "Unless we accept the Bible's teaching that woman was created for man, we cannot begin to follow God's plan for happy marriages. Denial of this foundational truth may be the first step of a rebellion against God's plan for happiness in marriage. . . . A man's role as leader is threatened when the woman refuses to give him the support he needs in the challenging task of undertaking godly leadership." (116) Thus it is women's own deep love of Christ that requires them to let men obey Christ's commandment to lead.

Here an extraordinarily talented and strong woman, who has her own daily radio show, guides a national organization, administers intensive lobbying campaigns, produces sophisticated videotapes, and is the author of many books, goes on to assure us that women need more guidance than men because, like Eve, they are more open to the spiritual world. Proof of that is the fact that there are more women psychics and more women teaching Sunday school. Weaving a curiously confusing rationalization, she then argues that because women are *more* spiritual (and thus more open to misdirection) than men, men should be the spiritual heads of both family and church. Yet it turns out that it is not only in the spiritual realm that women are more adept, but also in the realm of knowledge. In order to resolve a contradiction, LaHaye reasserts the kind of opposition she was earlier at pains to undo. The head now predominates over the heart, as women's emotions become the real source of danger:

> When the serpent approached Eve, it was not because she was less spiritual than Adam, but because she was more emotionally responsive to misdirection. A modern woman's susceptibility to misdirection is the same as Eve's, no matter how logical or brilliant she may be. It is partially *because* of the woman's interest in knowledge that God directs the husband to be the spiritual head of the family. Remember, a woman's weaknesses are pride and an insatiable desire for knowledge, both of which make her easily deceived. The husband's responsibility for spiritual leadership is a grace gift given by God for the wife's protection from deception. (118)

Quoting a 1980 article by Elisabeth Elliot in the *Moody Monthly*, LaHaye argues that this primary position of the husband is not earned, nor achieved, nor dependent on superior intelligence, virtue, or prowess, "but *assigned* by God."[16] It is leadership modeled on the metaphor of the body, though now the head is curiously again privileged over the heart, which was earlier so central. Yet the heads of women are discounted: "To submit doesn't mean to become a zero. The idea is to acknowledge your head. Every member of a human body obeys the commands given in the head. When the wife acknowledges that her husband is her head, she acknowledges that he is her source, her leader, her authority, and she voluntarily accepts the authority . . . gladly, not in rebellion, nor resignation, but in obedience to God. . . . It's glad and voluntary obedience, each respecting the other, each sacrificing himself for the other." (134, quoting Elliot) But LaHaye also recognizes that men have not conducted themselves particularly well in carrying out their responsibilities to their wives: "Women favor bigger government because they see that they can no longer count on men to provide their needs with regard to money, home, and child care." (121) In order to thrive, "a woman needs a husband who is truly Christlike," for she "does not fare well when treated as a means to an end or when given the dregs of a man's time." (122–23)

This confusing description of woman's subjectivity and identity is relieved by exquisitely sensual language as LaHaye describes Mary's reaction when she learned that she was to be the mother of God: "I imagine her breath was taken away when she looked into the face of God and held the One who had always known the heavenly realm as home. And I imagine the soldier who stood at the foot of the cross was breathless for a moment as he looked up into the bleeding, dying face of Jesus of Nazareth. That face, he realized, was the face of the almighty God who had knit him together in his mother's womb." (28) And in very real ways, this deep belief cements a family structure and provides the networks of community often missing in postmodern secular culture, for many of these women not only meet together for prayer, but they also keep track of each other's children, help give advice about mothering children and adolescents, and volunteer to baby-sit and help out new mothers. LaHaye, drawing on even as she distorts the work of Deborah Tannen, argues that while men need to compete, women need to form communities, though this female need is again used to enforce separatism and homogeneity, for LaHaye advises Christian women to avoid friendships with those who will be a spiritual temptation to them.

Because the primary definition of woman is mother, LaHaye redoubles her efforts to empower those women who have chosen to stay home or to work at part-time jobs in order to spend more time with their children. Not so coincidentally, this valorization of mothering within a religious community whose members increasingly participate in political activism that usually benefits Republican candidates also ensures that there are women available for such activist work. The activism of these women resembles that of the more liberal League of Women Voters, as both groups provide intellectual stimulation and rewarding friendships for women who often face the boredom that can accompany mothering, though both groups also include career women. In many places, however, the League has been weakened by feminism, as members have begun to devote themselves to careers. The involvement of Christian women who are taught that it is their duty to stay home helps address that problem.

In coming to terms with their duty to stay home if at all possible, something many women in fact want to do, and to be available to their children to teach them the morality based on absolute difference between right and wrong, a strategy that rests on the double elimination of contradiction emerges. First of all, contradiction and ambiguity are not allowed into a belief structure that claims such a rigid and clean distinction between right and wrong. If, however, a contradiction does happen to force its way in, as in the curious relation between knowledge and women, a turn to God resolves it, as in this explanation of why women should not be ministers: "My desire and purpose is to relate a woman's role to the authority of Scripture — the only absolute truth. God does not contradict

His principles." (208) It is not contradictory because — always already — God does not contradict himself.

And just as women cannot serve both God and feminism, neither can they accept abortion and homosexuality, because society's acceptance of those things is a result of its acceptance of Satan's biggest lie, evolution: "God's truth is that we came from God's hand. As His creation, we are valuable. If we believe this, we know that we have inestimable worth, and that we also have a responsibility to live as our Creator planned." (195) The solace and comfort of that earlier, gentle self-esteem have now turned into an increasingly insistent, unquestioning emphasis on absolute morality and the literal biblical narrative, leaving no place for any doubt, any ambiguous complexity that might obscure the clean lines between binaries. Because doubt might blur those lines and threaten this absolutist certainty, its slightest emergence becomes the focus of intense cultural work: "By doubting God's truth about creation, we have set ourselves up for a tidal wave of doubt that will destroy our very foundations." (195)

By this time, the exclusivity of this belief has become even clearer, for just as Christ shares with us his inestimable friendship and the deep love that proved itself when he died for us, even though he had no sin himself, our own deep gratitude and love now require that we sacrifice ourselves and trust him completely and unquestioningly. This kind of trust, turning ourselves completely over to him, will ensure that we are right and that we are not guilty of hatred or bigotry: "In the midst of opposition, conflict, and a topsy-turvy world, we will be found without spot and blameless (2 Peter 3:14)." The moving and understandable solace of this truth, the certainty to be found in the depths of our hearts as we meditate on this spiritual meaning, is then extended to politics: "We know that God's truth is found only in God's Word. We must defend that truth in our homes, in our schools, and in our country." (196)

Many readers who respect religious meditation and discernment will nevertheless feel brutalized by this abrupt move from spirituality to politics, by this collapse of the spiritual into the political. When one sees, for example, a huge ballroom filled with Christian Coalition members being courted by Republican presidential candidates singing "God Bless America" while swaying, hands in the air, with the intensity of a church service or revival, one understands why this collapse of religion into politics does not seem brutal *to them*. But the sensual experience dangerously joins religion to a very restricted form of patriotism. A firm body guided by a Christian heart has in one move been connected to the firm foundation of the nation threatened by chaos and fluidity. And we now discover that ethical behavior is only possible for those who know God (*this* absolutist God, for there are many other kinds of Christians whose God is not this one, and many deeply ethical people who are not Christians). A note of shrillness and resentment creeps into LaHaye's texts, her gentleness now gone:

> Our modern culture is blind! In order to maintain high moral values, all societies must know and revere God. It is impossible for America to ever win the battle for integrity unless we return to the Judeo-Christian ethic upon which we were founded. Our country has forfeited the firm footing from which it could attack lawlessness." (201)

The sweet, gentle, motherly tone of LaHaye's earlier consolations has now lent itself to absolutist, theocratic, judgmental politics, and many of us are simply excluded. Ideas and beliefs different from hers, even though they may be deeply ethical, are demonized and any kind of opposition to this narrow Christianity is blamed on Satan: "The world's problem — its lack of a firm foundation — becomes the church's problem when the church shoots itself in the foot by refuting the inerrancy of Scripture. When the church upholds the truth, light will shine, people will see, and righteousness will be lifted up. Remember, the devil is as crafty and subtle with his 'logic' today as he was in the Garden all those years ago." (202) It is this absolutism that the rhetorical and political sophistication of the Christian Coalition's Ralph Reed increasingly hides. LaHaye keeps worriedly returning to feminism, for it is now to be found, like Groothuis's work, even within the church, a most intimate enemy: "Nothing is sacred to feminists who view the church as just another frontier awaiting their arrival." (210) They mistakenly apply the standards of egalitarianism from secular life to the question of women's roles in the church: "Unlike the worldly feminist who lives only for herself, however, the Christian woman gives of herself. The two mind-sets could not be more radically opposed because the feminist wants to get all she can while giving as little as possible . . . feminism is nothing but childishness in a mature-looking package." (204) And in stark, clear terms, she finally excludes feminists from Christianity altogether: "No card-carrying feminist can go where Christ goes, for He came to give up his rights and lose his life." (204)

Here, of course, not only feminists but many other Christians have been excluded from Christianity. If you do not trust in (this absolutist)

God, you can *only* trust in government. It is either one or the other. Even though LaHaye's strict binary has left very few people pure enough to meet her standards, she has nevertheless, along the way, appealed to plenty of people for whom at least a part of her message resonates. And that resonance has been firmly grounded in the amorphous, powerful feelings one has for one's own family.

iii.

Another text by a conservative Christian woman, Connie Marshner's *Can Motherhood Survive? A Christian Looks at Social Parenting,* continues this construction of sacred intimacy by focusing on motherhood in greater detail. Formerly a national spokeswoman for Concerned Women for America, as well as editor of the *Family Protection Report* and chair of the National Pro-Family Coalition, Marshner's argument shores up the identity of a woman who may have chosen to return home, where she faced what feminists have long described: the fragmented self-identity imposed on mothers who are expected to participate in their own effacement in the interests of their families.

Not so surprisingly, motherhood lies directly in the narrative about craving significance. If postmodernity revealed the infinite processes of language that underlie the crisis of masculine identity, it also revealed the unraveling of the identity of Woman, and, in particular, the identity of mothers. Though man's crisis became world-historical, the failure to recognize the crisis of traditional women that occurred simultaneously with feminism's liberatory discoveries, the failure to provide solace for many women, has left the door open for absolutist religion. The discourse of religion, as Kristeva argues, "tried and proved over thousands of years, provides the necessary ingredients for satisfying the anguish, the suffering, and the hopes of mothers."[17] The reaction of many women to this crisis of identity has been to turn to a literal, absolute metaphor for femininity, to the absolute sacredness of motherhood defined in a very particular way. This kind of sacred motherhood is, again not surprisingly, constructed precisely where much of secular society's contempt and disgust have historically been focused, for mothers are at the same time idealized and despised. In this religious framework, children become the instruments of a guaranteed, sacred identity for women who have a deep and realistic fear that without such a guarantee, they will inevitably be judged against men and found lacking. Then they and their children will be left at great risk in a society based on masculine competition, whether built by free-market theorists or liberal institutions.

In Marshner's book, the crisis that implicates motherhood and religion is described very early in terms of both guilt and miasma: "If you are a mother, you feel exasperated and isolated and frustrated more often than you would like to. And maybe you think it's all your fault because you're not a good enough mom. But don't be discouraged: understand that the culture in which we live — all of Western civilization — is being enveloped by a miasma of anti-motherhood, and few of us can escape its effects."[18] She is right about society's contempt for mothers from both political directions, and it is significant that she finds that something about this crisis of motherhood is confusing enough to elicit a description of it in terms of a miasma, a poisonous gas or vapor once associated with swamps and putrid matter, with abjection.

Marshner's ostensibly simple use of the concept of miasma situates her argument directly in the terms of a misogynist cultural logic of purity. That logic rests on the privileged identity of the Pure Mother, and all other women are seen as abject or improper. She thus grabs hold of the Pure Mother produced by this kind of misogynist logic, but she does so in order to use the misogynist Pure Mother against misogyny itself. That is, after acknowledging that the female body has been symbolically coded in two different ways, the abject and the pure, she selects the pure one and builds on it. By doing so, she empowers herself to resist the very misogyny that produced the split in the first place. The problem with that response, however, is that her own empowerment and that of women just like her has now been situated directly in the realm of absolutist familiarity that simultaneously endangers a whole range of other women.

Marshner wrote *Can Motherhood Survive?* while she was eight months pregnant, admitting that she had returned home after having been out in the world debating feminists while acting like one. In order to return to her two neglected teenage sons and a toddler, she had to overcome the opposition of her feminist mother and at least initially her husband. She did so, however, as part of a frontline resistance to what she calls social parenting, "a public institution making sure that every child, even those not yet conceived, receives certain medical, dental, and psychological interventions, diagnosis, and treatment. Not parents. Not family." (93) She relates that to Walter Mondale's proposed Child Development Bill, vetoed by Nixon in 1971. It would have:

committed the federal government to establishing child advocacy programs in any locality that had more than five thousand residents. The programs would have delivered a full range of health, educational, and social services to all children — not just poor ones, but all children, on a sliding fee basis. The rationale was that Congress had recognized that such services were essential for all children to reach their full potential and therefore Congress was going to assume its responsibility to ensure that all children had what they needed. Parents were out of the picture. (105)

Though one might have imagined that these services would have helped parents and children, in her view, and in the view of absolutist conservatism in general, they rested on the volatile base of social parenting, in which the state took the place of God. Quoting Shakespeare, "the Devil hath power to assume a pleasing shape," she agrees: "Satan does have the power to assume a pleasing shape. Social parenting is not in accord with God's plan for the raising of children. Social parenting has the power to assume a pleasing shape." (65) It is described presciently and in almost Foucauldian terms as "the infinite industry of social parenting," or as other conservatives call it, social engineering. (92)[19] In Marshner's analysis, institutional child-care programs are strategically targeted to break the bonding between parents and children and to work in the interests of yuppies who want to avoid the full costs of child care. Other groups who have a stake in social parenting consist of "professionally credentialed members of the helping professions," pediatricians whose practices depend on children who catch more illnesses because of day care, professional poverty lobbyists, medical- and mental-health professionals, organized charity, and educators. (65) Marshner argues that mothers provide the most natural child care, and she accuses feminists of being hypocritical when they criticize her for that position at the same time they insist on natural childbirth. Why "natural" childbirth and not "natural" child care?

Diane Eyer's *Mother-Infant Bonding: A Scientific Fiction* agrees with Marshner about this contradiction, tracing feminism's own uncritical embrace of an ahistoric and romanticized mother-child bonding to argue that the movement to reform childbirth in the 1970s was based on an appeal to what was natural, which "acquired the connotation of being inherently good, even moral."[20] Bonding itself was drawn into this definition, so that what was "natural represented an existence free of commercialism and materialism. . . . Connected to this romanticized view of nature was religiosity that fit beautifully with the earlier Christian under-pinnings of the natural childbirth movement of the 1950's — a small but dedicated group for whom childbirth was a holy and heroic event rooted in the teachings of the Bible." (164) Eyer's critique of bonding in no way suggests that women and children do not or should not bond. It simply argues for looking at bonding *reflectively,* both sympathetically and crit-ically, to see what other interests and political agendas are involved.

These theories of natural bonding have, of course, made it possible to blame children's problems on the mother — she smoked, she worked in a dangerous occupation, she was not home after school, and so on. These are easy answers that preclude much more difficult questions about what is wrong with the arrangements within which women have to mother. These bonding theories, which closely resemble fundamentalist discourses about women, entered scientific discourse in the 1970s as part of political struggles between parents and doctors over the control of the territory of mother and infant. In this way, a particular religious argument about morality entered the relationship between medicine and power, and the bonding between mother and child became medicalized, with obstetricians and pediatricians viewing bonding in relation to their scien-tific authority, for they had taught women its importance. That lesson, Eyer argues, also helped doctors to manage their patients.

Marshner's religious insistence on bonding attributes any refusal to recognize the biblical importance she assigns it to secular reasons such as liberal guilt or, during the days of the Great Society, national embarrass-ment at falling behind Sweden, whose social services paradoxically force women into the workforce in order to pay for them. Another reason liberals support social parenting is their guilt about poverty. Poverty here is dealt with only incidentally in order to make a point about the need for morality, though at a later stage, some religious conservatives belatedly begin to address it as a problem in and of itself. But for Marshner, the reason one must be concerned about poverty is that it represents "the camel's nose under the tent for feminists," a cover issue used merely to advance the interests of feminists who oppose motherhood. It is not that poor mothers do not need their lives changed, but that only the church is capable of doing it: "The church — through its practical ministry and its preaching of Christ and Him crucified — can change lives; government programs cannot. . . . our help is in the name of the Lord, not in the name of Washington, D.C." (70–71) Feminists' arguments about the needs of poor families are simply attempts to absolve themselves of their own responsibilities and to attack other mothers like her: "In the name of helping the poor, the attack on motherhood continued." (105) And finally, referring to various programs like AFDC, she says, "All of these were couched in rhetoric of 'enabling the poor to achieve self-supporting status,' and together they add up to $2.7 billion a year of federal subsidy of the destruction of motherhood." (105)

Marshner connects the sacred status of the family to free enterprise, which is both part of human nature and divine law. As Pat Robertson says, the Eighth Commandment is God's recognition of the sanctity of private property. "Thou shalt not steal" is about taxes. It means that the "God of Jacob forbids a citizen to take what belongs to another citizen . . . to take from the rich and give to the poor." He continues, "What a man has accumulated was his. In God's order there are no schemes of wealth redistribution under which government forces productive citizens to give the fruit of their hard-earned labors to those who are nonproductive."[21] Marshner links the family to free-market economics by her discovery that feminism and Marxism are exactly the same thing, both directly traceable to Marx and Engel's *The Origin of the Family, Private Property, and the State*. She has now displaced the Cold War, from a focus on an external enemy to a focus on the enemy in the very bosom of the family, asking, "How do we come to be fulfilling the dreams of Karl Marx in the destruction of our families? The answer is alarmingly simple. . . . Ideas about women and the family which are fashionable today among liberal opinion makers can be traced to Karl Marx. . . . It's a feminist (read Marxist) principle that all relationships are political." (179–80) That Marshner equates social parenting with Satan and finds this satanic enemy in the bosom of the family would not surprise Elaine Pagels, whose study of Satan as a product of the relationship between Christianity and Judaism argues that Satan "is not the distant enemy but the intimate enemy." (49) In a curious and contradictory way, of course, other culture warriors of the Right make the same claim Marshner has just called Marxist; George Gilder praises Phyllis Schlafly for showing that "all politics is on one level sexual politics."[22]

This sacred nature of motherhood, or rather the tie between mother and child, is the basic kernel of absolute Christianity, the site that must be guarded in order to resist Satan's dangers at the very heart of intimacy. Marshner's description of the nature of motherhood accompanies a thoroughly middle-class narrative of child rearing that is strategically targeted at women for whom professional careers are a possibility, even more than at ordinary working women. Later, religious conservatism will reach out to other classes and minority groups. It is much easier, she says, for women with noncareer jobs to stop working than for women who have interesting careers like hers, which may, in fact, be Satan's most powerful weapon to seduce women away from motherhood. In this middle-class context, Hannah Papanek argued that because women's work is likely to be poorly paid, their production of cultural capital through activities like volunteering at school, working on school boards, chauffeuring children to lessons, and researching colleges and scholarships may be much more important to maintaining a middle-class position than their employment. The class nature of Marshner's focus on the child also suggests its historicity; as families become smaller and children more expensive, the burden on each one to be perfect is even greater.[23]

The ideal family implied in Marshner's narrative is a family with enough resources to make the choice to rely on only one wage earner, though she acknowledges here and there that this is neither easy nor often even possible, even as she instills a sense that any other arrangement will in some way scar the child. Of course it *is* true, as any working mother can tell you, that there is a serious shortage of good day care and that because women are usually solely responsible for their children, working and being a mother makes for exhausting, difficult, and tense days. But she blames the inadequacies of day care, and the difficulties for women caused by work situations organized around the needs of a generic worker with a wife at home, not only on feminists but indirectly on the minority day-care providers who work at wages below those of parking-lot attendants. The family addressed by Marshner may also be caught up in white flight from the minority influence of day-care providers. After noting that "tragically, in our postfeminist society, any task having to do with the care of children has been downgraded and robbed of all prestige" (76), she does not use that observation to argue for improvements in the way people doing those tasks are paid and treated. Instead she exploits the middle-class fears of falling out of that class. In studying Democratic defectors to the Republican Party in the 1980s, Thomas and Mary Edsall found that fear of falling out of the middle class was expressed in racialized terms. They quote a Democratic polling firm, the Analysis Group: "[N]ot being black is what constitutes being middle class; not living with blacks is what makes a neighborhood a decent place to live."[24]

Marshner indirectly echoes this fear in her worries about day care, for it may be, she warns her readers, that someday their own Christian-raised children will date and be friends with children poorly raised by day-care providers. Because religious conservatives have been "casting a wider net," the Christian Coalition's term for forming coalitions with other religious and racial groups, the racism in texts like Marshner's rarely shows up overtly. It instead works structurally, because one's religious life and social contacts tend to isolate the church members from those other groups. As one participant at a Concerned Women for America workshop told me with an air of disbelief when I asked whether one's teenager could date a Jewish teenager, "Your children never date outside their faith." Whether they date outside their race was a question I did not ask. The atmosphere in daycare centers and the effects of that atmosphere on your child's IQ are also problematic: "Adults give lots of commands and repetition and can pay but little attention to children's questions, let alone give thoughtful answers to them. In short, the whole atmosphere is more like the low-income mothers than the middle-class ones" (185), though she insists that this is not a criticism of lower-class women but an example of the values that guide the middle-class mother's care: "By the way, don't be put off by the socioeconomic descriptions: income level has nothing to do with mothering skills. . . . That 'middle-class mothers' happen to have the maternal skills that produce intellectual development is behavioral science's way of noticing that kids with attentive mothers tend to achieve more in life." (185–86) All of her claims do, of course, contain some truth, and they also reflect the anger of women whose skills in mothering are often discounted by academic specialists giving them advice. Yet there are many other truths, such as economic and racial circumstances, which cannot make their way into this discussion.

This is an ideal, symmetrical narrative of parenting in which the patient mother is always available and receptive to interpret and respond to every nuance of the child's development. Marshner here plays her trump card, for there is no narrative more deeply embedded in a mother's repertory of guilt than that she robbed her child of this kind of nurturing. She constructs a teleology to guide this perfect, attentive mother at every moment and to give each of these moments legitimacy, for the overarching narrative that gives meaning to this difficult, often boring and frustrating work is the knowledge that it is work raising a child for God. This is a narrative that redeems the mother's life from the frumpery or bored depression of the housewife looked down on by men and women alike. It also provides a compensating match for the symbolic rewards men get from masculine headship in the family, giving the mother a narrative to complement the man's Oedipal one. In the male Oedipal narrative, the end point—transcendence of some sort—assigns value to each step along the way toward that transcendence, and it makes each of the steps along the way mean something rather than being simply arbitrary.[25] In that same Oedipal narrative, the woman merely provides the spaces along the way through which the male hero has to pass so that his story will keep moving; her lack of agency facilitates his claim to it. Marshner leaves the woman in the Oedipal narrative—it is crucial that she still be available to facilitate the man's movement forward—but now there is a narrative for the woman who waits that is as important as that of the man who acts. Male and female are defined in terms of two different *functions* that cannot be directly compared. The woman now has duties that do not simply depend on her husband, who may or may not be a good Christian, but are instead duties to God himself. This narrative of the mother is located exactly where a feminist theory of female agency is also at stake, as it undercuts any notion of agency for women unrelated to motherhood. The loss of that agency is partially compensated by the intensity of spiritual and emotional passion.

As Marshner continues this redefinition of submission, she methodically dissects the advice feminists have given women about independence, reminding the reader that God does not help those who help themselves but instead helps those who depend on and submit to him. Just as the Spirit refuses to exalt itself, so should women: "Holy women do not exalt themselves, do not speak of themselves but respond to the needs of those they love." (158) And because it is in their biological nature to be receptive and to serve, women are more naturally suited to be close to him: "The essence of motherhood is response: our bodies respond to the first hint of pregnancy; our emotions and minds continue to respond. . . . Some of this is spontaneous and natural; some of it is learned." (158) In fact, Mary herself was selected by God because she "just followed where service led. . . . The essence of femininity is response. The church is feminine because it is a response to a call from God. So, for that matter is creation." (158) The potential problem this creates for Christian men will be discussed in chapter 4.

Because this kind of response is so difficult, the mother begins to take on the characteristics of the true hero, for "it is a decision of the will that enables a mother to submit herself to the reality of other people's needs." (158) Her decision is, in fact, more difficult than the man's, for he must simply overcome his desires to stay at home with his family (and history has shown us how strong those desires are, a fact George Gilder confirms, as he argues that men have to be bribed to commit themselves to their families): "Whatever his personal, intimate response to his family, his primary responsibility is to go out and earn money among strangers so that the mother of his children can minister personally to them." (159) But for the woman in contemporary culture, the most heroic of all decisions is the one to stay home, in particular to stay home as an act of rebellion: "This is a free country. But women are not free to be mothers." (12)[26] It thus requires great willpower, even revolutionary fervor, perhaps the kind feminism too requires, to lead a life of Christian dependency, submission, and response.

Marshner counters the emotions a woman might feel when she learns that it is her role to submit, especially in a culture influenced by feminism. Satan loves for women to feel self-pity about wasting their lives and talents, though that self-pity is totally misplaced, for this is a cosmic responsibility: "But if you're doing what God wants you to be doing, how can you be wasting yourself? If God thought of you from all eternity and created you so that this moment you could respond to the cry of that child, whom He also thought of from all eternity and gave to you and nobody else to mother — how can you be wasting yourself? This is what you were born for! . . . You were created by God, for all eternity, to comfort that baby and feed that family." (159–60) You must not simply do what God wants, but want what he wants: "There's glory in submission, not shame. . . . This kind of submission requires more strength than leadership because the challenge is not to compete with other people but to compete with the flesh and the Devil." (160) And she is probably right about the difficulty of that submission — ask any mother. How could this boredom mean worthlessness if it proves to mark such a great struggle for such a cause? Submission has become epic.

And the dimensions of this epic, even cosmic, struggle to submit increase when she describes the model for women's behavior: "After all, even God Himself did what He is asking mothers to do. . . . He took upon him the form of a servant . . . and became obedient unto death." (160) She will, in fact, be defined in *opposition* to a specific notion of self. Yet importantly she also has not quite done that. By erasing her own specificity and agency, she has activated what she sees as an even greater agency in Christ, the self that gives God glory. The woman has been provided with the most secure and legitimate self imaginable. She can experience a proximity to the Spirit that seems to be *greater* than that available to men, whose possibilities for submission are far fewer: "Our Savior Himself came into this world as a dependent." (135)

Marshner's strategy of redefining an active woman as dependent and submissive requires even further supplementation in heroic terms to make it convincing; it is a hard sell. It is probably inevitable that country music hits like Pattie Loveless's "You Don't Even Know Who I Am," about a housewife who walks out of a marriage, leaving the dirty laundry on the floor, or Martina McBride's "Independence Day," about a wife's violent rebellion against domestic violence, may foretell a plain folks American feminine mystique in the making. In attempting to forestall that rebellion, Marshner argues that even Satan knows that women are the most important, that their role is the most integral to his purposes: "Women, as the heart of the family, are always more vulnerable to Satan's delusions. . . . He knows that if he can get women thinking about themselves, they won't be thinking about other people, and they won't be seeing the dangers he's busy laying for children and men and society." (137)

In traditional society, a woman knew who she was, so she worried less and had more time to work on her relationship with God, and because the family's livelihood depended on agriculture, she actually did have it all. She could produce goods at the same time as she did domestic work for her family, and even though her responsibilities were "primarily repetitive domestic chores," could perform them calmly because she understood that that was what she was supposed to do. There was no unsettling questioning of the worth of such work. The symmetrical, perfect match between doing her job well and the success of the clan located her domestic behavior at the very center of public happiness and situated her as the exemplary hero of the early stages of capitalism: "And since whatever she did achieve benefited her entire clan, it benefited her as well. Free enterprise in its most original form." (140)

But today's women are destroyed by anxiety, as they question whether they are good enough and as they try to find their identity in accomplishments, paychecks, and titles. Marshner's text returns relentlessly to the miasma where ambiguity, doubt, and guilt show up for mothers, me included. For in spite of my recognition of the dangers of this absolutist logic, I often find myself reading painfully because of my own perceived failures as a mother in a society organized around women's sole responsibility for parenting; all my guilt buttons are pushed. In this logic, of course, which is not only religious but more broadly patriarchal, every mother should be ideal, never is, and is by definition always already a failed mother. Mother *means* failed. These failures are inevitable, but so are mothers' deep worries about them and their potential receptiveness to anyone who offers help. This may be the most important thing to understand about Marshner's argument—its appeal to deep, profound, inarticulable worries about children on the part of many women who may not necessarily be racists or bigots but who become involved in politics that have racist and bigoted effects because this rhetoric addresses them as mothers. Marshner's text plays every string of mother's guilt, which is notoriously resistant to rational argument, and she is right that the "biggest losers in most cases are children." (17) All our children have a very hard time in a world like this, but some have a much harder time than others.

Her description of the ideal mothering narrative not only makes me feel guilty, but it also highlights the difficulty of talking about motherhood at all without being trapped in the tangles of the narrative of mother's guilt or the narrative in which any woman without children or any lesbian is outside the frame of legitimacy. And it is true that many feminists have found it difficult at various times to be dialectical about motherhood, to valorize it at the same time they dissect its constraints. That has often left the identity of mothers in a void, just where it has left unanalyzed feminism's overreliance on the state for political redress. Marshner plays on both the feeling of a void and on guilt and unease while insistently countering any hint of doubt about the decision to return home, but she finally must turn to good and evil as cosmic concepts to calm those doubts. In doing so, she makes clear how important a logic based on absolute binaries is to her own decision, and at the same time, she also shows what a crucial role mothers play in reproducing this way of thinking. For after she has argued that needing help and being dependent is Christ-like and that "dependent is not a four-letter word," she cannot rely on having convinced us but must bring our interpretation under control by eliminating any possible wrong reading. This requires a turn to God: "To be content with this dependent role, she has to choose: resent the dependence or find grace in it. That's all there is." (145) That choice arises out of one's reasons for having children: "What is the purpose of having children? To give us satisfaction, ego gratification, contentment, a sense of accomplishment—or to give God glory and to give Him sons and daughters? One or the other must be the main reason. The answer should be easy for a Christian." (29)

The need for a clear judgment guaranteed by God always shows up in places where doubt — or perhaps more importantly, anxiety — threatens: "One, decorate it how you will with high-sounding rhetoric, comes down to this: 'I don't want to.' The other comes down to this: 'Yes, Lord.' Rebellion or submission. No other choice." (160) Such binaries are part of the epic and by now cosmic nature of a woman's will to submission: "This kind of submission requires more strength than leadership because the challenge is not to compete with other people but to compete with the flesh and the Devil. Boring? No way. It's the greatest struggle in the world, the same struggle that occupied every hero or heroine of the faith you have ever admired. There's glory in submission, not shame. That's the secret a Christian knows that the world does not." (160) The difficulty and anxiety of choices in a world hostile to women can be assuaged by a belief that eliminates questions: "Either God knows what He is doing or He does not. Since as a Christian I believe that God knows what He is doing, I consider it a privilege to share in the carrying out of His plan." (15) The literal word of God, channeled through evangelical preachers and discerned through daily personal and group prayer sessions does not lend itself to questioning.

But the fact that language is literal, not interpretive, must be learned, and the mother's most important contribution may be a lesson about language: "[T]he child will not learn that words mean something but rather will become distracted with too much context. If 'come' does not mean the same thing from everyone who says it, the child will suspect that other words mean different things depending on who says them. And then the child will spend precious time trying to interpret what is said and deciding whether it must be taken seriously rather than simply obeying." (38) One might think of this lesson in language to the young child as paradigmatic of absolutist religious conservatism in general.

Because there are only two possibilities, yes or no, and because "too much context" has been eliminated, the refusal to obey leads to nihilism, which in this framework nullifies the very possibility of ethical behavior. Any attempt to draw on ethical systems other than absolutist morality is simply eliminated from the frame, the refusal to obey proof that one has rejected all moral guidance. As Irving Kristol argues, the Right's culture war defends "capitalism, the American political tradition, and bourgeois civilization grounded in religious truth."[27] Marshner's seemingly innocent resistance to day care has now proven to be a defense of America's mission in the world, as Kristol acknowledges: "If you de-legitimize this bourgeois society, the market economy — almost incidentally, as it were — is also de-legitimized. It is for this reason that radical feminism today is a far more potent enemy of capitalism than radical trade unionism." (55)

The very principle of sociality is indeed threatened, as Marshner understands: "When the most fundamental human relationship, that of mother to child, is compromised, mind and flesh are disordered, reflecting the disorder introduced with the Fall." (194) Perhaps most important for the men who head right-wing churches, political organizations, and think tanks and whose very legitimacy depends on faith, faith itself rests on the mother. For we cannot learn how to be faithful to God unless our mothers provide us with the model for submission: "How can we believe in the self-giving love of a heavenly Father when we have not known such love from a human mother?" (195) Who can we have faith in if not our mothers?

iv.

A last example of this kind of motherly advice is Linda Weber's *Mom: You're Incredible!,* also written with questions for study and reflection in prayer groups and published by James Dobson's Focus on the Family. It appeals to women who may be having difficulty carrying out their resolve to stay home with their children or, if they work, which she acknowledges many must, to give their children priority, not the leftovers of their time, and the focus of her book is somewhat different. Whereas Marshner and LaHaye identify radical feminism as the greatest threat to the family, Weber expands that message to argue that it is a mistake for mothers who work at home and those who work outside the home to be pitted against each other, for the real issue is the kind of nurturing both do in their homes. While being home is not the ultimate goal, making an impact there is. Her book also shows the political usefulness of building coalitions in opposition to the target that secures the widest alliance among evangelical Protestants, conservative Catholics, and orthodox Jews: homosexuality.

Here, as they are for LaHaye and Marshner, gender differences are primary: "Dads understand lines, boundaries, and borders. . . . Dads will give their lives for lines. Moms, on the other hand, understand nuance, nurturing, and developing. Moms color in the blank spaces."[28] Her own concern about day care is that children do not learn the difference between lines and spaces; little girls stop playing dolls and nurturing and start acting like boys. And in her concern about the teaching of proper gender, she too turns to single mothers to suggest that they not give up, that they grieve their loss, that they cherish the relationships with others, that they admit their failures, move on, and keep loving. But she does not stop there, for it seems that the biggest problem that single mothers, as well as strong women in marriages, must acknowledge is that they may provide their children with an unbalanced image of gender:

> A domineering mother can be one of the most dangerous and damaging parts of any crisis. That negative influence probably accounts for as many disorders as any other factor in the lives of children. . . . One study states, "In homes led by dominant mothers, both girls and boys were likely to say that they disliked the opposite sex. Also these girls and boys were frequently disliked by the opposite sex." Many experts believe maternal dominance has a direct and extremely influential link to sexual disorientation: "Boys from homes in which the mother asserted herself as the leader exhibited more feminine sex-role preferences than did boys from homes in which the father was the leader." (124–25)[29]

Weber offers the following advice about resisting that impulse to be dominant (which is a perfect match for her husband's contribution to the Christian men's movement, to be discussed in chapter 4): "The Master Designer wrote His parenting manual, the Bible, with the intention that each child should enjoy the influence of both a mother and a father. The complete puzzle shows the necessity of the masculine leader to ensure the growth of a strong family." (143) For "a home with a healthy mom and a healthy dad wrapped around the Living Lord is a home not easily broken. It's a home where the sons grew like 'strong trees' and the daughters become like 'pillars adorning a palace.'" (144)

This perfect family relies on the leadership of the father, as Richard Strauss says in *How to Raise Confident Children*: "If a child knows beyond all doubt that dad is the head of the house, that mom speaks for dad, and that dad's authority backs up what she says, he will be more apt to obey and will have more love and respect for both his parents." (quoted in Weber 149) And if the family is to work, husband and wife must carry out different functions, not occupy equal positions. Weber advises women to pull back and let their husbands take their rightful positions: "So be a team player and love your husband — really love him. Make him your priority. Accept him. Let him lead. And help him succeed as a father. You'll win. He'll win, and most of all, your children will win." (151)

There could not be a clearer description of the "dominant fiction," the representation of the traditional family as the primary filter of truth and reality. A social order can only stay in place so long as it keeps producing subjects who will want to replicate that social order. It can only do so by bringing the desires and identifications of individuals into conformity with the desires and identifications that will ensure its continuation.[30] The neatness and orderliness of the family arrangements described in these texts no doubt produce many confident children, through their insistent and loving enforcement of one view of the world as the correct one and exclusion of beliefs that cannot be converted into this model. Concentrating on only the negative effects produced by such rigidity, and there are many, risks overlooking the important sense of confidence and security such training provides for many people. The problem is its exclusivity.

And even though women like LaHaye, Marshner, and Weber have reinscribed women into a family in which the father is the head, the admonition to women to be submissive and useful to men is double-edged. For this version of submission also threatens to undercut the equation between men and the anthropomorphic image of the Creator. Here it is *women* whose image is closer to his. The mother's Christ-like sacrifice is modeled directly on his: "How can we possibly imitate the Creator in our relationships if we can't learn from our mothers to give of ourselves, to offer ourselves in love to another, and to control our fleshly impulses for the sake of another?" (195) Though women learn in this misogynist structure to act in men's interests, it nevertheless is obvious that they also derive a great deal of power from this guaranteed identity. The threat to men posed by the resemblance between Christ and women will reemerge in the Christian men's movement, as we will see, for in many ways, these women have learned how to usurp the most important guarantee of meaning in this religious structure: the imitation of Christ.

TWO

The Heart of the Matter

IMPACT Records brings the melody of *romance* right into your living room. . . .
— liner notes to Kelly Connor's *The Heart of the Matter — Love Songs for Christians*

To all those who believe married love can be beautiful, exciting, and fulfilling
and to those who wish they could believe. — Tim and Beverly LaHaye

The intimate training women provide within the family is part of the
biggest prize in American politics and political economy: passion, here
the passion grounded in the belief in absolute sexual difference. Religious
conservatives like LaHaye, Marshner, and Weber have brilliantly drawn
on the decentered, deconstructed fragmentation of an information society and a global economy in which it seems impossible to find a center.
And they have done so as part of a more general construction of what
Lawrence Grossberg calls a "national popular," a conservative popular
culture that has influenced the terms of everyday life and the public language of what matters, moving the center of American politics far to the
right. The term "matter" here is important in two senses. First, it refers to
the very nature of materiality in general and the body in particular. And
second, it includes the way things come to matter, the way emotions are
learned and taught.

The texts of the last chapter depended on the reconstruction of everyday life, the broader level of familiarity defined not only by economic
criteria but by lifestyle and identification within the terms of a popular
imagination. By tracing popular culture's role in the increasing conservatism of American politics, Grossberg's study complicates postmodern
celebrations of popular culture's liberatory possibilities, with popular culture defined here in broad terms as all the kinds of cultural practices in

which people find themselves empowered by an identification and emotional investment, including books like the ones I have been following, as well as media, community involvement, and the activities of everyday life. That definition will be made more specific later. After a brief discussion of Grossberg's description of "what matters," I turn in this chapter to a text and videotapes that redefine sexuality within the sacred intimacy of the family: a book by Tim and Beverly LaHaye, *The Act of Marriage: The Beauty of Sexual Love;* a short video about abstinence for teenagers, *Wait for Me;* the second of two videos about the influence of homosexuals, *The Gay Agenda in Public Education;* and a training tape from the Christian Coalition's School Board Training Seminars.

An analysis of the emotional restructuring of everyday life by religious conservatives has to take into account the history of American liberalism after the Second World War, when the two political parties agreed not to disagree over economic strategies in a corporatist compromise among the competing interests of labor, capital, and government, an argument developed by Grossberg.[1] Part of liberalism's ideological construction at the time depended on a highly charged difference between democratic capitalism and the external threat of communism, accompanied by an internal threat of subversion. Communism was also thought of as a disease within liberal society itself. In this framework, pluralism marked America's difference from the rest of the world, in particular fascism and communism, even though pluralism itself was denied much real political significance. And in the 1950s, many Americans experienced the possibility of upward mobility not so much through the acquisition of cultural capital as through improvement in their economic circumstances. This meant that their upward mobility did not require that they renounce their regional and class identifications and tastes, their plain folks identities.

At the same time, upward mobility depended on a conservatism that focused on the family as the site of and reason for consumer spending, part of a larger commitment to consumption as the key to the fulfillment of the American dream of peace, prosperity, and protection from "godless communism." This political economy and national mythology set the context for everyday life, which was characterized by a commitment to consumerism, upward mobility, and a normative desire for comfort and success. But everyday life, while amorphous and seemingly generic, was not something a person simply chose to have. Instead you got to choose how to activate its maps, "what matters, where one invests." Everyday life is, in fact, a luxury because it is not available to everyone: "Only those who have the resources can live within its capitalized spaces. And while those resources are largely economic, they are also cultural and social and identificatory." (149)

The New Right in the 1980s mounted a direct attack on the compromise that had constituted that postwar liberal consensus, and the state began to abandon its role as the mediator between these various interests, openly embracing "its relations to capital and its commitment to act on behalf of the need for increased profits." (156) At the same time, a culture war — fought directly in the realm of popular culture — began to reverse the influence of the previous site of passion: the Left and sixties culture, or what Lawrence Grossberg calls the "rock formation." A new conservative alliance brought into power a wide range of diverse groups whose goal was

> to regulate the possibilities of pleasure and identity as the basis of political opposition and to dismantle the cultural and political field constructed in the 1960's. . . . The new conservatives have to regulate pleasure in order to reestablish the discipline they believe necessary for the reproduction of the social order and the production of capital (e.g., the family), [joined with] a sophisticated and strategic understanding of the place of media and culture in society. (10–11)

Yet central to this regulation of pleasure is a recoding, not an elimination, of it, as the marriage advice from the LaHayes will show. For radical conservatism moves pleasure directly and intensively into the sacred site of the family through the construction of what matters.

Contemporary conservatives, of course, argue that the last thirty-five years were a detour from what Newt Gingrich calls the "highway of American values." In that view, during those years history was rewritten to mock God, patriotism, and family values; as Missouri senator John Ashcroft said, "the infection of the mantras of the 60's affected the immune system of America. It began to accommodate the lowest and least rather than the best and highest."[2] This swerve away from the real America, in this argument, led to the loss of shared civic moral principles which were replaced by the privatized ones that resulted from the separation of church and state. It was not only cultural elites, however, who insisted on privatized values, but an activist liberal judiciary who banned religion from public life, while they mandated what is referred to as racial preference, protected the right to choice in *Roe v. Wade,* and produced activist environmental rulings that threatened private property. As Robert Bork said at the 1995 Christian Coalition convention, "A large part of our cultural confusion can be laid at the doorstep of the Supreme Court. . . . We must take back our culture from the courts."

Such a national popular can be assessed in terms of the way various practices achieve a coherence based not on what causes them or their specific rationale so much as on the similarity of their *effects*. As we have seen, the disclaimers of radical Christian women who may sincerely deny any bigoted intentions are in many ways beside the point, for the issue is not their particular intention so much as the way their activities join together with others' to impinge in a similar way on the same people. While the substance of beliefs and activities may be diverse, their effects are not.

In describing the historical shift in passion from the rock formation, to the Right and the popular conservative formation, Grossberg argues that it is neither academic discourse nor theological discourse nor even legal discourse that sets the tone for such shifts. Instead it is the popular culture of everyday life itself, which "seems to work at the intersection of the body and emotions . . . the source of its power, whatever it may seem to say, or whatever pleasures it may offer, can be identified with its place in people's affective lives, and *its ability to place other practices affectively."* (79–80, my italics) The question of passion is thus primarily about "the feeling of life," the history of struggle within and over the plane of emotions:

> For it is in their affective lives that people constantly struggle to care about something, and to find the energy to survive, to find the passion necessary to imagine and enact their own projects and possibilities. . . . Popular culture, operating with an affective sensibility, is a crucial ground where people give others, whether cultural practices or social groups, the authority to shape their identity and locate them within various circuits of power. People actively constitute places and forms of authority (both for themselves and for others) through the deployment and organization of affective investments. By making certain things matter, people "authorize" them to speak for them, not only as a spokesperson but also as a surrogate voice (e.g., when we sing along to popular songs). People give authority to that which they invest in; they let the objects of such investments speak for and in their stead. (83)

Here the popular songs will prove to be a collection of hymns and national anthems that are simultaneously and powerfully both religious and patriotic. Like Christmas carols or the national anthem or the school songs at sports events, they will unite us, for "we" all know the words. Thus a powerful group identity is called up, just as a passionate exclusivity is created, as Christmas always reminds those who are not Christian.[3]

Affect, or, as I have been calling it, the familiarity of sacred intimacy, organizes the emotions and narratives of life in many ways that are not overtly identified as religious. Popular culture establishes different moments of relative authority that are emotionally, if not overtly, connected to each other. For example, the Ten Commandments (through "Thou shalt not steal") are linked to the resistance to taxes which is linked to God's relation to a divinely ordained American global mission, for "God shed His grace on thee."

The importance of affective intensity, or affective individuality, is paradoxically related to the history of postmodernity, in which the supports of belief were fractured and deconstructed in relation to the rock formation and a postmodern economy. The 1950s of the liberal consensus, of the mythical family and idyllic small town, were also a time of the alienation and boredom of a middle-class youth culture. Young people's boredom interacted with an impossible narrative of history, into which they could no longer imagine themselves after the Holocaust and the bomb. Similarly they perceived a gap between emotion and meaning. In countering that boredom and especially that lack of a match between intense feeling and meaning, the rock formation mapped their alienation onto the way they lived their everyday lives, a mapping that also fit the transition to the suburbs, which produced a different kind of shock to the emotions. A sense of placelessness led to a feeling of perpetual transition, a new identity that was simultaneously a lack of identity. The sense of postwar economic optimism thus both coexisted with and contradicted feelings of terror, alienation, and boredom. It also accompanied an apocalyptic sense of anxiety in which the narrative of history was perceived to have been punctured by nuclear threat.

The organizing trope of signification, as Grossberg describes it, became the billboard. It could represent meaning that was neither true nor untrue, neither authentic nor inauthentic, but performative in the sense that a sign's meaning could be established only by what it did, and what it did could be assessed in terms of its emotional effects. (That those emotional effects also became the chief focus of the strategies of the free market will be discussed in chapter 6.) This ironically intense — while also alienated — rock formation of the 1960s eventually led, in the 1970s and

1980s, to a postmodern unwillingness to commit to anything, an "ironic knowing distance, coupled with a sense of emotional urgency." (212) Commitment or "mattering" that was tied to any particular cause came to be the most impossible thing of all, the thing to be laughed at:

> This is the era of the permanent smirk, the knowing chuckle, of jokey ambivalence as a way of life. This is the irony epidemic. . . . [It] does not celebrate or savage; it does not get its hands dirty . . . [it] is about avoidance. . . . [It] lives in terror of becoming . . . *anything*. . . . If everything is a pose, a sitcom riff, then you're still a kid, just goofing around. (217)

The success of Rush Limbaugh is closely related to, even as it recodes, this irony epidemic and will be discussed in chapter 6.

Underneath this irony was a constant sense of dread and unease, precisely because "there are no identifiable enemies and no grounds for confidence in the possibilities of change. Yet one [feels] threatened, under constant attack, simultaneously antagonistic and powerless" (219), as even pleasure and desire became risky. And within such a configuration that had no "anchoring effect" to link emotions and desires to meaning, it became impossible to care. Questions about how to make a difference had to confront the fact that there was no center against which to measure one's efforts. Postmodernity thus represented a crisis in people's ability to locate any meaning to which they could tie an empassioned commitment. In order to link passion to meaning, the reconstruction of everyday life by popular conservatism has thus exploited and reconfigured that sense of unease that it helped produce. In fact the strategy of traditionalist conservatism depends in part on the production of fear against which its own absolutist certainties can then function as an indispensable inoculation.

Ronald Reagan became the icon of this new conservative national popular based not on content but effects. Though he was not an authentic cowboy, or a traditional family man, or a churchgoer, the effects of his familiarity with the forms of popular culture, from Hollywood movies and the rhetoric of the common man to the vague language of everyday religious morality, were perceived as authentic. He knew how to speak the language of everyday life and of plain folks Americans, unlike academics, journalists, or other politicians who justifiably came to be known as the cultural elite, in part because of that fact. And this was true even as he constructed a millionaire populism in which corporations, millionaires, and ordinary people could feel themselves equal within the terms of that familiar Transparent American Subject. They were structurally situated in the same place, if that place was identified as opposition to the federal government.

The appeal of this conservative national popular was not an attempt "to win the minds of the nation, [but] a struggle over its heart and body." (255) And it was through "maps of mattering" that that struggle could then and now best be read:

> The image of mattering maps points to the constant attempt to organize moments of stable identity, sites at which people can, at least temporarily, find themselves "at home" with what they care about. Affect defines a structure and economy of belonging. The very notion of "the popular" assumes the articulation of identification and care; it assumes that what one identifies with (including moments of identity) matters and that what matters — what has authority — is the appropriate ground for identification. But mattering maps also involve the lines that connect the different sites of investments; they define the possibilities for moving from one investment to another, of locking the various fragments of identity together. They define not only what sites (practices, effects, structures) matter but how they matter. And they construct a lived coherence for those enclosed within their spaces. (84)

The intensity of mattering, while ideologically constructed, is nevertheless "always beyond ideological challenge because it is called into existence affectively." (86) And in postmodern America, where pessimism and a very strategic depoliticization had become the norm, affective investments increasingly became the most valuable political prize: "the condition of possibility for the optimism, invigoration and passions which are necessary for any struggle to change the world." (86) Thus the conditions of postmodernity described by postmodern theory — fragmentation, lack of a center, unease, fear — have proved to be precisely the resources drawn on to construct popular conservatism's conditions of possibility.

Here, in terms of these mattering maps, the work of the LaHayes, like that of other radical Christians, is articulated into a public agenda to be followed in the next chapter, a public agenda in which many different kinds of people with different kinds of religious and political beliefs nevertheless agree to the terms of religious conservative discourse: "It is in fact not a matter of what can be said but of what can matter, of what is worth saying, of what has some chance of mattering to people. It is the public language of what matters that is at stake" (162), literally, what has "value," or values.

ii.

The Act of Marriage, a book of advice about sexuality within marriage written by Tim and Beverly LaHaye, first published 1976 and reissued several times, insists on the rigidity of the family structure. But *inside* that structure, the practice of legitimate and physically satisfying sexuality is opened out in a way that may surprise those who imagine that evangelicals are simply uninterested in sex. What is developed in books like this one, and others that are even more attuned to postmodern life, like Archibald D. Hart's *The Sexual Man: Masculinity without Guilt,* is the sacred intimacy, not just of family feelings, but of an absolutist concept of heterosexuality itself in which sexual desire and activity are redefined in deep and intimate ways to fit the biblical interpretations legitimated in church communities and prayer groups.[4] This particular version of Christ's commands, along with the satisfying wholeness of homogenizing sameness, then provides a personal level of intimate familiarity with other Christians who have also been taught these same commands. The deeply emotional sense of belonging is in this way solidly attached to a real community that provides the basis for an emotional demand that the national community exactly replicate that familiar one.

Tim LaHaye's introduction suggests that the book be read only "by married couples, those immediately contemplating marriage, and those counseling married couples." He explains the need for such a book by noting that while most Christian books avoid the issue, most secular ones go overboard, advocating practices "considered improper by Biblical standards." In writing the book in a way that will allow Christians to trust his advice, he first legitimates his interest in sexuality: "To keep the facts that every couple needs to know from being offensive, I am writing this book with the help of Beverly, my wife of twenty-eight years."[5] Once the proper place for sexuality has been absolutely and clearly established as heterosexual, monogamous Christian marriage, the experience of satisfying sexuality can be opened up with great passion.

The key to this revalorized sexuality is the divine plan that allows the LaHayes to describe God's rules for sexuality: "The act of marriage is that beautiful and intimate relationship shared uniquely by a husband and wife in the privacy of their love — and it is sacred. In a real sense, God designed them for that relationship." (11) From the very beginning they define sexuality not as sinful but sacred and explain that lovemaking and procreation were ordained by God in the Garden of Eden *before* sin entered, God's first commandment having been "Be fruitful, and multiply, and replenish the earth." (11) This interpretation of sexuality counters the view that sexuality is unambiguously associated with Original Sin and the Fall. Here the sacred nature of sexuality in fact predates Original Sin: "This [commandment of God] necessarily includes the strong and beautiful mating urge a husband and wife feel for each other . . . and although we lack any written report for proof, it is reasonable to conclude that Adam and Eve made love before sin entered the garden." (11) Not only that, but God had created *all* the body parts before sin entered the Garden: "The idea that God designed our sex organs for our enjoyment comes almost as a surprise to some people." (11) They also draw on the Holy Trinity to legitimate the sacredness of sexuality, as long as it is within marriage, where sexuality is "undefiled because it remains a sacred experience." (13)

Just as Marshner reclaimed purity for the mother, grabbing it away from the impurities a misogynist culture had assigned to the maternal body, here the LaHayes reclaim purity for sexuality, and they do so in a way that allows for sexual pleasure that might be all the more sensual, especially for women. Because it is sacred, guilt need not interfere with its pleasures. The LaHayes remind us that God does condemn fornication, adultery, and homosexuality, for "God is the creator of sex. He set human drives in motion, not to torture men and women, but to bring them enjoyment and fulfillment. . . . What kind of God would go out of His way to equip His special creatures for an activity, give them the necessary drives to consummation, and then forbid its use? . . . Looking at it objectively, sex was given at least in part for marital enjoyment." (15) The Bible even approves of foreplay, and God "sees the intimacy practiced by married partners and approves it." (18) Judgment is reserved only for those "who violate His plan and desecrate themselves by engaging in sex outside of marriage." (18)

To "know" another person involves far more than an intellectual understanding. It concerns "the sublime, intimate interlocking of mind, heart, emotions, and body in a passionately eruptive climax that engulfs the participants in a wave of innocent relaxation that thoroughly expresses their love." (16) The metaphysical binary that opposes mind to body is here under intense cultural revision, for it is clear that mind and body cannot be separated in this version of knowing: "Some people have the strange idea that anything spiritually acceptable to God cannot be enjoyable," citing the example of a young woman he had counseled in one of his marriage seminars. She had resisted his advice to pray with her husband at night because she feared that would hinder their lovemaking. As it turned out, once she took his advice, their sex life improved: "To my amazement [she said], we found we were so emotionally close after prayer that it set the stage for loving." (16) As the LaHayes advise, communication is very important to women, and in this instance, because prayer is involved, women's needs are met because the man *has* to talk.

Yet in spite of the fact that their advice often draws on contemporary discourses sensitive to the circumstances of women, as it does here, two of their four main principles of lovemaking — (1) both husband and wife have sexual needs and drives that should be fulfilled in marriage, (2) when one marries, he forfeits control of his body to his partner, (3) both partners are forbidden to refuse the meeting of the mate's sexual needs, and (4) the act of marriage is approved by God — dangerously overlook the history of domestic abuse within families. They might, in fact, set the stage for more.

The book's first chapter, "What Lovemaking Means to a Man," suggests that sexual aggression is part of a man's nature: "God designed man to be the aggressor, provider, and leader of his family. Somehow that is tied to his sex drive. The woman who resents her husband's sex drive while enjoying his aggressive leadership had better face the fact that she cannot have one without the other." (23) Or vice versa. That sexual drive is almost immediately related to the man's sense of his manhood: "Whenever I find a fractured ego, I look for sexual frustration. . . . Success in other fields becomes a mockery if he strikes out in bed." (25) Part of the harshness of this is countered by his argument that the more a wife provides for her husband's needs, the more she will become the object of his love. He quotes one satisfied husband: "When you have a Cadillac in the garage, how can you be tempted to steal a Volkswagen off the street?" (29) And not only does sex make him love his wife more, but it also reduces friction in the home. The kids don't get on his nerves so much; he has an easier time concentrating; he is less prone to be edgy and hard to work with; and he will find it less difficult to retain lasting goals. It also makes him much more eager to spend his time at home: "The truly satisfied husband refuses to waste his business day on trivia; he wants each moment to count so he can get home to the wife and family who give all his hard work real purpose and meaning." (32)

And because a man is much more stimulated by visual temptations than a woman is and because he is driven by a "sex drive [that] is so powerful that sex often seems to be uppermost in his mind," it becomes clear that a sexually responsive wife is the key to a civil, orderly society in which men engage in responsible behavior. Now it is not only motherhood that guarantees the social order, but the wife's responsiveness to her husband's sexual needs. She will solve the problem of his greater responsiveness to the sexual temptations all around him by keeping his thought life pleasing to God: "Because she thinks more of his needs than her own tiredness, [she] will give her love freely to him." (34)

One does not have to doubt the sincerity of the LaHayes' description of their own marriage or the strength of their relationship, or trivialize the difficulty of keeping a marriage intact. Certainly it is not easy. Yet this description seems to infantilize men and to require that women accept that infantilization. One has to ask why an omnipotent God would have created sexuality in such a way as to make men less able than women to deal with it. Surely he would have foreseen the problem. This Christian advice book makes claims about men that would be called outrageous if made by feminists, but they are claims that will show up again in the Christian men's movement and in George Gilder's sociobiology, where the civilized man proves to be not only the hero but the exemplary victim in American civilization.

In another chapter, the LaHayes deal with what lovemaking means to a woman. It fulfills her womanhood (she will never accept herself as a woman until her husband accepts her as a wife); it reassures her of her husband's love; it satisfies her sex drive; it relaxes her nervous system ("As with a man, the female nervous system is intrinsically tied to the re-productive organs. God has made it possible for wives from all walks of life to enjoy a hygienically relaxing experience on their marriage bed. The act of marriage exists for the propagation of the race and personal enjoy-ment, it is true, and it does promote fidelity and fulfillment; but it also contributes a much needed relaxant to the nervous system." [45]). This curious "hygienically relaxing" experience is a woman's ultimate experi-ence, not childbirth, as some women might think, which is not a con-tinually rewarding experience. It is sex that provides the feeling of one-ness upon which a Christian marriage depends.

In spite of this strange, hygienic language, the LaHayes' description of women's sexuality provides a way to displace the guilt about sex that is part of the lesson women usually learn when Woman is divided in two: the good mother, presumably sexless, and the whore (the coding here covers the radical feminist, the lesbian, the overly sexualized welfare mother, the prostitute), whose sexuality is sinful. Rather than being repressed, here sexuality itself is divided cleanly in two: sacred sexuality (within marriage) and sinful sexuality (any other kind). Within such a frame, a good Christian woman can be both a good mother *and* sexual because sexuality has by now been purified. The sense of eroticism available within this configuration of sex for Christ should not be underestimated. Whatever the experience of a Christian woman actually is, the LaHayes determinedly construct a picture of a sexually satisfied Christian woman, drawing on a 1970 *Redbook* survey on sexual pleasure which found that "strongly religious women (over 25) seem to be more responsive," and that the religious woman "is more likely than the nonreligious woman to be orgasmic almost every time she engages in sex." (quoted in introduction, n.p.)[6]

The book provides detailed anatomical illustrations to teach sex without prudery or squeamishness, focusing in particular on the fact that men have not understood female sexuality, especially the importance of clitoral stimulation to enable women to have satisfying orgasms. Here the advice on sexuality is sensitive to the differences between women's needs and men's, insisting that women need more talk, more time in foreplay, and more emphasis on romance instead of fast sex. Husbands are then given lessons in how to do those things. Beverly LaHaye, among others, often refers to men's and women's different sexual needs in household terms: "Men are speedy microwaves; women tend to be slow-cooking Crockpots." (*Desires* 126) Another chapter, "The Key to Feminine Sexual Response," teaches a system devised by Dr. Arnold H. Kegel, who in 1947 developed a sequence of vaginal exercises to strengthen what they call the P.C., or pubococcygeus muscle, in women after childbirth and due to aging. The exercises are evidently well-known among doctors, and the LaHayes provide charts and advice for regular exercise to improve sex and help make the vagina "active."

In discussing the unfulfilled sexuality of women, the LaHayes argue that society has seriously shortchanged women in terms of recognizing their sexuality:

The strangest paradox in the realm of sexuality is the widespread idea that woman's orgasmic capability is less than a man's, whereas in reality it may be even greater. Equally difficult to understand is why such a pleasurable and exciting experience has been hidden from so many women while their male counterparts almost universally have tasted the delight of ejaculation. No research or tradition suggests that the male orgasmic capability has ever been questioned in any culture. Yet the tragic tale of female sexual frustration winds its way through almost every tribe and people, leaving literally billions of married women sexually unfulfilled. Fortunately there is no longer any reason to perpetrate this hoax on potentially one-half the world's population. (110)

In a selective interpretation, they argue that though it has been true of "almost every tribe and people" that women were sexually frustrated, this is a historical and changeable thing, unlike the simultaneous and opposite argument that because male dominance has occurred in "almost every tribe and people," it is eternal, natural, and cannot be changed.

And because women enjoy a greater capacity for love than men do, they usually try harder to be good and faithful lovers, yet "one thing has been obvious — far more women than men are willing to settle for a second-rate love life." (96) Ultimately, in this marriage training, improvements in sexual sensitivity and responsiveness on the part of both partners has one cause and one result: "God put the sex drive in human beings to inspire them to mate through marriage. If a single person satisfies that drive with a vibrator or other means, his or her major motivation to marry is destroyed. It is also dangerous because it creates an erotic sensation that no human on earth can equal." (289–90) Thus the pleasure of sex is designed by God to keep people — but, it seems, primarily men, who are less likely to stay — in monogamous, heterosexual, permanent relationships. And as it becomes clear that providing a satisfying sexual relationship that will keep men at home is a key duty, women's sexuality is recoded in terms of their pleasure as well. This pleasure is useful for keeping such marriages intact in an age when many women do not have to depend economically on men.

Such marriage training grounded in belief also has the very important capacity to build a mutual respect, friendship, and affection, because it includes a commitment to working to keep the marriage together:

Everything a Christ-controlled Christian does is spiritual. That includes eating, elimination, spanking children, or emptying the trash. Why isolate sex in marriage as if it were in a category all by itself? Many spiritual Christians pray before going to bed, then in a matter of minutes engage each other in foreplay, stimulation, coitus, and finally orgasm. Why isn't that just as spiritual as anything else couples do? In fact, we believe the more truly spiritual they are, the more loving and affectionate they will be with each other and consequently the more frequently they will make love. Actually, coitus should be the ultimate expression of a rich spiritual experience that continues to enrich the couple's relationship. (312)

The LaHayes have brought the question of what matters full circle by joining spirituality and sexuality. The title of Kelly Connor's *The Heart of the Matter,* an album of love songs for Christians, gives a name to the sexuality that is an expression of God's tablet inscribed in the intimacy of the heart and body. Heart and body are deeply and sensually involved in loving relationships watched over by a loving but demanding God — and the male leaders of his institutions.

iii.

The binaries that are so important to this belief come together in the oneness that defines marriage: two people united as one under the guidance of one God and ultimately one definition of the nation. The sacred sexuality described by the LaHayes is also the subject matter of abstinence training for young people and the passionate resistance to sex education in the public schools. This section will briefly describe several of these forms of intimate training, beginning with *Wait for Me,* a videotape distributed by Concerned Women for America.[7] A high-quality, innovative short film, it tells a story of the dangers of sex before marriage in which a young man dreams that he and several of his friends go to a party at the home of another member of their church youth group whose parents are out of town.

After arriving at the huge, expensive, stylish home full of teenagers and noise, the main character wanders from room to room in a daze until he encounters a stranger who proves to be an angel sent to guide him through this initiation into sexuality. Acted with great comedic flair, this angel, Gabe, proves his identity by instantly turning into an emcee under a rotating light at the Starlight Lounge, where "Kumbaya" is played as a dance tune, part of the witty and smart juxtaposition of various television genres throughout the video. After various scenes in which petting is narrated in a Howard Cosell play-by-play description and Rod Serling shows up to describe the Teenlife Zone, they move upstairs to the bedroom for the most important encounter in this hormonal challenge to the heart. There a couple embraces on the bed, though neither quite knows how far to go. The camera then moves in very close to situate the viewer as if in the girl's position. A series of almost surreal faces looks down from directly above, faces of people who have just learned she has had sex. Some are presented as caricatures, some as if they were real: in a black-and-white image, a parodic, shotgun-toting father rushes down the stairs and says, "That boy — he did — he did *what* to you?"; a caricatured Church Lady tells her self-righteously, "You'll rot in hell!"; a hip teenage girl, very impressed, says, "Cool!"; the girl's best friend says worriedly, "I thought you were gonna wait"; a very serious, dour pastor framed against a stained-glass window says in somber tones, "I'm very disappointed in you, Jenny"; a sleazy-looking guy with an earring and a leering sneer, licking his lips, says, "Will you go out with *moi?*"; two young girls giggle and ask, "So, can I like be your bridesmaid?"; her best friend asks, "What if you get pregnant?"; another girl says, "Come on, everybody's doing it"; her best friend asks, "What about AIDS?"; and finally, her boyfriend, lying on the couch and offering her flowers, says, "You're the only one I'll ever love." Then it is the young man's turn. The series of images going through his mind contains a few of the same characters: a CEO, perhaps his father or his future boss; the Church Lady again; another teenage boy — "How'd you convince her?"; a teenage boy who congratulates him; another teenage girl — "If it feels good, do it"; a guy who says, "Cool. Way to score, dude"; and finally the girl herself — "I can't wait till we're married." We are then transported into his grandparents' living room as they describe their long, happy marriage.

The girl is then transported to school where, standing in front of her locker as two friends ask whether she is going to the game, she answers, "I have birthing class tonight," and we see that she is pregnant. As they leave, and she says, "Oh Mom, I wish I'd listened to you; you're the only real friend I've got," she is transported home. No longer pregnant, she listens to her mother tell her about sex as well as, rather mysteriously, about her own regrets: "That's the horror of growing old. You bring all your yesterdays with you." She then reveals that she had sex with three men in college before she met her husband. He was different and never asked for sex before marriage because he was a Christian saving himself for "that special union of marriage."

But the mother is still filled with regret: "My past came chasing after me. I was paranoid that he wouldn't want me." Though he showed real love and accepted her as she was, she felt she had shortchanged him. While he could give himself fully to her, she could never again give herself the first time. And when her daughter says, "People don't think of sex that way anymore," the mother gives a moral lesson whose content is quite beautiful, even if its tone is stifling because of a cloying Hallmark effect very different from the rest of the video:

> The God who created you, cherishes you, intended for the union between a man and a woman to mirror His desire to love and nurture us. He gave of Himself once so that we could enjoy Him forever. And that's the way sex and marriage should be. Once you make the choice to have sex you can't go back and undo it. Saying you made a mistake and you're sorry is wonderful, but it won't make you a virgin again. That's why I hope and pray you'll wait.

In the video's most unsettling scene, we are then transported back to the couple in the bedroom, this time to see them in wedding attire as he carries her across the threshold. Placing her on the bed, he goes into the bathroom, and we discover that three aggressive, boisterous guys have suddenly appeared on the bed with her, as she shrinks from them, terrified: "What are you doing here?" "What do you mean, baby? You slept with me. We're a part of you forever. Forever and ever. A*men!*" Leering, laughing, threatening and wild, they have in fact taken over the bed.

From there the scene shifts again to Gabe, now a game-show host, and then as the camera moves back, we are shown several frames: the bedroom door through which we have been looking at the couple, then the lights, the scenery, the entire mise-en-scène. Gabe and Johnny are looking through that door into the bedroom with us: "It's easy to shatter an illusion and walk back into the real world. . . . But it's devastating when reality is shattered by a hasty decision, a thoughtless word, or a selfish act. . . . There isn't a thrill on earth worth dying for." Because the two have not been self-righteous characters in the video, the sincerity of their advice is especially appealing: "God says wait."

The film ends with the voice of the mother reading from the Bible, from Psalms 103 and 145, and though earlier she was annoyingly self-righteous, here the voice-over is beautiful, loving, comforting, resonant. One has to imagine hearing this from a number of different perspectives, in particular that of teenagers who may already have had sex voluntarily or who have perhaps been forced into sex:

> The Lord is compassionate and gracious. He does not treat us as our sins deserve, or repay us according to our inequities. He has removed our transgressions from us. The Lord upholds all those who fall and lifts up all who are bowed down. The Lord is righteous in all His ways and loving toward all He has made.

Religious conservatives are right to focus on helping teenagers remain abstinent and on addressing their cravings for significance. It is easy to see how important such advice is to young people who feel pressured to conform and who often have little guidance about the integrity of relationships or who lack the self-esteem to say no. As Gabe says, it should not matter what other people are doing or other people are saying: "So what? If we call ourselves a Christian, we won't go with the flow. God calls us to be separate from the world and He offers us the strength to be His examples." This kind of training may be most effective for teenagers who have very little structure in their lives because of poverty, but it is also effective for teenagers with absentee parents or with baby boomer parents who may have rejected religion for good reasons, yet forgot to put some other consistent structure in its place.

When abstinence training is left only to religious conservatives, however, vulnerable young people are also taught, in the depths of their most passionate feelings, the condemnation of difference.[8]

iv.

Within this configuration of sacred intimacy, the public school is at the very center of activism about sex-education and antidiscrimination curricula. Because the child guarantees the sacred gender of the partners in the marriage, the dangers to that child posed by homosexuals energizes absolutist conservatism. The Lambda Report, a group that monitors gay activism, produced two influential videos about what is called the gay agenda. The first, *The Gay Agenda,* was a hit among military audiences and conservative congressmen, but it could not be shown to families in church settings because it included tabloid coverage of provocative scenes from gay pride parades and the most extreme reaches of gay eroticism. The second, *The Gay Agenda in Public Education,* however, counters that difficulty by shifting to a much more discrete, professional focus on the influence of gay activists in the public schools.[9] The discussion thus moves from the immediate sexual dangers to children to the much more vague, omnipresent cultural dangers to the child's mind and his Christian identity.

The signature beginning of the video, like the ending, features a sunrise, the biblically coded light of Christ's promised return. As the feature itself begins, we watch a little girl on a playground, swinging in slow motion. Somber music accompanies this image of the innocence of childhood and the vulnerability of everyday life. But that idyllic, sweet image is suddenly interrupted by noisy clips of public schools in crisis: scholastic standards are in a free fall, budgets are mismanaged, campus violence is rampant, teachers are unqualified, classes are disrupted by protests, and students are barely able to read their own diplomas. In spite of this chaos, however, the voice-over tells us that public-school educators are diverting resources away from basic academics in order to promote the gay agenda in antidiscrimination and sex-education courses. The video then turns to concerned mothers and caring professionals, who are interviewed and shown in poses framed by family pictures or book-lined shelves. Their discourse is polite, articulate, and calm. Interviewees include Joe Dallas, a counselor whose book, *Desires in Conflict: Answering the Struggle for Sexual Identity,* is used to teach people that homosexuality is something that can be cured; Dolores Ayling, president of Concerned Parents for Educational Accountability, whose activism helped drive the superintendent of schools in New York City, Joe Fernandez, from office because of the Rainbow Curriculum; Edie Gieb, president of Parents and Students United, in Fairfax, Virginia, who fought Project 10, an antidiscrimination curriculum; John D. Hartigan, legal counsel for School Board 24 in Queens, New York; and Howard L. Hurwitz, Ph.D., identified only as a former high-school principal.

The video makes clear that the key enemy is public education. Pat Buchanan often sounds this theme as well, as he incites fear about the fact that secular education is transforming our kids into aliens, turning them against us and teaching them to question our ideas. While many of the concerns about public education — concerns about its inefficiency, its overloaded administrative layers, and its often unrealistic scenarios for adding information to the curriculum — are indeed important, the main concern of this video is the danger of intimate difference. It echoes Elaine

Pagels's argument that Christianity has historically defined the satanic not so much in terms of distant threats but in relation to intimate ones. The most dangerous characteristic of the satanic enemy is that though he will look just like us, he will nevertheless have changed completely: "How could one of *us* become one of *them?*"[10] This amorphous fear echoes throughout discussions of the public-school curriculum, as many of these activists very consciously learn their political strategies from groups they now oppose. One of the interviewees, a nice, intelligent mother named Edie Gieb, tells how she learned her activism from liberals, who well knew that if you get a child early enough, you can change society.

The video ends with a return to the playground, as slow-motion camera work captures other kids playing, then gradually focuses on another child on a swing, this time a beautiful blond boy. The image freezes on his face.

v.

To make a transition from this question of one's deepest concerns for the family and in particular for one's own children, if not those of other people, to the activism to be discussed in the next chapter, I turn finally to the crucial question of women's involvement in protecting their children from postmodernity by monitoring and running for local school boards. While the Christian Coalition has obviously influenced politics at the national level, its most intense activity is focused on the grassroots level. Training people to work at that level helps Christians who, during the period when fundamentalists shunned civic involvement, had allowed their civic muscles to atrophy. Beginning at the local level helps merge them back into citizenship and prepare them to run for higher office as they draw on their local experience.[11] The Christian Coalition conducts School Board Training Seminars around the country, and in conjunction with those seminars publishes a sophisticated leadership manual that consists of the following sections: "Dealing with Teachers Unions," "Education Reform and School Choice," "Academic Standards and Outcome-Based Education," "Winning as a Religious Conservative," and "Developing Your Campaign Plan and Message." Also available for purchase and use in one's church group are a set of videotapes entitled *Targeting Voters and Building Coalitions, Building an Effective Grassroots Organization, Developing Your Campaign Plan and Message,* and *Developing and Implementing a Fundraising Plan,* among others.

One of those videotapes features a talk by Shelly Uscinski, from Merrimack, New Hampshire, a mother of three children, with one deceased. Her concerns about a health curriculum convinced her to run for the seat held by the chairman of the local school board, which she won by three votes after a very bitter campaign. The election and the subsequent activities of the school board, such as attempts to teach creationism, have torn the town apart. A devout Catholic in her late thirties, small, with a deceptively shy demeanor and a determined steeliness, Uscinski's description of her treatment by liberals in the community shows how that opposition helped confirm her convictions and build community support for her. She was labeled a radical far-right Christian fundamentalist wacko attempting to take over local politics: NARAL and Planned Parenthood campaigned against her and called her the most dangerous woman in New Hampshire; she was accused of killing children because she did not want the AIDS curriculum taught in the first grade and of being a white supremacist; she was compared to Goering and Hitler; and she was accused of having an affair with the chairman of the school board. Because she had been pregnant at the time of her first marriage, at the age of seventeen, she was also reviled as a teenage mother and mocked because of the way she spoke, the way she held her hands, even the way she took notes during meetings. The accusation of extremism, much of it both misogynist and classist, backfired, however, because she does not look like any of those frightening things. And those attacks, in fact, aroused sympathy for her. She is quietly firm about the ultimate irrelevance of those attacks and insists that if one has lost a child, nothing else hurts.

However, she did go through a period after her election when, the day after school-board meetings, the stress would take its toll and she could not get out of bed. Gradually, however, she trained herself to deal with such hostile circumstances, and when friends asked how she could put up with it, she gives the answer in her videotaped talk:

> My children . . . my children. They're the most important thing to me in my life. And it's that simple. I could not sit back with the knowledge of what they wanted to teach my children. The assault has got to stop. We cannot send our children off on the school bus any more and trust that the schools are doing the right thing. Our children and our nation depend on us. And I hope and pray that we are not too late in turning things around for the better.[12]

Even the accusation that she was a stealth candidate for Pat Robertson came to look very foolish, because of her deeply sincere demeanor; she is open and forthright about her activities, not at all devious in the sense implied by the word "stealth." Interpreting her actions that way has more to do with the fact that liberals and those engaged only in secular analyses often do not understand how fundamentally linked these intimate questions of sexuality are to an absolutist worldview; Uscinski had never even heard of the Christian Coalition when she ran on her own. There is no stealth in her motivation, no question about why she does what she does. It is for our children and our grandchildren, she says; "we must have a seat at the table." Because this health curriculum took on things like sex education and AIDs education, "areas that were not any of their concern," it intruded into the sacred area of the family and was thus an attack on her deepest identity as "an average mother who stayed home and raised my children." After joining the board, she was able to get Planned Parenthood banned, the health curriculum sent back to study, and, as she boasts, the committees stacked in favor of conservatives.

What is clear is that the more she was attacked, the more the differences among beliefs came to be collapsed into absolutist sameness and the more a wide variety of people began to see those attacks as unfair. Many Christians then generalized those attacks into an attack on their own religious faith, even those who would never associate themselves with someone like Pat Robertson. Their Christian commitment was thus not to the letter of dogma but to the deep familiar feelings of family so amorphously appealed to and attacked. The homogenizing effects of such a discourse could be seen in Uscinski's rage at being asked to prove that she, a Catholic, was not a fundamentalist Christian, a question that, in her reading, sounds all too much like another kind of antidemocratic question: "Are you now or have you ever been a Christian?" Her supporters even had buttons made that said, "It's not a crime to be a Christian," and, "No religious test should ever be required to hold public office."

Though her attackers showed their own narrowness, her generalized faith also eventually revealed a similar narrowness after the Christian Coalition discovered her. She was invited to speak at the national Road to Victory convention in 1994, which she described as "Republican heaven," surrounded as she was by Dan Quayle and Pat Buchanan and Elizabeth Dole. Very different kinds of people of faith had come together in the hands of Robertson around the question of the deep, inarticulable love of children, in part driven into homogeneity by attackers who had themselves falsely homogenized them from the beginning.

Uscinski's unpretentious, if rambling, talk ends with advice that is also contained in the Training Manual, which also includes a collection of newspaper articles about her campaign. She advises activists to go door to door; *always smile;* take your children with you; forewarn your spouse that you are going to be out all the time and that the phone will ring all the time; make sure that you get people to register to vote; and perhaps most important, once you have discovered that there is an issue of concern to you, begin regularly writing letters to the newspaper so that you will have developed a concern about that issue before you run for the board. You have to awaken other parents in your town in order to organize opposition. Her message to her audience is one we will hear again in the next chapter. Politics is not so much about the public sphere as it is about the private one: "It's as important to know who's in the principal's office as it is to know who's in the President's office. Our children are our future."

When popular culture in all its forms is framed by the Bible as the book of absolute law, aided by the lack of knowledge on the part of secular critics, and when it works in conjunction with the absolutist morality of male-headed institutions like churches and political organizations, when absolutist belief saturates the deeply sensual experiences of community, and when it is organized within the extraordinarily sophisticated media resources of religious television, radio, and computer nets, the surrogate voice of God takes on a powerful interior/public resonance. It might be said to collapse the superego, the voice of God and the conscience, directly into the Imaginary, the personal site of individual, phantasmatic identity, which, of course, is what traditionalist conservatism wants it to do. And in terms of women's involvement, the formerly transgressive semiotic meaning collapses into the commandments of those in power. Putting one's heart in this God's hands is a serious matter for all of us who do not live in his absolutist Book.

THREE

Kitchen Table Politics: The Folking

of America

Who but a woman is as deeply concerned about her children and her home? Who but a woman has the time, the intuition, and the drive to restore our nation? . . . The women of this nation are at a crossroads of history. — Beverly LaHaye

I'm glad I didn't fit in with *that* group of people.
— John Brennan, about his time on MTV's *The Real World*

While the construction of passion on the terms of familiarity and sacred intimacy helps link the family to the nation, women's activism, symbolized as work done around the kitchen table, extends the lessons taught in the immediate family into public policy. This chapter follows several examples of that activism to show its range: a training workshop for prayer-group leaders of Concerned Women for America; the advice of a former cabinet member of the state of Virginia, Kay Coles James, on becoming a "strategic presence for Christ in the public sector"; the entrepreneurial activism of Star Parker in South Central Los Angeles; the anti-gay and property-rights activism of two Oregon women, Loretta Neet and Kathy Phelps; the advice of Rebecca Hagelin in a media-training workshop in the Christian Coalition Leadership Series; and finally a speech by Elizabeth Dole, in which her own personal religious witness becomes a performance on the well-funded, absolutist political stage of the Christian Coalition's national revival.

The almost quaint simplicity of the kitchen table could not be more deceptive, of course, for it is one of the most pragmatic, efficient, and emotionally coded tools for activism. It functions both in actuality and as a metaphor for the ability of these women to move beyond the intimate training within the family and address what they perceive as threats to the homogeneous community of which they are a part. In doing so, women's activism becomes a key element in the postmodern "folking" of America in which homogeneous groups draw together in a variety of ways that exclude people who are not like them. Women's grassroots organizing takes various forms: keeping phone trees, electronic networks, and mailing lists up to date; circulating petitions; monitoring local governments and school boards; establishing communication with the local press; and running for public office, among other things. It also depends on the reconstruction of the True Woman as Christian social reformer and the Abnormal Woman as radical feminist. As Beverly LaHaye says, "If you take an honest look at American history, you'll discover that women have often been in the forefront of social reform movements, especially ones that would strengthen and promote family stability. (You'll also discover that radicalized women have led some of the most morally corrupt organizations in America.)"[1]

The postmodern economy has produced working conditions in which workers must be as flexible as their work schedules, making it difficult for them to participate in community activities, as labor unions and political parties, too, have lost their ability to provide group identity. As a result, one of the only places to find anything resembling a community is the church, where participation does not interfere with the work week and where both adults and children together can interact with people of all ages. It is not only small towns that are cemented by churches, which often function as highly organized cells, but suburban and urban communities as well. These church communities also recognize that women have family responsibilities, unlike many other political organizations that see the political activist in generic terms — as someone who does not have responsibilities outside of work, does not need help with child care, and has no difficulty attending meetings at night.

Members of many radical conservative religious communities come together regularly not only to pray but also to learn how to run for public office and to distribute voters' guides that endorse candidates in such a way so as not to jeopardize the church's 501(c)(3) tax exemption prohibiting partisan political endorsements (though in relation to the Christian Coalition, that exemption is under challenge). These communities take advantage of the fragmentations and disruptions of postmodernity by means of the resources of postmodernity: electronic networks, the simultaneous downloading of organizing information through satellite transmission to individual church groups, even the development of alternative conservative media networks, such as National Empowerment Television and linkages between talk radio, grassroots organizing, and conservative national political leadership.[2]

Political activism is also legitimated by a belief in a narrow interpretation of natural law, which links the absolute morality of traditional religion to the need to reinforce that morality in public policy. Charles Rice, in a book published by the Ignatius Press and sold at the 1994 Christian Coalition convention in Washington, D.C., defines natural law in this way: "The natural law is a set of manufacturer's directions written into our nature so that we can discover through reason how we ought to act. The Ten Commandments, and other prescriptions of the divine law, specify some applications of that natural law. We ought to welcome those manufacturer's directions, whether written in our nature or on tablets of stone."[3] That version of natural law also sets the foundation for Regent University's American Center for Law and Justice, which provides free legal help for people who feel their religious rights are being violated. The secular, much more direct political use made of natural law will be followed in chapter 5, in a discussion of George Gilder's sociobiology, where it grounds absolute sexual difference in a sexual constitution more basic even than the legal Constitution.

Blurring absolute gender divisions causes us to fall out of being into nonbeing. Samuel A. Nigro, M.D., develops that argument first by quoting Thomas Carlyle: "Men and women are different, and sex outside of love and marriage is pollution." He then goes on, "If not in tune with nature and nature's God, existence is an agony because it is non-being. It becomes a journey among the dead and among the witless swindlers of the press and media and among the unstably dogmatic and arrogantly humble scientists who cannot get anything right. Without being there is neither pilgrimage nor a road nor even genuine sex."[4] As we have already seen, that sense of threat and the unease aroused by blurring gender differences also grounds many women's deep fears about postmodernity's challenges to traditional culture, a sense of threat that drives many of them into action, as Beverly LaHaye says: "Women instinctively have this desire to protect, comfort, and serve. I am certain this is a major reason why they have been so aggressive in social reform movements. They see their families and lives coming under attack and they cannot remain passive." (16) Describing women as inherently nurturing will, however, paradoxically legitimate their protective aggressiveness. That aggressiveness can then be seen not as abnormal for women, as is the manly aggressiveness of feminists, but as womanly, because it is now natural aggression or agency in defense of their children.

The founding of Concerned Women for America was a direct response to feminism, and in particular, to the National Women's Convention in November 1977, in Houston, which celebrated the International Year of the Woman. In describing the need for such an organization, LaHaye uses the familiar rhetorical frame of anticommunism, apocalyptic prophecy, and opposition to the socialist welfare state, attributing her motivation to the activism of women in Brazil in the 1960s. In her view, those women were responsible for the defeat of communism in that country. She does not tell us that their activism helped install a military dictatorship in 1964 that lasted twenty years and saw the torture and murder of thousands of Brazilians, as well as the exile of many clergy and laity involved in liberation theology, including Paolo Freire. To show the way resonance works, I have italicized parts of LaHaye's text to foreground the kinds of phrases she was using in 1964, which have now become common to political discourse. They need no explanation, their clarity coming from those shared feelings:

> Through the courageous actions and prayers of hundreds of thousands of women in Brazil, that nation was *saved from a bloody communist revolution!* Who but a woman could have led such a successful educational campaign against *Marxism?*
>
> Do you see the potential that the women of America have for bringing about a *restoration of our nation to moral sanity?*
>
> I sincerely believe that God is calling the Christian women of America to draw together in a spirit of unity and purpose to *protect the rights of the family.* I believe it is time for us to set aside our doctrinal differences to work for *a spiritually renewed America.* Who but a woman is as deeply concerned about *her children and her home?* Who but a woman has the time, the intuition, and the drive to *restore our nation?*
>
> The women of this nation are at a *crossroads of history. The battle lines are becoming more clearly defined. The forces of darkness are becoming darker. There is no neutral ground in the battle to come.* . . .
>
> In Brazil, *the subversives called themselves Communists; in America, they may call themselves feminists or humanists.* The label makes little difference, because many of them are seeking *the destruction of morality and human freedom.* (13–14)

That this is a battle over the definition of the human being in terms of the members of the traditional nuclear family is shown with stark clarity by the opposition between the True Woman and the lesbian, the woman who has all along lurked beneath the image of the radical feminist. LaHaye's description of the Houston convention is based on shocking stories by Christian women who attended the convention unaware that they would find a den of radical feminism:

> It was difficult for me to convey the feelings I experienced after listening to Gladys Dickelman unfold the story of the Houston convention. I was *nauseous and filled with despair* as I realized that those feminists were claiming to speak for all women in America. In my heart I knew that was a lie. Those feminists had managed to convince Congress to spend five million dollars of *our tax money* to hold state conventions and then this grand finale at Houston, which seemed to be a *Marxist/lesbian circus,* manipulated and controlled from the beginning by a dissident group of feminists who were *demanding federal intervention into our lives.*
>
> *My nausea soon changed to rage,* and I determined in my heart that I would do whatever was necessary to *raise up a standard of righteousness against feminism.* (28–29)

Nausea and nonbeing can be countered by rage and the insistence on absolute gender identity, the nausea arising out of the miasma Marshner discovered, the rage aroused by the "fatal woman," Lynda Hart's term for the mannish lesbian, who is also indistinguishable from the dangerous Marxist feminist.[5]

Such rage and nausea inspired an organization that claims to have six hundred thousand members and eleven hundred prayer and action chapters, its goal to see "the family restored and preserved as that bedrock institution of society consisting of individuals related by blood, heterosexual marriage, birth, or adoption."[6] Or as the *Washington Times* tells it, in a way that leaves no confusion about the definition of family values, "Family values, [LaHaye] says, is a married mother and father and children. It is passionately pro-life, virulently anti-homosexual, hostile to feminists. Period."[7] CWA's prayer and action meetings are an arm of the church rather than substitutes for church attendance, and these are their goals:

> Informed prayer for our nation and its leaders. CWA does this by informing Christians of issues that affect our Judeo-Christian moral

standards, exposing movements which seek to weaken the family structure, and educating members about the legislative process in order to encourage pro-family public policy. All of which must be encompassed by many prayers. . . . God will reward the chapter leader and those who faithfully meet for united prayer and action.[8]

The training document for women who want to become prayer chapter leaders, "Opportunities for Leadership in Concerned Women for America," was distributed at a leadership-training workshop at the national convention in Washington, D.C., in September 1994. The workshop drew on the familiar metaphor of the heart: "How to Use Your Servant's Heart for Leadership: cwa Opportunities in Your Local Area." The document gives women gentle support for fitting their activism together with their family responsibilities and their faith, encouraging them to "lead women in your area down the path of a great movement to make righteousness a standard for our families and nation."[9]

The prayer and action chapters are most effective when "they meet regularly to inform Christians of pertinent issues so that they can pray as a group and individually." And they are united in a statement of faith, with which a chapter leader must agree:

> We believe the Bible to be the verbally inspired, inerrant Word of God and the final authority on faith and practice.
>
> We believe Jesus Christ is the divine Son of God, was born of a virgin, lived a sinless life, died a sacrificial death, rose bodily from the dead on the third day and ascended into Heaven from whence He will come again to receive all believers unto Himself.
>
> We believe all men are fallen creations of Adam's race and in need of salvation by grace through personal faith in the Lord Jesus Christ.
>
> We believe it is our duty to serve God to the best of our ability, to pray for a moral and spiritual revival that will return this nation to the traditional values upon which it was founded. (3)

The duties of a prayer and action chapter leader are, first of all, to keep "prayer and her relationship with God and her family a priority" and to "become grounded in the Word of God." She is also to be the liaison between cwa and the women of her group, to plan monthly prayer and action chapter meetings, to keep "members praying, learning, writing, calling and motivated," to establish and activate a prayer/phone chain that the national headquarters of cwa can use to lobby Congress, to recruit new members and establish new chapters, to keep herself politi-cally informed, and, for those working at the state or national level, to go through leadership training at the Navigation Center in Colorado Springs. Increasingly, the fact that radical Christian groups are working in coalitions finds CWA members distributing Christian Coalition voters' guides and inserting them into church bulletins the Sunday before local and national elections.[10]

Women are advised not to volunteer to be prayer and action chapter leaders if they are doing so simply because they think they should, rather than out of their own discernment of God's call. They are also warned that activism can eat up their time, and they are given sound advice: it is a bad thing to be compulsive, you must learn to say no, no one is indispens-able, politics can present unique temptations because it is very heady, you should not look for glory and recognition but be willing to do what is needed, and, perhaps most important, you should not feel guilty when other responsibilities interfere: "If no one is there, it's up to God." Perfec-tionist women of all political persuasions will appreciate the power of this permission to say no. The central feature of the chapters is the priority of prayer, for Satan can derail us by making us so busy, getting us so excited, that we forget to pray and keep ourselves centered, again an important contribution to women living fragmented lives, who are here given a meditative focus and center. Other leadership positions available at the area or state level include monitoring the legislature and keeping mem-bers and the national organization informed.

The motherly face has also been expanded to include grandmothers, perhaps because of the fact that many Christian activists are now retirees. A May 1995 fundraising letter from LaHaye to CWA members features a series of photographs of Joyce Woodall, a sixty-seven-year-old mother of five (including Jim Woodall, the vice president of management of CWA, who gives some of the most rabid anti-gay talks one hears at CWA con-ventions), grandmother of seventeen, great-grandmother of one. She is shown sitting on a porch reading her Bible before being arrested. This new grandmotherly face counters another FACE, the Freedom of Access to Clinic Entrances Act, passed to provide security for health clinics that also provide abortion services: "As she knelt and prayed, silently and peacefully, Joyce . . . was forcefully lifted and led away." But, writes LaHaye, the FACE Act targets only one group of people as criminals, pro-lifers, while allowing every other group to protest legally. Joyce is, in fact, being criminalized for praying: "Because Joyce prayed in front of an abortion clinic, she's been charged with a federal crime and threatened with imprisonment."[11]

We have already seen how deeply personal and autobiographical one's relationship to prayer can be, and here it is as if Woodall's very soul has been criminalized. Though Concerned Women for America's appeal to conservative women is increasingly challenged by the hip conservatism of young urban women such as the Independent Women's Forum and the much more visible conservative congresswomen and journalists, it would be a mistake to forget the resonance generated by the arrest of this grandmotherly activist.

ii.

One of the most visible and effective members of Concerned Women for America, formerly its national pro-life spokeswoman, is Kay Coles James, who provides an African American motherly face for an organization that is overwhelmingly white, even though it has intensified its outreach to minorities. Like other African American conservatives, such as Alan Keyes, she is a master of the oratory and cadence of the black church and the Civil Rights movement. James, who was a member of the cabinet of Governor George Allen, senior vice-president of the Family Research Council, and assistant secretary for public affairs at the U.S. Department of Health and Human Services under George Bush, now serves as the Dean of Regent University's Robertson School of Government. She is described in a blurb on the cover of her autobiography, *Never Forget*, as "a strategic presence for Christ in the public sector." She tells a story about a trip to Mount Vernon with her children, who wanted to know how George Washington mowed all the grass in Mount Vernon's huge lawn. Sitting down with them next to the slaves' burial site, she resolved, "I will never forget where I came from."[12] And where she came from includes not only the black church but a public housing project; a segregated neighborhood in Richmond, where she faced demanding teachers in school and Klan rallies on the football field; an integrated high school whose racist teachers barely acknowledged African American students until their parents organized to force them to; a black college where she participated in sit-ins against the administration. At other times, she was involved in a fair-housing study that revealed blatant racism, a job in management at AT&T, motherhood, the near loss of one of her children, a position as the spokeswoman for National Right to Life, and finally her positions in government. All of this is given coherence by her resolve never to forget: "I haven't forgotten the racial slurs, the spit in my face, or the pin pricks I faced when I integrated the schools. I haven't forgotten being turned away from housing simply because I am black. And I most certainly haven't forgotten my childhood and the pain of going to bed hungry and cold." (177–78)

James's autobiography shows how powerful the consolations of religion can be, how deep the sense of self-worth to be gained from it. While attending a black college, Hampton, she was powerfully affected by the Black Pride movement, whose language was circulated through her evangelical Christian beliefs, her words resonating with LaHaye's:

> This discovery and celebration of my black identity was intimately related to my discovery and celebration of my identity as a beloved child of God. . . . *I am fearfully and wonderfully made!* I would tell myself over and over again. And my soul rejoiced to know very well the love my Heavenly Father had for me. It was so freeing, so exhilarating. It was with a sense of childlike wonder that I grasped the fact that God loved even a fatherless, little nappy-haired girl like me. He had knit me together in my mother's womb. He loved me even before I was born! It wasn't long before it dawned on me that not only had God created me, but He had created me black. . . . We knew that black is beautiful, and we knew why. God had created us in His image, and God did not create mistakes. (95, her italics)

In this powerful, personal rhetoric, James constructs her own version of feminism, differentiating what she calls the radical version from the real one:

> I am who I am. I don't have to change who I am to be equal to anyone. Why do I have to become like a man to be equal? I bear children; it is a part of who I am. And I don't need this 'right' to mutilate my feminine organs and kill my children in order to be equal to men. Maybe what we need to work on is getting the government and private sector to value women in their uniqueness, their strengths, and their needs, especially when they take on the role of mother. That to me seems a much more compassionate stance than killing their children. (168)

James's effectiveness is most apparent, however, in her public appearances, to which she brings her remarkable oratorical gifts, which join together a deeply personal relationship to the Bible, the folk tradition of storytelling, and the language of the Civil Rights movement. James's speech accepting an award at the national convention of Concerned Women for America in 1993, prior to the Republican takeover of Congress, is grounded in the most intimate language of mothers. She begins in a personal, kitchen-table way, wondering aloud how she could be rewarded for doing something it was her heart's desire to do. Receiving the award in front of such an audience is "like coming home. It's like family," she says, eliciting a standing ovation and tears. In fact, she says with kind humor, because she and Beverly LaHaye share so much in terms of their hearts' desires, they are "soul sisters." It is hard to convey the effectiveness of her performance style, however, without seeing it. Achieving an almost perfect match between the requirements of public performance and a personal sense of authenticity, she turns from humor — when she left Washington after the Democrats took over, she left a sign on her desk that said, "Rent. Don't Buy," a joke about her husband and Tim LaHaye founding a group called National Right to Wife — to seriousness, inviting the audience to join with her in the battle that is going on "out there." We're involved, she says, "in a cultural battle for the soul of this nation."

Expressing her annoyance at people who get discouraged — "to feel hopeless and be a Christian is sort of an oxymoron" — she draws on the unassailable, inarticulable truths that mothers know to remind them what this activism is about: "This is not about me. I'm out here every day for my kids. And for the grandchildren I hope to have someday." At the 1995 Christian Coalition convention, she managed to situate the discussion of the federal budget directly within the terms of a family, comparing welfare to the situation she and her husband would face if their teenagers showed up in the kitchen every month for a check, leaving them unable to pay the mortgage or the health insurance. Her response would be to call a meeting on Saturday morning to inform the children they had to give something back for that check. And though they would say she was mean, she, as the mother of teenagers, has heard all that before.

In recognizing the exhaustion the women in her audience feel as a result of their activism, she also knows that the thing that keeps all of them going is family, making a perfect fit between the Christian heart and the nation's soul: "You see, I love this country and I love my family." And she motivates the activists in the audience by relocating the grass roots, and in particular, women at the grass roots, at the center of religious conservatism. Women like her who hold government positions can only try to keep the government from doing harm — they play defense — but the real work must be done at the grassroots level, where the offense is carried out, where the ball is advanced, especially now that money will be allocated at the state level through block grants. And advancing is not just a matter of the next battle or the next piece of legislation. It is advancing in the domestic sphere, where intimate work is simultaneously cosmic: "We win the battle every time a little kid gets exposed to the gospel by his mom for the first time," every time a kid learns about the importance of family, every time someone exposes a friend to Jesus: "Ladies and gentlemen, this country needs revival." Standing ovation.

James also tells this predominantly white audience how she responds to the question she is often asked: "Kay, aren't you being used as a surrogate for the right wing?" The mocking face she makes at this question suggests that she and her audience consider it completely idiotic, but it made possible for her an Esther experience, a chance to prove her courage in the model based on the story of Esther in the Old Testament. (Esther, the wife of King Ahasuerus, saved the Jews of Persia by revealing her own identity as a Jew. The story is frequently cited as a model for women's unselfishness and devotion to God in the face of attacks on their beliefs.)

> Sir [James answers], you need to understand that I do what I do because I'm called on by God to do it. I don't look to the left wing or the right wing to see who stands with me. You need to understand that if you have a problem with what I'm doing, you're talking to the wrong person. May I suggest that you call God and then the two of you discuss it. And if He wants me to stop, have *Him* call me.

Her style is witty, full, in the best tradition of southern preaching and women's talk.

She then brings the story back to the difficulties facing women activists: "Are you prepared to throw off the spirit of fear, what your neighbor might say because you're getting involved in politics?" The fear of postmodernity is first constructed, then her listeners are powerfully inoculated against it, reassured that it is their sacred duty to fight the things they have been taught to fear: "See, we told 'em, y'all take politics and we'll just keep our churches and our families. Now they're coming after our churches and our families. Cast off that spirit of fear." The battle is far too important, the objects of fear far too dangerous, for timidity, and with gentle steeliness, she advises them that if they are not serious, if they are not dedicated, if they are afraid, they should go home. Then this mostly white, predominantly southern audience is reminded of its sacred duties in Civil Rights language, "If you can't keep your eyes on the prize, we'll still love you but go home. We have a job to do." Finally, she ends by placing her beautifully articulated, emotionally powerful message squarely in the middle of the absolutist framework with a slow, rolling, sensuous resonance: "I'm here [*beat*] and you're here [*beat*] because we love our country, [*beat*] we love our families, [*beat*] but above all we *love* our God [*beat*] and we're gonna be obedient to Him."

James's African American cultural difference has now been converted into the familiar, powerful terms of absolutism, and though it provides gentle persuasion for the loving acceptance of difference, it is difference that is acceptable only if it is converted into the family of the same. This is true even though her own family did not fit the ideal: "I remembered my own family—certainly not the perfect-Mom-and-Pop-with-two-sweet-kids-in-a-tri-level. But a family just the same. Even when it becomes fractured or damaged by the cares of the world, it is still the unit that was meant to give each of us a sense of who we are; who we can become." (173) Her strong familiar feelings about her family circulate through her own family history and are then included in an absolutist political agenda: "Any policy that ignores the central role of religion and morality in the healthy functioning of our society will fail in the long run. The strong religious character of African Americans is a strength and an asset, not a 'personal matter' to be ignored." (181–82)

James's role within conservatism is important, for like a number of other African American conservatives, she argues that conservatism is closer to African American traditions than is the welfare state, and in certain ways, she is no doubt right: "Black conservatives trace their roots to the post-emancipation self-help movement, when freed slaves relied on faith, family, and the black community to overcome the obstacles in their path. While supportive of some government programs, black conservatives prefer individual efforts by the business community and church leaders." (176) Her conservative principles match the blueprint of conservatism in general, as she argues that social programs try to convince African American young people that they are simply victims of racist society or an economic system, arguments that rob them of their confidence. The only thing that will work is strengthening families, disempowering bureaucrats, slashing the federal debt, stopping the nation's credit addiction, lowering taxes, and emphasizing the central role of religion and morality in a healthy society. She finds no place, however, to address corporate responsibility or the political exploitation of race as a wedge issue.

As keynote speaker at the 1994 commencement of Pat Robertson's Regent University, in Virginia Beach, James strategically differentiates herself from another segment of the African American community: "I've been to one too many conferences where they tell me it takes a village to raise one child. First of all, I disagree with the premise. It takes a stable, two-parent, intact family to raise a child. . . . These children in our country are not the nation's children or the government's children, they are our children." The family is always prior to government, and her message reinforces passionate grassroots empowerment:

> I have no over-glorified images of my government service. . . . Where we really make the gains in our culture is in our lives as wives, moms, husbands, fathers, friends and neighbors. In these roles, we are perhaps in the best position to have an impact on our world. You are the salt of the earth. You are the light of the world. In this same way I challenge you to let your light so shine before men that they may see your good deeds, praise your Father in Heaven, and if I may have the license to add, as a result, change our culture.[13]

Her address to the 1994 Christian Coalition Road to Victory convention was significantly entitled "Transforming America: From the Inside Out."

iii.

James brings her appealing, intelligent motherliness into the public sphere with powerful effect. Star Parker, another African American conservative, engages her audience very differently, with passionate, breathless, aggressive, at times vicious adrenalin-driven talks about being an entrepreneur; her activism has to do with connecting free-market entrepreneurship to biblical literalism. She speaks to such conservative groups as the Christian Coalition national convention, where her panel, Building Bridges into Minority Communities, was standing room only in 1994, and appears on conservative radio and television shows; she was also a featured speaker at the 1995 convention.

Having lived for three years on AFDC as a single mother in Los Angeles, Parker went on to earn a degree in marketing before founding the Coalition on Urban Affairs in 1992 to provide a conservative response to the Los Angeles uprising. The Coalition on Urban Affairs is described in its brochure as a grassroots network "to Inform, Impact, and Influence black America with a political, social, and economic agenda rooted in moral absolutes." The blurbs on one pamphlet, entitled *Commentaries of a Black Christian Conservative Radical Republican Right-Wing Woman,* are from Ben Kinchlow, of the *700 Club;* Pat Buchanan, who told her that her speech "showed a sense of justice rooted in the abiding moral truths that must remain the guiding principles of our cause"; and Rush Limbaugh, who told her that "after talking with her for more than an hour, I've come to the conclusion that Star Parker is one of the most intelligent women I've ever met."[14] Her other pamphlets include *The State of Black America: Is It Too Late to Turn the Tide from Socialism?, The Killing of a Race: Abortion and the Black Community,* and *A Culture of Dependency: The Morality of Welfare Reform.* Parker is also the founder of NFTA Publishing Corporation, which publishes a small magazine billed as "your source to Christian events and information" and claims to work with over three hundred pastors and thirty thousand church members in the Los Angeles area.

Primarily focused on entrepreneurial efforts in the African American community, Parker shows how absolutist the framework within which such restructuring of the community must be, beginning with a chapter in which the attempt to relate homosexual rights to African American rights is viciously, even frighteningly, denounced. She argues that the only doctrine of diversity Christians should honor is the division between Christ's kingdom and Satan's:

> David said that, *"Upon the wicked the Lord will rain coals, fire and brimstone and a burning wind, shall be their allotted portion." (Psalm 11:6)* So be the Word of the Lord anyway; but the proponents of wickedness had better stop trying to use blacks — else they'll find blacks gladly wearing their pre-owned servant uniforms to platter the brimstones, fan the fire, and serve the coals for a Master. (her italics)[15]

This absolutism is all the more unsettling because it is joined to legitimate discussions of racism, in particular the argument that the history of reproductive rights is thoroughly entwined with the racism of the early part of the century, in the work of Margaret Sanger, founder of Planned Parenthood. That argument has also been made by historians and, in particular, by Angela Davis, who has shown how the struggle for reproductive rights benefited middle-class white women and how the sterilization of minority women figured in that struggle. In that context, while reproductive control was thought of as a right for middle-class women, it was taken to be a duty for women of color.[16] But Parker collapses that necessary historical analysis into an absolutist condemnation of feminism, abortion rights, and gay and lesbian rights, and by doing so, participates in a political agenda that has no qualms about scapegoating people of color and, in particular, women of color. Parker's energetic advocacy of entrepreneurial opportunities in the inner city is important, but the moral absolutism of her proposals means that the empowerment she advocates for herself constitutes a direct threat to many other people, particularly as her advocacy becomes a part of a national political agenda. She has been a featured speaker at the last two Christian Coalition national conventions, where she argued for the abolition of the minimum wage and the use of the death penalty: "Cursed is he who keeps back His sword from blood." She also interpreted the story of the multiplication of talents in the Bible to be proof that "God is a capitalist" and ended her angry talk in this way: "Arise, O God. Judge the earth," after which she received a long, impassioned ovation from the audience.

Her pamphlet ends with an argument for dialogue about welfare reform, but "honest dialogue for welfare reform cannot seriously take root until African Americans admit to some fundamental truths about black dependence, and then come to the debate table to accurately analyze why this once embarrassing phenomenon has become so acceptable amongst blacks." Her willingness to open a dialogue, however, is deceptive, for she has already set the terms that must be accepted before it can take place. It will be a monologue: "Until we revive some absolute moral and sexual standards by which to govern our nation, welfare to work programs, job training programs, affirmative action programs, civil rights bills, hate-crime bills and gun-control bills will continue to fail."[17]

iv.

Oregon politics provide an exemplary microcosm of national politics, combining western and southern influences with a history of urban cosmopolitanism and progressive activism, rural resentments of liberal cities, and conservative suburbs. The state is caught in the middle of two contradictory attitudes about the federal government, one of which sees the need for federal oversight of civil rights and the environment, and the other of which is part of a western libertarianism that considers each person wholly responsible for his actions. This has become especially significant, sometimes violently, in relation to property rights, even though, like the rest of the West, Oregon owes the open spaces and scenic lands that inspire such passion to the fact that much of that land has been federally protected from private development. Divided between rural and urban interests, with a declining timber economy increasingly replaced by tourism and high-tech industries, Oregon is also a favorite destination for affluent migrants and retirees fleeing racially mixed urban areas, particularly California. Like corporations, many of these new Oregonians are eager to shed tax responsibilities for public services, a desire that matches a strong libertarian political streak among longtime residents. And because it is relatively homogeneous racially, like the Northwest in general, Oregon has long been home to white supremacist groups on whose map of the United States the ecologically and racially "pure" Northwest is referred to as God's Country.

Of special importance, however, to the resonating structures traced in this book is the issue of property rights, in particular the Wise Use movement, which links the absolute values of the traditional family to the absolute right to property in which a certain form of populism becomes confusingly melded to corporate interests. That right to property arouses deep passions that also saturate other political issues, as the work of two Oregonian women activists, Kathy Phelps and Loretta Neet, will help make clear. The Wise Use movement, which began in Reno in 1988, not only brings together various conservative interests, but it also has increasingly radicalized them through ties with armed citizen militia groups. As Tarso Ramos, who monitors the movement, argues, while the Wise Use movement remains distinct from white supremacist and paramilitary militias, it increasingly helps "launder" the involvement of such far-right groups within the electoral process. It also helps develop the climate for intimidation and violence against environmental activists and government workers. Such laundering can be defined in terms of a linkage "by crossover leaders, an increasingly overlapping constituency, and some common ideological views — most notably belief in the illegitimacy of the federal government and assertion of state and county 'rights' over federal authority."[18]

The question of the sacred nature of property has enabled antienvironmentalist activism and absolutist conservatism to come together in various ways, a predictable anticommunism also present, with environmentalists referred to as watermelons — green on the outside, red on the inside. The Wise Use movement has two major elements: on the one hand, right-wing ideology and the often legitimate concerns about the loss of jobs in a changing economy, and on the other, the "industry populism" of corporations involved in resource extraction and development. Ron Arnold, of the Center for the Defense of Free Enterprise, in Bellevue, Washington, developed the outline of the Wise Use movement in 1979, which would use industry money and support to create a movement that joined citizens and industry through grassroots organizing. Using corporate financing, Wise Use activists mobilized employees in timber and mining around "an industry agenda of deregulation that targeted environmental laws." (7) Blaming the real loss of jobs on environmentalists and endangered species, pro-industry citizen groups appeared throughout the West in what appeared from the outside to be a completely spontaneous movement.

Though Wise Use and militia movements in the West function separately from each other, the organizational resources of militia groups have often come directly from Wise Use attempts to take over local government and federal management of public lands, as counties are seen to be the most legitimate form of citizen government. As Ramos argues, "These views derive from the Posse Comitatus (literally, 'power of the county'), forerunner to the Christian Patriots and Northwest militia groups." (7) This claim of county rights constructs an "ideological bridge" between Wise Use and extremist groups; he quotes Eric Ward, of the Seattle Northwest Coalition Against Malicious Harassment: "Militias have taken up any number of entry points into communities, including land use, private property rights and anti-Indian organizing—all issues associated with the Wise Use Movement." (8) The influence of this conjuncture is expected to grow as the population of western states increases and property-rights adherents, like Helen Chenoweth and Larry Craig of Idaho, gain increasing political power. In fact, Craig is now a part of the GOP leadership, having been elected to head the Republican Party Committee, and is the fourth-ranking leader in the Senate, as well as the highest-ranking member from the Northwest. As long as the Republicans hold the majority, he will also serve as chairman of two subcommittees, one dealing with energy and natural resources, the other with agriculture.

The movement also has a slick national presence in the National Wilderness Institute, based in Washington, D.C. Its advisory board is headed by Larry Craig, and its corporate funding is evident in the glossy style of its publications and the fact that it makes available free legal help for people who feel their property rights are threatened. Individual subscriptions to its publication, *NWI Resource,* which is modeled on pro-environment publications like those of the Sierra Club and shows undisturbed wildlife and scenic mountain vistas, costs $25 for an individual, or a minimum of $250 for a corporation. Articles in its spring 1995 edition, subtitled *This Land Is Whose Land?* and distributed at the workshop offered at the 1995 Christian Coalition convention, included "The Magic of Property Rights" and "Protecting Your Property," as well as a pullout map designed to create an image of the entire nation threatened by environmental "takings" of property: maps of government lands, wetlands, habitat conservation plans, wilderness areas, wild and scenic rivers, protected natural landscapes, and the United Nations Biosphere Reserves.[19]

The charge that environmental regulations constitute an illegal "taking" of one's property is based on a literal reading of the Fifth Amendment that says that "private property [shall not] be taken for public use, without just compensation," a powerful rhetorical move described by Ramos: "As an organizing strategy, takings is a kind of deviant genius. It automatically puts environmentalists in the position of defending the federal government and appeals to anyone who has ever had any kind of negative experiences with the federal government, which is a hell of a lot of people." (5) It also handily fits into the rhetoric of dominion theology, which is suggested here by Pat Robertson: "As a follower of the son of God, assume the authority, power, and dominion that God intends for men to exercise over the rest of creation."[20]

While Oregon has been powerfully affected by the Wise Use movement, it has also long been the site of a variety of new religious movements, which range from Christian communes to the Rajneeshees, the Thaker Singh group, and the Scientologists, among others. Of particular interest in relation to radical conservatism was Shiloh, an evangelical Christian commune so named because it hoped to provide Christian communal living "until Shiloh come." It constituted one of the largest Jesus People movements of the 1970s, attracting disaffected college-age youth from the counterculture. Begun in Costa Mesa, California, in 1968, as the House of Miracles, the movement came to Oregon in 1970, when John Higgins purchased seventy acres of land in Dexter, outside of Eugene. While drawing on the culture of soft-rock music and other elements of sixties popular culture, Shiloh depended on gender hierarchy and individual responsibility for one's actions rather than a consideration of social circumstances. Though Shiloh collapsed in 1978 when its founder was dismissed, Marion Goldman's follow-up study of former members in

1987–88 found that many who had joined with relatively little religious commitment were intensely religious when they left, and almost all ended up in smaller evangelical churches that depended on high levels of personal commitment and religious activism. Their involvement in Shiloh had resocialized them in a way that replaced the religious or cultural beliefs of their upbringing, and in many ways, they were like immigrants who found a home among others like them when they relocated in evangelical religious communities.[21]

In political terms, the Republican Party in Oregon, once the home for mavericks like Tom McCall, Mark Hatfield, and other urban moderates, is now split between moderates, rural, and ultraconservative suburban legislators, many of whom are backed by the Christian Coalition and some by the even more radical Oregon Citizens Alliance (OCA), whose executive director is Lon Mabon, once a California hippie and commune member. Because of the visibility of the OCA, which has put initiatives on the ballot to make it illegal to recognize the minority status of gay and lesbians, and to amend the Oregon Constitution by labeling homosexuality "abnormal, wrong, unnatural, and perverse," Oregon is one of the few places where the Christian Coalition's entry into state politics was not protested. Though the OCA has since been discredited, it had earlier relied on pro-life and antihomosexual activists at the grassroots level to run third-party candidate Al Mobley for governor in 1990, a campaign that cost the moderate Republican, Dave Frohnmayer, the election. The OCA has since organized the state county by county and, even though anti-gay measures have been ruled unconstitutional, it continues to nourish its grassroots base, in many cases providing the networks into which the Christian Coalition was able to insert itself in alliance with other groups such as Christian Voice, Concerned Women for America, Eagle Forum, Lifesavers of America, and Operation Rescue.

Though the OCA has distanced itself from open connections to white supremacists and neo-Nazi organizations, it helped establish ideological bridges in Northwest politics. Steve Gardiner cites "One-World Government: Myth, Conspiracy, or Reality?" an article by Patricia Smith, the research director for the OCA, in which evidence for that conspiracy is drawn, on the one hand, from Phyllis Schlafly, of the Eagle Forum, and, on the other, from an organization called Police Against the New World Order.[22] This organization was founded by a former Arizona police officer, Gerald "Jack" McLamb, who is an associate of Lt. Col. (Ret.) James "Bo" Gritz and a leader in the Christian Patriot movement who recruits police officers and soldiers into the movement. Gritz is a former Populist Party presidential candidate who claims that Zionists are corrupting the world. Both McLamb and Gritz were present at Ruby Ridge.

To see how radical conservative women explain their involvement in this grassroots politics, I turn to an interview with Loretta Neet, of Springfield, Oregon, one of the working-class communities that passed its own anti-gay ordinance even though the statewide measure failed. The videotaped interview with Neet takes place in her home, at the kitchen table; the sun shines on the lawn outside, and children's noises can be heard in the background, the ordinariness of domesticity striking because of the substance of her politics. The two community-college students conducting the interview, for a class entitled Women on the Right, were both involved in anti-OCA activism, but their behavior with Neet follows the style of women's domestic talk, and it foregrounds the problem of analyzing the effectiveness of this motherly behavior.[23] The interview is conducted in a familiar tone, accompanied by laughter that helps put the participants at ease and the small talk that marks ordinary conversations among women. Such familiarity blurs our confidence that we can tell the "absolute" difference between community concern and hatred, ourselves and the dangerous Other. It is a troubling tape precisely because everyone is so nice and because nothing marks Neet, who is articulate, poised, trim, attractive, friendly, as an exponent of some of the ugliest politics in Oregon history. As viewers, we are unsettled because she seems to be just like us. Or at least us middle-class, married white women.

Raised in Montana and Oregon, Neet is the state communications director of the OCA and a born-again Christian who attends a nondenominational church and is a board member of the Oregon Christian Coalition.[24] She often refuses to give her name to people she does not know, and when asked why she is involved if it is so difficult, she gives the familiar reason for such sacrifices: she is a mother, and she fears for her children in this period of cultural disintegration. What, she asks, will it be like for them if things are already this bad in terms of violence and deteriorating schools? By comparison to conditions in many urban areas, Springfield, Oregon, could be considered a good place to raise children, except for its real problem, the lack of jobs. When Neet began working on a newsletter, writing letters, and handing out information to her friends, she was only reacting, she explains, to one simple question about the quality of her own mothering: "Why isn't anybody doing anything?"

Describing herself as a traditional feminist who fights pornography and crime in order to protect families and children, she also acknowledges that feminism has benefited women by focusing on equal pay for equal work and removing the stigma from jobs formerly held only by men. In spite of that, however, she describes secular feminists as radicals.

The OCA's focus on abortion and homosexuality, she argues, was not its choice but was forced upon it by the urgency of the moment, in particular by Governor Neil Goldschmidt's executive order banning discrimination in the public workplace, which the OCA succeeded in reversing in 1988. But in a motherly way, she wants the interviewers to understand that she does not hate homosexuals, and she insists that she is not taking anyone's rights away, for anti-gay activity is not about civil rights but about special rights. If one views the Constitution as literally, divinely inspired and, as such, grounded in the narrow natural law she espouses, then it is the traditional family, not the individual, which is the core unit that must be protected by the Constitution. Thus Neet is, in fact, "logical" when she claims that because the Constitution, as she reads it, grants human rights only in relation to the traditional family, it is therefore legitimate to allow people to vote on the constitutional rights of gays and lesbians. For their rights are, in this logic, "special." The dangers of that simple, clear logic could not be more apparent.

Neet's kitchen-table conversation and this familiar, simple logical framework can be juxtaposed to an article written by another OCA activist to show how powerfully this logic banishes ambiguity in order to achieve the simple, absolute clarity upon which people can act with great passion. Another Oregon activist, Kathy Phelps, of Eugene, is chairwoman of the Lane County Republican Party and headed Alan Keyes's presidential campaign in Oregon. She wrote this article in response to an unsuccessful attempt by moderate Republicans to remove the issues of abortion and gay rights from the party platform and bring about a compromise that might avoid splitting the party. Phelps responds with an argument that is key to the linkage between individual rage at the government, absolute morality, and corporate economic interests: "Although the intent [to compromise] seems admirable and harmless, removing these issues would destroy the basic foundation that the party is built upon: private property rights."[25]

In what initially seems to be a surprising move on the part of an activist concerned about the biblically mandated traditional family, Phelps focuses on an ostensibly secular issue: "Private property rights are, and will always be, the core of democracy." But following her reasoning helps contextualize the emotional and sacred weight given to property itself and the ease with which it intersects with narrow biblical readings of the Constitution. In establishing the context for her argument, she, like Neet, claims that liberal Supreme Court justices have in fact been political activists who acted unconstitutionally by creating an illegal preferred classification called "fundamental rights." This is her term for what is more commonly referred to as civil rights. That classification appears to "give selected groups or individuals legal infringements over another person's property. In doing so, the court adopted an erroneous theory that 'property rights' are somehow inferior to 'fundamental [civil] rights.'"

Phelps then sets out a states'-rights argument about what she sees as judicial activism, arguing that the federal judiciary acts illegitimately when it proceeds according to judicial *interpretation* rather than according to a *literal* reading of the Constitution: "Fundamental [civil] rights are court-established rights subject to whatever decree that a judge might issue. The court redefines these rights at will and forces its definitions onto the states. These rights now supersede all other rights and have unconstitutional amnesty from being regulated by the people, the state and the U.S. Constitution." Other strains of antigovernment ideology obviously resonate with this argument, in which Phelps identifies a federal tyranny based on "takings," on the unconstitutional misinterpretation of the Fourteenth Amendment: "No state shall . . . deprive any person of life, liberty, or property, without due process of law." Reading this amendment, one can only conclude that if there were ever a need for deconstruction, this is it, for what has just been legitimated in this sentence is an entire authoritarian and theocratic social contract that links life, liberty, and property together in an absolutist framework whose language is presumed to be transparently clear.

If we follow her reasoning, we can see how appealingly simple this certainty is. First, she argues, "there is nothing more sacred than the property of life." The elements of that sentence symbolically resonate: sacred, property, life. But the activist liberal courts have made civil rights more important than property rights, and thus those courts have made illegitimate, unconstitutional decisions about a person's very life. It is important to see what she has done here: life is defined as the life of members of the traditional family. The lives of gays and lesbians have been excluded from the category, as have the separate rights of pregnant mothers, though the life of the fetus is included. She has elaborated a concept of "special" rights that must be condemned, along with affirmative action.

Phelps then refers to what she calls "another private property injustice," which is the attack on people's religious beliefs in order to provide civil-rights protection for gays and lesbians. As she puts it, in terms that echo Neet's, granting civil-rights protection means "granting minority status to people for participating in homosexuality. This court-established minority would give homosexuals the full coercive power to use the law to force schools to teach children that homosexuality is a good thing, equal to race, gender and national origin." In a way that echoes the *Gay Agenda* tape, this means that parents' and students' constitutional rights to their religion are infringed on by the antidiscrimination efforts of schools: "Pupils have the constitutional right to have and to hold their values and moral standards without interference from the schools."

Phelps here follows the arguments of the movement called constitutional activism, in which a literal reading of a divinely inspired Constitution and Declaration of Independence links absolutist conservatism to Wise Use and militia movements. As Phelps argues, "The Republican Party, Oregon Citizens Alliance, Oregon Right-to-Life and Traditional Values Coalition are joining a growing movement to return our Constitution to the people. Regardless of a person's good intentions, no one has the constitutional right to strip a person of his or her choices concerning private property." And finally she returns to the metaphor of the heart that structured so much of the rhetoric of absolutist Christian women: "I would rather quit politics and hold my head up high than to pull the heart out of the very fabric of my party. If the Republican Party compromises what is right, then it stands for nothing."

This short opinion piece is revealing in terms of the resonance, the simple clarity that makes it possible to link a wide range of diverse political activism and violence, religious and secular, within a symbolic framework. Phelps's argument ends with the kind of absolutist commitment that shows how troubling this cohesion can be, as she situates her role as a mother within the utopian apocalyptic narrative in which activism is mandatory: "If 'we the people' don't stop this injustice to our society, our children and grandchildren will not taste the flavor of freedom. If you believe freedom is worth fighting for, join us in our battle to save the republic." We might once have dismissed this kind of logic as isolated extremism, but this particular version of "We, the people" is now legitimated at the highest levels of national politics.

v.

Another woman activist could not, at first, seem more removed from this style and prophetic language, though her political influence at the national level is based on the same logic and reaches an even broader audience. Rebecca Hagelin illustrates the sophistication and brilliant political strategy of the Christian Coalition and, especially, Ralph Reed Jr. Reed, the real genius behind the success of the Christian Coalition, emboldened by the successes of Republicans in 1994, for which the Coalition's organizing was partially responsible, later focused on intense voter registration and precinct organizing in preparation for the presidential election of 1996. He introduces Hagelin on one of the training tapes provided to local Christian Coalition chapters as part of their grassroots leadership training. This series of videotapes, entitled the Christian Coalition Leadership School Video Training Series, includes such offerings as Paul Weyrich on *Rights and Wrongs of the Religious Right,* Tim Phillips on *Voter Targeting and Issues Management,* Guy Rodgers on *Biblical Basis for Political Involvement,* and Senator H. L. Richardson on *Positive Confrontation: Learning How to Win.* Hagelin's presentation is entitled *Media and Spokesmanship.*

Raised in Florida, Hagelin attended Troy State University in Alabama and served as communications director for the Center for Judicial Studies and for Concerned Women for America; she also helped develop communications strategies for Pat Robertson and the Christian Coalition. The tape is a fascinating illustration of both her effectiveness and the difficulties southern women present for progressive analysis. As with the tapes of LaHaye, unfailingly the response of progressive audiences to whom I have shown this tape has been laughter, the condescension that allows an audience to see her as completely other, completely different. This exclusion of difference works powerfully in favor of the Right because it does not hurt Hagelin at all, but it does indicate to other women like her (or their daughters) what progressives think of them, and it also handily gives her a screen of invisibility. But, like LaHaye, Hagelin is very familiar and ordinary to anybody from the South. She is not at all "other" but represents the white, middle-class norm of decency: sweet-looking, with a gentle, soothing voice, deeply sincere, not at all what one would expect of a communications strategist. And that should perhaps tip us off. She is talking about a strategy whose audience will be people like her and whose motivation is deep religious belief. While leaders like Robertson and Reed may seem slick and manipulative in the way they use their belief for political power, the selection of women like Hagelin is a brilliant move, for her appearance suggests that there is not a false bone in her body, even though later events in her own family suggest a much more complicated story. Hagelin's parents, Alice Faye Redd and Dr. Henry J. Redd Jr., prominent and affluent members of their community, have since been involved in a scandal of major proportions. Alice Faye Redd developed what turned out to be a Ponzi scheme, in which many members of the church lost all their life savings; she is now in prison, though Hagelin argues that she suffers from manic depression and should be in a mental hospital rather than prison. Dr. Henry J. Redd Jr. has been allowed to continue to practice medicine to help repay some of the money lost by his wife.

Nevertheless, Hagelin presents a powerful image for this lesson in press relations. Dressed in a red dress with white polka dots and sporting a hairdo that is almost, but not quite, Big Hair, she looks and sincerely acts out the almost perfectly illustrative intelligent, decent, white southern woman who does not at all come across as puritanical or mean or even bigoted; she could be either from the suburbs or from a small town, and she is, of course, very nice. Small-town white girls like me know her well; in fact, many of us probably were her at one time or another. But one could not imagine a more powerful construction, for she and her message are anything but naive. And while a progressive audience simply ignores the message by laughing at her appearance, a radical conservative audience with fundamentalist or evangelical beliefs hears every word of her message about how to translate biblical principles into an effective media strategy that takes into account the blindnesses and interests of its secular audience and reporters.

She begins the tape in this way: "Hi, I'm Rebecca Hagelin. Pretend I'm with you in person." As she speaks, she often cocks her head in a way that suggests she does not pretend to know more than anyone else or to be talking down to anyone. Significantly, in the collection of videotapes I purchased at the Christian Coalition Convention in Washington, D.C., in 1993, she is the only woman featured, and again significantly, the only woman speaker is the one who teaches media strategy. Her lesson begins with advice about image, as she counters the public impression of fundamentalist activists as extremists, simple rubes driven only by their own absolutist readings of Scripture. Her training session is, in fact, essentially about avoiding the extremist image and learning professionalism. The qualities you must have "or appear to have," she says, are ones that reveal that you are honest, caring, intelligent; you must also be well-groomed, committed, and look like an achiever as you work to promote biblical principles. And though effective communication requires that you read about communication and the skills necessary to achieve the desired image, the best source of information is the one you read every day: the Bible.

Giving careful and clear advice to local chapters about how to conduct a media plan, she advises them to select a spokesperson after analyzing the strengths and weaknesses of their members. Molly Yard's media image, its coarse militancy, she argues, should tell you right away that just because a person is a good leader, she may not be the best spokesperson if she does not present herself well. You should develop a public relations plan, with flexible, written guidelines, which she explains in detail. But she also shows how crucial her own work and that of other women is as she tells us that one of the most important features of a communications strategy is personal contact with the press, giving explicit directions for developing a good press list and keeping relations with the press current. Never underestimate the importance of phone calls. It takes a long time to keep these relations solid; always focus on the image you want to project. And her communications advice for interviews presents us with a list of things to keep in mind: politeness, a soft answer, being wise as a serpent, sending thank-you notes, taping interviews so as not to be taken by surprise, admitting when you do not know something, refusing to say anything off the record, resisting defensiveness, being responsive, being aggressive but charming, and others. It is very clear the kind of strong woman who is being constructed here as the face of traditionalist conservatism: not Molly Yard but Beverly LaHaye, not the Marxist lesbian but the good girl as mother, not Angela Davis but Kay Coles James.

vi.

Another southern woman whose abilities in the public sphere are widely recognized, Elizabeth Dole, currently head of the National Red Cross, dangerously seals this powerful female figuration within a reconstructed popular culture centered on religious faith. Though Dole's husband was considered somewhat moderate, he restructured his politics to appeal to the absolutist Right in his presidential campaign. Elizabeth Dole was one of the featured speakers at the national Christian Coalition convention in

1994, whose "nonpartisan" roster also featured almost all of the Republican presidential candidates. What is striking about Dole, once again, is how ordinary her appearance is to anyone raised in the South or in a small town, even though she was educated at Duke, Oxford, and Harvard. Clearly a powerful career woman in her own right, Dole used her speech, described as personal testimony, to situate the importance of her career in terms of her own rediscovered biblical priorities. Her speech was a kind of public confession of the dangers of allowing your religious beliefs to take a back seat to your public career, a testimonial or witness in the tradition of revivalist religious discourse.

Dole, like LaHaye, Neet, James, and Hagelin, fits the role of the True Woman, the nice, gentle, polite woman with a soft voice and a deep kindness that saturates her presentation. Like James, she draws on the oral traditions of storytelling common in southern culture, and also like James, she shows how those storytelling traditions have always been deeply structured by biblical stories. Dole has enormous power to establish a public space for the kinds of arguments that have been made in a more coarse form at the grassroots level. If you were to listen to her talk to the Christian Coalition, whose leaders are determined to set the national agenda, and if you did not know who she was, you would not be able to tell the difference between her positions and those of Loretta Neet, so massively has theocratic language established the terms of contemporary public discourse. That people like Dole may not understand the climate in which their words are heard at the grassroots level, not only by absolutist fundamentalists like Kathy Phelps and Lon Mabon but by supremacists and militia groups, does not excuse the irresponsibility of these mainstream Republican exploitations of faith. The political issue that must be taken seriously by believing Christians is the dangerous power of the *resonance* of their words.

In her beautiful, articulate, elegant southern style (Julia Sugarbaker without the attitude), Dole begins by arguing that "we have come dangerously close to eradicating the moral underpinnings of a virtuous society," words like those used by small-town preachers who never imagined that they would be taking over the government but who saw their role much more modestly as moral advisors. Dole now joins that pastoral advice to a political message spoken to an audience already well primed to hear it: we must "put America back on the right track." Pat Buchanan, in another speech to the Coalition, says the same thing, yet his words, like those at the 1992 Republican National Convention, immediately set off our fears, because they are so pugnacious, angry, violent. Elizabeth Dole's sweetness, on the other hand, and her calm, motherly professionalism do not seem so dangerous, yet they are saying the same thing: there is one way. There is one kind of absolutist American biblical morality that must structure our politics. Either absolutism or nihilism.

And the thematic of the heart, not surprisingly, shows up, as she uses this public forum in a deeply affecting, personal way, telling us that she was asked "to speak from the heart about the difference Christ has made in my life." In order to do that, she establishes the setting in which her audience is to listen to her story, taking us back to her childhood home in North Carolina on Sunday, the Lord's day, which was reserved for "acts of mercy and necessity," where the "Gospel was as much a part of our lives as fried chicken and azaleas in the spring." Many of those Sundays were spent at her grandmother's house, where in the afternoon they had cookies and lemonade, played Bible games, and listened to her grandmother, Mom Cathey, read from the Bible. The 1960s rock formation Grossberg described finds itself powerfully matched here by a southern religious configuration that establishes a different kind of popular, affective investment. Mom Cathey, Dole's hero, devoted her life to her Christian faith, as did many of our own grandmothers. When her son was killed in an accident, Mom Cathey sent the insurance settlement to a missionary group to build a hospital wing in Pakistan. Though not wealthy, she gave whatever money she could spare to ministries at home and missions abroad. When she moved into a nursing home in her nineties, she did not see it as a sad thing but as an opportunity, telling Dole, "There might be some people there who don't know the Lord."

The Book of the World in its tactile, emotional sense marks Dole's experience of reading the Bible, for she now has Mom Cathey's own Bible, with Mom's handwritten notes in the margins, including the date and time they were written. Those notes provide a beautiful, spiritual diary of her grandmother's life, thoroughly inscribed in and by the Bible. And Mom Cathey establishes the standard for feminine behavior: "I can't remember an unkind word escaping Mom's lips in all the years I knew her or an ungracious deed marring her path. My grandmother was an almost perfect role model and I wanted to be like her."

The subtext of Dole's testimony is her discovery that the promises of feminism did not tell the whole truth, that in developing her own very successful career, she began to find that her career had become of paramount importance to her, a barrier to her total commitment to the Lord.

Being a perfectionist, she found that she wanted to be best at everything she did, but while she had a beautiful marriage and a challenging career, her life was "threatened with spiritual starvation." God led her to a sensitive and caring pastor who helped her find the joy of turning one's life over to Christ and letting everything flow from there. Psycholinguistic theory might suggest that such a move resembles the methods of analytic transference, in which an organizing metaphor that helps meaning cohere is constructed in a discursive relationship with a sensitive mentor. It is obvious that the depth and power of such structures of meaning, their importance in people's lives, must be taken seriously, but it is the *exploitation* of those structures by people building powerful political machines that is so troubling.

The story Dole tells is the biblical story of Esther, which everyone in the audience already knows but which she reinterprets in a way similar to the use of biblical passages by other radical Christians. Walter Benjamin described the way such stories work in his discussion of baroque Christian allegory. A superficial narrative reveals a deeper truth about the divine order of the universe and provides a lesson about that order. But because the interpretation of the allegorical fit between the two narratives is always site-specific and historically contextualized, this allegorical interpretation also constantly renews the biblical passage by reinscribing contemporary situations into the biblical narrative and the biblical narrative into the contemporary context. Of course Benjamin also points out what was essential to baroque Christian allegory: the necessity for a transcendent Judge to keep the historical and linguistic disruptions under control and the two layers together so they will match.[26] Religious institutions, Dole's pastor, the community Bible readings, all serve that function, making it possible to join a deeply felt, uniquely personal reading (Dole's personal, loving relationship to Mom Cathey) to the more general beliefs of this entire public audience and to radical political conservatism itself. The practice of turning oneself over to the Lord, trusting that he will inevitably reveal what he wants you to do, provides both solace and unquestioning certainty. Significantly, Dole moved her Bible readings into the upper reaches of the public sphere, organizing a Bible study group with other Senate wives.

By retelling the story in which God tests Esther, Dole traces the reasons for her decision to put Christ first and to "submit my resignation as master of my own little universe. God accepted my resignation." The story of Esther teaches her the power of dependency we have followed in the texts of Marshner and LaHaye: "I've had to learn that dependence is a good thing," and that power comes "from God, not from me. God does not want worldly successes; He wants my heart."

Were this story a personal testimony to encourage others to find meaning and coherence in faith rather than in empty competitiveness and materialism, Dole's performance would be inspiring and beautiful. But she is speaking in a context in which what she says must also be evaluated according to the stage upon which she says it, or its framing presuppositions. And that stage is a massively overdetermined political platform built for her by Pat Robertson and Ralph Reed, with their minutely and electronically organized grassroots networks, media empire, and ties to corporate-funded think tanks. The effects of what she says, the use she makes of her grandmother's faith in this context, reinforce the collapse of national politics into an absolutist Christian political agenda based on the words of "our saviour, the central figure of all history, the risen Lord, sovereign over all." Though absolutist Christians remind us that Martin Luther King and the Civil Rights movement also used biblical language, King did not have access to an entire political and corporate structure within which to make his language "literal." Dole continues in this vein:

> The world is ripe and ready, I believe, for men and women who recognize they are not immune from the predicaments of the day, men and women who are willing to accept the privilege of serving and who are ready to see that the providence of God may have brought them to such a time as this.

vii.

This intimate structuring of what matters has now brought the most personal, emotional, and spiritual feelings together with the Christian Coalition's attempts to control the agenda of the nation, not merely that of the Republican Party, a connection guaranteed by the motherly face that legitimates a politics whose effects impinge violently on groups excluded from its definition of familiarity. This motherly figuration has become the face of a postmodern folking of America in a flight from the cities that once provided the utopian model for the American Dream. That dream has now become the house in the suburbs. But though that house was once part of a middle-class American Dream, the middle class itself has now split in two. Many of those who would formerly have been able to imagine owning a house in the suburbs and sending their children to college are now holding relatively unskilled jobs whose wages have stagnated, if the job has not disappeared entirely. The other segment of the middle class consists of those with professional skills suited for the economy of an information society, with their wages increasing. Within this context, the American Dream increasingly reveals its exclusivity, as plain folks Americans and middle-class victims of supply-side economics join the "secession of the successful" from responsibility for the public good, though they do so in different ways.[27]

Those suburbs are increasingly the site of the privatization of everyday life in gated communities, neighborhoods with private streets, sidewalks, parklands, and recreational facilities. Surrounded by walls or fences, with supervised entrance gates to control automobile and pedestrian access, these neighborhoods rely on their own set of codes and regulations, rather than those of the city or county. Such gated communities take a number of forms: "lifestyle" communities built around golf courses, lakes, or country-club-like recreational facilities, usually for retirees or those whose children are grown; "new towns" that attract younger families; "elite" communities for the rich; and "security zone" communities determined by concern for personal safety and the protection of property and property values.

As citizens worried about crime, taxes, poor municipal services, and poor schools abandon the cities, the increasing popularity of gated communities, or what the Lincoln Institute of Land Policy calls fortress communities, reflects people's desire to retreat. As Roger K. Lewis argues, they want to "spend more of their tax dollars on themselves instead of others. Further, they take comfort in the social homogeneity of such communities, knowing that their neighbors act and think much as they do." (25) These fortressed homes were described by Faith Popcorn, whose market analyses predicted the possibilities of this trend, which she named "cocooning," and they led to the growth of take-out gourmet foods, home entertainment centers, and home security systems.[28] Lewis suggests that "people are not just seeking to escape from the problems of the city. They are abandoning the whole 'idea' of city — its culture, its physical form, its intellectual and commercial vitality, its complexity and unique capacity for accommodating disparate individuals within a shared environment."[29] (12) One might also see this retreat from public responsibility as part of the reconstruction of states' rights over federal responsibility, the Articles of Confederation over the Constitution, at least as it is seen to have been tainted by a liberal judiciary.

Such communities are, however, simply microcosms of the larger segmentations of American society according to income, race, and economic opportunity. And as the upper classes now send their children to elite private schools and determine their neighborliness according to property values, evangelical Christians retreat to communities of other born-again Christians, where they open private religious schools or school their children at home. Far-right groups escaping to "pure" places like the Pacific Northwest are only the most extreme version of this phenomenon based on achieving a sense of security that is highly dependent on purging difference and reconstructing communities of the same. These are handy structures, as well, for enabling global corporations and the wealthy to jettison their public responsibilities and any kind of commitment to the public good. In fact, that commitment has been redefined in terms of supply-side economics to mean that one's obligation to the social good is to become wealthy, an obligation to be traced in chapters 5, 6, and 7.

Just as the importance of the motherly face in humanizing this flight from public responsibility is now enacted by conservative women, the earlier success of Ronald Reagan's plain folks American language, which was made transparent, identical to the language of corporate interests, was guaranteed by another woman: his speechwriter, Peggy Noonan. Noonan's Irish family had moved from the city to the suburbs of Massapequa, Long Island, when she was young, part of an eastern suburban folking in which plain folks Americans defined their own identity in terms of ethnicity — white ethnicity. And the political trajectory Noonan followed repeats the story of other plain folks Americans. She went to Washington to campaign for John F. Kennedy, but she eventually changed her political affiliation, according to her autobiography, because of her feeling that the young, male Ivy League Democratic activists looked down on people like her. In an ironic rebellion against privilege, she went on to provide the popular voice that linked white ethnics and millionaires in Reagan Republicanism.[30]

The involvement of women in a backlash against feminism, the turn to conservatism, and a flight from the complexities of the city has obviously reflected many real problems for women, such as ineffective schools, poor municipal services, and crime. And it is obvious that movements other than feminism have become more successful in appealing to women. Yet these ways of solving problems have proved to be disastrous for many people who are outside the circle of "people like us." As the historian Nancy Maclean argues, in spite of the stereotypes of women's goodness, women have historically worked not only for the common good but often as an "agency in complicity" with repressive movements. For example, in the 1920s in Indiana, the Ku Klux Klan included a women's auxiliary, much of whose work consisted of reformist activities focused on helping other white women within the community. In particular, the wives sometimes encouraged vigilante moral action to punish those men in the community, some of them Klansmen, who were involved in domestic abuse. And though such activity was praiseworthy in terms of aiding white women, it had quite another, not so immediate effect, for it provided a "humanizing facade that rendered the Klan more insidious."[31] One might see the motherly faces of radical conservatism as a contemporary, more complex version of this humanizing facade, the human face of a very particular, exclusive — purified — notion of America as a national small town.

Feminizing politics means feminizing it in the image of the Pure Mother, whose image accompanies the reaffirmation of the patriarchal Father. If he will not or cannot reconstruct culture, she will do it for him. If the absolutist Christian nuclear family is threatened by angry cities full of violent minorities, socialist bureaucrats, radical feminists, blasphemous artists, scheming Jews, perverse homosexuals, and parasitic immigrants, who will compensate for men's failures, for the futility of Michael Douglas's violent rampage in the movie *Falling Down?* Who will be able to provide the human face of the postmodern backlash against postmodernity? As Beverly LaHaye says, and as she titled one of her books, who but a woman?

FOUR

Tender Warriors

We have been *in* a war but not *at* war! If we are to make a difference, it will require much more than we've been doing until now. — Bill McCartney

It appears that America's anti-Biblical feminist movement is at last dying, thank God, and is possibly being replaced by a Christ-centered men's movement which may become the foundation of a desperately needed national spiritual awakening. — Jerry Falwell

The advice and activism of Christian women that revalorizes traditional femininity in biblical terms has its counterpart in a growing Christian men's movement and in psychological counseling based on biblical interpretations of absolute gender differences. In addressing the difficulties faced by families trying to cope with the physical or emotional abandonment by men, as well as the emotional and spiritual needs of the men themselves, the Christian men's movement achieves a simple clarity: making promises and keeping them. This is joined to a pedagogy that teaches men the skills of communication and intimacy, filling a void for men who have heard contradictory messages from society and have tried, without enough guidance, to figure out how to be good fathers and husbands. The movement also speaks to many women trying to keep their families together in the face of men's abdication of responsibility. Dismissing all the men involved in this movement as angry white males too quickly homogenizes them, overlooking the fact that many of them are, indeed, interested both in looking for community and in learning responsible behavior. Another important goal of the Christian men's movement, the Promise Keepers, is to break down racial barriers among men, though the response to that appeal is reflected more in terms of African American clergy than attendees, who represent only 1 to 3 percent of the audience at Promise Keeper events.[1]

The Promise Keepers, a ministry to men only, is one of the fastest growing movements in the country, with a budget in 1996 of $115 million and a full-time staff of over four hundred. (Gardiner 4) Its organizational sophistication is part of its success:

> By the time Bill McCartney and crew make the trek to a regional stadium, Promise Keepers is thoroughly organized in the area. State directors, working with their own staff, in offices reminiscent of university athletic departments, have set up statewide networks of county level "task force" organizations. The county task force groups have in turn recruited and trained "ambassadors" (responsible for a local region or groups of churches) and "key men" (one per church). (Gardiner 4)

Promise Keepers events are postmodern spectacles: football stadiums filled with thousands of men, who sometimes sing hymns and at other times do the Wave or chant competitive sports cheers: "We love Jesus. Yes, we do! We love Jesus, how about you?" Huge screens show the speakers' and singers' faces as they perform on the raised stage at one end of the field; sophisticated sound systems magnify the hymns, which are played in very modern, culturally diverse musical styles, with some sung in Spanish; the words of the hymns are broadcast on the screen, even though most of the men already seem to know them.

The real goal of Promise Keepers is the step that follows the large events, the establishment of small groups of men who are encouraged to return to their own churches and communities and form small Bible-study groups. They are given advice about how to set up such groups by means of a multimedia package, *The Next Step: From the Stadium to the Small Group*. The small-group strategy resembles that of the women's study groups, but the terms used in describing them are unambiguously masculine. The general model of mentoring draws on baseball metaphors, and the description of the different kinds of groups men need are described in this way: "Adrift" — the Life Raft Group; "Feeling Good" — the Yacht Group; "Battle Weary" — the Destroyer Group; "Deep and Long: Where Are We?" — the Submarine Group; and "Refreshed, Refueled, Refocused" — the Carrier Group.[2]

The general message of the Promise Keepers is a charismatic one of ecumenical unity and nondenominational appeals for spiritual revival. As

Hans Johnson argues in *Church and State,* Promise Keepers has "managed to draw support not only from evangelical and fundamentalist churches but also from some mainline Protestants and Roman Catholics who would be wary of more overtly political and narrowly sectarian organizations such as the Christian Coalition."[3] Promise Keepers also attempts to avoid denominationalism in its magazines: *New Man, Charisma,* and *New Ministries.*[4] In fact, as Steve Gardiner argues, the ecumenical appeal to a generalized spirit of Christian revivalism may, in fact, make Promise Keepers more appealing to members of mainstream churches, nonreligious progressives, and charismatics than to fundamentalists themselves, many of whom have been critical of Promise Keepers because of its resemblance to secular new age pop psychology and its charismatic appeal to a very loose notion of doctrine.[5]

Though Promise Keepers began with help from James Dobson's Focus on the Family ministry as well as Bill Bright's Campus Crusade for Christ and is part of a well-financed, sophisticated coalition of evangelical groups bent on influencing public policy, it is relatively autonomous in terms of direct political affiliation and receives most of its income from tickets and the sales of books, videotapes, and other paraphernalia. This autonomy, however, "points to the possibility that this is the real thing: an independent cultural movement that will produce *as an outcome* a broader base of support of Christian Right politics." (Gardiner 9)[6] Thus honoring the seriousness and anxieties of men, which these gatherings address in powerful ways, also requires taking account of the way those needs are exploited in the interests of what Gardiner calls their hegemonic effect: "their ability to create space where the ideas of Promise Keepers become part of the cultural repertoire of the participants." (Gardiner 5) As I have argued, that repertoire is one that legitimates absolutist masculinity, Republican political power, and corporate interests (see chapters 5, 6, and 7). That many men are looking for some form of coherent identity and integrity does not have to lead to absolutist bigotry, but the Promise Keepers are powerfully shaping it in that way.

This chapter follows advice books for men in which masculinity is revalorized and masculine intimacy is taught within a sacred, absolutist frame: Stu Weber's *Tender Warrior: God's Intention for a Man* and, briefly, his *Locking Arms: God's Design for Masculine Friendships; Seven Promises of a Promise Keeper;* and, though it is somewhat less absolutist, a book of advice by a Christian psychotherapist, Archibald D. Hart's *The Sexual Man: Masculinity without Guilt.* These books are used in men's groups in local churches, many of which also send busloads of men to large Promise Keeper conferences across the country, like one in Boulder, Colorado, in 1994, attended by fifty-two thousand men who gathered to listen to, among others, James Dobson, Bill McCartney, and Charles Swindoll, who rode in on a Harley-Davidson. Other conferences have been held at Anaheim Stadium (attended by fifty-two thousand); at the Hoosier Dome, in Indianapolis (attended by sixty-two thousand); and in Saint Petersburg, Florida, in 1995 (attended by fifty thousand). The cost of attendance is fifty-five dollars. A Promise Keepers conference that hopes to attract a million men is being planned for the Washington Mall in the spring of 1997; the original plans were to hold it in conjunction with the 1996 election. My discussion also draws on my participation in a Promise Keepers gathering at Autzen Stadium in Eugene, Oregon, in August 1996, where Stu Weber was a featured speaker. A representative of Promise Keepers made press passes available following a discussion of the event by the university senate. The response came in part because strong local opposition to the event had been couched in terms of the unconstitutional use of university property for an event that excluded women; opposition to Promise Keepers because of their condemnation of homosexuality could not be framed so clearly in terms of the constitution. The local paper was flooded with letters, both pro and con, and a vigil in opposition to the event took place on the first night of the conference. Media coverage was for the most part favorable, focusing on the general theme of male responsibility. Such negotiations are part of an increasingly successful strategy to dispel opposition by both the media and mainline churches.

Randy Phillips, the president of the Promise Keepers, says in *Seven Promises of a Promise Keeper,* a collection of essays published in 1994 that set out the framework of the movement, that "today's American men are looking for answers, and they are looking to Jesus to provide them." He describes the movement this way:

> We are at the threshold of a spiritual awakening. Though the "time of God's favor" has been generously extended to all people in all times through the cross, church historians have noted that there have been specific seasons of God's increased favor throughout history. Scholars use such terms as *outpouring, awakening, movement,* and *revival* to describe those unique periods when God bestows His grace and power in unusual measure upon a people to extend his kingdom on

earth. There's a growing consensus among Christian leaders that we are now, once again, in such a time. . . . God's Spirit is calling men to rise up! And they are! They're growing into a new and deeper intimacy with Jesus, and through His power they are seizing the spiritual initiative in their homes, churches, friendships, and communities.[7]

Within this exhilarated spirit of revival, masculinity will be reclaimed not just from feminism but from a definition of spirituality that associates it with women, who have historically been the most active church members even as leadership positions were held by men. This masculinity will also, of course, be connected to a cultural war, as Wellington Boone writes in the same volume: "The prayer that sparks revival begins long before the countryside seems to awaken from its slumber in sin. It starts when men fall on their knees and cry out to God. That's where intimacy with God takes place. . . . as we are transformed, the course of a nation can be changed."[8] Such a transformation will depend on reviving a form of masculinity that brings together courage and moral character in a deep personal, masculine intimacy with God:

When we're alone with God, there are no more distractions to the development of intimacy. It's just us and Him. The rest of the world must wait.

True prayer is not a rhetorical stream of eloquent words. It is the expression of a deep longing for God that is born out of love. . . . Scores of people have found Him in saving grace but have not yet come to know Him in intimacy, the place where He begins to impart a sense of divine separation for His purposes. (27–28)

In teaching men how to achieve this heroic intimacy, Stu Weber's *Tender Warrior* draws on everyday life and popular culture in a narrative addressed to the other men of the sixties generation and their sons, the men who were not antiwar or pro–sexual liberation (or who have repented if they were). Weber, who grew up in Yakima, Washington, also brings to this spiritual project two experiences that will attune him to the shifting political and regional sources of imagery in contemporary American politics: he fought in Vietnam as a Green Beret, and, as a native of the West, his everyday experiences had more to do with hiking, camping, and hunting in its mountains and deserts than with urban activities. He now serves as the pastor of the Good Shepherd Community Church in Gresham, Oregon, a suburban community outside Portland; he and his wife, Linda, who have three grown sons, founded the church together. They also write, speak, and conduct Family Life marriage and parenting conferences across the country.

Though warrior and military metaphors saturate his book, Weber's appearance is that of any mild-mannered, clean-cut, middle-class white man—ordinary and nice. In fact, the cover of an issue of *Christianity Today* that contains an article on the Promise Keepers features a picture of Superman in a business suit, his family and his house behind him, as he takes off his coat to reveal the letter *S* on his chest.[9] Weber resembles the Christian clients described by Archibald Hart, a psychotherapist in Los Angeles, who "offers a sane view of what it means to be male, sexual and normal," according to the blurb on the jacket of his book. Hart's clients are the good men who "make up the middle of the road. They are the mainstream men. Mostly they are married, fathers, church-going, God-fearing, decent, hardworking, honest men doing ordinary living."[10] But Hart adds an element to this description that suggests a particular difficulty for good men trying to remain good: their "mental sexual sound-track never matches the high moral tone of their behavior." (64)

The cover of *Tender Warrior* features a line from the book that will frame Weber's advice: "Every man's purpose, every woman's dream, every child's hope." Discussion questions are included at the end of each chapter, as they were in the books for women; these consist of practical, concrete assignments related to everyday life. The book opens with Weber situating his story within the biblical apocalyptic frame, which is always threatened with bursting, the fears it constructs helping energize the passionate intensity of attempts to find and correct evil. These are fears, however, that will then be superseded by the dynamism produced by the shift from the tragic apocalyptic narrative to the optimistic, comic one. For the exuberance of this masculine revival will make it possible for men to be at the same time mature, responsible adults and adventurous men whose heroic actions can be described in the language of adolescent fantasy. Weber begins right in the middle of both apocalypse and adventure: "The present time is of the highest importance — it is time to wake up to reality. . . . The night is nearly over; the day has almost dawned. . . . Let us arm ourselves for the fight of the day! (Romans 13:11–12)."[11] He then tells us about his own discovery of reality, first sharing stories of near misses in Vietnam, where he narrowly escaped death several times, once when he was called back to Nha Trang just before the rest of his camp was "blasted from the face of the earth." But a wake-up call of equal importance that was almost as shocking came at a dangerous moment in his fifteen-year marriage. When his wife, Linda, had finally had enough of his behavior, he saw something completely unexpected in her eyes: "Deep anger. Hot anger. . . . It was absolutely clear—there would be some changes in our relationship, or our relationship would change. Things were never going to be the same." (17)

These crises that made him face his vulnerability and immaturity are then generalized to the crises faced by the men around him. What confuses them is the fact that there is a missing gender, and that missing gender is Man, a claim that seems strange in light of the fact that men are everywhere; they have the best jobs, they make the rules, they run the government, as we all know. However, because men have few models of responsible male behavior to guide them, even the "normal" men of Archibald Hart's study may find themselves anxious about masculine identity. The problem of articulating the definition of Man is similar to the problem of the search for a representation Marshner faced. In the face of the changes in secular and popular culture, heterosexual men who want to behave responsibly find only a blank to mark their identity. At the same time, secular and popular culture have inflicted serious damage on men's ability to develop intimacy. Archibald Hart reports the response of one of his clients, who comments that all men seem to think about sex a great deal of the time: "It seems clear to me that much of our male desire for sexuality is a misplaced desire for intimacy, having gotten the two confused in our culture in puberty." (76)

Working his way into these lessons for men, Weber does what traditionalist conservatism in general does so brilliantly: he uses postmodernity against itself, turning to television to establish a common framework, in particular the television series he watched as a boy in the early sixties, *Wagon Train*. This series will provide the images and stories he needs for reconstructing masculinity, and his retelling of it will connect popular culture to the frontier iconography of Manifest Destiny and biblical iconography, as *Wagon Train* becomes an Old and New Testament epic of divinely inspired masculine adventure:

> [S]tocky, fatherly Ward Bond astride his mustang, squinting wind-chiseled features into the horizon. With a quick look back over his shoulder, he would raise a rawhide-gloved right hand in a beckoning gesture and call out, "Wagons, *ho-oh!*"
> Then the great caravan of canvas-topped prairie schooners bearing

clear-eyed pioneers would begin rolling inexorably behind while the theme music filled our living room and stirred my young heart with a thirst for adventure.

But the guy *I* really wanted to see came galloping up next. Clad in fringed buckskins and a wide-brimmed black hat, he rode up alongside the wagon master at the head of the train. As the theme music rolled on, the black and white screen filled with the image of the lithe-limbed, cleft-chinned, raven-haired Robert Horton as Flint McCullugh.

The Scout. . . . He was the first to smell danger, dodge the arrows, hear the muted thunder of far-away buffalo herds. . . . It was up to him to spot potential hazards, discern lurking enemies, and pick out the best and safest trail for the train to follow.

It's always the image of Flint McCullugh that swims into my mind as I think about the role of a man as provider for his family. Now, that wouldn't make much sense if you thought only of the traditional definition of "provider." In our culture, when we think of provision, we think of food on the table and a roof over our heads. Actually, the emphasis in provision is *vision*. The *pro* part of the word indicates "before" or "ahead of time." "Vision" obviously speaks of "sight" or "seeing." (21–22)

Here the Scout is the chosen son of the wise father, the New Testament Son who is to lead civilization, represented by older men, women, and children. The concept of provider is thus displaced from its domestic usage to a public one that reveals its importance to civilization itself. Interestingly, Weber has to make a leap to reinscribe the homoerotic Flint McCullugh, played by Robert Horton with a kind of Victor Mature–like beauty, into his frame. The bachelor Flint McCullugh was, in fact, unencumbered by a family, as were the heroes of most sixties Westerns, like *Bonanza, Maverick, Have Gun Will Travel,* and *The Rifleman,* most of these currently playing as reruns on Pat Robertson's Family Channel. For the most part, those television shows were about families of men, though ironically they may have helped form a whole generation of feminists, for many of us girls, left with a choice between June Cleaver and Flint McCullugh, decided, like Weber, to emulate McCullugh and seek adventure.

Another feature of popular culture shows up with familiar regularity in Weber's description of the frontier man—the popular iconography of Frederick Jackson Turner's frontier thesis, which I will trace more fully in chapter 6 as a model for conservatism's dynamic entrepreneurial political economy. Turner, whose address to the American Historical Association in Chicago in 1893 set the terms for the historical study of American identity and the American West until fairly recently, argued that the receding frontier had been the formative influence on the character of American democracy. Though in actuality, the frontier may have been very different from his description, his thesis nevertheless rhetorically established the almost mythological outlines of American identity. (He had, in fact, taught rhetoric and oratory before becoming a historian.) American identity, as he saw it, was forged out of the encounter with the frontier, a performative struggle that identified a man as an American and initiated him into America's social contract. In this thesis, all true Americans are immigrants who have been provided by God with an empty continent upon which to define themselves and their unique democracy. The original inhabitants were obstacles to that definition and the divinely inspired national project. The true portrait of the American pioneer is represented by the image of the settler standing at the Cumberland Gap looking out over the wilderness valley; the wilderness, vision, and destiny are all framed in that stance.

That image also links the pioneer and the Christian man, for his vision (always double because it is also pro-vision) determines the path to be taken through a dangerous but exhilarating wilderness, the key to his family's survival and, by extension, the survival of civilization. These frontier themes are intensified in the personal narratives of writers, like Weber, who actually live in the West. Weber's detailed stories of hiking, camping, and hunting in the mountains and deserts of eastern Washington and Oregon add an easy familiarity and love of the outdoors to the linkage between natural American identity, *Wagon Train,* and the Bible. The familiar iconography of the frontier is also given metaphoric resonance by such layerings of personal experience, popular culture, and the religious theme of wandering in the wilderness. In a way that suggests that Weber's writing is a male romance of the frontier in which the participants are a man, the land, and himself, an equivalent, perhaps, of the female Harlequin romance, Weber gives a long quotation from Harold Bell Wright, described merely as an "Early Twentieth-Century Novelist":

There is a land where a man, to live, must be a man. It is a land of granite and marble and porphyry and gold—and a man's strength must be as the strength of the primeval hills. It is a land of oaks and cedars and pines — and a man's mental grace must be as the grace of the untamed trees. It is a land of far-arched and unstained skies, where the wind sweeps free and untainted, and the atmosphere is the atmosphere of those places that remain as God made them — and a man's soul must be as the unstained skies, the unburdened wind and the untainted atmosphere. It is a land of wide mesas, of wild rolling pastures and broad, untilled valley meadows — and a man's freedom must be that freedom which is not bounded by the fences of a too weak and timid conventionalism. In this land every man is — by divine right — his own king; he is his own jury, his own counsel, his own judge, and — if it must be — his own executioner. . . . In this land a man, to live, must be a man. (23)[12]

This kind of man is not going to like government controls on "his" land very much, even if it is federal land belonging to us all, and he will require a very inspiring version of domestic responsibility. For now the provider role must be inscribed in a way that firmly reassigns the sole responsibility for vision, or agency, to men, given the inroads made by feminism. If men are to be able once again to lead their families and American civilization, their roles will have to be fundamentally reconstructed. Weber first compares his project to that of the secular men's movement led by Robert Bly, which he sees initially to be similar to his, for both Christian and secular men recognize that the purity of masculinity has been diluted: "Each rightly realized that tepid water samples from the contemporary stream of manhood were hopelessly diluted and polluted. What each of them longed for was a long drink from the icy headwaters of masculinity." (35) Both groups looked around at contemporary manhood and found no models, so they turned to history and searched through the "murky shallows of [the] nineties, eighties, and seventies," arriving at the "dark turbulence of [the] sixties," and refusing to "linger at the compelling but deceptive currents of the fifties and forties." These were all superficial, inadequate models, and what drew men on were the "ancient tributaries of legend, myth, and tribal lore" as the waters "grew wilder and sweeter." Here, however, Bly and the secular men's movement made the mistake of stopping too soon, for in spite of the fact that they had, in fact, reached the headwaters of Man, their depictions of true masculinity were not pure. They had not gone far enough toward the origin to discover what lay underneath true masculinity — the mother spring, the Genesis Spring: "the taste of Original Man. Undiluted. Untainted." (36)

We are now situated firmly in the logic of purity. The absolutism of this model reveals that the true value of masculinity lies in pure masculinity without mixture, pure masculinity as the nature of man, "the nature of a man." (37) And if one keeps going back, as Christian men do, it becomes even more obvious that the truths of pure masculinity are to be found in the Story of Stories, the Book of Books: "Think of the Bible as the owner's manual for your masculinity." (37) That owner's manual, the Book of natural law, proves that nature and human nature are Judeo-Christian in their very essence. Nature is a blueprint that reveals the fingerprints of the Author, and it provides a steadying coherence, because it links the Four Pillars of manhood to other natural phenomena: the four points on the compass, the four seasons of the year, the four elements. Those Four Pillars of manhood are king, warrior, mentor, and friend: "Four undergirding life rhythms throb in the veins of every male-child." (38)

This throbbing language of purity is always troubling, given this century's history of tribal nationalism based on the purity of blood. Weber's book makes no concession to such worries nor to the various supremacist groups in the Pacific Northwest. The cover of the book, in fact, looks as if the Tender Warrior and his family came straight out of the *Nibelungenlied,* the thirteenth-century German epic poem based on the legends of Siegfried. A background of bold blocks of color brings into chiseled relief the images of a family, their solid figures in black edged with silver. The man, with enormous muscular shoulders, is at the center and holds a huge silver sword in his right arm, in front of the family unit like a shield; his left arm shelters his wife, who looks down at their child in her arms. The iconography is that of medieval chivalry and knighthood, an aristocracy in which there is no distinction between the nobility of body and the nobility of character; Weber's second book, about male friendship, refers to modern man as a knight whose armor has rusted.

In these Four Pillars of manhood, the king, of course, is God, but he legitimates Adam, his earthly son, who is destined to rule "with all power and authority" and who is instructed beside the Genesis Spring to "have dominion." (40) The most crucial of the four identities, however, and the one that gets most of Weber's attention, because it has endured the most abuse from feminists, is the warrior. Here the warrior is strategically and importantly linked to Jesus in the process of shifting the image of Jesus from that of a passive, loving God to militant warrior. The definition of Man then becomes essentially Christian, though as we will see, an Israeli soldier helps provide a masculine face: "Jesus Christ is the ultimate Man. Maximum manhood. The perfect Model. The complete Hero." (207) He is not meek and mild, as he has often been represented; in fact, he even closes the Bible "on a white war horse, in a bloodspattered robe, with a sword in His mouth and a rod of iron in His hand. The book ends with a roar, not a whimper. Within the epistles, the mature believing man is often described in militant terms — a warrior equipped to battle mighty enemies and shatter satanic strongholds." (41) Like Christ, a warrior is not a brute but a protector who acts out of high moral standards. When Jesus is called a peacemaker, it is not because he is a pacifist but because he will "establish that peace from the back of a great white horse as the head of the armies of heaven." (41)

This military version of Jesus has to be reestablished if men are to be drawn back to spirituality, a remasculinization of Christ that is crucial to Weber's efforts to draw men to religion, for he recognizes the difficulty of asking men to submit to Christ when submission is a model for women: "Many of us fear that . . . if we fully yield the reins of our life to Christ, He will take away our manhood. Victims of a demasculinized portrait of Christ, we have forgotten that His perfect blend of divinity and humanity was expressed through existence as a man." (209)[13] One of the reasons men think of religion as feminized, Weber suggests, is that the image of Jesus has been thoroughly distorted. Weber insists here on making the finite absolute, in the way Adorno and Horkheimer warned us about, for he must discipline and control the figuration of Jesus so that he can be represented by only a certain kind of man: "Even the single most famous portrait of Jesus makes Him look more like a pouting model for Breck shampoo than a man. Doesn't it? His eyes aren't toward you. The face is thin and aloof. The long hair is waved and feminine." (208)[14] It would seem that even Renaissance paintings were not Christian enough, in Weber's terms, and he turns to a warrior who ironically could not imitate this kind of perfect man because he is not a Christian, though his virility and military identity seem to overcome that difficulty. While on a trip to Israel, Weber's driver was a twenty-five-year-old, dark-eyed, virile soldier just released from the hospital where he had been convalescing from wounds suffered in the Yom Kippur War. After this encounter, "that pale, limp-wristed Galilean faded like a bad dream and the laughing, dark-skinned Son of David took over the picture in my mind." (209)[15] These military metaphors are important, for the military will prove to be the other place where men are expected to be submissive without being feminized, where, in fact, that submission makes them even more masculine.

The other two roles for men are mentor and friend. As mentor, the Christian husband is the subject who is supposed to know, who is supposed to have the vision that others will follow, and as friend, he is also expected to be a lover. The concept of lover, however, is carefully circumscribed, for it is "never to be prostituted by the isolated erotic." (43) That is, it is never to be interpreted or acted upon in any way other than within heterosexual, monogamous marriage. As a friend and mentor, the man must make commitments and keep them, which means that he must be a promise keeper and refuse sexual liberation, which taught men that they could simply be uncommitted, footloose, absent. Weber here focuses on one of the consequences of sexual liberation that feminists, too, have analyzed: the fact that, in many cases, men benefited more than women — the Hugh Hefner, Jack Kerouac model. But for Weber, Christian masculinity is about the heroic power of staying, of keeping one's promise and making a sacrifice for another. It would be hard to argue that this is not an important message for men. He also connects that "staying power" to the fidelity a husband owes his wife, for the marriage promise means that "the toxin of comparison [of one's wife with other possible partners] has been utterly neutralized and washed away by the sacred anti-toxin of a promise." (61)

Men thus imitate Christ when they keep their promises by sacrificing themselves for their wives and children, for Jesus "not only models staying power, He provides it for the asking. He not only shows us what the Ultimate Man is like, He rolls up His sleeves and helps us get it done. That's why real men don't run. Real men stay and stay and stay." (66) In fact, many wives and mothers pay the registration fee for men to attend Promise Keeper or Family Life gatherings. And Weber returns relentlessly to his central point: we cannot get men to fulfill their promises and commitments to women and children unless we affirm their masculinity, unless we provide them with both actual and figurative masculine privilege. Today's men suffer from being expected to be unnatural men, while natural men, warriors, and kings are criticized and suspect. This leaves a void in men's identity, the space of representation marked by a blank: "Without [warrior and king], we are hollow men. We are men without chests." (48)

The problem for Weber in addressing that void is the need to find a way to bring together two seemingly contradictory things: warrior virility and the tenderness and commitment needed to keep a family together. Real men, Weber argues, must even learn to speak "woman":

> Let me ask you this question: What would your business look like if you applied the same amount of mental and emotional energy to it that you do to understanding your wife? Am I far off the mark when I say that most of America would be bankrupt?
>
> Use your head, men. Think it through. Work hard at it. Don't give up. *Understand.* Become a student of your wife and live in light of that knowledge. (121)

His discussion of what women require from men was inspired by a poem he received from a woman in his congregation, which showed him the despair that can come from a Christian marriage that is simply required and not developed. The woman's poem was entitled "Life in a Tomb" and goes like this:

> The emptiness of 20+ years.
>   The loss of hope.
>   The battle for joy with a good man
>   a man content to be alone
>   (but he needs me to be the keeper of his house,
>   the mother of his children)
>   a companion but no communion.
>   How can one endure contented
>   with so little
>   amidst so much material?
>   I worry for my soul
>   living without love. (117–18)

He uses the poem to emphasize the kind of things men must learn, for their relationships with their wives must be *action* plans. Love has to be shown, demonstrated, verbalized, expressed, "woven into real words and real deeds. How does a man love a woman? He learns to know her needs and consistently speaks her language in meeting them." (125)

Suggesting that Christian men may have read more women's writing about women than have most secular men, Weber, however, firmly keeps this advice within the frame of absolutist biblical teachings about male headship: "He is an initiator and she is a responder. That's masculinity and femininity in the proverbial nutshell." (120) These are the natural roles that will determine the relationship within the marriage, though it will be made especially strong because of the woman's responder role: "When Linda responds with such joy and warmth it almost makes me ashamed at how seldom I exert myself in that direction. But the fact remains . . . when I as the lover and initiator attempt to speak her language and penetrate her world, she is all I've ever dreamed of as a woman in response to me." (128)

Weber's most emotional description of the way he values his wife comes in a description of the birth of their first child: "What I wanted to broadcast was, 'Hey world, this is my wife, this is my *woman,* this is my miracle worker. Look what she has done!'" But even for men who do not have children, the pride in one's wife is to be nourished and celebrated: "Do battle with hell itself for the sake of your woman and your marriage. Polish the treasure where you live and forget the mythical one at the end of Hollywood's rainbow. All you need is under your own roof if you'll only acknowledge it and cherish it." (129)

The armor of this Tender Warrior also hides a masculine need for relationships with men, the desire to touch and be touched. These emotional and spiritual needs for relationship show up in sports: "The inner drive to touch and connect won't be denied. What's the first thing they do when a great offensive drive explodes in a touchdown? They look for someone to touch." (70) And though some people refer to those touches as high fives, he calls them chicken hugs, because men are not supposed to embrace in front of everybody even though they are every bit as emotional as women: "Real men need one another. Real soldiers love each other." (176) But here Weber has to pause to make a crucial distinction between the adjectives "tender" and "soft" in order to free up the possibility of masculine love for the virile men of his audience. Hugging men in football, or homosociality, can all too easily appear to be and threaten to become hugging men homoerotically, an interpretation that must be rigorously forestalled. "Tender," he argues, is linked to the Latin word that means to stretch out, or extend, and he links that definition to expressions of love, kindness, affection, and compassion. The word "soft," on the other hand, means mild, effeminate, easily yielding to physical pressure, unresistant to molding, untrained for hardship. He carefully assigns the gender mark of the masculine to "tender," and the feminine or effeminate marking to "soft." His complete lack of defensiveness about such tenderness is, of course, partially enabled by the fact that the book's opening has already proved his own virility in the descriptions of his battle experiences as a Green Beret, and surprisingly, he criticizes the John Wayne model of male heroism: "The celluloid hard guy is hard-core. Scornful of sentiment. One dimensional. And phony as a guy in a cheap gorilla suit. Hollywood folks wouldn't know a Tender Warrior if they saw one." (69) They know only two types of heterosexual men, the hard-core lover and the effeminate liberal, and neither is sufficient.

After the definition of tenderness has legitimated masculine emotion, tenderness is movingly described in discussions of Weber's own friend-ships and his relationships with his sons. These are especially striking because they seem so different from the usual behavior men have learned from a culture that makes male emotional display and communication suspect, cultural training that leaves friends, wives, and children emo-tionally abandoned. As he describes his reaction to his son's birth, it is easy to see the power in a child's life of such a father, and it is clear he means it: *"I love you. I will do anything for you. I will never leave you. You are mine. And I am yours."* (77)[16] One of the most intense moments at the Promise Keepers conference in Eugene came during Weber's talk about fathering. The most critical observer of the Promise Keepers would have been moved by the deeply emotional response of many of the men in the stands when Weber asked all the teenagers and very young men to stand. Then he asked their fathers to do so. When it was apparent that many of their fathers were not there, Weber asked that someone nearby stand and offer support. Finally, he asked all the others of all ages who had come with their fathers to stand; they did so and most embraced. Because it is so rare to see middle-aged men being embraced by their older fathers, teenagers wrapped in the arms of theirs, it was deeply moving. The inten-sity of the emotion felt by men at these moments cannot be underesti-mated, especially for men whose culture has robbed them of intimacy and emotional expression.

Any easy dismissal of this intimate advice to men would be a mistake, and any attempt to counter it has to recognize the deep needs it speaks to. bell hooks, from a different political direction, speaks of a contemporary yearning for meaning on the part of many different groups. Hers is a term that will have to take into account a yearning for this kind of masculine love between fathers and sons.

What becomes so unsettling, however, is the same combination of solace and absolutism that shows up in LaHaye's writing. For accom-panying these deeply moving passages about love and friendship and these beautiful encounters is the rigidly structured gender argument that situates tenderness within an absolutist cosmos. Weber first strategically reconstructs the feminist critique of men's abdication of their responsibilities, even as he duplicitously begins to define feminism as a desire for male headship: "Our culture is so horribly confused at this point. Many are being swept away by the whirlpool of role confusion. I personally believe the more militant side of the feminist movement is a frustrated revolt against unmanly men — men with little or no concept of providing, protecting, mentoring, and loving — against tyrant men who have abused their caring responsibilities." (92) In setting out these absolute gender differences, he must criticize the tyrant in order to reestablish the legitimate male head. And in doing so, he argues that leadership is not something men can unproblematically enjoy, for things have not gone well between men and women: "Men bear a primary responsibility for this sorrow between the sexes." (118) He quotes Dr. Richard Halverson, chaplain of the United States Senate: "It is my deep, settled conviction that *one hundred percent* of the responsibility for the sustenance of the marriage relationship belongs to the husband." (118) Men who make unjust demands on women are condemned as un-Christian men who have not submitted themselves to God.

Recognizing that a postmodern climate of expectations about gender equality will structure an audience's receptiveness to his teaching, Weber says that one of the questions frequently asked at his Family Life seminars is whether it bothers his wife that "the man is the head of a woman." Before answering that question, he must first patiently set out the reasons masculine privilege is necessary. First he turns to the work of both Sherry Ortner and Carol Gilligan to argue for the essential necessity of male leadership. As he quotes Ortner, "The universality of female subordination, the fact that it exists within every type of social and economic arrangement and in societies of every degree of complexity, indicates to me that we are up against something very profound, very stubborn, something we cannot root out simply by rearranging a few tasks and roles in the social system, or even by reordering the whole economic structure. . . . I would flatly assert that we find women subordinate to men in every known society." (94) Anthropology and biology thus match Scripture: "How then should we respond to it?" asks Weber. "Accept it and live it. Trust it and obey it. Take the orders, and follow them. As men under authority." (94)

This Marine-like version of male leaders who take orders from the Commander grounds his rhetorical frame: "Boys and girls, men and women, are simply naturally profoundly unquestionably thoroughly DIFFERENT." (101) But this is not inferiority or superiority "any more than blue is superior to green or green is inferior to blue or water is superior to air or air is superior to water." (122) Women need to nurture and to savor relationships and memories; men need to conquer and provide. That is a lesson that comes literally and directly from the Bible, whose truths do not come to us hermeneutically through interpretation but literally through revelation: "Every major tenant [*sic*] of our faith is a matter of *revelation* not explanation. We know what we know by taking Him at His Word. We apprehend His intentions and affirm our allegiance by believing what He says." (88) And what he says is that "woman was made for man, not man for woman." (108)

The husband is the head, the director, the chief, the foremost. Male leadership is part of the original plan: "Were the apostle alive today, he might be shot for saying that, or certainly vilified in the media as a small-minded bigot and a sexist. But that's the Bible. It just says it." (90) This allows Weber to retell the story of Adam and Eve so that the Fall proves to be Adam's fault rather than Eve's. The fact that it is his fault makes him responsible for taking charge now. Adam allowed Eve to sin, and that abdication of his leadership role made his sin far more serious than her surrender to Satan's seductions. The real lesson of the Garden of Paradise was the abdication of male leadership, not the sinfulness of woman; the man's duty is to be responsible. We are also situated in the generic requirements of tragedy here, as George Gilder will remind us in the next chapter. In the classical Greek story of Oedipus, the man is not so much guilty as responsible, as responsibility and guilt are broken apart into two different concepts. Women like Jocasta and Eve are assigned guilt but not responsibility, and men can only be guilty if they fail to act on the responsibility that is their duty. Guilt for Eve is action; for Adam it is inaction.

When men abdicate leadership, that unmanly behavior also feminizes them in the eyes of their wives. Citing Pierre Mornell's *Passive Men, Wild Women,* Dr. Howard G. Hendricks in the Promise Keepers volume describes what happens when men who are active out in the world of work during the day return home and become inarticulate, inactive, lethargic, withdrawn, and passive. This feminization of their behavior drives women crazy: "In the face of his retreat, she goes wild."[17] This example might also suggest that women simply want men to help out at home or work out a way of sharing leadership. But it becomes proof for Hendricks that women demand that their husbands take back the sole leadership role. Dr. Tony Evans, in that same volume, calls this kind of feminization of men a "misunderstanding of manhood that has produced a nation of 'sissified' men who abdicate their role as spiritually pure leaders, thus forcing women to fill the vacuum."[18] In responding to that feminized male behavior, Weber has a suggestion: "Men, as husbands you have been given a trust — a stewardship, a responsibility, a duty — to husband, or manage, or care for the gifts of your wife. *If you abuse that trust, you fail at the very heart of your manhood.*" (92) By condemning the abuse of male power, however, he has also subtly collapsed two things into one. The authoritarian behavior of a tyrant and the refusal to keep one's wife from claiming equal agency have now become wrongs of equal significance. The heart of the matter now clearly contains a phallus, and its owner is duty bound to resist Eve's claims of agency. Tony Evans's Promise Keeper advice is far less subtle:

> [S]it down with your wife and say something like this: "Honey, I've made a terrible mistake. I've given you my role. I gave up leading this family, and I forced you to take my place. Now I must reclaim that role." Don't misunderstand what I'm saying here. I'm not suggesting that you *ask* for your role back, I'm urging you to *take it back*. . . . Your wife's concerns may be justified. Unfortunately there can be no compromise here. If you're going to lead you must lead. Be sensitive. Listen. Treat the lady gently and lovingly. But *lead!* (79–80)

This kind of dangerous certainty lurking beneath advice about masculine leadership is accompanied by a disconcerting paternalism as Weber bases his advice on 1 Peter 3:7: "You husbands . . . live with your wives in an understanding way, as with a weaker vessel, since she is a woman; and grant her honor as a fellow heir of the grace of life." (120) The definition of "weaker vessel" does not simply refer to physiology: "She is the fine China, not the stoneware. She is a finely-tuned sports car, not a '66 Chevy pickup with mud flaps. She is more fragile, more sensitive . . . a magnificent creature who by design requires provision and protection and care." (121–22) As men learn to cherish this delicacy, fragility, alertness, and sensitivity, however, they must also come to understand that women are much more influenced by the nature of their bodies than are men. Cyclical changes and PMS produce depression and irritability that men must learn to cope with: "It's chemistry, pure and simple." (123)

The differences between male and female bodies, even if those differences make neither of them inferior or superior, nevertheless guarantee that one of those bodies is the universal subject. The other's identity is determined by its connection to nature:

> What do you see, after all, when you look at the vehicle of a man's physical body? What was it made for? Check it out. In contrast, what does a woman's body tell you a woman was made for? Every 28 days or so her body tells her she was made for life and its sustenance. Her breasts remind her that she was made for giving life and nurturing life. What does a man's body tell you? Not a thing! Why? Because the purpose for a man is out on the horizon. A man was made to be a provisionary, a wagon scout out there in front, looking ahead. Their purpose isn't inside. (212)

This means that biology requires that the wife must sacrifice her agency so that the man can lead and save both family and nation. Again suggesting the way this model of gender is deeply influenced by military discipline, Weber quotes a "vivacious, intelligent woman in our church" who told him, "I know now why my husband is such a good leader . . . because he first learned to be a good follower [in the Marines]. . . . What a wonderful day it was when I finally let him lead." (93) And his own wife, Linda, says in the acknowledgments of her book, *Mom, You're Incredible,* "Although I had started developing other ideas [for my book], my husband, Stu, said, 'Mothering needs to be first.'"

But though women would seem to make the exemplary sacrifice when they give up their agency, that has already been surpassed by a superior masculine one. Weber turns to C. S. Lewis, whose writing is a frequent source of legitimation for radical conservatism's view of natural law: "It is painful, being a man, to have to assert the privilege, or the burden, which Christianity lays upon my own sex." (95) If it is the case that male headship is a tragic burden laid on men, the problem becomes how to deal justly with its inevitability. If it is inevitable, we must stop wishing it were not so and simply get on with it. Weber inserts that inevitability into the terms of the imitation of Christ: "Husbands, love your wives [*exactly*] as Christ also loved the church *and gave Himself up for her*" (96, his brackets); the church was Christ's bride. Weber has remasculinized the imitation of Christ. For as the women's texts showed, because submission is a part of their very nature, women appear to resemble Christ more closely than men do; Christ submitted to his father's will. Weber here averts two serious possibilities: one, that women will be seen to have been created in the image of Christ in a much more direct way than men; and two, that Christ in his submissive character might appear to be more feminine than masculine. The virility of both Christ and Christian men, the tragic nature of their sacrifice for the sake of civilization, has, however, now been made clear: "The mature husband understands servant-leadership. Just like Jesus." (97)

The effectiveness of Weber's strategy here is that, in a powerful sleight of pen, assigning all the blame to men has also justified arguing that all our effort must now be devoted to reconstructing men's traditional position in the family. The pressing issue, not so surprisingly, will be fatherhood, and in an emotional sweep, fatherhood links patriotism, Pilgrims, and nation. For the Pilgrims were "men who I believe understood manhood and fathering. . . . They were truly patriots — a word drawn from the root word for father. And for all of our politically correct 'multi-cultural' rejection of this heritage, the canyons and valleys and mountain peaks of our nation still echo the song of the pilgrim fathers. The best of who we are can be traced back to their godly fathering at the dawn of our nationhood." (145) By our own actions as fathers, he tells his readers, "good, bad, and ugly — we are actually affecting the leadership of the twenty-first century! What an awesome power!" (150)[19]

Even if you were not fathered well, there is another Father waiting. The reader can be born again: "Flint McCullugh never spent a day rootin' around where the train had already been. He was too busy envisioning the future. Take that approach. Climb a tree. Dream a future. Draw a plan." (151) The most important result of revalorizing fatherhood is to make it possible to release our "arrows," our children, into the world as a part of our responsibility to evangelize. More children remain in the faith, he argues, if their fathers are active Christians than if only their mothers are. This revalorization is not simply good for our individual families; it is of world-historical importance: "As time draws to a close on this darkened planet, surely every arrow must count." (168) The anxiety aroused by a darkening planet, part of the tragic apocalyptic narrative, has from the very beginning been framed by the utopian revivalism of the comic narrative. The book opens with an epigraph from Romans 13:11–12: "The night is nearly over; the day has almost dawned. . . . Let us arm ourselves for the fight of the day!" (13)

Once the specific responsibilities of men within the family have been covered, Weber turns again to male friendships, whose model is the military:

> "Your love to me *was more wonderful than the love of women.*" What words are these? Perverted words? Twisted words? The words of some pathetic sexual deviate? No. A war-hardened veteran penned these words after his best buddy fell in battle. They were written by a warrior, with the piercing grief only a soldier mourning for a comrade-in-arms could begin to understand.
>
> Twisted words? No. They are words straight and true—a swift, clean arrow shot from the heart of Scripture. David wrote these words after the death of his friend Jonathan on the bloody slope of Mount Gilboa. (171)

Here Weber attempts to bypass the model of homosocial bonding in which male relationships are circulated through a woman—for example, in a movie like *The Fugitive,* in which the characters played by Tommy Lee Jones and Harrison Ford are connected by the figure of the murdered wife. Though she had to be absent, nevertheless she was necessary to the plot in order to bring them together. For Weber, even that much intervention by women is eliminated, for this is "a desire for friendship with nothing between," a soul mate, a friendship whose true model is that of Ranger buddies in war. Though a man is willing to die *for* his family and home, "something inside us longs for someone to die *with* . . . someone to die *beside* . . . someone to lock step with. Another man with a heart like our own." (172) If one cannot find these because there is no war or dangerous, satanic communism abroad, then perhaps the challenge of waging a cultural battle with evil within the nation will provide that same wartime bonding.

Because true manhood and true friendships have to be tested in war, just as true American identity must be tested by battling a wilderness, the deployment of fear produces the sense of danger that requires such a warrior—cultural deterioration, crime, perverts, plagues—and the scapegoats ready at hand. The character and courage of the soldier will be determined by the dangers of his opponents. For if those evils are not deadly and world-historical, then only mediocre men will be needed to fight them, not this kind of warrior, whose persecution by secular attacks on him will prove the merit of his cause.

Tender Warrior's inspirational story of male friendships in the struggle against evil has proven to be situated not only in military discipline but squarely in the mythologies of everyday life made available through popular culture. The book ends with a description of a painting reproduced on the cover of the magazine published by James Dobson's Focus on the Family. Weber describes his experience of standing mesmerized in front of the full-size painting, of four men on horseback. What held him there was the fact that "these men had tamed the beasts beneath them . . . and within them" (213), and unlike the image of the solitary Marlboro Man, they were riding together across the frontier:

> They had understood that masculinity was made for connection. They rode together upstream. Fully equipped to face the elements. You could see their breath on the cold fall morning. They rode together as friends and soul-mates and warriors, against the force of the current, into the cold wind and *exhilarating* in it. (214)

The story behind the painting gives it an even more powerful effect, however, for these men were not only excited friends riding across the frontier; they were also religious men with a calling: "Willing to face the obstacles. Willing to buck the current and the wind and the dangers. Willing to die, if necessary." (214) The painting had been commissioned by Focus on the Family to honor four lay churchmen killed while flying back from a ministry retreat: "Four laymen protecting—through their ministry involvement—the spiritual values of a whole nation. . . . Men who were other-oriented, not self-oriented. Men on a mission paying the price." (214) A western imitation of Christ.

Weber ends the book by reconnecting that highly emotional adventure to the personal experiences of everyday life, joining the romance of the Wild West, the Marines, and moral absolutes of Christian fatherhood as he asks his readers to join him in a similar adventure:

> Men, you and I need to own for ourselves the same clarity of vision that so marked the life of Christ. We need to give ourselves up for our brides and *the* Bride as He did. So that the family might be healthy. So that the people might live well. So that this nation might continue to experience His favor and remain the land of the free. There are some little guys and gals out there who need Big Bompas. There are some women out there who need clear-eyed provisionaries. Men who face the worst hell has to throw at them and stay and stay and stay. There's a world out there that needs some Tender Warriors. It's

every man's purpose . . . every woman's dream . . . and every child's hope. It's the definition of a man. I want to head down that road with all my heart. But I want some Ranger Buddies to walk with me. Will you come? Let's do it together. (214–15)

This is not what religious discourse used to sound like. It has now been thoroughly recoded into virile outdoor adventure, the television western, the experience of Vietnam, and absolute moral values heavily laced with male hormones.

Yet while the warrior masculinity of the adventurer has been reaffirmed, so has his emotional and spiritual nature. Perhaps the most unsettling experience for an outsider at a Promise Keepers gathering is the unexpected beauty of thousands of male voices singing a hymn like "Amazing Grace" a cappella, with a soulfulness totally unexpected in a football stadium. But, in the very same moment, one is chilled by the uncanny presence in the cultural air we all breathe after World War II of images of other stadiums, other large gatherings of men singing. Thus the most moving aspect of the Promise Keepers is simultaneously the most frightening one, this seductive, unsettling equation between solace and certainty.

ii.

One of the Promise Keepers, Wellington Boone, takes Weber's adventure one step further in order to contain everything, not only Original Sin but birth, within the orbit of traditional masculinity. For now the harrowing dangers to be faced by the new Christian man, the dangers revealed by the tragic apocalyptic narrative and the dynamism enabled by the comic, utopian one, take Boone to a place where he can control the site of the greatest danger of all: female sexuality and, in particular, birth. In his lesson to men, this renewed masculinity becomes a masculine pregnancy to surpass the centrality of the female role in reproduction. This revival is now described in the terms of a masculine pregnancy with God as the Father. Having submitted themselves to the church as bride, as Weber advised, and having translated submission into masculine terms, the men's movement has now paradoxically *become* the bride impregnated by the Father, and it gives birth: "Our changed lives are obvious. Like a woman who is pregnant and nearing the end of her term, we Christian men are about to burst forth with the coming of the Lord in ways we have never experienced. *I believe that the church is in travail and that God is about to birth the next great awakening. And it will start with Promise Keepers on their knees in prayer."* (31)

After women are methodically defined as essentially nurturant and pro-creative, that definition is surpassed by a greater kind of birth, in which men provide the womb. The apocalyptic narrative now *promises* to burst rather than threatening to do so, in a bursting that will not signal Armageddon but will usher in the Millennium, the thousand-year reign of Christ on earth. This birth and its euphoria are made even more exciting because they are included in a military context and because they are spoken by a football coach, Bill McCartney: "We're in a war, men, whether we acknowledge it or not. The enemy is real, and he doesn't like to see men of God take a stand for Jesus Christ and contest his lies (see 2 Cor. 10:3–5). But almighty God is for us. . . ."[20]

Russ Bellant, in *Front Lines Research,* provides more background on McCartney's involvement with Promise Keepers. While assistant football coach at the University of Michigan at Ann Arbor, McCartney became involved with the Word of God community, led by Jim Berlucci, whom McCartney describes as one of the most important influences on his life. WOG was involved in a controversial movement called "shepherding/discipleship," in which each person in the group submits totally to the head of the group: "Members were required to submit their schedules in advance and account for every hour of every day. Marriage partner, movie choices, jobs, and other decisions also had to be approved by this leader." On leaving Michigan, McCartney joined the WOG-linked Vineyard church in Boulder, whose leader, John Wimber, describes his purpose as "power evangelism," in which "self-conscious members of God's army [are] sent to do battle against the forces of the kingdom of darkness. . . . One is either in God's Kingdom or Satan's." (7) The pastor at McCartney's church, Rev. James Ryle, sees the Promise Keepers as what Bellant calls "the fulfillment of the biblically prophesied end-time army described in the book of *Joel* — a terrifying army from which there is no escape. . . . Ryle says he has a vision of Promise Keepers purging America of secularism, which he considers 'an abortion' of godliness." (8) Bellant quotes Ryle: "Never have 300,000 men come together throughout human history except for the purpose of war." (8) The PK mentoring structure is similar to the Word of God shepherding/discipleship model, but most groups are not rigid and members do not feel themselves manipulated to such a degree.

Such exuberance comes as a great relief in the face of anxiety about a man's identity, for now this world-historical male adventure legitimated by Christ means that men need not work through the kinds of questions that have been asked by feminists about the cultural training of men and the very nature of the American social contract. Instead they can transcend that, ignore it, and reestablish the identities they grew up with. As Weber says in his more recent book,

> When you get right down to it, you'd just like to enjoy being a man, wouldn't you? We'd just like to be and do what men were *made* to do. Something down deep inside us just wants to be a man. Remember when men were men? And women women? And the differences were obvious? Remember when you didn't have to wonder? And weren't criticized for being a man? Can you remember when little boys couldn't wait to grow up and become men? When young men wore masculinity like their home team's colors? Maturing into manhood was like earning a varsity letter. It was a glad, grand thing to be a man. It was good to be part of the fraternity.
>
> But now in a culture that wants to elevate a higher standard of so-called diversity, we're destroying diversity in its most beautiful and elemental form.[21]

Though these emotionally powerful gatherings are attended by many men who reject the Christian Right's political agenda, and though the speakers rarely make overtly partisan or even, at times, identifiably right-wing arguments, at other times there is little question about their agenda. At the Eugene gathering, one of the featured speakers was John Hagee, whose book, *Bible Positions on Political Issues,* was on sale in the big tent. It includes chapters on the key issues for a conservative Christian like himself and his ministry, the first dealing with abortion, which is subtitled "The American Holocaust." The next concerns homosexuality and AIDS, subtitled "Alternative or Abomination"; a chapter on the feminist movement, "War against America," includes this advice to men, "If you have a problem that involves a woman, go to her husband, not to her."[22] There is also a chapter that describes the agenda of the environmentalist movement:

> to control the U.S. economy through governmental regulations and to control the birth rate in the U.S. through abortion and restrictive population control methods. . . . to redistribute the wealth of America to third world nations through the control of the United Nations without interference from the United States. (75)

The book concludes with a final chapter on capital punishment, in which Hagee assures us that God favors it and, in fact, mandates it.

Though it may be obvious why he devotes chapters to abortion, homosexuality, and feminism, it still may not be clear to some readers why the environmental movement deserves condemnation in such absolutist Christian terms. Hagee's version of the environmental movement, however, shows how smoothly this absolutist framework can work, as it helps legitimate the rhetoric of the groups discussed in the last chapter. The major players in his version of the environmental movement are what he calls the Conservation movement, which includes such groups as the Audubon Society and the Sierra Club; the "Radical Green" sector, made up of people who vandalize things to protect spotted owls and other endangered species; the "deep ecology" sector, "which links the movement of the New Age and the occult," primarily through their concept of Gaia; and "the eastern establishment and liberals in America and Europe," whom he calls "the New World Order crowd," including the members of the Council on Foreign Relations, the Trilateral Commission, and the Club of Rome. All of these groups "hate the free enterprise system . . . portray all businessmen as evil, greedy villains, . . . and want to stop all industrial growth (i.e. your job) through restrictive environmental laws." And they do this "so they can control the economy, the government, and you." (87) A key point in his analysis is that environmentalists imagine that they can influence nature, when in fact, such a goal denies that God is completely in control:

> Jesus Christ stood on the bow of a boat in the Sea of Galilee and said, "Peace, be still!" and the wind and the waves obeyed him. Gaia didn't do it. Witchcraft didn't do it. The Son of God did it. He is not nature, he is above nature. . . . God will use nature to announce the Second Coming. . . . I believe God knew from the beginning that some pagan cretins were going to come along with a doctrine about nature worship and the spirit of the earth. And God will prove to anyone with the intellectual capacity of a stump that he is in absolute control. (89)

And, finally, the Christian men's movement also finds itself synchronized with attacks on affirmative action and the Supreme Court, though now Justices Clarence Thomas and Antonin Scalia are seen to have changed the Court's direction by bringing the focus back to the original intent of the Founding Fathers. That original intent had to do not simply with Christianity but with conservative Judeo-Christian morality, as we have seen. The chief legal counsel who argues absolutist conservatism's cases before the Supreme Court, Jay Sekulow, is Jewish, and he heads the American Center for Law and Justice, associated with Pat Robertson's Regent University. In concluding this chapter on the revalorization of religious masculinity, I want to describe the definition of American culture held by the increasingly effective ACLJ, whose chief opponents are the ACLU and other liberal organizations, like People for the American Way and Americans United for the Separation of Church and State.

As Jay Sekulow explains in the Center's publication, *Casenote,* the ACLJ's mandate is to provide free legal help for religious people all across the country who feel they have been discriminated against because of their religion. To make such help available, the ACLJ has launched the Religious Liberties Project, the Economic Liberty Project, the Family Life Project, "to defend the family from direct and indirect attacks," and the Human Life and Reproduction Project, which "will stand against euthanasia and the bio-ethics of death."[23] Its Office of Governmental Affairs monitors legislation and directs litigation on a number of fronts, and the ACLJ filed an amicus brief on behalf of the state of Colorado in opposition to extending civil rights to homosexuals.

Keith Fournier, a Roman Catholic who is executive director of the ACLJ, writes that the definition of the family "is not open for vote or judicial alteration."[24] The determination of the ACLJ to reverse the judicial activism that has strayed from that truth is based on what Fournier describes as the inextricable relations among the Constitution, the family, and God:

> The unlimited God Himself was incarnated into our limited capacity and through that action removed our limitations, elevating us to a new level of relationship. God, who is family, expanded His family through the first born, Jesus Christ. Jesus became the bridge that brings us into a family relationship with God. With the birth of Jesus the birth of the first "domestic church," the Holy family of Nazareth — father Joseph, mother Mary, and son Jesus. They are a model showing us the incredible connection between family and church. . . . the family has been, and will be, the first church, the first government, the first school and the primary social structure of all civilizations. By God's royal design the family is the driving force in history.

The intimacy of the family has now been carefully and sensually situated at the very center not only of the Declaration of Independence but of the Constitution as well. Defined as the basic truth of the social contract put in place by the Founding Fathers, a new revolutionary fervor is required to reverse the cultural changes of the last thirty-five years and to return to America's true foundation. It was the judicial activism and cultural forces of the last thirty-five years, Fournier says, that produced a "religious cleansing in the American Republic." Though one might see America in the 1990s as a decaying, desperate, post-Christian society that has forgotten its origins, "it may be more helpful to think of it as *pre-*Christian."[25] What will bring it back to Christ will be the ability of Christians to engage in the public marketplace of ideas *as Christians:* "As long as America remains free, we will be able to take our message into the marketplace where it can compete head-to-head with all the other ideas clamoring for the minds of Americans."

The structure of clarity has come full circle with this proposal for a free, democratic marketplace of ideas. For here the discussion can only begin *after* the terms of debate have been firmly grounded in a legal framework that is fundamentally theocratic, even while, in a case of reverse mirroring, Fournier describes it in the familiar language of open debate and the democratic clamoring of ideas. After the amorphous vagueness of passionate clarity has made it possible to propose a logic that equates Church and State while renaming that equation democracy, the equation is then sealed with passions and certainties that are fully capable of making real democracy impossible.

FIVE

Postmodern Hunters and Gatherers

Capitalism begins at the mother's breast, with the feminine belief in the sanctity of every life, enshrined in the family and equal before God. — George Gilder

Tolerance, it seems, ended where respectability began. — George Mosse

When I hear the word "dialogue," I usually turn off my hearing aid.
— Irving Kristol

George Gilder's *Men and Marriage,* originally published, in 1973, as *Sexual Suicide,* provides another kind of lesson about intimacy, this time settling the sacred intimacy of Weber and the Promise Keepers directly into the secular biology of masculine sexuality and free-market politics. And as it turns out, even though this is a natural biology of the sexes developed through evolution, it is not the kind of evolutionary natural history described by Darwin and condemned by many conservative Christians. Instead, Gilder's sociobiology shifts the site of evolution squarely into culture to provide an evolutionary natural history of capitalism.[1] Postmodern American entrepreneurial capitalism will prove to have evolved naturally and inevitably from the earliest forms of society to its contemporary fulfillment. Therefore, it can function in this political economy as the universal model for civilized human nature, now that history has "ended."

In spite of the archaism of Gilder's views, his influence on the broader parameters of traditionalist conservative public policy has been enormous, and he is now a major figure in discussions of the possibilities of cyberspace and technology. Currently editor of the technology supplement to *Forbes* magazine, he is also a founder of a think tank in Seattle, the Discovery Institute. Funded by philanthropic grants, individual and corporate contributions, and individual dues, the Discovery Institute brings together multidisciplinary public-policy scholars and writers to publish reports, articles, and books, as well as "to devise applications of the Institute's long-term proposals that elected officials and other policy makers can use even in the short term, and to show how 21st century humanity can benefit from the principles, policies, and practices advocated by the Institute and its fellows."

The Institute functions as a high-tech collection of people interested in conservative economic thought and the future of cyberspace, a dizzyingly surreal combination echoed in Newt Gingrich's flights into the ether of techno-utopian language, to be discussed in the next chapter. It is Gilder's recognition of culture's importance in harnessing the unpredictability of entrepreneurial capitalism and a digitized global economy that makes him so interesting and influential. Not only did he merit a cover story in *Wired,* the hot, hip magazine of techies, but his book *Visible Man: A True Story of Post-Racist America* was a book-club selection of the Progress and Freedom Foundation, which evolved out of Newt Gingrich's course, Renewing American Civilization. As Po Bronson said in the *Wired* article, "George Gilder's past presents [a] problem to the many fans of his technological prophecies. Because amid all the people who hold libertarian views on technology, there are still deep chasms under the surface that yawn open the minute the topic of conversation switches away from technology."[2] The man who merits a cover story in *Wired* also writes for the *American Spectator,* and his publications, which include *Wealth and Poverty, Naked Nomads, Life after Television,* and *Microcosm,* reflect that chasm. The futuristic works are firmly grounded in a framework that is far from futuristic and that now structures much of the policy language of conservative politics.

This chapter will focus on the side of Gilder that coexists uneasily with his image as a cyberspace guru in the socially liberal world of *Wired* readers: that is, his remarkably regressive sociobiological explanation for human behavior. Gilder first absorbs Freud's reading of the unconscious, particularly in *Civilization and Its Discontents,* but he then converts it into *Capitalism and Its Discontents.* In the process, he develops a cultural and political agenda that will compensate men for the sacrifices capitalism demands of them. But while Freud argues that the discontents of civilization required the internalization of aggressive drives, Gilder's theory advocates the release of those drives into public discourse, where they are externalized and where they directly target scapegoats: gays, immigrants, people of color, and women.

And while postmodern theorists have used Freudian theory to describe the cultural force that is needed to maintain the illusion that gender differences are absolute, Gilder wants to make Freudian theory literal, to use it as a prescription for the way a society *should* be and to legitimate its real and symbolic violence. In order to do so, he first readily accepts the postmodern argument that culture is constructed, then goes on to methodically and relentlessly use that insight to construct what we might call capitalist second nature. This is Horkheimer and Adorno's term for the historical form of capitalist culture that calls itself natural and claims to be built out of archetypal human nature.[3] Gilder's project is in essence a response to Stu Weber's concern that there is a missing gender, and that this missing gender is Man. For as Gilder describes the stakes of this cultural reconstruction, "In all its specific expressions, manhood is made, not born."[4]

In reconstructing culture for Man, Gilder is also working out a theory of human identity. Like the sociobiology of Lionel Tiger, Gilder's theories originated in criticisms of quantitative methodologies in economics and sociology because they excluded the specificity of the individual subject: "The aggregation of many entities is assumed to nullify the singularity of each case." (160) Sounding as if he has read Foucault or feminist theory or eco-criticism, Gilder finds that this quantitative research claims that "what is measurable and aggregatable is more important than what is not. . . . the requirements of the social science model all too readily become the parameters of a social ideal. Measurable rationality, sexual homogeneity, environmental determinism, and credentialism all subtly change from heuristic simplifications to social goals." (161)[5] In Gilder's view, we cannot understand society if we look for explanations in the work of economists and sociologists who "avoid the murky domains of psychology and religion, affiliation and aspiration. Warped and webbed with family and ethnic loyalties, sexual drives and religious commitments, unconscious compulsions and spurious public rationales, the behavior of the sexes in society would completely confound the social scientist without the use of heroic simplifications." (159)

Gilder tells us that he published *Sexual Suicide* because he was disturbed by efforts to deny and repress sexual difference and, in particular, because his studies had taught him the importance of "the redemptive joys and crucial functions of marriage and family, the roots of human civilization." Those roots lie, as do Weber's, in a logic of purity in which gender absolutes are recognized and revalorized, while mixtures or dialectical relationships are demonized, then forcibly eliminated: "The differences between the sexes are the single most important fact of human society." (vii) The target of the book is made clear by Rush Limbaugh's blurb on the cover: "Timely when originally published, *Men and Marriage* is essential now given the warlike climate of male-female relationships, unfortunately fostered by radical feminism." Gilder's introduction to the 1993 version suggests that though some people may think feminism is dead, feminist beliefs saturate liberal society, and they even threaten conservative attempts to reform the welfare state. As he argues in a more recent article in the *American Spectator,* even many Republicans continue to be seduced by the "welfare feminism that is the regnant ideology of government." They, too, lose sight of the central fact of sexual difference when they advocate jobs programs for female welfare recipients: "We must eliminate all government programs, from coed job training to affirmative action, that fail to face the crucial differences between the sexes that make marriage possible."[6]

Gilder's importance lies in the way he provides a basis of stability in order to free up the infinite change necessary for entrepreneurial capitalism, and he does so by linking marriage to the economy. In his schema, it is not simply religious faith that should cause one to believe in the traditional family. In fact, he argues in a chapter in Newt Gingrich's college textbook, to be discussed in the next chapter, that a person need not actually be religious but must have faith in religious *culture.* So it is not absolute morality alone that requires marriage. Instead, marriage is necessary because of the *link* between faith in the dynamism of a free-market economy, faith in one's procreative energies and prospects, and religious faith, all of which come together in a utilitarian organization of society. Marriage is used in the interests of the market and the market is used in the interests of marriage, the linkage between the two kept intact by means of a political agenda based on a sexual constitution that privileges discipline over pleasure, which can only occur within the traditional family: "When people lose the power of sexual polarity, they also lose their procreative energy and faith in themselves and their prospects. . . . The advocates [of sexual liberation] may indulge a lot in what they call sex. But it is a kind of aimless copulation having little to do with the deeper currents of sexuality and love that carry a community into the future." (xi)

Gilder's sociobiological project, like the nostalgia of Gertrude Himmelfarb and Newt Gingrich for the Victorian era, has parallels in late-nineteenth-century Europe during the development of industrial capitalism. The changes of that period, as was true of the history of American fundamentalism, were resisted by the very class responsible for those changes. George Mosse's history of that period draws on the concept of "respectability" to describe a configuration of attitudes and behaviors through which the European middle class in the eighteenth and nineteenth centuries constituted its class identity. Respectability links national identity, economic identity, and familiar behavior in an amorphous way that is similar to the familiarity I have been following in earlier chapters. As Mosse says about the middle class, "Side by side with their economic activity it was above all the ideal of respectability which came to characterize their style of life. Through respectability, they sought to maintain their status and self-respect against both the lower classes and the aristocracy. They perceived their way of life, based as it was upon frugality, devotion to duty, and restraint of the passions, as superior to that of the 'lazy' lower classes and the profligate aristocracy."[7] The middle class could ostensibly dispense with economic or even racial criteria as bases of cohesion, for even though those criteria remained fundamental, they no longer had to be made overt. The middle class could instead define itself in terms of a "lifestyle that first became largely their own and eventually that of all settled and ordered society." (Or as Gilder describes it, all civilized society.) Respectability came to be enforced as normality, "everybody's morality." (4) Its contemporary reconstruction in America provides a simple, commonsense frame for inserting the sacred masculine intimacy Stu Weber describes directly into free-market capitalism. It will be up to Gilder to claim that capitalism is biologically natural to the human organism.

The center of nineteenth-century respectability was the nuclear family, which provided the disciplinary possibilities for countering the massive social changes the middle class had itself initiated: "The travails of industrialization seemed unending; so did the need to keep control in a nervous age, to find firm structures for a bewildering world. Again and again we will find men and women reaching out to grasp a 'slice of eternity,' whether embodied in nature, the nation, or religious belief, in order to counteract 'the vibrations of modernity.'" (Mosse 8) The disciplinary nature of this search for a slice of eternity, which Gilder's utilitarian morality resembles as it reacts to the changes brought about by postindustrial

capitalism, was related to techniques of restraint and moderation imposed by police and educators and based on a distinction between normality and abnormality. Development of these educational techniques
had moved from the clergy into the realm of medicine; in twentieth-
century America, the clergy has emphatically joined back in. In that earlier
era, the containment of social passion and the enforcement of morality
required an ideal that could make them cohere, and nationalism was up to
the task: "Nationalism absorbed and sanctioned middle-class manners
and morals and played a crucial part in spreading respectability to all
classes of the population, however much these classes hated and despised
one another. Nationalism helped respectability to meet all challenges to
its dominance, enlarging its parameters when necessary while keeping its
essence intact." (9) The most serious challenge to that respectability and
its nationalism was the revolt of the younger generation prior to the First
World War, repeated in the American context in the 1960s.

The key link between nineteenth-century European respectability and
that of the late twentieth century in America is an emphasis on manliness.
The respectability of the earlier period was influenced by the Evangelical
and Pietist revivals in Europe in the eighteenth and nineteenth centuries,
in which true manliness was the center of a spiritual and national revival.
Such manliness was often represented by the iconography of medieval
knighthood, which provided a model of nobility in which masculinity
and moral character were indistinguishable: "Manliness was not just a
matter of courage, it was a pattern of manners and morals." (13) The
renewal of masculinity also depended on valorizing male friendships,
even as extraordinary energy was expended to rid them of homoerotic
overtones, in part through a symbolic link between sodomy and national
catastrophe. The latent erotic aspects of personal relations among men
were emotionally and powerfully projected onto the nation and religion
in a way that displaced or exorcised eroticism: "The importance of such
male friendships as a social and political force cannot be overrated. They
provided a home and a shelter for modern man. Yet for all their latent
homoeroticism, such Germans and Englishmen were for the most part
heterosexuals, good husbands and family men. . . . the eroticism inherent
in male friendship did not exclude sexual normalcy." (89)[8] But these male
groups, like sports, could also pose a danger to respectability because they
threatened to take precedence over the centrality of the family; the Promise Keepers counter a similar danger by redescribing men as Family Men
and building their male bonds around that definition.

In the European version of respectability, war functioned as both a symbolic and an actual site for men's deepest experiences of community, a camaraderie in which friendship was superior to all other human relationships. This was the case even if, as Mosse points out, the sentimentality of war accounts was often due to the fact that most were written by officers. And in the Freikorps texts he cites, war was the one place where genuine, unsuspicious contact among men was possible in a context of discipline and struggle for a nation at risk: "Wartime camaraderie was regarded as the cell from which a new nation pure in body and mind might develop." (126) And war also made available a stereotype of maleness that was "both sensuous and stripped of all sexuality." (129)

As we saw in Weber's text, it is no accident that in contemporary conservatism, the most proper civilized warrior is the military man, like Weber or Colin Powell, or that Vietnam has become a litmus test to divide members of the baby-boom generation in terms of a binary between discipline and pleasure. "Can it be," asks Mosse, "that camaraderie at the battlefront—for years the site of horror, strife, and chaos, was actually seen in the postwar world as an education in respectability, a finishing school for masculine manners and morals?" (128) And though many veterans, like Weber, articulate that education, others who have not fought in a war have close connections to military communities or come from military families, like Ralph Reed, Newt Gingrich, and Phil Gramm. The state of Virginia, which is the home not only of the Pentagon but of Pat Robertson's Regent University and the Christian Coalition, and Jerry Falwell's Liberty University, is also home to many active and retired military families. Tim and Beverly LaHaye founded their church in Robert Dornan's Southern California, which is also home to a large military population. And Ross Perot's Electronic Data Systems, from which he made his fortune, exclusively hired retired U.S. military officers at the management level. This is, however, as much about believing in the military as about actually having served there.

The nineteenth-century renewal of manliness connected to discipline and the camaraderie of wartime did not have to do simply with national defense but with domestic organization: "Nationalism and respectability assigned everyone his place in life, man and woman, normal and abnormal, native and foreigner; any confusion between these categories threatened chaos and loss of control." (16) And those places were assigned in relation to a national stereotype of the citizen that was identical to the middle-class stereotype of manliness, which sealed an entire structure:

> The ideal of manliness was basic both to the self-definition of bour-
> geois society and to the national ideology. Manliness was invoked to
> safeguard the existing order against the perils of modernity, which
> threatened the clear distinction between what was considered nor-
> mal and abnormality, which was interpreted in moral, medical, and
> aesthetic terms and influenced another binary, the genuine as op-
> posed to the artificial, the organic as opposed to stunted growth.
> Moreover, manliness symbolized the nation's spiritual and mate-
> rial vitality. It called for strength of body and mind, but not brute
> force — the individual's energies had to be kept under control. (23)

This form of respectability could enforce sameness in the midst of change:
"Nationalism helped respectability to meet all challenges to its dominance, enlarging its parameters when necessary while keeping its essence
intact." (9) In an age of change and dynamic economic performance, it
could provide ideals and unchanging values that would guide "the dynamic but orderly process of change itself." (31)

Respectability thus made it possible for the bourgeoisie to retain control of the social dynamic of modernity, just as Gilder describes the project of retaining control of the social dynamic of postmodernity:

> Ironically enough, it is the so-called reactionaries who offer the
> best prospects for continued American leadership in the world econ-
> omy in the new era of accelerating technological change. Just as the
> nuclear families of Western Europe unleashed the energies of the in-
> dustrial revolution, so the new miracles of modern technology are
> created and sustained by the moral discipline and spiritual incandes-
> cence of a culture of churches and families. In families, men and
> women routinely make long-term commitments and sacrifices that
> are inexplicable and indefensible within the compass of sexual hedo-
> nist values. Modern society, no less than any previous civilization,
> rests on the accumulated moral and spiritual capital embodied in the
> rock of ages. (113)

A number of other similarities link the manliness of these two periods.
Those who guarded nationalism and respectability, writes Mosse, "felt
menaced by the big city, the apparent center of an artificial and restless
age. Such cities were thought to destroy man's rootedness. They led to
alienation — and unbridled sexual passions." (32) And they served as the
symbolic site not only of life-draining bureaucracies but of conspiracies in

which immorality, subversion, and financial manipulation were linked together. It was also there that one found the extremes of wealth and poverty that led to sexual deviance. Within respectability's categories, stereotypes of sexual degenerates were "transferred almost intact to the 'inferior races'" who inspired the same fears. These races, too, were said to display a lack of morality and a general absence of self-discipline. Blacks and then Jews, were endowed with excessive sexuality, with a so-called female sensuousness that transformed love into lust." (36)

Because different ethnic groups were categorized in relation to manners and morals that revealed inner character, differences among people were not considered as "chance variations, but as immutable, fixed in place." (133) The implications of sorting people out according to a level field in which only their manners and morals were taken into account produced an inevitable logical consequence; nonwhite and ethnic groups were identified as abnormal according to the terms of respectability. And because respectability was identified with nationalism, the best and most proper citizens were, of course, the respectable ones. Within that definition of respectability, racism came to function as a "heightened form of nationalism." (41)

In the symbolic universe of respectability, in which cities were identified as sites of deviance and racial difference, the small town could serve as a symbol for the eternal values that stand outside time, and it could offer a way of life that fit human nature. In the small town the nation and manliness were at home, and its inhabitants could still recall the healthy, happy past that they wanted to restore: "The city was home to outsiders — Jews, criminals, the insane/homosexuals — while the countryside was the home of the native on his soil." (32) The opposition between small town and city was also exacerbated by the instability of rapid economic and social change, though that opposition had to neutralize a central contradiction:

The quest for rootedness which informed the bourgeoisie set it against its place of origin. Its members feared the impersonal monster they themselves had created: the monumental streets and buildings, the anonymous mass. . . . But above all the healing power of nature, symbolizing the genuine and the immutable, could serve to reinforce human control over a world forever on the brink of chaos, [countering] the speed of industrialization and urbanization — the need of men and women to annex a piece of eternity in order to keep their bearings. . . . Nationalism, racism, and bourgeois society all sought to base themselves upon nature in order to partake of its immutability. (137)

The fact that the nation, the race, and the class were grounded in nature provided another "slice of eternity" and gave meaning and order to individual lives. Such a belief also drew on the comic apocalyptic narrative: "By becoming a part of the nation and nature, Paradise lost might yet be regained." (183)

Regaining Paradise and eternity by means of manliness and respectability, however, required a chaste and modest woman who was linked to nature and who could guarantee sexual difference and the division of labor within the family. This chaste, motherly woman who was directly connected to eternal values "looked backward. . . . Woman as a preindustrial symbol suggested innocence and chastity, a kind of moral rigor directed against modernity — the pastoral and eternal set against the big city as the nursery of vice." (98)[9] However, "if woman was idealized, she was at the same time put firmly into her place. Those who did not live up to the ideal were perceived as a menace to society and the nation, threatening the established order they were intended to uphold. Hence the deep hatred for women as revolutionary figures, almost surpassing the disdain which established society reserved for male revolutionaries." (90) And because of the importance of woman's direct link to eternity and in particular to renewed masculinity, "by the start of the twentieth century the hatred reserved for lesbians seemed, if possible, even deeper than that directed toward male homosexuals." (91) They threatened society "to an ever greater degree than homosexuals, given women's role as patron saints and mothers of the family and the nation." (105)

While respectability was sanctioned as religious truth, nationalism infiltrated religion and bent it to its purpose, and in postindustrial America, the force applied to reconstructing respectability now gains energy from a new question about nationalism, one again created by the very groups attempting to control it. The identity of the nation as an entity defined by a certain land mass and borders is now threatened by multinational and transnational corporations whose global activities occupy the abstract space of the digitalized movement of capital. They are no longer national entities with national loyalties but stateless corporations with loyalties only to the stock and bond markets. A different model of abstract nationalism requires a different kind of American frontier, a speculative financial one, and in chapter 6, I will follow Gilder's construction of just such a frontier. Organizing difference into the sameness of respectability is also ultimately a matter of constructing a stable domestic base to free up unfettered global capital.

The other term whose definition has been made highly unstable by postmodern financial capitalism is "middle class," the definition of which, in an economy marked by increasing wage stratification, now rarely includes economic homogeneity at all. As the real wages of low-skilled workers have fallen dramatically in comparison to those of highly skilled workers, many people who in the postwar years would have been eligible for the dream of a home in the suburbs, a college education for their children, and even the purchase of a house have now been locked out of that dream. Unlike the term "bourgeois" in Europe, which meant, according to Engels, the class of modern capitalists, the owners of social production and employers of wage labor, the postwar American middle class was primarily working class, a point John Cassidy makes in his analysis of the contemporary disappearance of the middle class. While middle-class wages have fallen, "productivity, profits, and stock prices have all soared," he argues, with the result that "America is no longer a middle-class country; indeed, the term 'middle class' has lost its meaning." (14)[10] As income has been redistributed toward the rich in an unprecedented way, the country's class structure is now divided into four groups. Bounded on top and bottom by the superrich elite and an underclass increasingly abandoned by the rest of society, the middle class is now made up of two groups: highly skilled, educated professionals doing fairly well and a huge group of workers who are unskilled or semiskilled, their wages falling, their living standards declining, and their economic situation increasingly uncertain. As Cassidy argues, these people cannot be defined as middle class, if that definition means one who has a rising standard of living and a high degree of economic security. Seventy-five percent of American men, he points out, do not have college degrees, and as their wages have fallen, women have been under greater pressure to work. That pressure has also caused many women to fear that equal-rights legislation could cost them the gains made earlier in the century to limit working hours and improve working conditions; their circumstances are quite different from that of women entering professional careers. The process has also pitted those falling out of the middle class against the underclass for a smaller and smaller share of the economy.

In spite of this void at the heart of the middle class, absolutist conservative rhetoric constructs a symbolic American identity *only* in terms of respectability, or the symbolic common denominator of traditional values. Because the energy devoted to enforcing the purity of these concepts is in direct proportion to evidence that they are in transition and even false, this logic proves to be a phobic one. It insists on more force — more prisons, more capital punishment — for those who fall outside its terms of sameness. Similarly, the more the boundaries between genders prove to be porous — the more Gilder looks around him — the more phobically he insists that rigid gender identities be guarded.

And though Gilder might want to read Mosse's arguments about the importance of respectability as proof that his own arguments are correct, just as he reads the long history of male dominance as evidence that it is natural and eternal, Mosse is in fact tracing the roots of European fascism. He finds respectability to be far more unsettling as an organizing concept precisely because of its familiarity. As he says, "The analogies between past and present must have struck the reader at every turn, for this is a past that relates to everyone's experience of the present." (181) The question he asks, in light of the fact that all societies, not only dictatorships but also representative democracies, need cohesion is this: What price is worth exacting for the type of cohesion that is based on absolute familiarity and respectability? And in particular, how does that form of cohesion relate to tolerance of the outsider?

Gilder provides very troubling answers to these increasingly important questions, for his twentieth-century respectability methodically and relentlessly constructs an intolerance of the outsider through a *secular* intimacy that joins together free-market political economy and a biology based on absolute values. As Mosse writes, "Tolerance, it seems, ended where respectability began." (111)

ii.

Predictably Gilder finds a woman there waiting to put a face on this cultural war to reconstruct respectability: Phyllis Schlafly, whose contributions toward the defeat of the Equal Rights Amendment made clear that "she understood what was finally at stake in feminism. She was defending both the sexual and legal constitutions of the United States from their most serious attack of this century." (103) And she did so by joining the national defense to domestic defense: "All politics is on one level sexual politics." (112) As Gilder tells it, the defeat of the ERA was the moment when culture began to shift back to the right. It was also the beginning of challenges to the rule of federal law and an activist liberal judiciary, for it proved that people "still instinctively recognize that preservation of the sexual constitution may be even more important to the social order than preservation of the legal constitution." (105)[11]

Schlafly, like Lynn Cheney, Helen Chenoweth, or the conservative women who formed the Independent Women's Forum and who do not fit the soft, motherly mold of Beverly LaHaye, is given wide latitude to be harsh and unmotherly in her public persona, while aggressive feminists are condemned for similar behavior. This kind of latitude is similar to the permission given to warriors to be tender; just as a man can be tender only if he has first proved his masculinity, women can be aggressive only if they have first proved their identity as true women. It is almost as if a template has been put over American culture. The things feminists want can now be defined as positive, but only because they are located within the overarching terms of absolutist morality. Men can now act tenderly and women can be aggressive because such behavior is kept safely under the umbrella of God's judgments about true gender identity.

For both Schlafly and Gilder, the challenge to absolute gender differences produced the crisis in contemporary America, a crisis represented by the bands of roving barbarians who have abandoned their family responsibilities and turned them over to the welfare state. And it was caused by sexual liberationists: radical feminists, homosexuals, unattached males of every class, biotechnologists developing contraceptive and reproductive technologies, socialist academics, and cultural liberals who gave us the culture of the 1960s. Before analyzing the category of barbarians to show the simultaneous racism and misogyny of this structure, I want to follow Gilder's description of the sacrificial social contract of civilized society.

Feminists have argued that in the social contract of Western civilization, social cohesion has required the sacrifice of women, who have been the objects of exchange by men. Gilder, on the other hand, methodically reverses that argument to focus on the real victim of capitalism's discontents — men:

> The man renounces his dream of short-term sexual freedom and self-fulfillment — his male sexuality and self-expression — in order to serve a woman and family for a lifetime. It is a traumatic act of giving up his most profound yearning, his bent for the hunt and the chase, the motorbike and the open road, the male group escape to a primal

mode of predatory and immediate excitements. His most powerful impulse — the theme of every male song and story — this combination of lust and wanderlust is the very life force that drives him through his youth. He surrenders it only with pain. This male sacrifice, no less than the woman's work in the home, is essential to civilization. (171)

To see how this reversal of the sacrificial social contract occurs, it helps to follow the dual process that structures Gilder's argument: the evolution of capitalism's natural history and the nature of masculine sexuality. He first identifies the origins of archetypal sexual difference in the ur–sex roles of hunter-gatherer societies. In those societies, there were two groups: the group of men, a unit made up of individuals; and the group of families, a unit made up of women and children. The groups encountered one another only when the male became "an occasional visitor seeking sexual release and sometimes displaying little interest in young children." (30) This primal arrangement produced a situation in which "the closest tie in virtually all societies, primate and human, is between women and children. But the next most common and strong connection may well be the all-male bond. . . . The real business of life was among the men and among the mothers and children." (34) Because the men in their group were hierarchical and competitive, those energies had to be released. This remains a feature of contemporary culture, whether in the form of "a team, a political club, an entrepreneurial company, a military venture as well, a motorcycle gang, a criminal conspiracy, a religious movement, or a revolution." (34)

The next stage of human development was agricultural society, a superior form of social organization that, however, revealed the seeds of the contemporary crisis, for this shift was psychologically damaging to men. While the woman in agricultural society got to keep her natural role as mother, the man had to sacrifice his natural role of hunter. This is the first glimpse of the internal tension between the contradictions Mosse describes: the dynamic of *change* and the eternal constancy of *absolute values*. As Gilder says, this presents the problem of "what to do with the males. . . . Virtually every community has to respond to the new anxieties of the male when deprived of his central hunting and warrior roles." (31)

The subsequent and final stage in this evolutionary, natural history of capitalism marked the end of the evolutionary process. It brought into being the ideal form that had governed that process: "With the industrial revolution . . . a better world did in fact arrive on earth. Perhaps the most cataclysmic event in history, it changed every aspect of human society." (35) Every aspect, that is, but absolute gender difference; only the sexual liberationists of postindustrial capitalism will later threaten to do that. Here industrial capitalism both created and depended on the nuclear family:

> The virtues of this arrangement, which also prevailed in colonial America, go beyond the effective harnessing of male sexual and economic energies to the creation of family units. By concentrating rewards and penalties, the conjugal household set a pattern of incentives that applied for a lifetime. Benefits of special effort or initiative were not diffused among a large number of relatives, as in the extended family, and the effects of sloth or failure would not be mitigated by the success of the larger unit. In general, the man stood alone as provider for his wife and children. He was fully responsible for the rest of his life. Such responsibility eventually transformed large numbers of pre-industrial men, living in a 'moving present,' into relatively long-term planners, preparing for an extended future. (36)

This basic outline is appealingly clear, concise, and absolute, and in an age in which people feel thoroughly overwhelmed by too much information, clarity takes on a special significance. Recognizing the need for clarity, Gilder exploits it.

In describing the psychological damage to men caused by this highest form of natural history, capitalism, he comes to the surprising conclusion that it is not simply the welfare state that feminizes men by robbing them of their provider role, as Frankfurt School and neoconservative critics alike have argued, but the very structure of capitalism itself. Gilder's argument joins Stu Weber's to establish the necessity for devoting all of society's energies to the reaffirmation of masculinity. To do that, he must first address the fact that the monogamy upon which capitalism's dynamism depends has introduced a new, troubling element into the natural gender differences of masculinity and femininity. In its natural form, masculine sexuality is frequent, compulsive, and brief. However, that form is not well-suited to the disciplined stability required by a market economy; for that kind of stability, it will have to be domesticated. But domestication creates a serious problem, for monogamy constitutes "a draconian imposition on males of the long-term rhythms and perspectives of female

sexuality. Men were made to feel that their identities as male were dependent not chiefly on religious rituals, or gang depredations, or hunting
parties, or warfare, but on work initiative, love, and responsibility for a
wife and children." (37)

The need to domesticate masculinity produces an inherently contradictory male identity. For even if monogamy is an unnatural state for men, it
is, nevertheless, the key to neutralizing the tension between the two natural components of masculinity — the warrior and the civilized man:

> The human race met the challenge of transition from hunting to
> agriculture and from agriculture to industry in part by shifting the
> male pursuit from game to women. Through the wombs of women
> men could partake in the future of the race. But the hunter in man
> did not expire; his hunting energies were applied to higher and more
> extended endeavors: from the seasons of crops to the life-spans of
> domestic animals to the prolonged phases of invention and manufac-
> ture . . . society became strongly dependent on the institutions by
> which the hunter is domesticated — chiefly now the institution of
> marriage. In general, across the range of modern life, marriage be-
> came indispensable to socializing the mass of males. (37)

Marriage thus becomes the pivot between nature, represented by women,
and culture, represented by men, in capitalist culture. Because it recon-
ciles the concrete and the abstract, marriage is the center of sociobiology,
for neither nature nor culture can be studied in isolation. Marriage is not
simply about ratifying love; it is also the instrumental conversion of sex
"into a biological and social continuity. The essence of that continuity is
children. Regardless of what reasons particular couples may give for getting married, the deeper evolutionary and sexual propensities explain the
persistence of the institution." (15) Children become the literal mediation between nature and culture, and they make it possible for nature to
become second nature.

Not only do children embody this mediation, but they also entice
warrior men into civilized adulthood. As "the desire of men to claim their
children thus emerged as the crucial impulse of civilized life" (37), the
love for specific children through marriage allowed a society to "evoke
long-term commitments from its members." (17) In fact this is the only
way society can evoke commitment to women. Gilder sets out the clearest
and most rigidly exclusive reconciliation imaginable, for the fact that
children are the "incarnation" of this union of nature and culture also

means that monogamous marriage and procreation provide the *only* terms of human identity and human rights. This version of the absolute bedrock of marriage is echoed in contemporary policy discussions that shape national policy, such as one by David W. Murray published in the journal of the Heritage Foundation. Like the discourse of earlier centuries, Murray condemns illegitimate children as bastards. Historically, he argues, to be a bastard was to be a child still in nature, not culture: "Children 'out of wedlock' are ill-fitting stones."[12] They were outside of "society's cultural infrastructure, its bridges of social connectedness" in a traditional society that was "composed of only two kinds of people — relatives and strangers." (10) Those bridges of social connectedness, which Murray wants to reestablish by reestablishing the traditional family, depended on marriage. Those outside of traditional marriage are alien: "To be a kinsman is to have a human identity; in the absence of kin relations, one is an alien and a potential threat." (10–11) And not only is the bastard a threat in terms of violence, his illegitimacy is also a threat to the social contract and its economy: "Three remarkable things become one at a wedding: love, legitimacy, and property coalesce as social forces upon the legal union of man and woman." (15) As a result, "creating conditions for the appearance of such vital and valuable forms is perhaps the most effective, and the least intrusive, task of social engineering. Helping people to marry helps society to remake itself, to restore in each generation that delicate but essential web on which our humanness is enacted." (15)

If this appealingly clear organic unity of nature and culture is to remain undisturbed, however, gender differences have to be strictly enforced, because it is up to women to guarantee the male socialization that can carry it out:

> The power of a woman springs from her role in overcoming these socially and personally self-defeating ways of men. She can grant to the man a sexual affirmation that he needs more than she does; she can offer him progeny otherwise permanently denied him; and she can give him a way of living happily and productively in a civilized society that is otherwise oppressive to male nature. In exchange modern man gives his external achievement and his reluctant faithfulness. It is on these terms that marriage — and male socialization — are based. (Gilder 17)

However, in postmodern America, sexual liberationists have distorted this difficult process of male socialization, and their influence impacts two different groups of men: on the one hand, the unmarried, illegitimate barbarian males who have remained uncivilized warriors; and on the other, the respectable middle-class men whose internal warrior identity has now been turned into impotence. Each kind of masculinity must be repaired.

But repairing the damage presents many dangers for both men and women, because the reaffirmation of masculinity, or the discovery of Weber's missing Man, will have to find its material directly in the resources of paranoia. As Gilder has already shown, archetypal warrior sexuality has been under siege from the earliest stirrings of the Industrial Revolution. Keeping in mind that for Gilder sexuality is literally the same thing as the ego, this means that paranoia must be inherent in masculine biology and capitalism. Paranoia, in fact, proves to be the very essence of masculine identity, something no feminist has to say because Gilder has already done so. And this victimization, surprisingly, is here caused, not by women or the welfare state or minorities, though they are blamed for it, but by capitalism itself. The way Gilder deals with this masculine victimization is similar to Weber's revision of Christ, in which he reconstructed Christ's virility to erase the possible femininity of his submission to the Father. Gilder bases his capitalist model on that Christian structure by requiring that the man's lessons in civilized submission, his socialization, come through the Father's masculine world of work.

But a danger is introduced here. The socialization that makes it possible for a man to enter the masculine public sphere must by necessity be filtered through a woman. She must, as Gilder told us, overcome his "socially and personally self-defeating ways." A perfectly procreative and feminine woman, the Pure Mother who is like Mary, the immaculate mediator between Father and Son, must draw a man into monogamous marriage and fatherhood in a way that does not feminize him but instead civilizes him. This precise and perfectly balanced Oedipal arrangement, however, rests on an extremely unstable site. There is a very thin line between the action of *civilizing* a man in the interests of the virile market economy of the Father, and the possibility that he might be *feminized* by a woman. And in a period of economic and cultural transition like the present, those two possibilities are inevitably confused, which means that enormous pressure must be applied to women to keep them from playing around with this immaculate site of Pure Motherhood and masculine socialization. If this paranoid masculinity is to be civilized, the woman must be simply a filter to pass on the Father's requirements; she must not introduce anything foreign into that site. Women must be symbolically and at times actually forced to embody the proper, pure phallic mother who passes on the Father's law.

In such a rigid model of socialization, a man learns that only the most masculine Father, even if he is a tender one, deserves to master him. If that mastery should be seen to come from an improper woman or a feminized source like the welfare state, a man will experience his identity and perhaps even his body as constantly out of control. If the line separating the two sites does not hold in such an absolutist model, neither does his identity. He will perceive himself to have been feminized, not by a virile Christ or a virile capitalist Father, but by an improper woman, by a feminized bureaucracy or by someone structurally located in emasculated categories: a Jew (anti-Semitic stereotypes reflect a small, verbal, feminized Jewish man), a person of color (racist stereotypes include the undisciplined and overly sexualized man of color, who is closer to nature, as are women), or a homosexual (homophobic stereotypes find effeminate, overly sexualized men and murderous dykes).

And while even in traditional societies the line between being civilized and being feminized is thin, in a period of change, that boundary will inevitably be experienced as dangerously permeable. Its permeability will feel all the more threatening if an absolutely stable identity has been promised and demanded. That is, the more a man is promised pure masculinity, the more he will find his identity under siege everywhere, the more he will need divine sanction to purge the uncanny enemy now settled into his body. Masculinity, already under great stress because of economic conditions, has been made all the more paranoid and vulnerable by being described in absolute terms.

Gilder moves on to argue, however, that it has not been the initial false *promise* and simultaneous *requirement* of absolute identity that causes the problem, as I would argue, but the absence of a cultural system that will *guarantee* it. In developing his argument that men are society's exemplary victims, he focuses on the one aspect of masculine sexuality that makes it so dangerously susceptible to humiliation and failure: it depends on successful performance. Women, whose bodies literally signify their sexuality and their relation to procreation, enjoy access to the deepest roots of both nature and civilization: "The central position of the woman in the home parallels her central position in all civilized society. Both derive from her necessary role in procreation and from the most primary and inviolable of human ties, the one between mother and child. . . . She is the vessel of the ultimate values of the nation. The community is largely what she is and what she demands in men. She does her work because it is of primary rather than instrumental value. The woman in the home is the last bastion against the amorality of the technocratic marketplace when it strays from the moral foundations of capitalism." (168–69) This means that "regardless of any anxieties she may have in relation to her sexual role and how to perform it, she at least knows that she has a role of unquestionable importance to herself and the community. Whatever else she may do or be, she can be sure of her essential female nature." (9) It is not the woman herself, of course, who determines that value, but her womb, which constitutes the basic unit of value from hunter-gatherer society: the *tie* between mother and child. For it is "through the wombs of women that men can participate in the future of the race." (37)

A man's body, on the other hand, "is full of undefined energies," which means that "fear of impotence and inadequacy is a paramount fact of male sexuality." (11) For "the man . . . has just one sex act and he is exposed to conspicuous failure in it." (10) The male sexual predicament "has a tragic quality that is difficult to adapt to egalitarian formulas. Men must perform. There is no shortcut to human fulfillment of men — just the short circuit of impotence. Men can be creatively human only when they are confidently male." (10) The subtle but firm elimination of "egalitarian formulas" will remain unchanged from here on out. This "inferior sexuality, this relatively greater sexual insecurity" means that sexual intercourse is much more important in men's lives than in women's. This is not simply because sex is pleasurable but because it is "an indispensable test of identity. And in itself is always ultimately temporary and inadequate. Unless [a man's] maleness is confirmed by his culture, he must enact it repeatedly, and perhaps destructively for himself or his society. . . . It is only when men are engaged in a relentless round of masculine activities in the company of males — Marine Corps training is one example — that their sense of manhood allows them to avoid sex without great strain." (11)

The combination of sexuality and identity works in the truest performative sense. It cannot simply "be," it must also "do." And it must be affirmed in that doing by all of culture; otherwise the penis is limp, the identity blank, the gender hollow. Only culture, only an admiring, receptive audience, can ensure the value of their performances, the success of their erections. While women are born, men must be made. And as we have seen, it is only through the proper woman within monogamous marriage that this erection can be made both dependable and literal, because it leads to a child, who allows undefined masculinity to be inscribed into nature. While feminism has argued that women have been excluded from the realm of culture, Gilder argues that men have been excluded from the realm of nature:

> Although his relationship to specific children can give him a sense of futurity resembling the woman's, it always must come through her body and her choices. The child can never be *his* unless a woman allows him to claim it with her or unless he so controls her and so restricts her sexual activity that he can be sure that he is the father. . . .
>
> Even then he is dependent on the woman to love and nurture his child. Even in the context of the family, he is sexually inferior. If he leaves, the family may survive without him. If she leaves, it goes with her. He is readily replaceable; she is not. He can have a child only if she acknowledges his paternity; her child is inexorably hers. His position must be maintained by continuous performance, sexual and worldly, with the woman the judge. The woman's position, on the other hand, requires essentially a receptive sexuality and is naturally validated by the child that cannot ordinarily be taken away. The man's role in the family is thus reversible; the woman's is unimpeachable and continuous even if the man departs.
>
> The man's participation in the chain of nature, his access to social immortality, the very meaning of his potency, of his life energy, are all inexorably contingent on a woman's durable love and on her sexual discipline. Only she can free the man of his exile from the chain of nature; only she can give significance to his most powerful drives. (13)

Gilder has strategically established a link between masculine vulnerability, the constantly threatened humiliations of impotence, and the need to banish women from the workplace. First of all, he argues that impotence is the least publicized epidemic of the 1970s, yet it becomes clear to a reader that with age, exhaustion, and stress, men whose identity depends on the model he describes will find that it is not simply civilization that relentlessly victimizes them, but their own bodies as well. And second, the rigidity of Gilder's categories of nature and culture allows him to use his praise for the woman's deeply grounded feminine identity as a way to banish her from the realm of culture, or the marketplace. Feminist discussions of male privilege have concentrated only on the economic imbalances in the workplace, he says; they have overlooked women's natural power in the family, where "deeper female strengths and male weaknesses are more important than any superficial male dominance." In fact, "conventional male power . . . might be considered more the ideological myth. It is designed to induce the majority of men to accept a bondage to the machine and the marketplace, to a large extent in the service of women and in the interest of civilization." (17–18) The tables have been completely turned. The victims of the social contract are masculine; the myth of male dominance is false.

iii.

Within this social contract, in which men are at such risk, some sort of bribe is needed to compensate men for agreeing to retool their warrior roles and enter the world of work. One of these, as we have seen, is the certainty that they can claim the paternity of their own children, their physical and spiritual link to immortality. This bribe to men requires rearranging society so that women, too, will be susceptible to bribery, for the only way women will allow men to claim their children is if men are the providers, as the Promise Keepers insist. The kind of force needed to get women to participate has already revealed the basic and unalterable tragic fact of masculine sexuality for Gilder: it cannot be affirmed in situations of equality. Women must *need to be provided for* before they will submit to *needing a provider;* it is only in that way that a man "can feel equal to the mother within the family and he can join it without damage to his sense of himself as a man." (37)

Men's insecurity in the family is exacerbated in the workplace, for women are also "socially superior," and they know it. For this reason, their presence, and in particular their success in the workplace, constitutes a humiliating threat, demoralizing and estranging the men around them: "Not only is she less likely to want to marry, but the man realizes that if he marries her his role in the family would be inherently precarious. Enduring procreative love becomes difficult, because it places the man in an impossibly inferior position. Amid squalling infants, even his residual role of providing sexual services at once becomes more difficult to perform and declines in importance." (41) This disturbance unsettles the exquisite symmetry an absolutist political economy requires, for society "is an organism. Removing those young women causes problems elsewhere," causing barbarian behavior in the streets: "If [men] cannot be providers, they resort to the primal male assets, wielding muscle and phallus for masculine identity and attacking the fabric of society." (41)

There is another important gender contradiction Gilder must deal with, for he has to account for the problem capital itself introduces into his absolutist sexual constitution, a problem he recognizes right away. The logic of money is the source of the greatest paranoia, because if money is to be available for circulation, exchange, and the infinite increase of profit, it can have no content. In this sense, money is like language. In order to circulate and change as history does, words, too, have to be made up of *lack*. They have no inherent content or *fullness*, because their meaning depends on their ability to circulate in relationship to other elements in linguistic and cultural systems. In the case of money, this free-floating circulation introduces an especially dangerous instability, for as postmodern theory has argued about meaning in general, money is in its essence *amoral*, or at the very least relativist. It can just as easily sell a crucifix as a shovel, a prostitute as a book of virtues. This infinite floating will obviously also undercut the absoluteness of gender: "The provider role is performed with money. But unlike the warrior's emblems and hunter's game, money lacks gender. Women can get it as well as men. The provider role, therefore, is losing its immediate sexual correlation." The fluidity of money will clearly pose a real danger to the renewal of civilization, for if men are to find the security to perform, in all the meanings of that word, the provider role must have a sexual correlation or men will neither work nor wed. It is up to culture to affirm the masculinity of that role so that money again "acquires a kind of concealed sex in the context of marriage." (47)

The instability of the sexual correlation between masculinity and money is made glaringly visible by the successful, single career woman, whose position will prove to be the equivalent of the threat represented by the welfare mother and the lesbian. They do not need men. Dan Quayle's attacks on Murphy Brown were not just about keeping babies safe but about preserving the success of male "performance," along with political economy and civilization. Though most women's working conditions are a far cry from Murphy Brown's, her sexual and economic power (as Connie Marshner also sees) symbolically jeopardizes the entire social structure: "In a world where women do not say no, the man is never forced to settle down and make serious choices. His sex drive — the most powerful compulsion in his life — is never used to make him part of civilization. . . . If a woman does not force him to make a long-term commitment — to marry — in general, he doesn't." In this sense, Murphy Brown, the lesbian, and the "welfare queen," to whom I will later return, symbolize the greatest threat to civilization: the young man's "problem is that many young women think they have better things to do than socialize single men." (47)

Active women — and *any* kind of activity by women other than proper procreative activity is immediately coded as aggression — take on an increasingly sinister cast. Because "males always require a special arena of glorified achievement from which women are excluded . . . their concern with sexual differentiation is obsessive." Yet that very necessary competition among men becomes deadly in the marketplace when "aggressive and competitive women, unconcerned with motherhood, produce more ruthless men — and a society so competitive that it disintegrates. Men, on the other hand, when passively preoccupied with childrearing, become incapable of effective sexual behavior and paranoid about aggressive women." (43) Masculine paranoia has been doubled in this unisex workplace, and the cause of the harshness of capitalism can now be pinned squarely on women. The consequences of this imbalance are not happy ones either for men or for career women, and Gilder's tone becomes increasingly resentful of women who are able to set the terms of sexuality: "Your young lady lawyers with brisk smiles and medicated wombs, your tired and hungry heiresses with advanced degrees . . . all those career women whose wombs are shriveling . . . can command the sexual tribute of men aged from their twenties into their sixties. But watch out when they get older than this." (53) Even though, because it is unnatural, their temporary dominance cannot last, it is offensive to men: "Liberation enthrones young women as a sexual aristocracy. For a span of some fifteen to twenty magical years, many of them are sexual princesses who can dictate terms to the world." (55)

While the incursions of women into the workplace are psychologically destructive, masculine identity is most deeply threatened in sports, where girls and liberals are systematically destroying male confidence: "sports are probably the single most important male rite in modern society." (120) Embodying a "moral universe," sports, like war, provide the most important site for primal masculine initiation rituals through "the indispensible sensation of competition in solidarity." (121) Sports are particularly important during adolescence: "At a period in their lives when hormones of aggression are pouring through their bodies in unprecedented streams, boys learn that aggressiveness must be disciplined and regulated before it can be used in society." (121) One can certainly agree with him about boys' need for activity, while at the same time recognizing how girls need it too and wondering why conservatives, then, opposed midnight basketball for inner-city teens and young men. But Gilder is really on the trail of a clear, unambiguous metaphor for masculine privilege in this discussion of sports. First he argues that putting money into women's sports is simply a way of rewarding inferior athletes when merit should be the only criterion. Here we have to remember his absolutist binary frame: there are only two absolute categories, pure masculinity and pure femininity, and the possibility of only one winner. This means that the only way to compare athletic accomplishment is to compare men to women: "In other words, millions of potential male athletes are losing opportunities to athletically inferior women, exclusively by reason of sex. Some of the excluded boys, who might have had satisfying athletic careers as their bodies mature, instead turn to alcohol, drugs, and crime." (122) (By this time, we have come to expect that bad weather is caused by feminism.)

But sports gives Gilder the terrain he needs to attack what always lurks just beneath the surface of his assaults on any woman who is not a nurturant mother: the lesbian. In sports, he argues, we find the unfeminine athlete who wants to be just like a man; that desire is the real problem with allowing women into sports. Women test absolute sexual difference because they do not act like women. In a thoroughly predictable move, he turns to the example of Jarmil Krtochvilova, of Eastern Europe (the string of signifiers—female athlete, dyke, ugly, Eastern European—could not be more mechanical): she "can run almost as fast as a male adolescent. But her achievement is flawed as an athletic performance because it is less a natural and beautiful fulfillment of the female body than a perversion of it." Her performance extinguishes "every hint of femininity." (122) And however spectacular their performances, Billie Jean King and Martina Navratilova's lesbianism "casts a pall on their skills as somehow unnatural and masculine in spirit." (123)

Because Gilder's logical frame allows only two absolute definitions of gender, sports now serves as a metaphor for the futility of women's liberation. In his analysis of pure merit in sports, Gilder wants judgments to be made according to male standards of ability. Here women will, of course, always be found lacking. Their gains can then be characterized, not as liberation, but as bondage to the male conditions of that activity: "By submitting to male values, they symbolically affirm male superiority and betray the higher possibilities of their sex." (124) Plug any issue into the binary framework, and you get the conclusion you wanted.

Women in the military predictably set up a serious challenge to sexual absolutism, given the centrality of war to masculine affirmation. Gilder's tone shifts again here, as he invites us to imagine "strapping young corporals reacting instantly in crisis to melodiously trilled female commands." The very monstrosity of these unsettled gender differences drives him into excessive style: "sultry detectives belted in karate follow firepersons glossy with bright red lipstick; . . . mascaraed West Pointers march on with hard-hatted construction queens and hod carriers, glamorous dealers in corporate leverage, lesbian mayors, women dunking basketballs, and space cadettes, actually tumbling in space." (137)

iv.

The original title of *Men and Marriage* was *Sexual Suicide*. The relationship between the two titles brings together other issues that have to do with the suicide of sex and sex as suicide. Gilder's earlier title was also related to race, or at least to minorities who do not follow the rules of respectability, and to the fear that the proper kind of Americans, respectable white ones, are not committed to their biological duty to procreate. To show what this means on a number of fronts, I want to first follow Gilder's discussion of homosexuality, then show how sexual suicide relates to questions of welfare and crime, and finally turn to Gilder's description of the implications of abortion and reproductive technologies for masculine psychology.

In his deployment of the fear of sexual suicide and apocalyptic social breakdown, a funny thing happens on the way to absolute values. As in the description of the sultry detectives and the space cadettes, the medicated wombs of career women, or the "glimpse of breasts shifting softly in a silken blouse" (187), at various points Gilder's style abruptly takes on a fevered intensity. The most striking symptomatic language comes when he describes gay culture:

> In the hothouse cruises of many male homosexuals — short-term, intense, violent, abandoned to the rule and worship of the most worthy phallus; moving from body to body to hungry body with scarcely a glint of human recognition behind the beckoning flesh; repeatedly coupling and climaxing, all beneath a clinging, heating,

and lubricating blanket of anonymous steam; pulsing to the rhythm of the hunt and the chase, with no fear of procreation, of entanglement and usually no expense—these men can enact for free the ultimate male fantasies of hedonistic and ecstatic sex. This circus of the senses repels most men, particularly the ones well socialized by women, and even offends many homosexuals who lead discrete and civilized lives. (69)

In spite of his claims that such sensuality repels him, it seems instead to entice him: "In some sections of town [normal men] will meet homosexuals on every street corner, genitals pressed like vultures against their jeans." (72) The gay male has become one of the men who gets to do what other men wish they could. The heterosexual version will be the man who has abandoned his family. The rigidity of absolute, phobic morality inevitably means that lots of things will not fit inside its rigid boundaries. They will, in fact, "bulge" against their strictures, their attractiveness all the more tantalizing because of the strict categories that produced the bulge's dangerous attractiveness in the first place. And it is not only homosexual but heterosexual promiscuity that eerily threatens: "The dank and dingy massage parlors, the fetid half-hour hotel rooms, the menacing mince of the streetwalker, the glower of her pimp in the shadows." (70) Like prostitution, however, "homosexuality thrives less because men want it than because they cannot help themselves." (70) It is a matter of discipline.

   Dangerous because it might contaminate those true bonds among men, homosexuality is like alcoholism, "a profound predisposition, possibly physiological in origin." Just as the heterosexual male can resist his desire to commit adultery, however, men can learn to control their homosexual urgings, which, like the temptation to adultery, will never disappear. Many homosexuals "have clearly been recruited from the ranks of the physically normal," and in the "course of initiation they have undergone a passionate experience of discovery and conversion." (71) Their homosexuality, however, is fully remediable:

In actuality, any man can be homosexual, but no man has to be. . . . Indeed, in some ways, homosexuality is more in accord with masculine nature than is heterosexual courtship. The sex drive of the young male is not only promiscuous; it also tends to merge with the male impulse to affiliate upward to worship power. Since male sexual power is embodied in physical endowment and prowess, young men with sexual confusions and anxieties, fears of inadequacy primed by rejection from women, can react passionately — and in a homosexual environment addictively — to the naked bodies of aroused and powerful men. Homosexuality can therefore feel more natural to many men than their comparatively laborious, expensive, and frustrating pursuit of young women. (73–74)

Though homosexuality may, in fact, be as natural as heterosexuality, it must be transcended, with great difficulty, in the interests of civilized nature: "Civilized society is not more natural than more degenerate social states. It represents a heroic transcendence of the most powerful drives of men. It is a triumph of aspiration and worship, salvation and conscience, over the compulsions of the flesh." (76) And at another point he says, "A major goal of every civilization must be to bring these compulsions under control by the force of aspiration, worship, and reason. It is not easy." (70) The importance of culturally reconstructing heterosexuality makes it all the more imperative to ensure, as Kathy Phelps and the Oregon Citizens Alliance want to do, that the state condemn even a neutral discussion of homosexuality. For even if homosexuality is not defined as abominable, a neutral discussion will indirectly condone it, abandoning those confused young men who are in recovery.

Jacqueline Rose points out a curious contradiction between the phobic, rigid superrationality of conservatism's obsessive ideology of freedom. She argues that this emphasis on freedom is, paradoxically, a *fear* of freedom.[13] One could not have a better example than in the description of the heroic measures Gilder has to exert to keep sexual freedom foreclosed, as its dangers bulge and seethe, threatening from all sides in the form of the gay man and the aggressive liberated woman. There is another way this fear of freedom works in Gilder's rhetoric, for just as he later reconstructs the image of the shopkeeper to give it the aura of adventure and destiny, here he rebuilds the image of the family man. He must be able to call upon the adrenaline rush that results from confronting the seductive homosexual. The greater the danger, the greater the symbolic reward from overcoming it. This family man can, like Weber's Tender Warrior, now have an adventure in the middle of what has been presented to us as a relatively boring working life. He can fight a culture war whose military terminology resolutely keeps that adventure alive: "Unlike the economic or political utopia, the sexual revolution can be practiced in one's own

home. . . . In theory [it] is utterly misconceived, and in practice it is evil."
(78)

Though Gilder spends a lot of time on male homosexuality, lesbian
sexuality did not initially seem threatening, because he has situated it
safely within his absolute categories, almost as an afterthought. Characterized as excessive femininity, lesbianism "has nothing whatever to do
with male homosexuality," for just as gay men offer a caricature of the
sexuality of single men, "lesbians closely resemble other women in their
desire for intimate and monogamous coupling. They most often explain
their practice by denouncing the meat market of heterosexual single life
and by proclaiming their own need for feminine tenderness and trust."
(73) And in fact, "lesbianism is a relatively trivial aberration." (74) This
dismissal is deceptive, of course, because the lesbian has been with us
from the book's first pages and from Limbaugh's statement on the cover.
She is the masculinized, aggressive, dangerous radical feminist, the fem-
Nazi who is always on the verge of turning into the Dyke. Her monstrous
independence sets up a murderous threat to the entire symbolic system
that is under such careful construction. As Mosse says of the lesbian in the
earlier era of respectability, she threatens "women's role as patron saints
and mothers of the family and the nation." (105)

v.

Sexual liberationists provide a tantalizing and alluring foil that emboldens
the civilized man to fight, but firmly in Gilder's sights is another target—
the dark, barbarian hordes of men acting out the uncivilized warrior's
desire to flee family responsibilities:

> Biology, anthropology, and history all tell the same essential story.
> Every society, each generation, faces an invasion by barbarians. They
> storm into the streets and schools, businesses and households of the
> land, and, unless they are brought to heel, they rape and pillage,
> debauch and despoil the settlements of society. These barbarians are
> young men and boys, in their teens and early twenties. If the truth be
> known, all too many of them are entirely unsuited for civilized life.
> (39)

Arguing that he is simply expanding on what he first heard from Daniel
Patrick Moynihan, Gilder finds that the only way to ensure that these

uncivilized warriors mature into civilized men is to rebuild the moral and legal obligations of monogamy. For though many of these single men are unemployed and living in poverty, in fact, "crime, like poverty, correlates far better with sex and singleness than it does with race." (64) Modern society is especially vulnerable to the outlaw: the alcoholic driver, the bearer of AIDS, the pusher, the guerrilla, the computer criminal, the mugger. "The real contribution made by individual men in their work, particularly at this stage in their lives, rarely exceeds the real damage they can do if their masculinity is not socialized or subjected to female patterns." (40)

This requires a number of conservative responses. First of all, it means ending all government programs targeted to both men and women, for "society thus has a much larger stake in employing young men than in employing young women. The unemployed man can contribute little to the community and will often disrupt it, but the woman may even do more good without a job than with one. Her joblessness may spur new efforts to induce a man to work, supporting her own crucial role as a mother." (40) This also means that we must put an end to affirmative action, because it puts more women in the workplace, and as we saw in terms of white-collar jobs, the unisex workplace can be demoralizing to young men: "In general, men are happiest working with other men in challenging and virile activity. At its best, the job can be an important mode of initiation to manhood. The male group at work can counteract the influence of the peer group on the street." (40) One problem with women in the workplace is that, like the home, the law, and social services, work becomes identified with women, which robs it of its paternal coding and its ability to entice men into it by affirming their virility.

And because women are the central civilizing influence that holds society together, their influence is so deeply valued that it must be isolated in its proper sphere. The absoluteness of their worth determines the absoluteness of the requirements for their behavior: "In general, taming the barbarians of any race requires not only that work be made available, but also that women be largely unavailable without marriage." (82) And in groups like the Black Muslims, "because the males are clearly dominant . . . they can afford to submit to long-term patterns of female sexuality." (83)

Gilder's view of welfare draws on this utilitarian notion of marriage with methodical bluntness, for he sees welfare primarily as a threat to the group of men homogenized as angry white males. Welfare qualms and frightens nearly every lower-class man. He does not resent the subsidized women and children themselves. It is the notion of the male deserter, lovin' and leavin' — in the glamorous pattern of every male fantasy hero — that makes the lifelong husband and worker, with after-tax earning little greater than welfare, feel like a cuckold. He remembers all the sexual opportunities forgone, all the payments dutifully made, all the disciplines arduously observed, and the image of the fugitive fathers tears at the very ligaments of his identity.

He feels that the social contract by which he has ordered his life has been broken. The society that entwined his sexuality in social cords — reaching from the depths of his psyche into the womb of a woman, and then into the future of mankind — has betrayed him. It has failed to maintain the civilization to which he has given his life as a man. It has used his money to subsidize the primal mode of male behavior that he painfully relinquished. (87)

Compassion for people in poverty, efforts to alleviate the difficult circumstances for men, women, and children living in poverty, are here entirely secondary to the wounds inflicted on the affirmative masculine identity of working men, many of whom work fifty or more hours of drudgery for very low wages. These men also find that their wives' unhappiness with marriage is encouraged by the lure of welfare available to those wives if they leave. And if men are unhappy in their marriages, the example of other family deserters encourages their own irresponsibility.

Gilder again predictably exploits the legitimate resentments of working men in a postmodern economy that has turned them into movable units to keep companies lean and investors happy. The circumstances of these men are not good, as Gilder admits, but culture will have to force them to give up their desire to flee: "The male role means bondage to the demands of the workplace and the needs of the family." Most of sociological research, he says, finds that men's work is "already too hard, too dangerous, too destructive of mental health and wholeness. It all too often leads to sickness and 'worlds of pain,' demoralization and relatively early death. The men's role that feminists seek is not the real role of men but the male role of the Marxist dream in which 'society' does the work." (173) These candid admissions about working conditions are, however, used strategically to attack feminists, not to address those conditions, just as at other points, concern about women is used to attack minorities.

This instrumental use of marriage becomes even clearer in Gilder's 1995 discussion of welfare reform, where he characterizes welfare as leisure living for women who receive massive benefits and do not want to give them up. This means that the real problem with the welfare culture is not poverty but "the women's skewed and traumatic relationships with men and boys," a totally unnatural situation. Unlike gender arrangements in civilized society, women in the welfare culture have the income and the connections to the public sphere represented by government, while the men are economically subordinate: "Favored by the feminists dominant at all levels of government, this balance of power virtually prohibits marriage, which is everywhere based on the provider role of men counterbalancing the sexual and domestic superiority of women." The incomes of black women, in which he includes both earnings and welfare payments, have "far exceeded the short-term value of marriage, and far outpaced the earning power of marriageable young men." (*AS* 25)

But this imbalance in income caused by feminists also causes the perversion of African American gender relations. For it is still true that even though black women have greater economic security, the men are stronger:

> Nonetheless, the men retain greater strength, aggressiveness, and sexual compulsions. By threats, violence, and remorseless pressure, these males extort beds, board, money, and other comforts from the welfare mothers. As night falls on an urban culture without marriages, the ghetto games of musical beds account for a large share of innercity violence. All programs addressed to relieve the condition or upgrade the employability of welfare mothers will only ensconce more fully these welfare "queens" on their leisured thrones and render the men still more optional, desperate, feral, and single. (*AS* 25)

The way to produce a faceless Other could not be clearer. Just as the definition of "human being" excludes those who are not properly procreative, here the construct of respectability, defined by the lifestyle of the traditional Christian family, excludes lots of other improper people; "feral" means savage, characteristic of an animal that has reverted to the wild from a domesticated state. All criteria except respectability are eliminated in the evaluation. Neither poverty, race, nor downsizing corporations can be taken into account now that all value must be evaluated according to the absolutist frame of respectability. Because race, poverty, and gender have been excluded as mitigating factors, Gilder need not hold back his contempt for poor women: "They are on welfare in the first place because they would or could not get jobs that remotely compete with welfare benefits. On the whole, white or black, these women are slovenly, incompetent, and sexually promiscuous." (*AS* 25)

Gilder then shifts his focus to government efforts to track down deadbeat dads, and he predictably finds that these are actually attacks on masculinity to divert attention from women. For in garnishing child support from men, women find yet another reason not to marry:

> With garnishees substituting for husbands, women lose the last economic reason to marry and domesticate the fathers of their children. Their best strategy is to seduce as many men as possible and then summon the constabulary of the welfare state to collect child support payments from the few who find jobs or win the lottery. After systematically destroying the family, the welfare state offers to replace it with government coercion and DNA tests, requiring that men support women and children without marriage. . . . With young women commanding power over income, sex, and children without marriage, why should they marry? (*AS* 26)

The woman on welfare has now become the symbolic equivalent of Murphy Brown, for both reveal the low opinion of marriage Gilder really seems to have. We already know that men are not much interested in it, and these women make it clear that if they could support themselves without it, they would not be much interested either: "However you slice it, marriage suffers from any welfare reform that enhances female employability and income above men's. Thus the current feminist reforms promote the violence and poverty for which marriage is the only workable remedy." (*AS* 26)

The solution for poverty can only come from traditional marriage, because the organic resources of a family's economic stability are provided by the market: "The only welfare reform that makes a long-term difference is a private economy that grows faster than the public dole. This means abandoning the idea of lifting the 'truly needy' above the poverty line." And much more fundamentally, it means doing away with all programs that do not "face the crucial differences between the sexes that make marriage possible." Unless we abandon those programs, the invasions of barbarians will continue to threaten us: "Unless they are tamed by marriage and the provider role, men become enemies of civilization, and revert to their primordial role as predators. . . . To fear young black males has become a mandate for survival on the streets of American cities. This unspeakable social tragedy — with all its infuriating reverberations for law-abiding black citizens — is the inevitable harvest of our misguided social policies. It will continue as long as welfare feminism is the regnant ideology of government." (27)

vi.

There is another way Gilder's concerns about marriage involve race, concerns reflected in the original title, *Sexual Suicide*. For he argues that there are ghosts upon which the successes of the American economy rest, as Americans consume "the meals that would have gone to our prevented or aborted babies." (174) The welfare state, in this view, will eventually self-destruct as fewer workers are made to pay more and more taxes to support "the child-free aged." (174) The younger workers will begin to work less productively because their taxes take so much of their income, even as their wives bear fewer and fewer children. The welfare state thus deters both work and childbearing. But one has to slow down just a bit here, because we have just been following an argument about too *much* childbearing among African American women. And there is also another kind of childbearing that presents a problem. In the past, increased immigration was used to address the problem of taxing too few workers to support too many older people. The problem with that solution, for Gilder, is that the immigrants themselves turn into welfare recipients; then their family structures, too, are destroyed by welfare. Peter Brimelow, who makes similar claims about immigrants, introduces the term "unskilled worker" as a new code word for race in his proposal to limit immigration. The problem for both Brimelow and Gilder is no longer that Americans are not reproducing but that the wrong kind of people are; sexual suicide means racial suicide. And it is sexual liberationists, and in particular radical feminists, who have produced a culture in which hardworking, respectable people are having fewer and fewer children. Those hardworking, respectable people are predominantly of European heritage.

Early-twentieth-century resistance to the suffragists and to women's demands for contraceptive rights is being repeated here in a very familiar way. In 1905, at a time when immigrants were arriving in record numbers, Theodore Roosevelt assessed the crisis facing the nation as one caused by white women who demanded reproductive rights, and he based his argument on the need to maintain race purity. White women's behavior was seen to risk the racial suicide of the nation: "wilful sterility — the one sin for which the penalty is national death, race suicide."[14] That very concern about willful sterility, about who was reproducing, led to a double-pronged interpretation of reproductive rights. The unskilled and the nonwhite, then as now, were considered to have a duty not to reproduce; the skilled and the white had a duty to do so.

Gilder comes to the end of his book with an ominous chapter about the "sexual suicide technocracy," which brings fears of race and homosexuality together with a concern about the dangers of biotechnology. (179) Initially his critique is devoted to the kinds of worries feminists, too, have had about the male-dominated institutions and corporations that control reproductive technologies and biogenetics. But for Gilder the danger is not that this technology is male dominated or dominated by the market but that it liberates both men and women from their natural reproductive responsibilities, their fundamental human natures. His sights are set most strategically on women, of course: "The fact is that there is no way that women can escape their supreme responsibility in civilized society without endangering civilization itself. The most chilling portent of our current predicament, then, is the conjuncture of a movement of female abdication with a new biochemistry, which shines direct and deadly beams of technocratic light on the very crux of human identity, the tie between the mother and her child." (177) As Mosse said about the earlier stages of respectability, the threats to capitalism are ones it has itself caused. Gilder argues that it has now endangered itself by making "technically possible for the first time in human history a change in the very essence of sexuality." (179) It threatens to open history back up after it has ended in the perfect American specimen.

The enormous power to change human nature and by extension capitalism itself again arises out of the fundamental amorality of money. This time what is at risk is not simply male psychology but the very matter of the human body, a threat so great that the market must now, paradoxically, be superseded by the naturalness of capitalist *culture*. Culture must protect biological gender from the logic of capital. Biotechnology is a threat to masculinity because it threatens the basic unit of hunter-gatherer society: the *tie* between mother and child. As we remember, it is not exactly through women themselves that civilization is continued; it is instead "through the wombs of women." The womb has become an eerie, womanless agent, not the woman, really, but "the space of woman": "Technological ventures into the space of women . . . are both more advanced and more portentous than any prospective adventure of astronauts." (179–80) That this might be a problem for women is secondary to the aroused paranoia of the threatened man. If the tie between mother and child is severed, men will be made redundant, optional. And just as the LaHayes infantilized men, Gilder represents men as incapable of self-discipline: "The power of women over men could gradually pass away," liberating men "to celebrate, like the ancient spartans or the most extreme homosexuals today, a violent, misogynistic, and narcissistic eroticism." (183) And men might also return again to the all-male groups like the Marine Corps, whose goal of creating a solidaristic group of male killers relies on killing the woman in the man: "That is the lesson of the Marines. And it works." (183)

Worry about liberation from procreation circles back not simply to a racist fear of men in groups, as we saw with the barbarians, but to a homophobic fear of the eroticized male body that masquerades as a concern about armed men: "The male physique, far inferior to the woman's in a sexual society, would become superior in a sexual-suicide society in which the state manages reproduction. The women's breasts and womb would lose their uses. The male body would become the physical ideal and lend symbolic authority to the male command of other instruments of power. The technocracy, a dominantly male creation in the first place, would remain in the hands of a male minority." (184)

After describing the frontiers of biotechnology, including cloning, in vitro fertilization, and sex selection, Gilder returns much more directly to everyday life to focus on the psychic damage inflicted on affirmative masculinity by contraception and abortion. Even though "the usual assumption is that opposition to abortion on demand stems from a puritanical aversion to premarital sex, combined with a religious superstition that feticide is murder," the real reasons for opposition have to do with the "erosion of male sexuality." Showing how the simplest act of independence on the part of a woman sends shock waves throughout this balanced system, Gilder argues that though women may have thought they were simply expressing their determination to have some control over their own bodies, in fact they were "striking at one of the most profound male vulnerabilities":

Few males have come to psychological terms with the existing birth-control technology; few recognize the extent to which it shifts the balance of sexual power further in favor of women. A man quite simply cannot now father a baby unless his wife is fully and deliberately agreeable. . . . Male procreativity is now dependent, to a degree unprecedented in history, on the active pleasure of women. (107)

The psychological consequences of this change have not been adequately recognized: "Throughout the centuries, men could imagine their sexual organs as profoundly powerful instruments. . . . Male potency was not simply a matter of erectile reliability; it was a fell weapon of procreation. Women viewed male potency with some awe, and males were affirmed by this response." (107) But now, that true potency has been lost both symbolically and in reality. The origin of that loss can be located in *the slightest trace of reciprocity* or equality between men and women: "The male penis is no longer a decisive organ in itself. . . . a man cannot validate his procreative powers, his role in the chain of nature, without the active, deliberate, and now revocable cooperation of a woman. A man's penis becomes an empty plaything unless a woman deliberately decides to admit a man's paternity." (107) The resistance to abortion has proven to be not about the life of the unborn, as we might have expected, but about masculine psychology and the sexual constitution.

And the same need to reaffirm the centrality of male control over procreation means that the importance of guns can be talked about in such a way as to suggest that the gun is the literal replacement of the threatened erection. It is as if Gilder has taken Lacan's argument about the hollowness of phallic authority and made it literal. Lacan argued that culture could provide the dominant fiction of male superiority and absolute gender difference to "prop up" that sagging authority. Gilder constructs an argument that agrees that phallic authority has been made hollow, but he then demands that that authority be literally remade in all its potency, and he shows us how the necessity of such reconstruction can be seen in men's relationship to guns. (Or at least respectable American men's relationship to guns. There seems to be no concern for the psychological needs inner-city men have for guns, nor consideration of the psychology of all those gunless Japanese, Canadian, British, and Norwegian men.) First Gilder includes the compulsory racist fear of barbarians: "the ultimate nightmare of almost every man is to witness helplessly the rape of his wife."[15] But the real reason men cling to their guns has to do with the fact that by clinging to the gun, they cling to their ego, which, as we know, is their sexuality: "The obstinate refusal of many males to support gun control is not chiefly a product of conditioning by the weapons industry. Rather, millions of men fear gun control because they are losing life-control; they are losing the sense of a defined male identity and role in the family." They cling to these weapons as totems of masculinity and participate in rites like hunting in which guns are symbols of their continuing role as protector and provider in the family. In this sense, the guns "have a virtually religious import." (106)

The absolutist clarity of Gilder's framework has now become much more ominous. He has carefully and strategically handed over to conservatism a structure in which masculine self-affirmation, patriotic duty, the condemnation of equality, and guns are inextricably linked. This is quite a legacy for a wealthy Harvard graduate safely sheltered from the consequences of that linkage.

vii.

Gilder has also left a legacy for attacks on critical thinking in general, for his sociobiology is grounded in the condemnation of professional doubters and academics engaged in defamiliarizing absolutes. That condemnation derives from the fact that, in his logic, the true thinker is the entrepreneur, a kind of philosopher-king engaged in the perfect form of praxis. For entrepreneurial activity joins abstract ideas and practical activity in the world, not simply in the library (though if you have ever been around an entrepreneur, you know how disengaged from the world they, too, can be, as they are linked to it only by their digitalized electronic screens). But because entrepreneurs make more money than academics, resentful academics try "to impose their own visions by law, usually favoring socialism and other forms of rule by intellectuals." (161)[16] Were the public not fooled by these elitist socialist academics, people would see what anthropologists have long told us: that the three things Gilder is most concerned about, patriarchy, religion, and private property, are "universal in all human societies." (162) Elitist academics can only recognize intellectual property, most of which attacks capitalism, and they look down on actual property and especially on working people (by which he usually means respectable businessmen). These academics are unable to understand that society and the economy are the same thing. Even more problematic from his perspective is the fact that academics reject the two most important truths necessary for understanding human nature and society: "The most crucial characteristic of modern social-science methods, in fact, is an inability to register the differences between the sexes or the existence of God." (163)

Gilder can now pragmatically dismiss any issue that might be identified as politically correct by opposing it to his own traditionalist political economy. First, in a familiar way, he defines humanism itself as a mistaken religious belief in "a cooperative, communal, egalitarian, secular, nonsexist, nonhierarchical and rational society." (164) The result of this binary choice between humanism and true religious culture then presents us with a choice between good and evil, absolute values or chaos. In this purifying logic, which requires that the side not chosen be completely purified out of the system, the elements in the negative list are eliminated from consideration. In fact, for Gilder, the condemnation of discrimination is the most telling sign of this mistaken humanism, for it is only by protecting sociobiological differences that "spring from human reality" that "ordered freedom" can be fulfilled. Any view that argues for economic planning, income equality, bureaucratic rationality, and sexual liberation "requires a totalitarian state." (164) Just as Marshner's binary between social parenting and Christian parenting eliminates things that look appealing, such as health care for children, Gilder dismisses the things in the humanist list, and he again introduces the Cold War as a disciplinary warning. He cites C. S. Lewis to show that an attempt to achieve things in the humanist list would entail "nothing less than the abolition of human nature" (164), something only totalitarian states and their supporters would want.

Gilder not only requires a choice on the part of his reader between the two beliefs, but he also suggests that it is the reader's duty to oppose the improper one, which includes equality. The absolute, unembarrassed certainty produced by such a division helps explain the tenor of attacks on affirmative action in Gilder's world, for marital status, personality, religious beliefs, morality, and motivation are "incomparably more important than race, ethnic origin, or even short-term income in defining the prospects or social contributions of a person." (160) The field of evaluation has been made completely level, with respectability the only criterion to assess value.

The anti-intellectual implications of these binary absolutes are extended in further attacks on academics. For Gilder, the attack on critical thinking is grounded, as always, directly in sexual difference. This time that difference shows up with a vengeance in coeducational schools, where feminists have given boys a "head start in emasculation." (120) The paranoid, even phobic, fear that structures affirmative masculinity now finds that boys have been damaged because mechanical and technical masculine knowledge is downplayed "in favor of the feminine realms of writing and high culture." (118) The skills of critical thinking are sectioned off as feminine, as he cites a book by Patricia Cayo Sexton, *The Feminized Male: White Collars and the Decline of Manliness:* "School consists almost exclusively of sitting down quietly for long periods among adolescent girls, at the behest of a female teacher, and reading and writing materials of little interest to most adolescent boys." (118) The result of this emasculation is that "the most feminine boys prevail in school and tend to go on to college and into the best jobs. Meanwhile the most aggressive and masculine — the ones who cannot sit in one place for more than ten minutes without severe nervous strain, relieved only by dreams of cars and football games — these boys tend to drop out and take the lowest-paying work." (118)

In this familiar rhetorical move, the issue of social class is brought up, but only because it can be used as a weapon against feminism. He takes this even further, as Mona Charen has also done, by arguing that sexual harassment is, in fact, caused by feminism: "And what do you know: some of the dropout males end up at construction sites whistling 'oppressively' at upper-class feminist women as they amble by, their breasts jouncing loosely in their shirts. 'Gee whiz, these brutes are treating us as *sex objects!*' say the feminists in their books and magazines, pamphlets and speeches." The working man in a relatively low-paying job "cannot feel himself the oppressor of women who seem to embody everything the world has denied to him: options, money, style, easy sex, freedom." (119) The dishonesty of this passage is blatant, even as it recognizes the very legitimate issue of class difference. The fact that there are working-class women who are sexually harassed or that affluent men harass women is simply off the radar.

And the feminized men who have remained in academics and gone on to college (Gilder, like his father, is of course a Harvard graduate) "are harassed as 'grinds' . . . by the more masculine boys," and because they are often alienated from their masculine natures and technical experience, their sexual anxieties "sustain billion-dollar markets in porn and prostitution." (119) Because they cannot deal with real life, they turn to abstract ideas and symbols, but the worst mistake of these feminist men has been to separate language from action: "In academic life, words are enshrined to the point that many feel all wars are settled, and all deeds accomplished, through arguments and speechmaking. The academy is often merely a repository of disembodied words . . . but there is hardly an act, deed or object in sight." (119) Students get restless about this condition, but certainly no more so than Gilder. Different kinds of words have now been divided according to gender for words, like his, in which absolute values are made literal, are masculine, while words spoken by academics are feminized, the language of critical thinking recoded as the dangerous place where women sweep men off their feet, make them lose their reason, smother, and devour.

viii.

Gilder's logic of purity rests on the ultimate delusion of absolute certainty. Jacqueline Rose's description of the certainty that was also a feature of Margaret Thatcher's conservatism helps illuminate Gilder's. In Gilder's (and Gingrich's) conservatism, Britain is the slightly out of shape older relative who must now be replaced by the younger, more virile America. But both the British and American versions of radical conservatism rest on a claim to certainty and a language of rationality, consistency, and control. This utter certainty of judgment makes it possible, as Rose argues, to "release into our public fantasy life, with no risk of confusion, the violence which underpins the authority of the State." (59) A postmodern view of language sees it as the place where violence and sacrifice can be worked through in symbolic practices so that they do not explode into real life. That possibility of peaceful working through is countered by Gilder's insistence on the literal language of absolute certainty that instead legitimates the symbolic sacrifice of certain groups. The contemporary seductions of fascism can perhaps be glimpsed here in the "repeated and central terms of consistency, persistence, and sameness, the refusal of any possible gap between reality and intent . . . in this form of rhetoric a denial of the precariousness of language itself, the insistence on the utter coherence of the word." (61) This kind of absolutely clear, literal language, whose intent is the total elimination of ambiguity, gives a name and a place to "the invisible adversary," which as we have already seen is an inherent part of its own identity. And it makes fear "a central component of strategy." (62)

The dictionary defines "clear" in this way: free from anything that dims, obscures, or darkens; unclouded, free from flaw, blemish, or impurity; free from doubt or confusion; free from qualification or limitation, absolute; free from contact or connection, disengaged.[17] Gilder's absolutism is perhaps "clearly" set out here, for the absoluteness of his categories rests on a purification process which must weed out impurities, doubts, and, most chillingly, darkness. We have seen how that works in his absolute binaries, and in another revealing way, the above definition suggests that such clarity requires a lack of contact, that it comes from a refusal to engage or to be engaged with things about whom phobic clarity is claimed; to "clear" an obstacle means to pass by, under, or over it without contact; to "be in the clear" means to be free of dangers but also of burdens. The question to be asked in contemporary America as we look at this kind of absolutist framework is this: What represents the greater threat — the supposed relativism of postmodernist versions of meaning that see it in terms of an ongoing, if messy historical process, or Gilder's transcendent absolutism, whose need for order constructs a system built on the very edges of symbolic cohesion and at risk of pushing the entire social order over into violence?

ix.

I'll return to these questions in the final chapter, but I want to end this discussion of Gilder's absolute binary system by following another argument that shows how easily the absolute clarity of binary oppositions leads to extremism. It is an op-ed piece entitled "Baptist Apology Signals Western Decline," written by Samuel Francis in the *Washington Times,* where he was a regular columnist at the time the article was published. After a furor developed over it, he was fired by the *Times,* but he has continued to contribute a regular column to the *Chronicles* and to publish his own newsletter, the *Samuel Francis Letter.* The opinion piece published in the *Times* concerns the 1995 public apology for slavery by the Southern Baptist Convention. Founded in 1845 by splitting off from northern Baptists over the issue of slavery, the Southern Baptists are now the most influential religious denomination in the South.[18] The apology read, "We lament and repudiate historic acts of evil such as slavery from which we continue to reap a bitter harvest," and then went on to call on Baptists to "genuinely repent of racism of which we have been guilty, whether consciously or unconsciously."[19]

In order to analyze that statement, Francis immediately describes that apology as part of "a modernist, secularized and social radicalized vision of Christianity that breaks with their own traditions and history as well as with the historic meaning of the New Testament." (30) Though he is a secular writer, this description suggests how deeply entwined religious and secular absolute values and public discourse have become. For he has here mechanically reproduced the same kind of familiar absolutist binary choices: either one believes in a socially radicalized, false vision of Christianity, or one believes in the real meaning of the New Testament. What identifies the Southern Baptist statement as socially radical, as Francis sees it, is that it contradicts true biblical literalism. Thus this statement is not really about the Bible at all; it is not really Christian, because it apologizes for something the Bible did not condemn. There, neither slavery nor racism are referred to as sins. There are

> at least five clear passages in the letters of Paul that explicitly enjoin "servants" to obey their masters, and the Greek words for "servants" in the original text are identical to those for "slaves." Neither Jesus nor the apostles nor the early church condemned slavery, despite countless opportunities to do so, and there is no indication that slavery is contrary to Christian ethics or that any serious theologian before modern times ever thought it was.

One might reasonably have decided to read that biblical passage historically and work through it as the Southern Baptists have. But in an absolutist world like Francis's, which lets in no ambiguity, such a choice would land you squarely in that "modernist, secularized, and social radicalized vision of Christianity." Such a choice would have introduced doubt into the clear opposition between what is literally true (what is based on a model of language as utterly coherent) and what has been interpreted and is thus false (what is based on a hermeneutic model of language that sees it as the historical sediment of cultural struggles). Racism and slavery have essentially disappeared as things to worry about in and of themselves, their disappearance helped along by the mechanical predictability of absolutist arguments, in which a demon is found nearby upon which to blame disturbances. Here it is that pesky Enlightenment: "Not until the Enlightenment of the 18th century did a bastardized version of Christian ethics condemn slavery."

A reader of Francis's column might simply want to mourn what this says about racism in America. For one might have imagined that a Christian would feel called upon to stop and consider the implications of reading the Bible in a way that would find that only an improper, bastard Christianity would condemn slavery. And indeed such a conclusion would be deeply abhorrent to many Christians, as it was to the Southern Baptists. Yet for Francis, slavery or slaves or racism are secondary to the real issue: the purity of the belief system and the need to discipline Christians who are tempted by egalitarianism. The next turn in this logic of purity requires an even more overt claim about such radicalism, which is seen to arise out of the liberalism of the Enlightenment, "or its more extreme cousin, communism."

Francis's giant binaries that pass for thought now lead him to another conclusion: "What has happened in the centuries since the Enlightenment is the permeation of the pseudo-Christian poison of equality into the tissues of the West." We have here the "level" field in which special rights and affirmative action are condemned, for if the religious ideas of the Founding Fathers are to be renewed, or at least if a literal reading of their ideas is to ground a divinely inspired nation, then the influence on the Founding Fathers of the Enlightenment and its poisonous ideas of equality will have to be repressed. Those other documents influenced by the Enlightenment, such as the Declaration of Independence, seem to have miraculously escaped this taint. But Francis's rigid binary framework is, of course, driving his conclusions. And equality does not fit into them. Thus poisonous *equality* comes to mark the site of the demonic, which like communism can always be found in the vicinity of things that do not fit the binary.

And in a very unsettling way, just as Gilder has to exclude the concept of equality from gender and race relations, here Francis excludes equality from the entire system as he also provides evidence of what Lind calls the southernization of politics. Francis argues that the only reason it took the Southern Baptists so long to be contaminated by egalitarian thinking was that they were located in the South: "The Southern Baptists, because they were fortunate enough to flourish in a region where the false sun of the Enlightenment never shone, succeeded in escaping this grim fate, at least until last month." That the Southern Baptists are called *Southern* Baptists, not simply Baptists, is only the historical consequence of a split between those who supported slavery and those who did not, which the apology has attempted to redress. Francis, however, seems to have constructed a nostalgic picture of the days of slavery and the pre-Enlightenment Middle Ages.

This kind of rigidity and its racism reflect the same fear of freedom that haunts Gilder. The dangers represented by the freedom to doubt are obviously all the greater if one really believes that there are only two possibilities, completely exclusive of each other. As a letter to *Christianity Today* had to say about such a binary, "[I]f God is not both sovereign and loving, then he is less of a God than I have believed. If the future is not completely in his hands, that leaves me in a frightening position."[20] Francis's fear of falling out of a binary leads him on, as he relentlessly isolates the real danger represented by this apology, a danger predictably located squarely within the apocalyptic narrative. For if the Southern Baptists refuse to read the Bible literally, and if they question the absoluteness of master and slave, which the Bible itself does not condemn, then such questioning can only destabilize everything else in this system. It is a system that, at least in his fearful reading of it, is precariously held together like a house of cards perched dangerously on a card table. People must be forced not to shake the table or to pull a card out; either activity will cause all the rest to fall. This freedom to take a card or to shake the table has to be prevented because the language of master and slave is found "in the same places that enjoin other social responsibilities—like children obeying their parents, wives respecting their husbands and citizens obeying the law."

Francis lives in the same phobic land where Gilder has his residence, and in a wild but logically consistent conclusion, he finds something that will surprise an awful lot of Southern Baptists I know. Driven by his binary framework, in which there are only two possibilities, absolute values and socialist nihilism, we should not be surprised at Francis's diagnosis of the Southern Baptists: "If some [biblical] passages are irrelevant, why should anyone pay attention to the others, and if you shouldn't, why not sign up with the feminists, the childrens' rights crusaders and—dare I suggest it—the Bolsheviks? So much for 'Christian family values.'" Even the Southern Baptists are not pure enough for him.

Gilder and Francis act out a script the French philosopher Michele Le Doeuff calls the ideology of the century: Tocquevillian doxa. She isolates several features of that doxa that produce an inherently contradictory, volatile tension. One of those features is the horror of mixing, which we have followed in detail in terms of the codings of impurity and abjection. Another is a fear of solitude, or an anxiety at being isolated and left alone. Those obviously contradictory features show up in Gilder's sociobiology, where families are to be forcibly kept together in social groups by means of structures that condemn the mixing of categories and genders. Those two strangely incompatible features are accompanied by a third, the one Francis seems to have acted out with phobic élan: the fear that equality will produce uniformity.

Within this configuration, Le Doeuff isolates another feature of Tocquevillian doxa, one that takes us back to the question of folking. She argues that it rests on "circuits of solidarity," such as the kinds of communities and organizations we have been following. Yet those circuits quickly become closed, leaving nonmembers outside "in the limbo of indifference." For Gilder, gender inequality makes no "difference"; for Francis, it is the history of racism that simply cannot count. And the logic of both illustrates Le Doeuff's final observation about what one finds inside those circuits of preferential solidarity, in a society that turns its exclusive definition of democracy into a patriotic religion: "structures of vassalage which are as undemocratic as possible."[21]

SIX

Riding the Entrepreneurial Frontier

Pure capitalism is a system of extremes. It is capable of marvelous innovation — and stunning brutality. — Robert Kuttner

If you cannot establish the legitimacy of your own civilization, if you cannot talk about progress and decay, then you do not have any yardstick by which to measure where you are and where you are going. And if there is no yardstick, there is a long-term tendency for people to drift into barbarism and savagery. — Newt Gingrich

Communism is the philosophy of losers: people who cannot face the competition. That's what egalitarianism is all about. — David Horowitz

The Bible, guns, and radio made the difference. — Frank Luntz

Every month, those on the mailing list of Newt Gingrich's Renewing American Civilization receive a newsletter published by the Progress and Freedom Foundation, the research and educational organization supported by contributions from individuals, groups, and corporations, their contributions tax-deductible because the foundation is "nonpartisan." In the January 1995 issue, a front-page article by Dr. Robert Zubrin describes with simple clarity the terrain for conservative reconstructions of America, joining the exuberance of renewal to the thrill of the future reflected in the work of Heidi and Alvin Toffler. In "A New Martian Frontier: Recapturing the Soul of America," Zubrin retells the frontier thesis of Frederick Jackson Turner as an adventure story of which Turner, a University of Wisconsin professor, is the hero. He made a name for himself at the 1893 conference of the American Historical Association, held in Chicago as part of the celebration of the four-hundredth anniversary of Columbus's voyage to America. As Zubrin tells it, in tones of academic adventure envy, after "a series of stultifyingly boring papers on topics so obscure that kindness forbids even reprinting their titles . . . in one bold sweep of brilliant insight Turner laid bare the source of the American soul": the existence of the frontier. This inextricable dependence of soul and frontier brings the popular iconography of the American West in line with that of Christianity, then propels it into an entrepreneurial future.[1]

For Zubrin, and for what I will call the cowboys of American conservatism, the chosen sons who bring together the warrior and the civilized man in this adventure, Turner's thesis, developed just as the American frontier was declared closed, still describes the American character. As the twentieth century comes to an end, America again faces the question, What if there is no frontier? "What happens to America and all it has stood for? Can a free, egalitarian, democratic, innovating society with a can-do spirit be preserved in the absence of room to grow?" (22) When all the land has run out, what will happen to a culture built on development and private property? Zubrin argues that this question is important not just for Americans but for the planet: "Human progress needs a vanguard and no replacement [for America] is in sight." (22) Thus the recreation of a frontier is the most important task facing humankind today, as a biblical apocalyptic rhetoric of unease at threats of impotence and diminishing vigor joins the American cowboy story to describe the present historical moment and its dangers:

> We see around us now an ever more apparent loss of vigor of American society: increasing fixity of the power structure and bureaucratization of all levels of society; impotence of political institutions to carry off great projects; the cancerous proliferation of regulations affecting all aspects of public, private and commercial life; the spread of irrationalism; the banalization of popular culture; the loss of willingness by individuals to take risks, to fend or think for themselves; economic stagnation and decline; the deceleration of the rate of technological innovation and a loss of belief in the idea of progress itself. Everywhere you look, the writing is on the wall. (22)

Though Zubrin wildly suggests that such a frontier might be found on Mars, the conservatives I discuss here find a frontier much closer to home. Theirs is part of the internal postmodern frontier Grossberg describes, a frontier whose resources are the fragmented, global, digitalized economy

and the decentered postmodern electronic resources of financial speculation. In constructing an internal frontier out of that material, postmodernity is first acknowledged, then used to create an "authentic" frontier
space that is, like the old one, dependent on a rigid binary logic. Only the
terrain has changed—from geographical landscape to abstract mindscape. And on the postmodern frontier the popular imagination is reconstructed according to a performative logic whose signifying trope is the
billboard. (Ted Turner's career, we might remember, began when he
managed his father's billboard company.)[2] As we have seen, the billboard's truth can be assessed only according to its effects; it means what it
does. Such a signifying logic not so coincidentally fits Gilder's requirements for performative masculinity and utilitarian capitalism. In this context, Ronald Reagan gave the exemplary performance; his "authenticity,"
his audience's feeling that he was a nice man and a real leader, was never
troubled by the fact that everyone knew he was often confused and frequently lived in movie scripts. Instead, his performance proved that he
was acutely attuned to matters of everyday life and the billboard logic in
which what was true was what was effective.

I will make a similar argument about the way several other contemporary conservative heroes situate their narratives in the terms of the popular cultural memory, staking a claim to what Michael Rogin calls "the
countersubversive position at the center of American politics."[3] Ronald
Reagan was also the exemplary countersubversive hero, a role aptly suggested by the title of Rogin's book, *Ronald Reagan, the Movie*. Those
politics and their reconstruction of America work their way into the
exuberance of Gingrich and Gilder's entrepreneurial frontier. They also
show up in the exhilarated spirit of the other important frontier figure:
the affluent immigrant who sees an empty continent waiting to be conquered, that breathless new immigrant represented here by Arianna Huffington. Conservatism is finally located in the mass-mediated, postmodern frontier hero now "authentically" available to us not by way of the
movies but by radio—Rush Limbaugh as the Voice of America. What is
at stake is the postmodern construction of an emotionally powerful
American identity that rings clear and true, in spite of contradictions and
evidence to the contrary. And it rings true because it is articulated in the
immediately recognizable terms of popular culture and a particular kind
of familiarity.

Before turning to discussions of each of these postmodern frontier
cowboys who thrive on adrenaline, whether in the form of breathless

financial speculation, throbbing political ambition, heroic evangelizing, or the addictions of workaholism, I want to follow two discussions of Frederick Jackson Turner and William F. Cody, by Richard White and Patricia Limerick, their essays published in conjunction with a controversial exhibit, *The Frontier in American Culture,* at the Newberry Library, in Chicago, in the fall and winter of 1994–95.[4] Though the Turner thesis has been almost totally discredited by historians, both White and Limerick focus on its continued influence on popular culture. They argue that the academic discourse of historians has had almost no impact on popular understandings of the frontier.[5] There was and is no way to talk about the frontier without confronting Turner, as well as the other half of his story of the West, the theatricality of Buffalo Bill. As White writes, "By the early twentieth century there was no way to tell stories about the West, no way to talk about an American identity, without confronting either Buffalo Bill or Turner. They had divided the narrative space of the West between them."[6]

Turner's talk was part of the Columbian Exposition in Chicago, where Buffalo Bill also produced his spectacle twice a day. Its program, entitled *Buffalo Bill's Wild West and Congress of Rough Riders of the World,* described it in the words of Brick Pomeroy: "Wild West Reality . . . a correct representation of life on the plains . . . brought to the East for the inspection and education of the public." (quoted in White 7) This West, White argues, was already "a postmodern West in which performance and history hopelessly intertwined," as "the show and lived historical reality constantly imitated each other." (29) It was a representation of the West that became the reality for millions of people in the Gilded Age who flocked to the shows. The genius of Buffalo Bill "was to recognize the power of the mimetic, of the imitation in the modern world." (35)

The frontier narrative involved two different stories, whose lessons were essentially the same. Turner's frontier was a "peaceful settlement of 'free' land, framed as a sweeping explanation of the evolution of a uniquely democratic, individualistic, and progressive American character," (1) with the West described as something "we settled, rather than conquered." (1) Indians were marginal to his story, whereas in Buffalo Bill's story of conquest, they were central. Turner's story of the essentially peaceful, pastoral search for a better world through the settlement of an empty, virgin, free continent and the creation of a unique American identity was juxtaposed to Buffalo Bill's narrative of violent conquest, the heroes of each strain of the story different, though in contemporary culture,

they are collapsed into one another. The farmer, whose tools of civilization were the ax and the plow, subdues nature in a conquest free of guilt.
The scout, whose tools are the rifle and the bullet, was involved in civilization's conquest over savagery. He was a man with a "knowledge of Indians' habits and language, familiar with the hunt and trustworthy in the
hour of extremest danger." For Cody's scout, the bullet was, in fact, the
true "pioneer of civilization." (Wild West program, quoted in White 9)

Both Turner and Buffalo Bill, argues White, were geniuses at using the
frontier iconography of log cabins, stagecoaches, guns, horses and covered wagons, to place their narratives not in the West "but in popular
representations of the West." (13) Dividing the frontier myth between
them, they drew on the iconography already available in popular culture,
that familiarity helping erase the complexities and contradictions of history: "the very ubiquity of frontier icons allowed both Turner and Buffalo
Bill to deliver powerful messages with incredible economy and resonance . . . their success lay in their ability to mobilize familiar symbols"
and to give sophisticated form to what people already believed. (11)
Frontier stories turned into the official American ideology within which
"diverse groups of Americans have asserted their legitimacy in American
culture by clothing themselves (both literally and metaphorically) in
frontier garb and revising frontier narratives to accomodate their histories." (3)

Turner's thesis, White argues, turned into "an incantation" in which
American history textbooks repeated the argument that the move west
through various successive frontiers had created American identity: "In
settling these frontiers, migrants had created a distinctively American
outlook. Americans (gendered male) were practical, egalitarian, and
democratic because the successive Wests of this country's formative years
had provided the 'free' land on which equality and democracy could flourish as the integral aspects of progress." (12) In fact, many in the contemporary Wise Use movement attempt a literal reenactment of Turner's
thesis, as they stake claim to federal preserves and forests. The cabin built
with simple tools proclaimed self-reliance and connection with place, as
well as the courage to act alone and independently build civilization in the
wilderness, that courage also a part of the construction of whiteness.
Turner's thesis, as Limerick points out, describes a frontier that runs east
and west, completely erasing Mexico, and its point of view originated
from the direction of English-speaking white people. The frontier "was
where white people got *scared* because they were scarce." (73, her italics)

American identity itself was remade through the encounter with successive frontiers, as diverse people remade themselves into Americans: "The frontier is the line of most rapid and effective Americanization." (Turner quoted in White 13) Becoming American was thus always performative. Becoming American, White argues, meant performing the activities that constitute Americanness, a "regenerative retreat into the primitive, then a recapitulation of the stages of civilization" (15), echoing the Christian narrative of *The Pilgrim's Progress*. The way to become an American was to consent to do so, to offer one's loyalty, and then to undergo the profoundly American experience of settling the frontier. That narrative inevitably led to a contradiction, because the success of settling the frontier led to its end: "It eliminated the wellspring of primitivism upon which the western experience depended. The image of the future — a not altogether happy future — became the city." (46) This was a city and technology gendered feminine; a horse could be contrasted to the newfangled car, which could be driven by either a woman or a dandified easterner. In a theme that sounds familiar, the children of the pioneers who inherited the frontier thought of themselves as "a lesser breed" than the older generation. The pioneers had "disdained, in the Wild West program's metaphor, to crowd into cities to live like worms. But with the West won, with free land gone, urban wormdom seemed the inevitable destiny of most Americans." (10)

White isolates a particularly resonant feature of frontier ideology in the reinscription of the theme of victimization. For the narratives of both Turner and Buffalo Bill depended on the popular iconography of "images of valiant white victims overpowered by savage assailants, heroic victims and their rescuers and avengers." This iconography was also familiar from the captivity narratives of the Puritans. Such a narrative inverts the story of conquest, and, curiously, the "great military icons of American westward expansion are not victories, they are defeats": the Battle of the Little Bighorn, the Alamo, later Vietnam, and, more recently, perhaps Waco and Ruby Ridge.

In a narrative that also draws on Christian themes of Christ as a victim suffering for his people, Custer became the centerpiece of the "theme of the conquering victim." His slaughter justified "retaliatory massacre" in an "inversion of aggressor and victim that justified conquest." (39)

By means of this narrative, Americans could claim both uniqueness and innocence. They could deny the guilt of the move west, for they had settled the West through hard work, using the resources of a virgin, empty land which it had been their destiny to settle. And they could argue that they had not planned violence but had simply "retaliat[ed] against barbaric massacres." (27)

ii.

Two characteristics of Turner's frontier thesis are reconstructed with exhilaration and energy in Newt Gingrich's introduction to the book of readings for his course, Renewing American Civilization; in Arianna Huffington's chapter, "Twelve Steps to American Renewal"; and in George Gilder's contribution to that volume, "America's Entrepreneurial Spirit." The book itself was part of a four-year effort to "understand the Pillars of American Civilization," and it was accompanied by satellite and video courses taught around the country. The two characteristics of the frontier thesis that are insistently used to give free-market economics emotional resonance are America's innocence and its exceptionalism, which show up in familiar ways around the themes of destiny and vision already developed by Stu Weber. The collapse of frontier imagery into Christian imagery provides common symbols that can be mobilized with economy and resonance in a way that erases the complexity of both the frontier and Christianity. But most strikingly, the book situates the free market as the great adventure at the very soul of American identity; Christ and cowboy, the inheritor of the legacy of pioneer and scout, come together in the entrepreneurial adventure.

The editors' foreword to the book sets the stage for a grand revision of American history, providing us with the term "American Civilization": "The task we set ourselves [in this book and course] was to create a vision of the future, founded in the historic principles of the American idea, that could serve as an organizing paradigm for our nation's progress over the next several decades."[7] The emotional weight and symbolic coherence are already placed within the narrative frame of the inspired man of vision with an almost sacred duty to the nation. He is poised at the Cumberland Gap looking out over the horizon and responsible for leading the wagons through, or he is Flint McCullugh looking out over the plains, undistracted because he has to look ahead, to look over, to overlook the costs to the Indians or to nature of the movement of these wagons. Americans want to know where they are headed, not where they have been.

Gingrich's introduction to the book is adapted from a special order delivered on the floor of the House on January 25, 1993, which situates us in familiar territory: "Our generation has a rendezvous with destiny. . . . that rendezvous is to renew American Civilization."[8] The seriousness of the threat of moral disintegration and the welfare state places it in a military context, for previous threats have come from the Nazis and imperial Japan in 1940 and the Soviet empire in 1946. Strongly influenced by Margaret Thatcher, who also influenced Ronald Reagan, and vice versa, Gingrich goes her one better: "The future of freedom is at stake. . . . We are the only country large enough, complex enough, multiracial enough, to truly provide leadership for freedom across the planet. If we weaken, there is no one to replace us." (1) Threat, vigor, the dangers of impotence, are all laid out, along with the immensely satisfying assurance that we are special and the masochistically pleasurable, familiar dynamism of being asked to sacrifice ourselves for something so noble. For when Gingrich talks about American Civilization, he means just that. Western civilization, which means white European culture, has aged and weakened. It no longer has the energy to carry out this somber responsibility to spread freedom and unregulated markets. American Civilization, however, is different. It is not merely an imitation of Western civilization; instead it stands on the shoulders of Western civilization as its finest product. It is continent-wide, multiracial, more optimistic, future oriented, more open, it provides more upward mobility, has less class consciousness, is less racist, and has attempted to reach out to all people of all backgrounds to give them the opportunity to rise. Its story must first be retold correctly, then learned by all American citizens who will become performative Americans. *Knowing* what makes America and acting on that knowledge will make them *be* Americans, and only those immigrants who do will deserve to be real Americans. This story must be learned "because American Civilization is in fact a more powerful, a more human, and a more desirable form of civilization than the alternatives." (4)

The popular-cultural frontier thesis of forward movement requires the coherence of the postmodern internal frontier and its binaries in order to assess decay: "If there is no yardstick, there is a long-term tendency for people to drift into barbarism and savagery." (5) This means that we must teach "other-culturalism" rather than multiculturalism, which "assumes cultures are equal morally, and it assumes you can lump American Civilization in with other cultures and civilizations." (5) But all cultures are not equal morally, as evidenced by the savagery of Aztec sacrifice, the caste system of India, the oppression of women in Iran, the fact, as Dinesh D'Souza reminds us, that Africans, too, owned slaves. Our own unique identity as chosen nation, our own rendezvous with destiny, means we have a duty to reclaim that uniqueness and innocence and to distinguish "between our primary culture—American Civilization—and the rest." (5) In this rendezvous with destiny, renewing American civilization does not involve simply politics but "everything from what local schools put in the curriculum, to what you hear on radio and television, to what happens with our local club and your local civic organization." (7) Secular in its outlook, this framework obviously makes a tidy fit with the absolutist Christian message of Stu Weber, not to mention those of Pat Robertson, Tim LaHaye, James Dobson, Lou Sheldon, and others who are more overtly religious and argue that the Constitution was divinely inspired. The Five Pillars of American Civilization (pillars erect themselves with great frequency in this terrain) are personal strength of will, character, and integrity; entrepreneurial free enterprise, which is "a moral undertaking and an inherent part of the makeup of human beings"; a spirit of invention and discovery; a commitment to quality; and reliance on the central lessons of American history. (11)

But the terrain, the frontier land to be conquered, is different from the landscape represented by McCullugh or Turner, because here it is abstract. It is the digitalized speculative terrain of economic growth: "We need an economy that is growing so we can lead the planet and so that we can have the strength to project power and provide assistance overseas" (18), to improve health care, and to save the inner cities. Each of these important and moral projects depends on an economic problem thoroughly clothed in familiar frontier dress: "More is at stake than just America, or just our children. For 200 years we have been the last best hope of mankind. We have grown from a tiny strip of 13 colonies on the eastern part of the North American Continent to the most powerful universal civilization in the history of the human race. All across the planet people want to be more like Americans." They want human rights, the right to free elections, free speech, productivity, and prosperity, which are the essence of being American. "If we succeed in renewing American Civilization, we will be strong enough to help them learn the behaviors that make these rights possible." (22) The simplicity and clarity are breathtaking, and he takes it one step further by insisting on the connection between these things and absolutist morality. You either believe in (a certain kind of) God or you don't; you either believe in right or you don't, with George Washington himself cementing the economic, moral patriotism that has now become biological. Gingrich's own political strategy has since depended on the control of communications to further strengthen the sense of condensation and rhetoric. Drawing once again on a woman, Linda DiVall, a pollster for the Republican National Committee, Gingrich has enforced a strict, relentless monitoring of his party's message and rhetoric. That rhetoric keeps the message simple and extends the advice of George Washington, quoted in a chapter of Gingrich's book written by Stephen Covey and Keith Gulledge: "The foundations of our national policy will be valid in the pure and immutable principles of private morality. . . . there is no truth more thoroughly established than that there exists in the economy and course of nature an indissoluble union between virtue and happiness."[9]

Those familiar elements of American Civilization are then translated into discussions of entrepreneurial activity that becomes millionaire populism. George Gilder begins his essay by debunking the myth that the rich have come from backgrounds of privilege, arguing that on the *Forbes* Four Hundred list of America's wealthiest people we find ten people who never finished high school. Only 240 of the 304 who went to college graduated. This is a group that proves that "capitalism exalts a strange riffraff with no apparent rhyme or reason," a "democracy" of millionaires that proves the uniqueness of American Civilization.[10] Its free market will inevitably, if unregulated, provide the most fertile democratic ground of America's heritage. Gilder even dismisses Adam Smith's "invisible hand of the market" as being too negative because Smith thought that we engage in economic activity out of self-interest and greed; economic activity is a far more idealistic, democratic activity than Smith understood. For Gilder's project in this inversion of conqueror and victim is to defend the entrepreneur as victim: "America's entrepreneurs are not more greedy than Harry Homeless or Suzie Saintly. . . . In proportion to their holdings or their output, and their contributions to the human race, [America's entrepreneurs] consume less than any other group of people in the history of the world." (61)

These millionaires are a very special group of Americans, whose identity now becomes the basis of a newly defined, egalitarian populism: "a strange riffraff, to be sure, because they are chosen not according to blood, credentials, education, or services rendered to the establishment. They are chosen for performance alone, for service to the people as consumers," the rich having "earned their money by contributions to the commonweal that far exceed their income." (61) The hero here is someone who, like Jesus or Custer, has been viciously misunderstood in spite of his sacrifice for the common good. The most unfair insult of all is the accusation that he acts out of greed:

> Greed is actually less a characteristic of Bill Gates, the Chairman of Microsoft, than of Harry Homeless. Harry may seem pitiable. But he and his advocates insist that he occupy — and devalue — some of the planet's most valuable real estate. From the beaches of Santa Monica to the center of Manhattan, he wants to live better than most of the population of the world throughout human history but he does not want to give back anything whatsoever to the society that sustains him. He wants utterly unearned wealth. (61)

This self-sacrifice by entrepreneurs is best described by the title of an article by J. Hoberman on the movie roles of Michael Douglas: "Victim Victorious."[11] For Gilder, homelessness is turned into avarice and wealth into self-sacrifice: "If you want to see a carnival of greed, watch Jesse Jackson regale an audience on the 'economic violence' of capitalism, or watch a conference of leftist college professors denouncing the economic system that provides their freedom, tenure, long vacations." (61)

This populism of the millionaire, which elicits identification from those in far less comfortable economic circumstances because, like the lottery, it *could* have been they who won, for they had equality of opportunity, is, of course, predictably accompanied by an attack on education. Entrepreneurial creativity and invention have less to do with professional education than with the self-made man: "The fashionably educated and cultivated spurn the kind of fanatically focused learning commanded by the Four Hundred" (63), which comes from the kind of learning others find insufferably boring, such as tax codes, garbage regulations, the intricacies of building codes. This is a populism that also reaches into regions of the country often ignored or trivialized by academics, such as Sam Walton's Bentonville, Arkansas. Academic economic theorists, Gilder argues, simply cannot account for the suddenness of the entrepreneurial creation of wealth. Gilder's description of entrepreneurial activity moves the frontier theme forward into postmodernity, for Bill Gates, Michael Milken, and others like them "did not capture the pinnacle; they became it." (64) They become the phallus, defining American identity by their own identity, which is equated with their economic performance. This move will find its most glorious example in the persona of Rush Limbaugh.

For Gilder, these populist entrepreneurs have become our new American heroes: "In fact, of all the people on the face of the globe it is only the legal owners of businesses who have a clear interest in building wealth for others rather than spending it on themselves." (64) Only Bill Gates would stand to lose if he focused on his own consumption rather than on his consumers: "In a sense, Gates is as much a slave as a master of Microsoft." He is "tied to the mast of Microsoft." (65) In mixed phallic metaphors, he proves to be tied to the mast while at the same time he *is* the pinnacle. He not only *has* it, he *is* it.

The abstraction of this new frontier reestablishes the frontier's openness: "The landscape of capitalism may seem solid and settled and thus seizable; but capitalism is really a mindscape," a "form of change that never can be stationary." (65) Such entrepreneurial development can occur in its full fluidity and creativity only when political attitudes about the freedom of the market flourish and allow "volatile and shifting ideas, not heavy and entrenched establishments [to] constitute the source of wealth." (65) In an inverse materialism, value does not lie in things, which stay the same, but in the thoughts about them: "Much of what was supremely valuable in 1980 plunged to near worthlessness by 1990." (66) Though he argues that a materialist superstition "stultified the works of Marx and other prophets of violence and envy" who believed that "wealth consists not in ideas, attitudes, moral codes, and mental disciplines, but in definable and static things that can be seized and redistributed," he in fact might have found that Marx agreed with him. But Marx would have then used Gilder's claim as evidence that such abstractions are only possible because the material conditions upon which they depend are effaced. And Marx would also likely have agreed with Gilder that the survival of the capitalist system depends on the cultural enforcement of such idealized concepts. For Gilder, "the means of production of entrepreneurs are not land, labor, or capital, but minds and hearts." (67) And as Marx would have agreed, "every capitalist investment has the potential for a dual yield: a financial profit and an epistemological profit." (74)

The frontier is deliberately revised from a geographical landscape to the "mindscape of capitalism":

[A]ll riches finally fall into the gap between thoughts and things. Governed by mind but caught in matter, to retain its value an asset must afford an income stream that is expected to continue. The expectation can shift as swiftly as thought, but the things, alas, are all too solid and slow to change. (65)

As are employees. This is an America defined by an entrepreneurial mind-scape so rare and delicate as to have become a living thing. Its adventurers must be protected, cherished, nourished by the entire society: "The wealth of America is not an inventory of goods; it is an organic, living entity, a fragile pulsing fabric of ideas, expectations, loyalties, moral commitments, visions. To vivisect it for redistribution would eventually kill it." (67) The emotional weight of American frontier patriotism is brought to bear to protect the free market, as entrepreneurial economic activity and its fluid, living growth replace the corpses of industrial capitalism and the welfare state. Fluidity, not static identity, has become the valorized term.

This pulsating, throbbing America is also the site of America's compassion, as the frontier thesis of inversion now recalls the Christian narrative of the last who become first: "Even the prospects of the poor in the United States and around the world depend on the treatment of the rich. If the rich are immobilized by socialism, the poor will suffer everywhere." High tax rates and regulations will not keep anyone from being rich, but they will prevent the poor from getting rich: "But if the rich are respected and allowed to risk their wealth — and new rebels are allowed to rise up and challenge them — America will continue to be the land where the last regularly become first by serving others." (68)

Those risk-taking adventurers, those Christ-like entrepreneurs serving others, are the masochistic, self-sacrificing heroes of this new frontier, the rebels who distrust expertise and education. In true populist rebelliousness, they "prevail not by understanding an existing situation in all its complex particulars, but by creating a new situation which others must try to comprehend." Their enterprise is driven by an aggressive action, not reaction: "It entails breaking the looking glass of established ideas — even the gleaming mirrors of executive suites — and stepping into the often greasy and fetid bins of creation." (68–69) The daring cowboy entrepreneur steps into the purifying primitive, as Turner knew he must, this time into a dangerous world in which "belief precedes knowledge" and bankruptcies serve as an index of growth, a kind of Darwinian survival of the fittest. (69)

In this entrepreneurial mindscape, the bravest and the most successful are those who understand that "enterprise always consists of action in uncertainty," that large setbacks are a portent of large gains and stability a precursor of failure. (68) Their vision looks out over this mindscape of growth, not down at its debris. This dangerous uncertainty, however, is not the feminized *doubt* of hesitation or of academic deconstruction or relativism. It is the hormone-driven gamble of *risk*—the dynamics that have become so central to Republican discussions of the economy and the suggestive notion of dynamic scoring. Instability and surprise are the tropes of the entrepreneurial model, the diving board its metaphor. The heroic author of this activity is also revalorized, for the dynamic and integrated view of a company requires one unique adventurer, one CEO such as Bill Gates or Sam Walton, to understand and coordinate every aspect of it. Men are back.

Money takes on the value of natural resource, the fertile matter of growth. It is no longer the filthy lucre described by those who mistakenly imagined entrepreneurs were motivated by greed. Just as academics need free time and libraries, and scientists need laboratories and assistants, just as intellectuals need the freedom to write and publish, so capitalists need economic freedom and access to capital. With all this fluidity, uncertainty, and instability, one wonders why postmodernist theory and its fluidity should be so threatening to the story of America Gingrich wants to tell or to Gilder's Adventure of the Entrepreneur. But this postmodern fluidity of capital, the essence, the organic "matter" of American identity—wealth—can only flow if the free market and its need for fluid ideas are, paradoxically, *guaranteed,* made static, by absolutist ideas about the sacred nature of the market economy, as Gilder already taught us. So alongside this Wild West entrepreneurial freedom in the mindscape of American entrepreneurial capitalism lies the necessity of religious values, not necessarily because of religion itself but, instrumentally, even crassly, because of the discipline religion enforces:

> Entrepreneurs, though many are not churchgoers, emerge from a culture shaped by religious values. The optimism and trust, the commitment and faith, the discipline and altruism that their lives evince and their works require can flourish only in the midst of a moral order, with religious foundations. Secular culture has yet to produce a satisfactory rationale for a life of work, risk, and commitment oriented toward the needs of others—a life of thrift and trust leading to investments with uncertain returns. Secular culture, in the name of charity, can only summon envy; in the name of service, can only offer coercion; in the name of giving, can achieve only the sterility of income redistribution. (76)

Though it seems not to matter whether or not one actually believes in God, it does matter whether one believes in religious culture: "The value of a society's good ultimately derives from the values of its people. . . . But the religious culture ultimately shapes the moral order in which entrepreneurs thrive or fail, defines the order of value that informs the prices and worth of a society's good." (76–77) Though entrepreneurs are not sinless — "They bear scars and have inflicted many" — nevertheless, "more than any other class of men, they embody and fulfill the sweet and mysterious consolations of the Sermon on the Mount and the most farfetched affirmations of the democratic dream." (77) The risk-taking cowboy has been integrated into the narrative not only of the frontier but of the Bible, the cowboy entrepreneur as good shepherd, as both find themselves comfortably within the narrative of nationalism. America is the only hope for global civilization, in whose interests the cowboy shepherd must be allowed to roam free. Its idealism is now grounded in one almighty principle, the creation of wealth:

> Bullheaded, defiant, tenacious, creative, entrepreneurs continued to solve the problems of the world even faster than the world could create them. The achievements of enterprise remained the highest testimony of the mysterious strength of the human spirit; confronting the perennial perils of human life, the scientific odds against human triumph, the rationalist counsels of despair, the entrepreneur finds a higher source of hope than reason, a deeper well of faith than science, a farther reach of charity than welfare. His success is the triumph of the spirit of enterprise — a thrust beyond the powers and principalities of the established world to the transcendent sources of creation and truth.
>
> The single most important question for the future of America is how we treat our entrepreneurs. If we smear, harass, overtax, and overregulate them, our liberal politicians will be shocked and horrified to discover how swiftly the physical tokens of the means of production collapse into so much corroded wire, eroding concrete, scrap metal, and jungle rot. (78–79)

The obvious fact that there are no jungles in America returns us again to the racism of this hormone-driven digitized mindscape.

The final essay in Gingrich's book of lessons for renewing America provides a frame for the adventure of the new, affluent immigrant who sees the American Dream as the quintessential adventure in the history of civilization. The new immigrant need not take more seriously the difficulties of those who were here first or who came before. She is called upon instead simply to renew the abstract frontier enthusiasm that comes from facing an empty continent waiting to be developed. In her contribution to the linkage between deep emotional feelings and a political agenda, Arianna Huffington, the wife of multimillionaire Michael Huffington and formerly a follower of the New Age guru John-Robert, now appropriates the religious framework of the Twelve-Step Program for the entrepreneurial renewal of America. Huffington heads the Center for Effective Compassion, uniting both secular Americans and religious ones, both the affluent and the not-so-affluent. In a way that is reminiscent of Gilder's sociobiology, she begins by telling us of her training as an economist and of her realization that James Carville's "It's the economy, stupid" was an inadequate slogan for the renewal of America. The crisis America faces is not an economic deficit but a spiritual one.

She, too, strategically distances herself from the tragic apocalyptic narrative, arguing that fire and brimstone preachers used to chart the decline of America, isolating all the things that were wrong with it. What they failed to do was chart a vision, and she situates us directly in the comic apocalyptic narrative. Though her framework is secular, the spiritual deficit is described in the same kind of monotheistic terms used by absolutist religion: "One thing we might say is that ours is a culture in search of a central idea." And her language repeats references to Pascal's description of an identity with a God-shaped hole at its center, though she translates it into existential terms. America suffers from an existential vacuum, a "*spiritual* deficit that has produced this hole in the heart of the American Dream."[12]

In order to explain how America can repair that vacuum and how she will situate her own Twelve Steps within that process of renewal, she sets out a theory of four instincts. The first three are survival, sex, and power. But it is the fourth that is the most important in contemporary America. Without it, more is demanded of power and pleasure than they can possibly supply, and their pursuit is inevitably disappointing: "Nothing can ever be enough when what you are looking for is not really what you want." (219) And what people really want is expressed by the Fourth Instinct, which rebels against meaninglessness at the center of culture:

It is a relentless natural longing that leads us beyond our first three instincts. . . . It is the instinct that strives for spiritual fulfillment, and seeks a context of meaning and purpose for "ordinary human life." The Fourth Instinct reunites us with our true nature, and guides us by our true interest. It is my belief that this instinct is the key, not just to personal renewal, but to the spiritual regeneration of America. For the moment we begin to change and regenerate our lives, the world starts changing with us. (218–19)

After a long period of "wandering in the wasteland of humanistic hubris," a contemporary version of the frontier and biblical wilderness, however, Americans have begun to search for and find purpose in their lives. (220) That purpose can be outlined according to the Twelve-Step Framework, which offers "some of the oldest truths and most fundamental lessons of American history, rearranged in twelve specific steps." (220) Like Peter Brimelow, the South African immigrant who now recommends restricting nonwhite immigration, and Dinesh D'Souza, who tells us there is no more racism, Huffington is a quick learner and is already an authority on the most enduring truths of American Civilization. The Twelve Steps, as she rephrases them in terms of national recovery, introduce the twelve sections of the article. They are:

Step One: We admit that our country is on the wrong track and that we, as a nation, have lost our way.

Step Two: We resolve to expand the national debate beyond what government can do for you, beyond what government can do to you, beyond even what you can do for your government.

Step Three: We concede that economic empowerment is not enough.[13]

Step Four: We contend that what is wrong with America extends far beyond the economic underclass and the inner city.[14]

Step Five: We acknowledge a Power greater than ourselves.[15]

Step Six: We admit that we are One Nation Under God — as is the whole planet.

Step Seven: We embrace as principles what earlier generations assumed as facts.

Step Eight: We reclaim a broad vision of responsibility.

Step Nine: We restore service to the heart of our civic agenda.

Step Ten: We commit ourselves to challenging the popular culture of nihilism, cynicism, and materialism by actively creating and promoting a spiritual counterculture.[16]

Step Eleven: We need to articulate a vision for the future — and we need to live that vision.

Step Twelve: We must commit ourselves to living in *coram Dei* (in the face of God). (220–25)

This is a program for Mere Spirituality, a term from C. S. Lewis, its rousing list of steps seen not as a sermon but as a challenge: "In our battle against the corrosive trends of our society, we must demonstrate that we have not only economic truth on our side, but moral and spiritual truth as well. That is the legitimacy that nations are built on. America *is* a Christian nation. It is also a Jewish Nation. It is a Muslim nation." (226)

Huffington concludes,

I was not born in this country, but I was blessed with the privilege of emigrating to these shores. It was this experience that allowed me to see how unique this land of ours really is. Another writer who hailed from abroad captured the essence of our miraculous country. "America," wrote Luigi Barzin, "is alarmingly optimistic, compassionate, incredibly generous. It was a *spiritual* wind that drove Americans irresistibly ahead from the beginning." It is time we caught the spiritual wind again. (226)

iii.

These various cowboys and one cowgirl would surely disagree with one another on any number of specific issues, but they share a coherence within the superrationalistic logic established in and by popular culture where things come to "matter." To repeat Lawrence Grossberg's argument, "By making certain things matter, people 'authorize' them to speak for them, not only as a spokesperson but as surrogate voice" (83), with affect constituting "the plane or mechanism of belonging and identification (of which identification, constructed through ideology or psychological interpellation, is only one form." (84) In terms of these resonating themes, "it is in fact not a matter of what can be said but what can matter, of what is worth saying, of what has a chance to matter to people. It is the public language of what matters that is at stake." (8)

In Rush Limbaugh's construction of a particular kind of populist affective mattering, his most important contribution to conservatism has been a performative populism that fits comfortably with Gilder's inverted narrative of conqueror and victim, Weber's Christian hero and servant, Huffington's wealthy immigrant. Like Reagan, Limbaugh is able to bring together widely divergent audiences, in part because of his understanding of the language and imagery of popular culture, particularly the popular culture (and "everyday life") of middle-class suburbanites and small-town residents, though his appeal extends far beyond those groups. As Grossberg argues, "it seems that people need not agree with the ideology or the specific projects of the ascending conservative alliance in order to find themselves drawn into its discourses and positions." (161)

Limbaugh has brilliantly positioned himself in the space in which post-modern theory has also found itself, within a model of signification that cannot take itself too seriously because it has discovered that it is hard to find a center against which to make meaning. In his tracing of American culture after the Cold War and its threat of global terror, Grossberg reminds us that in contemporary popular culture, terror has become boring and boredom terrifying. At the same time, the economic circumstances of Americans are increasingly incomprehensible and uncertain. Within this context, young people and popular-culture figures such as David Letterman "exhibit an ironic, knowing distance, coupled with a sense of emotional urgency" (212), an urgency of unease. He cites a promo for Letterman's show: "An hour of celebrities talking about themselves constantly interrupted by commercials. Hey America, the pride is back." (214) This is a sensibility in which "everything can be taken seriously and simultaneously made into a joke." (217) Within this context people are not rendered passive but actively and aggressively indifferent. As a teacher says about his students, "They don't have to make commitments; they don't have to listen closely; most importantly they don't have to believe anyone. And the only thing better, it appears, is to get them to laugh at the idea that anyone would even try." (215)

Limbaugh's smirky, adolescent performance style, repeated and "dit-toed" by mature adults who presumably teach their own kids better manners, exhibits a deep seriousness that pretends not to be serious by laughing at its own pretensions. Seriousness is thus made acceptable because it is now perfectly attuned to exploit a postmodern sensibility already available, using that permanent smirk in what Jacqueline Rose calls right-wing ideology's "specific economy of aggression and its defenses." (69) And like a cocky adolescent just jokin' around, Limbaugh constructs a populist resentment of elites and, ferociously, of Big Sisters who attempt to claim the place reserved for chosen sons. Limbaugh and Ronald Reagan are seen as the symbolic leaders of conservatism. Limbaugh opens an article in the Heritage Foundation's *Policy Review,* with Reagan's acknowledgment of that similarity: "Now that I've retired from active politics, I don't mind that you've become the number-one voice for conservatism in our country."[17]

To try to make sense of Limbaugh's appeal, the son who has replaced our Uncle Ronald, himself the chosen son in his generation, I want to focus on the way Limbaugh's rhetorical style frames a performative construction of "authenticity" within the internal postmodern frontier. That is, within this culture of irony and the smirk at anything that might suggest belief or commitment, Limbaugh establishes a passionate belief in the very things he admits he is constructing. And he centers that belief on the truth of his own identity, simultaneously achieving what Jacqueline Rose sees as the psychopolitics of right-wing ideologies that "harness fantasy to reason, giving reason to . . . the flashpoints of the social, the very points where reason itself is at its least secure." (69) Within the postmodern sensibility, the *constructedness* of that superrationality becomes the most dependable thing of all, the thing that matters most, a fact openly and proudly acknowledged. Though poststructuralist theorists have imagined that pointing out the constructedness of meaning was somehow subversive, in this specifically mass-mediated American context we could not have been further from the truth.[18]

In following Limbaugh's version of his career as performer of truth, I draw on his second best-seller, *See, I Told You So* (or SITYS, as he refers to it), as well as, occasionally, his *Policy Review* article. In *See, I Told You So,* he first assures his audience that everything he tells us is the Truth, beginning a sophisticated process of inoculation. And as he says, good satire has to be constructed somehow on the truth. But of course you laugh; it's ridiculous to expect someone, in this day and age, to tell the truth. And after all, he's a *media* star interested in *politics.* The ironic postmodern terrain, the frontier, has been prepared: "In time — in fact, before you finish digesting this sage guidebook — you will come to the inevitable conclusion that I am right, have been right, and will likely continue to be right in the future. You will find that the information is accurate, the explication sound, the analysis penetrating, and the format profound. I predict you will, before too long, even begin to enjoy this. Don't be afraid. It's okay. Really."[19] He then turns to a strategy common in other conservative texts: drawing on a wildly postmodern pastiche of things taken out of context.

Because the logics of the media and popular culture work this way, too, pointing out contradictions proves to be fairly useless. He has already accepted into his rhetorical style the neutralization of contradiction through laughter. Here his epigrams come from, among others, Voltaire (whom his fundamentalist Christian listeners condemn as an Enlightenment humanist beloved by Francophile socialists), Thoreau (a hero of environmentalists, whom Limbaugh despises), Thomas Paine (a radical often criticized by the Founding Fathers, whom Limbaugh reveres).

He ends, of course, with that sage Rush Limbaugh, in a style reminiscent of high school: "Isn't it amazing that these guys knew all this . . . without having to listen to me?" The reader has been inoculated against complexity, injected with passion but also with an accompanying silliness that assures us that Limbaugh has no authoritarian intent to dictate the truth but simply wants to situate himself at the level of the ordinary reader and have a good time. He thus takes the stage squarely in the popular sensibility in which we have all been fooled much too often. We do not take anything seriously: "I'm a nice guy — a harmless little fuzzball with a strong live-and-let-live credo. The furthest thing from my mind is to carry out some devious master plan to 'take over the airwaves' and impose my views on anyone." (1)

Thus he has subtly moved from the postmodern sensibility in which nothing much is to be trusted to a media context in which absolutely nothing is to be trusted, to a retroactive reinscription of both that begins to show what passion — what "mattering" — propels him to colonize these two deceptive areas. The passion he arouses will ironically prove to matter all the more precisely because passion and commitment have been made suspect. He begins the construction of a double populism that joins his own persona to that of his audience, for if he is to be taken seriously, if he is to matter to these people burned once too often, he must offer them something that is both true and fun. And what he offers is an ability to partake, guilt free, in the very essence of Americanness at a moment when cultural discussions of American identity show it to be the site of great struggle. Not so coincidentally, his message picks up themes of uniqueness and innocence that we have already seen set out by Stu Weber, Gingrich, Huffington, and Gilder: "America is being stripped of its soul." (111)

The essence of American identity on this stage *is* Rush Limbaugh. All the self-effacing jokes at his own expense can never really scratch the serene, smirking success of this poor boy made good, precisely because he has the touch of gold, the mark of Truth. He achieves more and more success as his audience grows. Every book is a best-seller, his newsletter rakes in money, and politicians flock to his door. Within a postmodern culture of indecision and doubt, he is the exemplary confident, forward-looking American, his success purely, simply, cleanly a function of hard work and excellence and nothing more: "My incomparable level of performance, and the preparation it requires, is hard work—as is staying knowledgeable, motivated, passionate; and ready, willing, and able to articulate my core beliefs." (3)

Belief and value are now clearly defined: media constructedness in the abstract, digitalized space of corporate and entrepreneurial creation of wealth equals the articulation of *core* beliefs equals the organic "matter," the natural resources of the free-market frontier, what "matters" both emotionally and biologically. Wealth, subjectivity, democracy, constructedness, equality of opportunity, not of outcome, are precisely, super-rationally cemented together. These core beliefs, as well as their tidy simplicity, are familiar, their emotional resonance that of frontier iconography erasing the complexities of history: "America is the greatest country on Earth and in history, still abounding with untapped opportunity for ordinary citizens. No other nation on the planet presents its citizens with such a gift—the promise that they can pursue whatever dream they have, with whatever talents they have, with all the effort and savvy they can marshal, and their reward will be the possibility of the dream realized. This is a social contract unique in history . . . and liberalism is indeed a massive tax on those very dreams." (9) This is constructing a "mattering map" with a vengeance: "I am absolutely confident in my view that what I have accomplished, though unique, is illustrative of what is possible in this country—for you!" (9)

He continues, "My story is nothing more than an example of the Original American Ethic: hard work, overcoming obstacles, triumphing over enormous odds, the pioneer spirit. . . . It is my heartfelt belief that, no matter what your status in life, you can learn about what's possible for you in this country by studying me. And if you attain even a fraction of my level of excellence, you will have arrived." (11) This tongue-in-cheek self-construction, symbolically as well as in reality, this billboard of Rush Limbaugh on Times Square, is true only if it succeeds. You don't ask whether Coca-Cola, or IBM, for that matter, are "true"; you ask whether they succeed, whether they create wealth. And succeed Limbaugh does. Yet in spite of that success and the accusation that liberals are the ones who want to be victims, he is exemplary victim, most misunderstood, target numero uno: "We've got to begin by having an honest and open debate about the problem—without name-calling and *ad hominem* attacks." (111) Liberals will tell you, for instance, "that I am motivated by hate and bigotry. The truth is that I have profound love and respect for all people" (117); "I practice the same standard of civility that I live in my personal life. . . . I try never to be cruel. . . ." (35) In fact, he says, in his early days in talk radio, he stood up to a station manager who wanted him to engage in insult radio; he refused then and refuses now. (The mind reels.)

The victim position familiar from Turner's frontier thesis becomes increasingly important: "I take it personally when people tell me the American Dream is a thing of the past. What does that attitude say about anyone [me] in this era who succeeds? Somehow, they must have cheated." (13) Like Noonan before him, Limbaugh universalizes the slights he suffered personally to slights against the American people, establishing his credentials and passion as a millionaire populist: "This needs to be discussed in a psychological sense. Today, so much of America is under assault that achievers are under assault. The Democratic Party has so successfully exploited class envy that people hold the wealthy and successful in contempt. The Democrats are breeding resentment. They have many people believing that anybody who is doing well is a cheater, a crook, selfish, and/or doing something unfair and unjust. I am now enjoying success in my life. That doesn't mean I don't remember what it was like to struggle." (17)

Though we could feel sorry for people who are suffering, he says, that would not help them. What they need is psychological inspiration so that they believe they can succeed. Or as his boss, Roger Ailes, said when asked if his own employees were unionized, "They don't need a union because they have me as a role model." Far better for Limbaugh to be a good example, for it certainly wouldn't do any good to sit around and wring his hands. The Bible assures us that poverty will never be eliminated, bad things do happen to good people, and life is full of risks. In a world of uncertainties, people need a cheerleader, like Reagan, like him, someone "who can make us feel good about ourselves and give us the confidence to be ourselves again." (18) When were we ourselves? He is not specific, but one can guess—before affirmative action, before gay rights, before feminism, before environmentalism, before government regulation of corporate activity, and so on.

His most powerful performative act in this argument is thus to equate attacks on him with attacks on his audience, who are, his surveys tell us, between the ages of twenty-five and fifty-four, upscale and educated, more than 60 percent of them with at least two years of college. When the book was published with updated material in 1994, they numbered 4.6 million at any moment of his broadcast and 20 million per week. (20–21) Thus these attacks on him inevitably *increase* and strengthen the loyalty of his audience, who in defending him are defending themselves. These attacks really "matter": "I don't mind being dismissed, disparaged, castigated, maligned, and reviled for my views, my achievements, or my continued audacity to breathe. I have thick skin — and the satisfaction of knowing that I am right. . . . Nevertheless, I am growing weary of the critics of my show who feel it is obligatory to impugn *you,* the audience. You are called 'followers,' right-wing zealots, reactionaries, bigots. You are described as my 'minions,' easily provoked dimwits on the fringes of society whom I can whip into a frenzy at my whim." (19) Well, of course, he *can* do that, as evidenced by his ability to get his fans to jam congressional switch-boards and fax machines. But he brilliantly includes his audience within his invincible, misunderstood ego, their dittohead identity proving their independence: "One of the most consistent threads in their erroneous analysis is misjudging, misunderstanding, and underestimating you." (20) And again, of course, he is right; many people have misjudged them, but many others have not. He continues: "Despite claims from my detractors that my audience is comprised of mind-numbed robots, waiting for me to give them some sort of marching orders, the fact is that I am merely enunciating opinions and analysis that support what they already know." (*PR* 5) He validates the thoughts of the silent majority that is no longer so silent. Jacqueline Rose describes this mobilization of a fear of the group: "the only group that can be trusted . . . is the one that tells you to trust only yourself." (220)

An impenetrable binary curtain slams down here, so that *no* criticism will be acceptable. The more criticism, the more he is proven right; the more criticism, the more money he makes. Thus, in what might be called the happy-paranoid logic of the millionaire populist, criticism is always already a sign that he is right (and rich), his critics wrong. "If you criticize [liberals'] behavior, and they call you a pig, a bigot, or a fascist, their consciences must be bothering them; they take the offensive because deep down they know they're wrong." (93) Richard Hofstadter did not antici-pate the effectiveness of a humorous version of the paranoid American in the countersubversive tradition, but he did recognize its claim to certainty: "It is nothing if not coherent, far more coherent than the real world, no room for mistakes, failures, ambiguities, if not rational, intensely rationalistic." (quoted in Rose 61)

However, though Limbaugh argues that talk radio is "the ultimate form of being in control on radio" (34), and that "my show is not about what my audience thinks, or what my callers think, or what my readers think. It is about what I think," he can also argue that this control is not authoritarian because it is so perfectly matched to the "real." (21) In the mindscape of capitalism, "symbol" and "real" prove to be the same, as marketing has become transparent, as if persuasion were not going on. Language is utterly coherent and literal. Rose describes Thatcherite conservatism in a similar way: "The repeated and central terms of consistency, persistence, and sameness, the refusal of any possible gap between reality and intent . . . and then, as the inevitable corollary for those who see in this form of rhetoric a denial of the precariousness of language itself, the insistence on the utter coherence of the word." (61) In this corporate media space, Limbaugh, as a favor to his audience, becomes the Transparent American Subject. His truth, the creation of wealth as the equivalent of democracy, morality, and normality, is connected without gap to the core beliefs of a certain, historically specific populism, a pure reason of profit clothed in the emotional iconography of popular culture: "Conservatives understand — intuitively, in most cases — that what has made America a great nation is the commitment of its people to a set of fundamental, core values. Among them are belief in God, monogamy, devotion to family, law and order, self-reliance, rugged individualism, commitment to excellence, and rewarding achievement." (398) One nation under God. Resonance. He is quite securely in the same secular and religious space as the earlier versions of natural law. I know who you are, he says to his audience, and *I speak you,* I perform you: "the ones holding everything together without whining about the lack of federal funding or burning your neighborhood down. With the help of God and your family. You've been portrayed as selfish and greedy, your desire to live a moral life and teach your children virtue laughed at, sneered at, scorned. You have to pick up the pieces and pay more taxes for failures of liberal social experiments." (22) By my humor I save you from the accusation of self-righteousness, unfairness, contradiction, bigotry.

There are other important victims with whom both he and his audience are allied, but he must expend a little energy on making that point, because historically, when populism targeted people who did not work, it targeted the wealthy. But as White argues, nonworkers are now, not the wealthy, but the minority poor and radical whites. That leaves the wealthy to be revalorized by Limbaugh: "In a free-market environment, or one even approaching it, wealth is constantly being created, and usually it is without victimization, without pain." (67) If there is, indeed, victimization in a welfare state, however, it is most likely the kind John Adams warned us about: "It must be remembered that the rich are people as well as the poor, that they have rights as well as others, that they have as clear and as sacred a right to their large property as others have to their's [*sic*] which is smaller, that oppression to them is as possible and as wicked as to others." (quoted in Limbaugh 314) He continues by equating his listeners' position to that of the millionaire: "Do you realize that if wealthy people are not secure in the enjoyment of their property rights, no one is?" (315) And in this frame in which the creation of wealth is the most natural human activity, envy is the only explanation for criticism. He enumerates some of those targeted in this "shameless exploitation of the politics of envy": "Today it's pharmaceutical manufacturers, the cable-TV industry, insurance companies, physicians, and chief executive officers of major corporations Clinton is targeting. Tomorrow it may be you." (60)

But though he is able to tell the truth about the economy, he has not yet played his trump card on the mass-mediated internal postmodern frontier. He knows the truth about the media construction of reality:

> Without question, presentation, packaging, imaging, and superficiality are all extremely relevant in the political world. As a person whose livelihood is dependent not only upon the message, but its critical delivery, I will readily admit that in the real world, form, though not as much as substance, does indeed matter. I've told you countless times that I attribute my success both to my political views and my "reportedly" entertaining way of presenting them. With my background I am uniquely qualified to address the interrelationship between substance and form, am I not? As an expert in both form and content — in both delivery and substance, in both entertainment and profundity — I must tell you that the two should never clash. (320)

The true Transparent American Subject, the millionaire common man, can only speak true words that express the real: "Because my show, though it contains various styles, never — let me repeat this — *never* betrays the truth. What drives my show is truth, truth in both form and substance. And my audience consists of those who have the courage to believe and live the truth." (320–21) This word and this subject are thus always already fair and just: "I always say my views and commentary don't need to be balanced by equal time. I *am* equal time. And the free market has proved my contention." (*PR* 5)

Criticisms of him and accusations that he is racist, homophobic, and sexist therefore *cannot* be true because, ipso facto, the free market reliably guarantees the goodness — the truth, the democratic, moral, fair nature — of whatever it blesses. It would not bless bad things; that is its very logic. Racism, homophobia, and sexism are bad things, therefore, they are not what I do, because the inherently democratic market, sanctioned by God and natural law, *does* bless me: "A program like mine could not have sustained such enormous growth and popularity for so long if I were a racist or a bigot." (271–72) Having proved liberals wrong on substance (or on what "matters") and insisting that people need "to understand how the world really works, not how we would like it to work or wish it would work" (138), he can now read liberal attacks on him and his audience for what they are: *"Lies have become facts. Lies are facts."* (322) "If I were truly what my critics claim, I would have long ago, deservedly, gone into oblivion." (*PR* 5)

iv.

Bringing psychoanalytic theory and a study of psychopolitics to these claims of absolute truth leads to the most important question about this Christian cowboy populism whose resonances give such different groups coherence: Why do exploited people move to the right and not to the left? How do we disentangle the legitimate and the dangerous in trying to assess populism? Analyzing such questions either in terms of a concept of history that does not recognize the importance of popular culture or in terms of a concept of rationality that does not account for the un-conscious and fantasy — on the part of both Right *and* Left — leaves us stranded, mumbling in fury at the successes of the Right. For those suc-cesses are not about empirical facts so much as about the name of America itself. As Rose argues, a critical analysis of right-wing ideology has to be aware of the way the analysis melts into what it criticizes. For example, my description of Limbaugh's omnipotence all too easily becomes a mir-ror image of his description of liberalism.

Following Kristeva's description of the social contract of the West as one based on sacrifice, Rose extends it: "It is the characteristic of a right-wing ideology such as this one not to threaten the social, but to act out its most fundamental symbolic economy" (63–64), or as Thatcher did, to lay bare the underside of legitimate power. Right-wing belief "threatens the social by making that economy too blatant — the object of a renewed investment by the very drives it was intended to regulate or keep underground"; it exploits the fear upon which it rests. (64) The criticisms of political correctness that make it far more acceptable to utter racist words than to criticize racism is an example of such a renewed investment. In right-wing ideology, violence "can operate as a pole of attraction at the same time as (to the extent that) it is being denied." (64) This results in the paradox of a political identity in which subjects can "take pleasure in violence as force and legitimacy while always locating 'real' violence somewhere else." (64) "Real" violence can thus be located in the very groups conservatism targets by building more prisons, hiring more police, outlawing other sexualities, executing more people.

Making overt those things formerly kept hidden so that the collective identity could cohere both socially and psychically, absolutist conservatism reveals "the worst of a phallic economy countered, and thereby rendered permissible, by being presented as a masquerade." (66) This is a masquerade of phallic femininity in Thatcher's case, as well as those of Beverly LaHaye and other conservative women. In the case of Limbaugh, it is the masquerade of a powerless pinnacle: "I'm a nice guy — a harmless little fuzzball with a strong live-and-let-live credo. The furthest thing from my mind is to carry out some devious master plan to 'take over the airwaves' and impose my views on anyone." (1)

Taking seriously Rose's warning about simply basing our analyses of fascism on its European history, and remembering how handily the label Nazi is used by those on both left and right to describe their opponents, I nevertheless want to juxtapose European history to the contemporary American context to show both their similarity and their specificity. Klaus Mann's novel *Mephisto* is a fictionalized account of a historical event, the career of Mann's brother-in-law, Gustav Gründgens, who was an actor involved with Mann and his sister Erika in antifascist political theater in Frankfurt before the war.[20] Gründgens then followed his personal ambitions in utilitarian fashion to become the head of Hitler's State Theater in Berlin. The actor's willingness to separate performance from effect joins the novel's other central theme: power's dependence on its actors, on those who theatricalize and "stage" it. While those in power require their actors, those actors are, in fact, themselves spoken by power. The stage upon which they speak helps determine the effects of what they say, in spite of their personal intentions. While Grundgens performs for a totalitarian state, Limbaugh, the chief actor of a mass-mediated traditionalist conservatism, masquerades as powerless. Yet at the same time, the effects of his performance work in the interests of the stateless global corporation represented by Ed McLaughlin and Roger Ailes, the entrepreneurial requirements of Gingrich and Gilder, and the absolutist mandates of Stu Weber's masculinist God. No longer on the stage, but in the radio studio, one might imagine Limbaugh speaking Grundgens's lines that end Mann's novel: "What do men want from me? Why do they pursue me? Why are they so hard? All I am is a perfectly ordinary actor. . . ." (263)

SEVEN

God's Intentions for the Multinational Corporation: Seeing Reality True

[The corporation's] creativity mirrors God's. That is the standard by which its deeds and misdeeds are properly judged. — Michael Novak

Discover the principles of government and establish the practice of public policy upon a foundation of truth revealed by God in nature and in the Holy Scriptures. — *Regent University Graduate Catalog*

The traditionalist conservatives of the previous chapters have developed a narrative of market fundamentalism that claims that the market, when allowed to work freely, will naturally provide the best and fairest of all possible worlds. The focus of this chapter will be on an argument made by Michael Novak, of the American Enterprise Institute, who spiritualizes the multinational corporation. In Novak's argument, the corporation is defined in spiritual terms as a natural extension of God's natural law, with the belief in the corporation and the protection of corporate activity legitimated by this image of the corporation, saturated with moral passion. The passion aroused by that image justifies an admonition to Americans that it is their religious and moral duty to export unregulated free enterprise to the rest of the globe. After following Novak's logic, this chapter will examine the graduate catalog of Pat Robertson's Regent University to see how Novak's lesson is taught in Protestant evangelical terms.

In the 1980s, a particular configuration of conservative political activism had enormous consequences not only for domestic U.S. politics but for foreign relations. That configuration, partially a result of restrictions placed on the CIA during the Carter administration of the 1970s, brought together conservatives of all stripes to support the Nicaraguan Contras.

They reacted to the congressional ban on Contra funding by developing elaborate and sophisticated networks of religious organizations, conservative nongovernmental agencies, anticommunist groups, and business interests, their activities carried out with the implicit cooperation of the military in the Caribbean basin and Latin America.[1] Prior to the 1980s, of course, many of these groups had already been active, though relatively invisible, in particular, evangelical and fundamentalist conservatives, whose activities had been little noticed since the Scopes trial of 1925, as well as anticommunist and nativist Republican activists, after the defeat of Barry Goldwater in 1964. The spark of Contra funding provided the occasion for a practice run that led to the flowering of those networks that moved contemporary U.S. politics so far to the right.

The concept around which these groups came together was the euphemistically named "low-intensity warfare," in which both conservative Catholics and evangelical Protestants became involved on a cultural level. For example, Pat Robertson's *700 Club* featured the Contra leaders Adolfo Calero and Enrique Bermudez, the anticommunist leader General John Singlaub, and the Reagan administration official Elliott Abrams on its television broadcasts. Many other conservative groups supported anti-Sandinista schools in Nicaragua, funded progovernment messages on Nicaraguan radio, and ministered to Contra troops with the message that they were under divine sanction in their efforts to kill communists. These activities specifically targeted at Nicaragua were also linked to other activities throughout Latin America, in particular, attacks on progressive politics and liberation movements. Evangelical churches had separated themselves from the mainstream World Council of Churches in 1974 to form their own organizations, energized by Billy Graham's 1974 Lausanne Covenant, in which evangelicals from around the world, including many from the Third World, came together in the interests of extending Christ's dominion over the globe.[2] A similar conservatism was felt in the Catholic Church, where Catholics who had supported liberation theology saw the church hierarchy turn against priests, nuns, and laypeople who supported liberation movements. Conservative groups also supported a born-again evangelical leader in Guatemala, Efrain Rios Montt, who was responsible for the murders of thousands of Guatemalans.

The most important feature of this confluence of different conservative interests was its ability to bring religion together with corporate interests, where a secular message was carefully crafted in ways that made it practically indistinguishable from the absolutist religious one. This was made possible by the open turn to the reconstruction of culture, with culture seen as the most powerful tool with which to mediate the direct imposition of power, translating global military force into economic theory and mediating it through the mythology of the traditional family. While the reconstruction of U.S. domestic culture seemed to be simply an internal U.S. matter, it was in fact part of a much wider agenda, for the emphasis on the traditional family simultaneously legitimated the imperialism of multinational capital as a universal truth expressed by God's natural law. In fact, as many of its adherents, including, in particular, the Catholic moral philosopher Michael Novak, claim, the multinational corporation proves to be the privileged carrier of the truth of God's law. Not only does this argument divinely legitimate the corporation, but it also demands the political will to build cultural institutions whose disciplined citizens will ensure domestic tranquillity and the expansion of multinational capitalism across the globe.

Before turning to the details of Novak's argument in order to describe the way imperialism has been recoded as Christian duty, it is important to reemphasize the symbolic logic of these powerfully emotional right-wing arguments, which brilliantly link the personal space of the traditional family and religious faith to the global imperative to spread multinational capitalism. In a form of cultural literalism, culture must be constructed in such a way that it will match the "real." That is, reality can only be understood — we can only "see reality true," as Novak will advise us — if it is interpreted according to the general religious framework of conservative Judeo-Christianity and the Ten Commandments. This version of natural law thus has an important, inverse relation to what the Left has called imperialism. Because, in the traditionalist conservative narrative, the end of history has proven that capitalism and the traditional family are inherent in reality itself, the critique of "imperialism," as the Left had defined it, was made essentially irrelevant. Or rather, what had been called imperialism was redefined as a *good* thing mandated by God. Corporate activity and the export of U.S. culture are now overtly and without apology defined as the highest expression of God's will, the missionary extension of his culture to the rest of the globe.

This turn to the reconstruction of culture, as we have seen, is evidence of the Right's recognition of culture's power, of its understanding that ideological arguments are far too abstract to move people, that collective fantasies and the passions they generate have much more to do with what matters in people's lives. Countering the seductiveness of these "natural" feelings is one of the most formidable projects for critics of traditionalist conservatism, for those arguments about what is natural make the quintessential contemporary imperialist strategy strikingly clear—it has to do with the construction and export of the real. As Fredric Jameson argues, "the most crucial terrain of ideological struggle in our time" is the claim that "the market is in human nature," a claim that is inseparably linked in religious economic conservatism with absolutist claims about proper sexual identity and behavior.[3] That construction of reality makes a determined and relentless move through the space of a constructed familiarity grounded in a symbolic traditional nuclear family, or what Kaja Silverman calls the "dominant fiction." This dominant symbolic frame or resonating image offers not only "the representation system by means of which the subject typically assumes sexual identity . . . but forms the stable core around which a nation's and a period's reality cohere." (41) A phantasmatic Imaginary subjects people by providing the filter of hegemony, of a belief in "reality": "The collectivities of community, town and nation have all traditionally defined themselves in relation to the family" (42), and even more, in relation to a constructed *belief* in a certain kind of family.

Not surprisingly in this collective fantasy, in which the natural is collapsed into the economic to produce what comes to stand for reality in popular culture, advertising too is engaged. A Liz Claiborne magazine ad for Realities perfume provides an example of how clearly—and, paradoxically, opaquely—the two fundamentalisms, economic and the "natural familiar," are joined. The ad consists of a black-and-white photo on tastefully heavy white paper that mimics an actual family photograph. We as viewers might have snapped the picture. In the photo is a very contented heterosexual white couple, she in the tub, he perched on a tiny chair while the baby, naked except for tiny socks, stands by the tub peeking over the side. Both parents are lovingly focused on the baby's reaction. The bathroom appears to be in a fashionable, tastefully understated but comfortable single-family home, and the couple's relaxed pose suggests that this family ritual is an everyday part of their yuppie/traditional family lifestyle. The father, dressed casually in jeans, leans over in an almost motherly way to catch the baby's reactions. The photo suggests a completely unhurried life, marked by the signs of an egalitarian sharing of parental duties. It even suggests gender ambiguity made acceptable because of its safe location within this frame; looking very boyish and more like a house husband while the wife looks like a career woman, the man sports a haircut that is noticeably longer than her short, stylish one. Under the picture is a caption whose implications will be made clearer in this chapter, a caption whose concision makes "literal" what we are expected to accept as reality. Bringing economy and the "natural" family together, while collapsing those two systems into one and sealing them with the passionate, unquestioned emotions of familiarity, its certainty and sensuality assure us of its simple clarity: "Reality is the best fantasy of all."

ii.

One story of this export of American reality to the rest of the world, Latin America in particular, is that of Michael Novak, who holds the George Frederick Jewett Chair in Religion, Philosophy, and Public Policy at the American Enterprise Institute, where he is also director of social and political studies. The AEI's Internet home page describes its research focus:

> AEI policy research combines intellectual rigor, practicality, and deep appreciation of the virtues of private markets and limited government. Its scholars appear every day in the leading national newspapers and on television public affairs programs, testify frequently before Congress, and speak regularly at academic, business, and professional gatherings throughout the country. AEI scholars are cited and reprinted in the national media far more often than those of any other policy research institute.[4]

Authors and commentators whose work has appeared under the auspices of AEI include Irving Kristol, Charles Murray, Richard Perle, Lynn Cheney, Jeane Kirkpatrick, Richard John Neuhaus, Peter Berger, Ben Wattenberg, Norman Ornstein, William Schneider, Robert Bork, and Dinesh D'Souza, among others.[5]

Novak, in *Toward a Theology of the Corporation* and *This Hemisphere of Liberty: A Philosophy of the Americas,* published by the American Enterprise Institute Press, patiently develops a moral philosophy that reclaims the definition of reality from Marxism and, in particular, liberation theology, and its focus on the exploitation of laborers and resources. In part, he draws on a series of encyclicals by Pope John Paul II on benevolent free-market capitalism and in opposition to liberation theology. He addresses the pope's criticisms of the brutalities of the market by providing a moral identity for the corporation. His argument also attempts to distinguish his own revalorization of the corporation from what he calls radical capitalism, or individualistic capitalism motivated only by individual will and not held in check by a "strong juridical framework . . . and ethical and religious norms."[6]

This Hemisphere of Liberty consists of a series of lectures given in Latin America, several of which were also translated and published there, most in *Estudios Publicos* in Chile. In the acknowledgments, Novak dedicates his book to those in Latin America "who have invited me to lecture . . . and directed my eyes toward our common destiny." He tells us that the book is part of an ongoing project to build cultural bridges between North and South America, which have already been naturally tied together by geography and the Creator. Such cultural bridges might help bring together "those who think in Latin and Catholic terms and those whose cultural context is rather more Anglo-Saxon and Protestant." (*THL* 6) This project is to be carried out in the interests of liberty, which is "the true destiny of this hemisphere, and through it, of the world." (6)

Novak's immersion in the American mythology of popular culture shows up early, and not too far behind is the iconography of the North American West and its frontier mythology. For Novak sees this hemisphere as the pioneer hemisphere, its model of liberty far surpassing that of Europe because it is based on the concept of the individual's liberty to create wealth. Because that concept was outside the experience of both aristocratic European intellectuals and socialist thinkers, they were unable to conceptualize it as they framed their notions of liberty. Key to their inability to understand this new commercial political system was the fact that they were unable to notice and describe the historically unique and innovative form of the corporation.

In Novak's telling, the story of imperialism is turned on its head; Hegel is back upright, and Marx flipped over. Now, rather than revealing a long history of the destruction of native peoples and the natural environment, the story of the expansion of North America's sphere of influence and in particular the release of the full energy of corporate and entrepreneurial activity recasts that expansion to present it in its "true" light, uncluttered by multicultural revision. Because, in Novak's view, the further expansion of the entrepreneurial corporate economy provides our only chance to save the globe from poverty and the violence of tribalism, that moral imperative allows Novak to clothe his economic project in religion. This version of the market is, in fact, the *only* hope for good.

Like all arguments, of course, this one ultimately rests on belief (which in many ways precedes the facts used to justify it, an argument to be developed more fully later). Another version of the free-market economy, for example, is told by Eric Hobsbawm, who describes the economic circumstances at the end of the twentieth century, in which broad parts of the world and various segments within the First World have simply been discarded by the global economy as "economically uninteresting and irrelevant." As he says, "the belief, following neoclassical economics, that unrestrained international trade would allow the poorer countries to come close to the rich, runs counter to historical experience as well as common sense."[7]

But Novak's powerful rhetoric, which casts the free-market imperative in moral terms, makes it not only possible but necessary to ignore the kinds of contradictory historical evidence Hobsbawm provides. In fact, Novak's argument is an example of a feature that shows up often in contemporary traditionalist conservative rhetoric: a kind of postmodern reverse mirroring. That is, the same words, like "liberation" here, come to mean opposite things to Left and Right. Novak is interested in "liberating" Latin America from poverty by means of a North/South version of trickle-down economics, even though he adamantly resists that label. He describes it in terms that are almost Freireian: empowerment of the grass roots. But in this dizzying if increasingly familiar description of a world in which up is down and down is up, making grassroots economic empowerment possible requires releasing economic energy at the top.

The entrepreneur, like the corporation itself, fits smoothly into Novak's moral schema because of the admirable simplicity the metaphor of the entrepreneur provides for Novak's logic: he is the simple vehicle for the expression of the Logos of God. In setting up the homology between entrepreneur and God, Novak reminds us that the essence of God is his identity as Creator. If we ask ourselves what an entrepreneur does, it is obvious that his activity, too, is defined by creation—the creation of wealth. Thus within natural law and the culture that expresses that law, entrepreneur and corporation prove to have been created in the very image of God. In fact, the corporate structure is even characterized by seven signs of divine grace ("a suitably sacramental number"). If we come to an appropriate understanding of those signs of grace, he tells us, we will gain insight into "God's ways in history," of which two are especially important. The first is, of course, creativity: The corporation's "creativity mirrors God's. That is the standard by which its deeds and misdeeds are properly judged." And the second is liberty, which "unleash[es] economic activism."[8] The radical simplicity with which Novak joins together traditionalist religion and the economy is breathtaking, for with God as the model for the corporation, he can easily and clearly make the logical claim that the unregulated free market is now part of a divine mandate.

Having thoroughly recast the concept of enterprise to give the literal match between economy and religious morality a smoothly reasoned rationale, Novak proves that he does not hold a chair at the American Enterprise Institute for nothing. With power relations now entirely erased from this neat symbolic structure, along with the fact that corporations are not democratically controlled, the individuality of the common man has been made structurally equivalent to the individuality of the corporation as person. This is a phenomenon that has become all the more pronounced in the United States with the decline of political parties, as corporations have become the mediating institutions of North American politics. In his discussion of the concept of corporate individuality, William Greider argues that for generations, the ongoing project for corporate lawyers has been to establish the full citizenship of corporate business entities. He refers to the origins of such a definition in an 1886 Supreme Court decision, which declared that

> corporations would henceforth be considered "persons" for purposes of the Fourteenth Amendment — the "due process" amendment that was established to protect the newly emancipated black slaves after the Civil War. Fifty years later, Justice Hugo Black reviewed the Supreme Court's many decisions applying the Fourteenth Amendment and observed that less than one half of one percent invoked it in protection of the Negro race, and more than 50 percent asked that its benefits be extended to corporations.[9]

The slippage from one kind of "person" to another provides the basis for one of the most powerful features of the corporation: its ability to exploit not only the religious rhetoric of natural law but the populist rhetoric of the common man who feels himself to be oppressed by government and burdened by taxes. For now, as a "person," the corporation, too, can patriotically draw on the language of plain folks Americanism to claim to be oppressed by government and burdened by taxes. This use of U.S. national mythologies of the individual is, of course, particularly hollow and even phobic because of the fact that multinational corporations can no longer even be called American.

Novak's intellectual trajectory here is similar to that of other traditionalist conservatives, as he revalorizes Adam Smith and dispenses with Marx. As Novak reminds us, Adam Smith described enterprise as "the cause of the wealth of nations" and "foresaw a world united by commerce, as neither religion nor military power nor political imperium could unite it." (*THL* 12) In this logic, in which layers are collapsed into each other, commercial self-interest comes to equal civic interest, with civic interest defined as the development of capitalist society: "To love such a system was, in a way, to love themselves." (*THL* 13)

The requirement that North Americans love themselves because of the moral validity of their economic interests is accompanied by a reminder of the uniqueness of North America; it is the land of the chosen people. In a predictable move, Novak turns to de Tocqueville, who, he tells us, described the United States as a nation that "alerted Europe to a new tide in human history, a tide deep and wide and directed by Providence, that would soon, or eventually, sweep the whole world." (*THL* 20) The energy for that sweep would, of course, come from the "moral virtue of enterprise," the free and voluntary nature of commercial organization, in particular the corporation, the radically original and productive innovation of this dynamic new type of nation. (*THL* 25)

The corporation is fundamentally connected to the very soul of this nation, liberty. But this is not the liberty conceptualized by anticapitalist intellectuals and theologians, who missed its true essence, but the liberty to create wealth, and even more, the moral obligation to do so:

> If no one can create wealth, then poverty is simply a fact, but if a society knows how to create wealth, then poverty is immoral. Second, the cause of the wealth of nations is the human mind. . . . Thus economics is both a moral art and a social art, addressing the proper and just arrangements of social institutions, oriented toward maximizing personal economic creativity, for the sake of the common economic whole. (*THL* 26)

It was academic specialization, in which a science of economics severed economics from its proper place in moral philosophy, that caused the loss of Adam Smith's simple, coherent notion of economy and morality, Novak argues.[10] Moral subjectivity, the relation between the definition of the human being and the natural law of God, is thus the very ground of enterprise: "Clearly, the exercise of personal economic enterprise is close to the moral center of the human person." (*THL* 29)

This economic system can slip smoothly into the framework of things

Catholics already believe, but it also shares something with the postmillennial apocalyptic narratives of people like Pat Robertson — that is, it provides an "incarnational ethical strategy" for "living well-ordered lives within history." (*THL* 65) One does not simply have to await the Second Coming, as earlier Christians were wont to do as they retreated from the world into prayer; hampered by that otherworldliness, those Christians left the most important matters of culture to others. Catholics now, Novak advises, should learn from the Jewish people, who were able to take part in history at the same time they awaited the Messiah. Through this incarnational ethical strategy Novak also attempts to reclaim Catholic social teaching from the concept of human rights advocated by liberation theology by redefining human rights in the terms he finds to be inherently grounded in the Logos of Jesus Christ: "the personal economic initiative is a fundamental human right [and] to exercise that right is to fulfill the image of God inherent in every man and woman." (*THL* 33)

Having laid out the connection between ethics, Christ, and the "intellectual and moral virtue" of enterprise, Novak turns, as most traditionalist conservatives do, directly to culture: "Instruction in the virtue of enterprise consists, too, in alertness to social obstacles to enterprise." (*THL* 33) The very survival of this nation and the health of the nations of Latin America, in fact, depend on such instruction:

> Whoever favors the right of personal enterprise must take responsibility for surrounding it with a political system and a moral-cultural system that allow it to flourish.
>
> This is the fundamental reason that economists must not be concerned solely with economics and that men and women of business must not be concerned solely with business. Every economic system depends on the political system and the moral system within which it is embodied. Therefore persons in business must take responsibility for politics and for the moral-cultural system. Not to do so would be suicidal. (*THL* 94)

Carrying out that instruction, reconstituting the social order in which human beings will be able to "see reality true," (*THL* 7) can take place only by means of a system of capitalist institutions designed "to liberate the creativity of the human mind. It is a mind-centered system." (*THL* 44) The poor can be helped only if the attempt to do so is not based on questions of materiality and labor but on ideas. The new Catholic social teaching must discount what Novak calls the nineteenth-century Marxist nostalgia, in which it was labor that was seen as the source of value. He argues that it is the entrepreneurial creativity of mind, not labor, that gives the human being its "historical fertility." (*THL* 44) Capitalism is thus not defined, as we might have expected, by the resources of capital but by the resources of economic liberty: "Only if we can make an affirmative theological judgment about democratic capitalism can we develop a plausible theology of the lay world and a theology of work." (*TTC* 31)

The most humanitarian act of all is thus to allow all, especially the poor, to "exercise their God-given 'right to personal and economic initiative,' to become in fact what they have been created to become, namely, creative." (*THL* 45) Novak reverses the analysis of poverty in Latin America to argue, not that the North has played a fundamental role in producing that poverty, but that it has provided the very model which will help cure it. And it has done so through the "civilizing practices of markets." (78) In fact, in a way that equates market exchange with language, he argues that God made nations diverse and unequal so that each would have to make up for its own lacks by trading.

But nations can do this only if enterprise, in its expanded moral and creative capacity, is left unfettered. The liberal intellectuals of the "new class" in the United States, the workers in the knowledge industry, those who argue for welfare-state solutions to poverty, have simply used the poor as "a rhetorical instrument of [their] own power," and in their own interests, they have favored "a 'managed' poor, rather than a self-sufficient independent poor." But there is no other road to helping the poor than the passage he advocates through culture, by means of the export of the reality of natural law:

> It is crucial, therefore, to understand that human capital includes moral capital, as well as intellectual: skills of the human heart, as well as skills of hand. In economic life, as everywhere else in human life, the primacy of morals is a fundamental, demonstrable law of human prosperity. The primacy of morals is an empirical, as well as a philosophical, principle. (*THL* 34–35)

In another reverse mirroring, Novak has now arrived at his real advice to those who think of themselves as ethical, moral, and deeply concerned about poverty in Latin America: they can only help by producing wealth. Within the context of North/South relations, it is the very concept of humanitarian ethics that now requires that corporate activity be supported, which means freeing corporations from regulation: "The sources of poverty may be as much in nature and in culture as in economic structures. If the Kingdom of God in this world demands the elimination of poverty, it may also impose correlative demands on the production of wealth." (*TTC* 14)[11] The production of corporate wealth has become the very source of goodness itself:

> Not only is it possible for an economic system to be suffused with moral purpose and religious belief, Max Weber argued that democratic capitalism is distinct from other commercial systems in the world *because of* the religious and moral value it attaches to commerce. It is one thing to tolerate commerce and to regard it as a vulgar necessity. It is another to regard it as the fulfillment of a vocation from God and a way of cooperating in the completion of Creation as God intended it. (*TTC* 38)

American businesses abroad do not represent simply an economic system but also a political and a moral-cultural system. "They are, willy-nilly, agents of democratic capitalism, not of free enterprise alone. Moreover, unless they succeed in establishing on foreign soil at least some of the political culture and some of the moral culture in which alone democratic capitalism can be incarnated, they are doomed to lose spiritual legitimacy." (*TTC* 36) Though he acknowledges that one must be aware of accusations of imperialism, that concern is overridden by the moral imperative involved; he reminds businessmen of their moral duty to alleviate poverty — on his terms:

> Direct political interference on the part of American enterprises abroad would be fiercely, and properly, resisted. So would a sort of tacit moral-cultural imperialism. Yet the international war of ideas cannot be evaded. . . . No person of conscience can remain indifferent to hunger and poverty. The great intellectual and moral argument of our time is not whether we should do all we can to raise the material wealth of all nations but what we ought to do and how. The greatest irresponsibility of all would be to pretend we know nothing about how to produce wealth, or that the knowledge was not implanted on this earth by the Maker of all things, so that His creatures, by trial and error, would in due course discover it. (*TTC* 36)

Thus Novak has laid out what he considers to be a true hermeneutic, not a relativist one. If one interprets the world and God's will correctly, eventually the true form of human nature will be uncovered, and it will be determined by the absolute idea implanted by the Maker on this earth. The Maker's natural law surprisingly even proves to have something to say about the welfare state: "I advise intelligent, ambitious, and morally serious young Christians and Jews to awaken to the growing dangers of statism. They will better save their souls and serve the cause of the Kingdom of God all around the world by restoring the liberty and power of the private sector than by working for the state." (*TTC* 34)

Weaving together moral responsibilities with the responsibility to support the creation of wealth, the natural resource of democracy and liberty, Novak has described the most important role of culture, by which the feelings of familiarity can be seen as *secondary* to the truth of natural law: "To be happy, one should not take feelings as one's guide; on the contrary, one should set one's moral compass to acting with integrity and train one's feelings to delight in that: first the substance of the act, then the feelings." (*THL* 25) Cultural training must ensure that the "natural" choices of people of integrity will be rationally chosen by means of individual discernment and moral deliberation, not simply because of one's emotions. Of course, the cultural training he advocates, the cultural training that defines religion in general, will already have produced the feelings which precede the discernment and the substance of the act. They will, in fact, be the gauge by which to assess, out of many possible choices, the "true" moral answer.

In a curious way, many analysts on both left and right have been influenced by Blaise Pascal, the Jansenist theologian who has been influential for traditionalist conservatives, even if only anecdotally, and for leftist analysts by way of the work of Louis Althusser. Pascal described the way our interior reasoning is determined by the network of symbols, language, and meaning within which we live, a symbolic universe into which we are born which "writes" our internal language. This suggests why Beverly LaHaye and Ralph Reed have turned to Pascal, who understood that cultural training must precede political reasoning. As Slavoj Žižek quotes Pascal,

> we must make no mistake about ourselves: we are as much automaton as mind. . . . Proofs only convince the mind; habit provides the strongest proofs and those that are most believed. It inclines the automaton, which leads the mind unconsciously along with it.[12]

For both Pascal and cultural training of any kind, reasoning has already been written in the body, which is crucial to the experience of belief, where "reasons reveal themselves only to those who already believe — we find reasons attesting our belief because we already believe; we do not believe because we have found sufficient reasons to believe." (319) Belief is thus secondary to training and ritual, as Pascal argued: "Leave rational argumentation and submit yourself to ideological ritual . . . *as if* you already believe, and the belief will come by itself." (Žižek 320) Within such a configuration, conversion is "a formal act by means of which we recognize what we have already believed." (321) It is the "belief before belief." (321) In this respect, it is no wonder Novak is fighting a cultural war, for belief must be taught before it is thought — so that, in fact, it can be thought. And for Novak what is to be thought depends on a reconstituted social order that will let us "see reality true." (*THL* 7)

iii.

While Novak has been absolutely clear about the need to revise Catholic social teaching in terms of political economy, another influential attempt to reconstruct reality comes from Pat Robertson, whose Christian Coalition's numbers and political impact were strengthened when Ralph Reed Jr. developed a strategy of "casting a wider net" to link evangelical Protestants with conservative Roman Catholics, Jews, and minorities. The linkage between Catholics and evangelical Protestants has at times been a very tense one, made evident at the time of an agreement between Cardinal O'Connor and Pat Robertson about a pro-life and traditional-values political agenda. Yet while Catholics and evangelical Christians compete for influence both domestically and around the globe, with evangelicals having made serious inroads into formerly Catholic strongholds, Novak and Robertson share a deep affinity in terms of the export of reality. The cultural mandates advocated by Novak can be traced, in a specifically fundamentalist Protestant form, through a turn to Pat Robertson's instructions in the virtue of enterprise grounded in natural law. A very brief examination of the catalog of Robertson's Regent University's graduate program shows how seriously Robertson takes the mandate to reconstruct culture.

Located in Virginia Beach, Regent University, formerly the Christian Broadcasting Network University, includes a graduate school that consists of schools of communication and the arts, business, counseling and human services, divinity, education, government, and law. Regent University is the site of the American Center for Law and Justice, which fights the ACLU on questions of the separation of church and state, drawing on the very latest technological and media resources; its most prominent representative, Jay Sekulow, has argued cases before the Supreme Court as well as various state and federal courts. The ACLJ also funds legal teams to fly into communities where conservative Christians feel they have suffered discrimination on religious grounds. Regent is also the site of the Founders Inn and Conference Center, a Georgian-style luxury resort that provides lodging and offers regular conferences for families and business people, all of these advertised through glossy, state-of-the-art publicity and brochures. A conference aboard a cruise ship, Victory at Sea, was planned for 1996. An ad for the Founders Inn, referred to enigmatically as "the only four-diamond hotel in Virginia Beach," might best introduce the multiple levels on which Robertson joins together God and enterprise, in particular by showing how misguided it is to imagine that traditionalist Christians are all simply poor, unsophisticated hillbillies. The ad features shots of sumptuous rooms, elegant restaurants, expansive gardens, and a beautiful indoor swimming pool. Its text, like the Liz Claiborne ad, claims a literal link between culture and reality. Here God and the dollar are joined in a remarkably unselfconscious way: "Once you experience our grand hotel, you'll be a believer."[13]

As the chancellor of Regent University, Robertson sets the tone for the graduate catalog by setting forth the school's mission:

> Our nation and our world are faced with tremendous challenges — challenges that sometimes can seem insurmountable. But know this, the plans of God will not be thwarted! God is doing remarkable things through those who desire to serve Him. This is why I founded Regent University — to provide you with a place to sharpen your skills and prepare you to help transform the world through Christian leadership.[14]

Of particular importance to the project of transforming the world, as the program of the College of Communication and the Arts shows, is Robertson's understanding of the power of media culture:

> Two of the most powerful mind-molders of today's society are the mass media and the arts. Societal values, beliefs and behaviors are greatly affected by both the personal and mediated communication of individuals from diverse social, political, professional and religious groups. . . . The College of Communication and the Arts is

committed to creating a "think-tank" environment for aspiring communication scholars and experienced faculty who seek to understand human communication with biblical wisdom and perspective. (41)

Courses offered in this school include Theology and Communication, Doctoral Seminar in Rhetorical Studies, Doctoral Seminar in Political Communication, and Doctoral Seminar in Media Effects/Studies. The School of Radio, Television, and Film is "dedicated to fulfilling the need for leaders with a biblically based perspective in the mass media." (45) Its course offerings include "recent semiotic and post-modernist critical perspectives" as well as Religious Broadcasting, International Radio, The Business of Interactive Media, Television Advertising: Theory and Production, Advanced Motion Picture Production, and Introduction to Multimedia. The Institute of the Performing Arts has as its mission "to be a beacon in reclaiming the performing arts for the glory of God." (47) It offers such courses as Writing Christian Drama for Stage and Screen and Advanced Camera Acting.

The framing mission of the university is to bring religion and culture together, as Novak advocates, and the School of Business's statement tells us that it participates fully "in Regent University's vision to transform society through Christian leadership. For us, that vision means preparing men and women to build dynamic organizations that provide life-improving products and services in a way that points to the life-giver, Jesus Christ." (59) One track, of special relevance to the missionary export of Christian enterprise, is called Entrepreneurial Tentmaking, which is "designed to prepare men and women to start businesses in other cultures that have the potential to revolutionize nations economically and provide platforms for spiritual revival," particularly "in an era when many nations are closed to traditional missionary outreach." (61) Another track is Media Management:

> It appears critical that committed Christians increase their penetration into the management of the nation's and the world's media. . . . This track is to prepare students to assume key management positions in TV and radio, production houses, print media, and public relations agencies. (63)

The Nonprofit Management track, "grounded in Regent University's mission of preparing the way for a day when 'the glory of the Lord will cover the earth as the waters cover the sea'" (62), teaches skills of leadership and management within nonprofit organizations. Missions Management prepares students for roles in churches and agencies engaged in mission work in both the United States and abroad. These courses specialize in "topics relevant to the field of work evangelization and global outreach" (64) and prepare students to "think and act strategically in planning and implementing programs that contribute to completing the great commission," or preparing the world for the return of Christ. This Missions track, with its "professional education, training, and empowerment of the Holy Spirit for Global Evangelization (Missiology)," trains mission leaders for evangelism and leadership in cross-cultural contexts in order to impact "all levels of world cultures and societies with the truth and power of the gospel." (80)

Of particular importance to the focus of this chapter is the Robertson School of Government, which offers interdisciplinary training in law, history, natural science, government, economics, and international affairs. Its interdisciplinarity rests on natural law, which is "ordained both for nature and for human society." (117) The theocratic nature of these courses is obvious, with all the dangers implied by that term, for here those who are training for careers in government service in the public sector are also being trained "to implement biblical worldview principles in current affairs with political effectiveness." (116) The religious frame of the School of Government firmly reinforces the structure of clarity discussed in earlier chapters, as it "seeks to equip men and women with a biblical foundation, a Christ-centered framework, and Spirit-infused skills for government service and public policy impact." (116) Its broad goal is

> to study public affairs in a unique way—integrating biblical principles from law, history, natural science, government, and economics in studies of public policy and government. . . . The United States of America is a nation founded upon biblical principles. Our founders espoused biblical views, and our founding documents reflect this influence. . . . It is the goal of the Robertson School of Government that this heritage be restored, renewed and enhanced in America, and that this heritage also be planted and nurtured in other nations. All areas of human endeavor need Christian influence and witness; the various fields of government service are presently in particular need of Christian influence. Ultimately, in every nation, the future well-being and perhaps the survival of freedom and democracy de-

pend upon enlarged Christian participation in public affairs. . . . A righteous foundation in every nation is critical to individual and societal well-being. (115)

Theocracy, the literal match between public policy and the divine mandate to assert Christian dominion across the globe, is the very ground of this institution, whose aim is to "discover the principles of government and establish the practice of public policy upon a foundation of truth revealed by God in nature and in the Holy Scriptures." (116) The mandate does not stop with providing instruction but extends to finding graduates leadership positions within government both in the United States and around the world. Students in this program, says the catalog, "are characterized by their strong commitment to the Bible as the Word of God, and a strong commitment to restoring government to biblical principles, in order that it may fully protect inalienable rights and properly facilitate the good in society." (116) To that end, students are also given instruction in multiculturalism as seen through the lens of evangelicalism. Courses include Cultural Anthropology (from the Christian perspective); Latin American Political Culture; Hemispheric Integration; Inalienable Rights and Liberties, which includes the biblical perspective on inalienable rights; Foundations of Natural Science; Race, Sex, and Politics; New International Economic Order; and Computer Modeling.

Finally, the political danger suggested by the literal collapse of the public sphere into the double fundamentalism of God and the dollar represented in Regent's catalog finds its most stark illustration in the mission statement of the School of Law, whose goal is "to build a course of study upon God's revelation in the Bible and in the natural world," a version of legal interpretation that presupposes that "God, the Creator of the universe, impressed upon His creation an objective legal order that man is bound to obey." Cultivating a "healthy fear of God," its purpose is to nurture and encourage "law students, practicing lawyers, judges, legislators, government officials, educators, and others to recognize and to seek the biblical foundations of law. . . ." (128)

iv.

The mission statements and course descriptions from Regent's catalog rest on a clear and passionate set of homologies whose symmetry must be held together by cultural institutions that will enforce the match between reality and (this) God's intentions. The clarity and passion to be gained by such a symmetrical, all-embracing view of the cosmos are obvious, as Novak's moral philosophy shows. Both Regent University and Novak's moral philosophy make clear the effectiveness of the tidy fit between market fundamentalism and religious fundamentalism, where natural law provides a unifying umbrella that can often smooth out the contradictions between social and economic conservatives by means of passion.

Fredric Jameson has described this match between market and morals as a form of "'politics' [that] now means simply the care and feeding of the economic apparatus (in this case the market rather than the collectively-owned and organized means of production)." (283) It may be that because the languages of Left and Right have collapsed into reverse mirror images of each other that, as Jameson says, we have everything in common, "save the essentials." (283) Yet while it is helpful to frame traditionalist conservatism in this way, what Jameson's critique misses may point to the element a progressive analysis must address, the element with which this book has been concerned. And that element is signaled by the most opaque, if most important, word in that sentence: "simply." For if Novak's moral philosophy and Robertson's graduate-school catalog have anything to teach us, it is that the cultural work of reconstructing the passions and emotions is precisely where political belief is formed, where the collapse of absolutist religion into politics occurs — in those places where things are felt before they are thought or believed.

In one sense, Novak's moral philosophy, Robertson's missiology, history, and law *are* "simply the care and feeding of the economic apparatus." And yet in another sense, that care and feeding has been achieved, not only at the level of the public sphere, though it works there too, but at the most intimate and sensual levels of the domestic one. Novak's and Robertson's reality depends, at the most fundamental, unspoken level, on the cultural work of modern traditional women discussed earlier, their centrality the very bedrock of traditionalist logic. But Jameson's sentence rushes past the work that concerns the feelings of intimate familiarity on the terms of natural law. That work is missed, even though his choice of the domestic terminology, "care and feeding," symptomatically acknowledges it. At the very heart of this version of natural law, upon which an entire political structure is built, is the requirement that women be kept precisely where they can make it all possible.

Though that profoundly ambiguous word "simply" flies past far too quickly in Jameson's sentence, it is, like the role of proper women, at the heart of this ambitious, global missionary project. What a close study of these right-wing texts may teach critics of traditionalist conservatism is to go through, not around, questions of both religion and gender. For if those of us working to counter the Right's global intentions don't know that imperialism rests on feelings, as well as on ideology and economics, if we don't understand that the political is profoundly sensual — that, like religion and family feelings, it has to be felt before it is thought — both Novak and Robertson do.

EIGHT

Warriors and Babies

When a scription on the limits of identity comes face to face with abjection, it enters into competition with biblical abominations and even more so with prophetic discourse. — Julia Kristeva

Sometimes I give myself the creeps. — Green Day

The contemporary revision of America's story that attempts to correct the history of the last thirty-five years has tried to reconstruct man as warrior, and that reconstruction not only has handicapped the development of a populist movement that does not succumb to supremacist nativism or anti-Semitic conspiracy theories, but also has made it very difficult to deal with the legacy of another traumatic event in American history: the Vietnam War. This final chapter will return to the rhetoric of man as warrior in several ways: by following the stories of several elite Vietnam veterans; by examining an important recent study of warrior films, pulp novels, and combat games; and by analyzing the rhetoric of threatened masculinity in the work of a far-right Christian conspiracy theorist. The final section of this chapter will then return to the role of traditionalist conservative women in this reconstruction by following the story of a young pro-life activist who survived her mother's attempt to abort her. The two strands of the book, the reconstruction of motherhood and the reconstruction of masculinity, will come together in the issue of abortion.

My discussion of the popular discourses of masculinity with which the chapter begins is motivated in part by Eric L. Santner's study of memory in contemporary Germany, in which he describes both the historical necessity as well as the costs of giving up concepts of identity that have proved to be so destructive. If the forms of American masculinity are to be changed, a long process of working through change will be required. And specifically in relation to this consideration of American warrior masculinity, Santner's turn to the work of the German novelist Christa Wolf is useful. Wolf writes, "Perhaps there should be at least an intimation of the difficulties in matters of 'compassion' also regarding compassion toward one's person, the difficulties experienced by a person who was forced as a child to turn compassion for the weak and the losers into hate and anxiety."[1]

Resisting the changes in masculinity has been the project of the conservatives in earlier chapters, but one writer who neither is a traditionalist conservative nor resists these changes in general nevertheless ends up reconstructing warrior masculinity almost in spite of himself. This is Robert Timberg, whose study of elite warriors, *The Nightingale's Song,* tells the stories of John McCain, Robert McFarlane, James Webb, Oliver North, and John Poindexter, all of whom graduated from Annapolis, served in Vietnam, and made it to the highest levels of Republican politics. Timberg also is a graduate of Annapolis and a Vietnam veteran, and is currently deputy chief of the *Baltimore Sun*'s Washington bureau. In this book he shows how the lingering effects of Vietnam continue to lock American political discourse into a binary opposition between warriors and everybody else.[2]

Timberg argues that Vietnam, because it shattered the belief in good wars inherited from World War II, "bruised American society like nothing else in this century."[3] He quotes Lance Morrow:

> Nineteen sixty-eight was a knife blade that severed past from future, Then from Now: the Then of triumphant postwar American power, the Then of the nation's illusions of innocence and virtue, from the more complicated Now that began when the U.S. saw it was losing a war it should not have been fighting in the first place, when the huge tribe of the young revolted against the nation's elders and authority, and when the nation finished killing its heroes. (140)

The war was accompanied by fears aroused by an almost apocalyptic sense of social change that threatened to rupture the American imagination: in the summer of 1965 Watts burned; in 1968 Martin Luther King and Robert Kennedy were assassinated and other cities burned; Lyndon Johnson announced he would not seek reelection in the face of the widespread, often violent protests against the war; many people also faced the deaths of their sons and friends in Vietnam. While the focus of this chapter is on the chasms in the identities of military men and those who wished they had been, the assassinations also show what other definitions of America were shattered.

Timberg begins by focusing on the pain felt by returning veterans, arguing that antiwar protestors made a strategic error by not understanding the complexities of those who had served, "as if by a simple act of labeling they could transform them into beings different from and less worthy than themselves, with less reason to live." (90) And as has been true all along in this painful, dangerous binary logic, Right and Left continue to provide reverse images of each other. Here both sides passionately claim the mantle of populism. John McCain, one of the most reasonable, nonjudgmental observers of Vietnam even after having spent years in a North Vietnam POW camp, does not express anger at the choice many people made to protest an unjust war, as Timberg himself does, but argues that he fought for their right to do so. What McCain does condemn, however, is the injustice of the class privilege that saved some people but not others from a war they did not believe in. McCain reminds us that "those who were better off economically did not carry out their obligations, so we forced the Hispanic, the ghetto black and the Appalachian white to fight and die. That to me was the greatest crime and injustice of the Vietnam War." (235) Or as Timberg says, McCain's anger was directed toward "a system that put the burden of service on the poor and the powerless, then through mismanagement, duplicity and political cowardice allowed nearly sixty thousand young men to die for vaporous national goals." (234)

James Webb, former secretary of the Navy, expresses similar anger, but his populist sympathy nevertheless remythologizes the warrior in a series of Vietnam novels, which Timberg describes this way:

> Many of the veterans [depicted in these novels] are not in Vietnam to save the world for democracy. Most are simply unlucky. . . . They do not come from privileged homes so they never knew they could beat the draft. Not that many of them would have chosen that course had they known about it. They are throwbacks to earlier days, when young men joined the service because they understood, however vaguely, that it was expected of them, especially in wartime, consciousness-raising not yet having trickled down to the poor and uneducated, both black and white, the ones who fought and died in Vietnam. (227)

The more privileged Annapolis graduates, like Webb and McCain, speak in the interests of those who know that they are at the "end of the line. That no one cares. They know." (Webb quoted in Timberg 227)

The Vietnam divide was also the occasion for the construction of another internal postmodern frontier whose authenticity could be opposed to the shifting illusions of culture. This came in the form of military training at Annapolis for the elite men of Timberg's study, where reality was constructed by means of intense initiation rituals, rigorous physical challenges, and male bonding. That belief in the military and in masculine identity became more real than the reality of an America unsettled by struggle and contradictions: "The price was high: your youth, at times it seemed your soul, for a slogan—duty, honor, country." (24) And while these idealistic young men were taught that more was expected of them than of other men, they were also taught that they deserved greater recognition for their service. Timberg cites Ron Benigo, another Naval Academy graduate who described midshipmen as "applause-seekers": "I believe we had visions of being someday at that critical moment when what we did would change the course of history." (30)

But Vietnam went unmourned for most veterans: "However painful their individual wartime experiences, they knew they had to put Vietnam in a safe place, let it scab over and get on with their lives." The silence, the inability to work through the experiences of the war, was often made more difficult as veterans found themselves working beside people who had opposed the war or who had avoided the draft, and their resentment was exacerbated by the fact that "those who opposed the war [had] long since been accorded the role of spokesmen for [their] generation." (255) It was not only Democrats, however, who were seen to be hypocrites but Republicans as well. David Stockman and Dan Quayle, for example, avoided the war, as did others who became what Timberg refers to as "chicken hawks," adamant supporters of the Contras, the invasion of Grenada, and the Persian Gulf War, "men whose testosterone gland abruptly began pumping after age twenty-six, when they were no longer vulnerable to the draft." (89)

Many of the men who served in Vietnam "would never see America and many members of their own generation the same way again, especially as they watched their old tormentors and fellow travelers prosper in the aftermath of the war." (91) As a Navy chaplain, Bob Bedingfield, told Timberg, "What it does is dislocate loyalty. It says that I can never believe in the system again. That's now part of the means by which I interpret the world I live in." (91) Another veteran, Milt Copulos, hospitalized for three and a half years and given the last rites seven times, says, "There's a wall ten miles high and fifty miles thick between those of us who went and those who didn't, and that wall is never going to come down." (91)[4] Of course it was not only veterans but also those who opposed the war who learned things about the system that would never allow them to trust it again, but here Timberg, Copulos, and Bedingfield articulate the reactions of the warrior male whose identity provided a metaphor for a nation that was nostalgic for the clarity of World War II. Personal betrayal and a deep sense of national shame were combined, as in Timberg's description of the evacuation of Saigon: "The next day and a half ranks with the most ignominious episodes in the history of the nation." (219)

The sense of national shame took another turn in relation to Ronald Reagan's revalorization of Vietnam in the 1980s. In arguing that Reagan's characterization of Vietnam as a noble cause helped produce even greater cynicism, especially for those who had been trained in unquestioning belief, Timberg uses the analogy of the behavior of nightingales, as described by Barbara Feldon. A nightingale, she says, will not sing unless it has first heard its song from another nightingale: "The moment it hears any part of a nightingale's song, it bursts into this extraordinary music, sophisticated, elaborate music, as though it had known it all the time. And, of course, it had." (quoted in Timberg 16) The song Reagan sang was immediately recognized by veterans: "To the men of the armed forces, he had a single, unvarying theme: I appreciate what you have done. The whole nation does. Wear your uniforms with pride." (17) Though it was a woman, Peggy Noonan, who wrote many of the best lyrics of that song, it was Reagan who seemed to be the real thing, after years of betrayal by politicians and bureaucrats. He was "a politician who stood for something, who insisted the men who fought in Vietnam were deserving of honor. Equally important, he declared that a nation should never send its sons to die in a war it was unwilling to win." (237)

Yet this illusion of reality led to another betrayal of warrior masculinity: "He looked like a President and acted like one, at least in public. The private Reagan—passive, incurious, often befuddled—was the dirty little secret at the heart of his presidency" (285), even if "whatever his other failings, Ronald Reagan always talked a good game." (337) Rage at the discovery of falsity seems to be proportional to the level of authenticity promised at the start, and in Timberg's reading, Reagan's promises of revalorizing the military betrayed the military a second time when Reagan abdicated his responsibility to oversee those working for him. Basically incurious about issues, "he knew what he knew" and stuck to it. (286) His refusal to run his own presidency left the activities of the National Security Council to rogue cowboys who made a mockery of military procedures and national honor, a natural result of the fact that Reagan never mastered the intricacies of issues and depended on advisers to tell him the facts as well as what they meant. Timberg cites David C. Martin and John Wolcott's study of Reagan's participation in the antiterrorism activities of his administration: "Involvement in foreign affairs was episodic, anecdotal, impulsive, and rarely decisive. It was no wonder that the staff of the National Security Council later concluded that the best way to serve Reagan was to do the job for him." (340) The Academy graduates, North, McFarlane, and Poindexter, who took it upon themselves to do what Reagan would not, had updated the warrior song to mean that if something needed to be done, the warriors would have to do it themselves. As Timberg says about the flexibility of the song's lyrics: "At times the lyrics seemed to enter a scrambler once they issued from Reagan's lips, only to emerge in versions that resonated to the individual tastes of the listening audience. Much like Reagan himself, the Nightingale's Song could be anything you wanted it to be." (340)

The ambiguity of Reagan's song about Vietnam was at the heart of his message to veterans: "Not that [Reagan] or the three Naval Academy men who would soon be working for him did not know by then that incompetence, cynicism, and double-dealing had gone into America's failed commitment to South Vietnam." (16) Thus Reagan's acknowledgment of the sacrifices of veterans during the war was true, but that truth was linked to the lie that the war had been noble. While that version of the war functioned as a kind of life preserver for many veterans, most also knew full well it was hollow. And it was a lie that helped prevent a national mourning for those men; the illegitimate revalorization of the war again overshadowed the legitimate recognition of their sacrifices, leaving veterans and those who had opposed the war locked in brittle hostility.

Timberg's book helps explain warrior masculinity by showing how difficult it is to escape the doubleness he criticizes, how difficult it is to refuse to respond to the song he hears even while he tries to come to grips with it. The blurb on the cover, which describes the men of Iran-Contra, reveals the unsettlingly double resonance of the song: "They are secret sharers, men whose experiences at Annapolis and during the Vietnam War and its aftermath illuminate a generation, or a portion of a generation — those who went. They shared a seemingly unassailable certainty. *They believed in America."* The phrase blurs the issue of America's failure by collapsing two things into one: America failed them by sending them to fight a war that was wrong; America failed them by not acknowledging their sacrifices. Like the song, the writer of this blurb exploits the amorphous feelings of personal betrayal over the more abstract anger that the war was fought at all.

Timberg himself is ultimately unable to work through that sense of personal betrayal, because he is still imaginatively locked into warrior masculinity, in spite of his very moving descriptions of the effects of Vietnam on many men. Though he came to hate the war, he finally had to admit to himself that he hated the war's critics even more. As Gilder has already shown, to be bested by a cowardly man and defeated by the weaker, feminized brother puts a warrior male in the most shameful position of all. And even though Timberg despised the duplicity, illegality, and incompetence of the Academy graduates who were involved in Iran-Contra, at a crucial point he is simply unable to respect the complexities he has painstakingly taught us and finds himself standing up for a member of the warrior tribe, Oliver North. North, he relates,

> tried to bring home six Americans who had been held hostage in Leb-anon for periods ranging from several months to several years. . . . Wearing his other hat, he attempted to keep a guerrilla army that was largely a creation of the United States in the field, which meant ensuring that they had beans, boots, Band-Aids, and bullets. Along the way he lied to Congress and may well have defied it, depending on how Boland II is interpreted. . . . Equally important is what he did not do. He did not gas Jews. Not even close. Anyone who does not understand the distinction is a fool. As for those who know the difference and persist in comparing North to a Nazi, one wonders what lies beneath such bluster and rhetorical overkill. Many, one suspects, are running scared, hoping to avoid a long overdue show-down with a part of themselves purposely and deservedly obscured for decades.
>
> Something about which they would just as soon not have to an-swer tasteless questions. (452)

The reader trying to follow Santner's advice about the need to mourn along with men their traumas of lost identity, trying to understand Viet-nam from the point of view of Timberg and of my own brother, a Marine veteran, is simply shut out, because the circle of those who can talk about men's loss has been so narrowly drawn. For while Timberg has already acknowledged that the decision to go to war in Vietnam was the result of cynicism and incompetence, and while he has described Ronald Reagan's ignorance about issues on which he gave absolute, even apocalyptic pronouncements, here, in a moment we might call jammed mourning, he is unable to avoid repeating that same mistake himself. Though he has told us that the country should have evaluated the cynicism and incompetence that led to Vietnam, he has also avoided asking the same kinds of questions in relation to military involvement in Central America. Complexity has dropped out, as his warrior identity lets him pay attention only to his warrior buddy and the sibling rivalry of warriors, civilian technocrats, and male antiwar activists.

What is most troubling about Timberg's loyalty to Oliver North is the exclusivity produced by warrior discussions that leave out many other tasteless questions to be asked about both Vietnam and Nicaragua other than the one about who was a warrior and who was a coward. Those questions have to do with the lives of the Vietnamese and the Central Americans, with whether or not women and pacifists have anything to say about war, with whether or not it is really easier to lose one's child than one's life, and, finally, with the economic interests served by the war. Here, at the most elite level, warrior mythology has blocked Timberg's imagination, leaving him unable to work through this personal trauma and getting in the way of a renewed populism by exclusively restricting its participants to legitimate members of the warrior tribe.

ii.

These Annapolis chosen sons, still bitter at their brothers who did not go to war, became prominent in national politics. At an everyday level, Vietnam also influenced images of the warrior for ordinary men, in what James William Gibson, in *Warrior Dreams: Paramilitary Culture in Post-Vietnam America,* calls the New War culture, a "cultural or imaginary New War going on since the '60's and 1970's":

> The New War culture was not so much military as paramilitary. The new warrior hero was only occasionally portrayed as a member of a conventional military or law enforcement unit; typically, he fought alone or with a small, elite group of fellow warriors. Moreover, by

separating the warrior from his traditional state-sanctioned occupations — policeman or soldier — the New War culture presented the warrior role as the ideal identity for *all* men. Bankers, professors, factory workers, and postal clerks could all transcend their regular stations in life and prepare for heroic battle against the enemies of society.[5]

Gibson traces the New War shift in movies, from around 1971, when Clint Eastwood moved from *Rawhide* to *Dirty Harry,* to 1974, when Charles Bronson appeared in *Death Wish,* to the 1980s, when Rambo, the soldier betrayed by bureaucrats, asked, "Do we get to win this time?" and to the influence of the techno-novels of Tom Clancy, a favorite of Ronald Reagan and Secretary of the Navy John Lehmann. He argues that during this same period, men's pulp fiction featured increasing violence that read like hard-core pornography, though it was the penetration of bodies by bullets that was described in sexualized language. Because of the importance of Gibson's book, I am going to follow it at length.

Like Frederick Jackson Turner's American creation myth, Gibson's term for the story in which an independent gunman defeats the evil enemies and founds a new society, Rambo movies provided a focal point for many people, though they were dismissed by others. But critics who mocked Rambo missed the point, for there were many people who did not: "Rambo was a worker and a former enlisted man, not a smooth-talking professional." (10) In fact, the more liberals laughed, the more Rambo's importance was proved, and it could not be separated from defeat in Vietnam. In a period in which men lacked confidence in government and the economy and when gender and race relations were changing, men began to fantasize about a warrior culture at the same time that "the whole modern world was damned as unacceptable." (12)

Earlier westerns and World War II movies had presented wars that were nearly always virtuous, wars won by American soldiers who were part of a larger organization they trusted, wars that were relatively safe and attractive, with tiny red dots of blood marking the injured or dead. But in New War movies, even those not specifically about the military, movies like *Dirty Harry, Red Dawn, Conan the Barbarian, Missing in Action,* and *Mad Max,* disenchantment had set in, as Americans realized that the war movies and westerns had been illusions. (Gibson notes that in the first four months of 1968, sixty Americans in Vietnam either killed themselves or someone else playing fast draw with their pistols.) In the

New War movies, disillusionment with the neatness of earlier war stories became apparent, as did disillusionment with official and legal authorities, who were now presented as despised symbols of a war that had been lost not by soldiers but by the CIA and corrupt, cowardly, liberal politicians. Just as in Timberg's biographical study, government officials represented a system that was never again to be trusted, and the warriors like North felt called upon to do what the police and the legal system failed to do.

These movies and novels featured male characters whose families had been destroyed, and as a result their revenge took place from within all-male warrior tribes in which there were no mothers and especially no older females who could remind them of a time when "the warrior was not an imposing figure, but a mere boy." (37) Because the families of New War heroes were no longer present, the stories frequently involved a search for substitute fathers and sons. They could thus be born again as warriors without women, and they could live in tribes where comradeship did not depend on reciprocity:

> These all-male warrior tribes present a radically new vision of male "reproduction" and maturation without parents and without all the conflicting feelings of dependency, love, hate, and disappointment that childhood and adolescence entail. The bonds between men result exclusively from the mutual recognition of one another's martial accomplishments. (37)

Violence in New War movies was savagely carried out by enraged warriors whose appetite for destruction could not be satiated, as war appeared to go on endlessly: "Indeed so great is the hunger for killing that the New War appears to be a war without end." (30) Gibson compares the image of war in these movies to the stories of the prefascist Freikorps in Germany, volunteer armies of disbanded soldiers from World War I who were organized by officers into roaming, largely autonomous groups. They were hired by the socialist chancellor Ebert, partially because he did not trust the largely working-class army, to put down strikes and to help bring order to revolutionary Germany in 1918. Motivated by a desire for revenge, they believed that Germany had been betrayed in World War I, "stabbed in the back" by communists, civilians, and weak and indecisive socialists, but primarily, as Barbara Ehrenreich says, "they fought, most of all, because that was what they did."[6]

Like the Freikorps stories, New War stories were not about setting up a new order but more basically about the experience of rage and destruction: "The New War culture portrayed the warrior as the epitome of masculine power and self-development, and combat as the only life worth living." (32) In these stories "nothing is created other than the pleasures of battle and the renewal of the warrior" in a war of vengeance without end. (117) But the rage with which this endless war was fought was more reminiscent of infantile than adult rage, even if it expressed the "very essence of the new warrior and constitute[d] a significant part of his popular appeal." (48)

The most intense, overt rage in these stories is directed at women, especially the most deadly of them all, the mother, her power displaced onto various black-widow women, such as the beautiful enemy agent James Bond finds in his bed or the various wily, castrating female terrorists. They must all be eliminated: "For the sad fact is that there can be no equality with black widow women, only domination or subordination." (63) The impossibility of equality also structures the image of the society the warriors have lost: "The point is clear: the desirable future for these men is a return to a prefeminist past." (54) And while the suffering of good women is presented in great detail, they too are usually destroyed for getting too close.

New War popular culture also includes fantasies of killing parents, wives, and children, followed by guilt over those very fantasies, which is assuaged by projecting the blame onto the enemy, who provides this warrior with his symbolic boundaries: "The enemy is the most important figure in all war mythologies because without him neither society nor its heroic defenders would exist." (65) In a free substitution among Indians, North Vietnamese, Russians, terrorists, older enemies like the Japanese, all of the enemies come to resemble one another when they penetrate boundaries that should be impermeable. Metaphorically, an apocalyptic national crisis is often figured in terms that suggest sodomy, in which the enemy sneaks up from behind or attempts to penetrate the hero's armored safety. Such penetration, if it succeeds, produces what the enemy wanted all along: chaos. The hero must thus always fight on two fronts, against both the enemy and the establishment. In this world, liberalism is heavily coded as a sign not only of duplicity and moral corruption but of cowardice and character defects as well.

These contests with the enemy are ultimately resolved with the hero reclaiming his control of the hardened armor that is his body, control that is emphasized by being juxtaposed to what happens to the enemy's body:

"While the paramilitary warrior's body remains hard and intact, the rup-
tured body of the enemy confesses its evil by exposing all its rotten spilled
fluids." (111) The death of the Other, and especially the pleasure taken in
viewing his destruction, proves the hero's virtue and control. Often at
such moments, the bloody liquids and pulpy, viscous remainders of the
enemy's body are purified and cleansed by apocalyptic fire.

But the hero, like the villain, is locked in a tragically self-referential
world: "The villain must transgress the parental law to feel that he is alive,
while the hero must deny that he ever had parents at all." And because the
evil villain, like the hero, is characterized by murderous rage that violates
all the boundaries of the body and society, his defeat requires that the hero
call upon constant self-denial and personal sacrifice, reflected in the hard,
mean look and controlled power of actors like Stallone and Schwarzeneg-
ger. Not only the phallus but the entire body is hardened, and killing
becomes a ritual appropriation of the enemy's power: "Only by killing the
enemy [can he] release the rage accumulated from a life of emotional self-
denial." (80)

This mirror-image evil enemy who keeps interminably returning is the
hero's only guarantee of his own identity as the embodiment of purity and
self-control. And though the hero suffers for all men, he is like a little boy
in a warrior's body, his anger, fear, and desire totally beyond his control:
"The New War is a playpen for men, a special one without the drag of the
supervising mother." (117) And though these battles and heroic feats
seem to be about masculine self-control, transgression proves to be the
same thing as regression for both hero and enemy:

> The evil one always wants more, because what he ultimately desires
> is to defy the laws of society, and seeking that solitary pleasure takes
> him down the road of cerebral insatiability toward childish regres-
> sion. When the hero and his mirror-image villain face off, their con-
> frontation may be seen as the hero's attempt as an adult to control his
> own regressive child-like nature. (80)

This is a scenario in which the hero seems to reenact the "narcissistic,
omnipotent child, the one who says, 'I need nothing and no one needs
me'" (80), a blocked, stagnant view of society:

> It is truly a dark, tragic vision. Social stagnation masquerades as
> restoration and social progress. Psychological regression wears an
> armored suit of maturity. Undeveloped and emotionally dead per-

sonalities appear as the height of individualism. An aesthetic of sexual violence is presented as realism. These inversions create powerful traps. There is no easy exit from the New War. (117)

But the adventure stories of the New War culture also spilled out of movie theaters and the covers of pulp fiction into reality. When the body counts increased in the New War movies and the distinction between cop pictures and war films disappeared, Hollywood filmmakers hired firearms-industry consultants and gun dealers to help them find props, real weapons that were linked to another form of popular culture, the stories and advertisements of gun magazines which reproduced the image of the armored warrior:

> Combat weapons and the concentric rings of power they create are not only a means of aggressive self-expansion; they also function as "body armor." But the enemy is always imagined to be more dangerous than the body armor developed to keep him away. Thus, the gun magazines' obsession with weapons and their lethal ranges can also be read as a discussion of fear — fear of an unbeatable, unstoppable enemy. The warrior is deeply afraid that no matter how many weapons he has, the enemy will penetrate each and every ring. No matter how many enemies he kills with his sniper rifle, carbine, and pistol, he will still be left alone to face just one more with his knife. (89)

The New War also showed up in other places, such as mock-combat war games that began with the National Survival Game (NSG, Inc.), founded in New Hampshire in 1981 as a form of woodsmanship and play. Influenced by New War movies and by the entrepreneurs who entered the field, these games very quickly changed from games to war games in which participants, often dressed in combat fatigues, went into the woods (or more recently, indoor commercial warehouses) to play war; kills were registered when an enemy was hit with a splatter of paint. The rapid growth in the popularity of these games resulted from Lou Grubb's invention of the "constant-air" paint gun, powered by ten-ounce canisters of CO_2 that could shoot over four hundred rounds of paint at full power. Eventually paint guns were refined into semiautomatic models that cost from $250 to $500; participants could also buy extended barrels, noise suppressors, high-capacity magazines, and scopes, which added to the cost. Even land mines eventually became available, with ads for these toy weapons increasingly mimicking the ads in gun and military magazines.

As Gibson reports, "By 1986, there were over forty paramilitary playing fields in Southern California alone," and over a thousand throughout the country. By 1988, "well over two million highly armed men in camouflage and face masks had fought at least once in mock wars and one million of them continued to play at least four times a year." (135)

Most of the participants were white, in their mid-twenties to forties, many were educated, and few were veterans; veterans in fact tended to stay away. In many ways, Gibson argues, these playing fields functioned as equalizers, where a battlefield performance, not an occupation, could make the man. They also made possible a male initiation ritual, in which a man could pass into warrior adulthood by means of a regression to child-hood: "On fields full of children in camouflage equipped with rapid-fire big kids' toys and lots of ammunition, the line between play and violence gets awfully thin." (139) That experience fed into the shift from an imagi-nary New War to the real nightmares of what Gibson calls War Zone America, in which popular culture indirectly legitimated a variety of su-premacist groups and others who "lived their own versions of the New War" in actuality. (13)

Another feature of the New War popular culture was Robert K. Brown's *Soldier of Fortune* magazine, founded in 1975 in Boulder, Colo-rado, just before the fall of Saigon. Brown had been a member of the Army Special Forces in Vietnam in 1968, where he commanded a Green Beret unit and knew the world of covert action through his work with Special Operations Groups, which operated outside the regular military chain of command. SOF billed itself as the magazine of "the independent warrior who must step in to fill the dangerous void created by the Ameri-can failure in Vietnam." (7)[7] The magazine became an important source of information for veterans of Special Operations and provided publicity for their causes; General John Singlaub, who had been fired by President Carter and founded the World Anti-Communist League (WACL), con-tributed to it. The beginnings of *Soldier of Fortune* also coincided with President Carter's attempts to clean up the CIA, efforts eventually reversed by Reagan and William Casey, who expanded covert operations. SOF's reporters covered the training of the Contras, the Afghanistan resistance, Angola, Mozambique, and South Africa, and at times participated in the training. Gibson argues that SOF was given tacit recognition as a publicity arm for American foreign policy while it also developed the image of the elite warrior and his arduous training and adventures, providing a particular position for its readers. *SOF* "was written *as if* the reader was a soldier or mercenary who might go off to war *tomorrow.*" (147)

During this period, the sale of military weapons increased exponentially, powerfully affecting the mythology of the New War: "It is as if the myth can be touched and held in the hand." (82) The weapons advertised in gun magazines included semiautomatic versions of the M16 used in Vietnam, guns imported by European manufacturers who advertised in *SOF*, and a legal Uzi that had a longer, sixteen-inch barrel and could be sold as a semiautomatic carbine, made available by Israeli Defense Industries. The countries of Eastern Europe, as well as China, also marketed what Gibson calls "the devil's own favorite hardware, the infamous AK-47" (7), the rifle used by the North Vietnamese and by terrorists around the world. And arms dealers brought out generic brands of ammunition "at discount prices often selling them in cases of 500 or 1,000 rounds. . . . In less than two decades, millions of American men had purchased combat rifles, pistols, and shotguns and begun training to fight their own personal wars." (7)

SOF's paramilitary journalism also added fuel to criticisms of the liberal media, for many of the participants at the *Soldier of Fortune* conventions in Las Vegas argued that the coverage by their warrior-reporters was the only reporting that told them what was really going on; that coverage rested on the assumption that any kind of leftist movement was evil and that possession and knowledge of firearms was essential to a man's role as a citizen. This journalism also taught him that if liberals continued to constrain the forces of liberty, irregular forces might have to step in. The readers of *SOF* were given a chance to play out their illusions at the annual conventions in Las Vegas, where they could participate in seminars on global danger spots and combat techniques, war games, training sessions in knife fighting, shooting matches featuring assault rifles, combat shotguns, and combat pistols, parachuting, rappelling from the tenth floor of the hotel to the poolside below, and paint-ball games. They could also wander around a Combat Weapons Exposition, a trade fair for gun merchants. The conventioneers saw the world as "a very dangerous, threatening one: the enemy was everywhere and he was on the march. . . . And always, there was Vietnam, a bitter reminder of failure; its mere existence, together with the lingering question of unaccounted for missing-in-action U.S. soldiers, indicated that the old world order premised on American power was gone." (158)

An underlying sense of anxiety, however, circled around the relationship between the real warrior and the play one: "How much war does it take to make a warrior?" (167) Conversations at the convention often had to do with the distinction between real warriors and weekend wanna-be's: "the wanna-be problem was like an atmospheric condition, a desert wind that charged the air and made everybody a bit on edge." That anxiety was both countered and reinforced:

> The Soldier of Fortune convention was, then, a model of how to keep people enthralled by and permanently mobilized for war. Conventioneers were idealized as the vanguard of good Americans, men who would defend the traditional values of the Founding Fathers and the frontier creation myth. They were made to feel that they were members of an elite, privy to confidential information, alert to the machinations of the news media and liberals at home and of encroaching Communists and aliens from abroad, and charged with the responsibility of remaining perennially vigilant and ready for war against the evil ones at a moment's notice. Further, in providing an array of "militia" units to join, *sof* channeled men of widely different financial resources and interests into real political activities, all the while providing entertainment and fellowship—and even religious transcendence. (166–67)

Gibson traces one other feature of the New War culture: the recreational experiences available in places where the distinction between wanna-be's and real warriors could be decided, short of actually going to war. Combat shooting schools that were open to civilians made it possible for them to earn high grades for marksmanship: "A man with such credentials would never be mistaken for a wanna-be." (170) Gibson himself attended Jeff Cooper's American Pistol Institute (API) in Paulding, Arizona. Cooper, a former Marine lieutenant colonel who served in World War II and Korea, and a Stanford honors graduate with a master's in history from the University of California, is also on the NRA's board of directors. He describes his political philosophy succinctly as opposition to CLAMS: congressional Left, academics, media. The institute is located at Gunsite Ranch, with nine pistol, six rifle, and six shotgun ranges on its 853 acres. As Gibson reports, by 1992, over nine thousand "would be gunfighters" had attended for various kinds of training: pistol, police shotgun, battle carbine (AR-15, Mini-14, or AK-47-type semiautomatic), submachine gun, or long-range rifle. Attendees were usually a mix of mostly civilians plus men and women from local and state police units, federal agencies, and military operations units (171).[8]

Basing his teaching on a "philosophy of violence" and holding his lectures in a building named Revelation, Cooper teaches the attendees that each man is morally obligated to defend himself, his family, and the larger society against criminal attack, and he is morally charged to redress any assault. Mastery of the martial art of pistol shooting will transform students into men of courage, and an armed man is one whose identity is certain: "I want to become more powerful through learning to kill." (176)[9] In order to master pistol shooting, however, the initiate must wholeheartedly surrender his agency and turn himself over to the elder. It is this ritualized surrender to a harsh, demanding regimen that verifies the elder's legitimacy: "Since the masters survived this same ordeal in the past, they must know what to do." (187) After successfully going through the rigorous, even terrifying training, the warrior's feelings and the experiences represented in the New War movies are literally reproduced in the very substance of the bodies of these elite participants, the training's lessons comprehensible only after the fact:

> Then it hit me—the week of intense training had created conditioned reflexes and an adrenaline rush strong enough to break through all the inhibitions that normally keep aggression under control. As a result, I'd loved the power of destruction. I'd loved the sensory distortions of time. I'd loved the adrenaline rush and that feeling of being so close to death, the "you're dead and I'm not" unspoken dialogue between shooter and target. I'd loved the way my mind and body worked together, remembering moves without consciously trying, dancing in one seamless flow. I had become the *armed man*—a reborn warrior. (189)

Gibson suggests that after such initiations, the group had in some sense been turned into a tribe whose totem was the gun, whose organization did not depend on external factors but upon this very training, the paramilitarization of the body. The shooting experiences out in the desert pushed the seduction of those movies and their heroes a step further, imprinting it in the conditioned reflexes of the body and its bodily ego, renewing the themes of New War mythologies all the more powerfully because they have now been experienced as "real." In an imaginative world with a warrior at its center, the training enabled participants to overcome constraints on aggression that had originated in childhood:

In a world where most men have no real power or control over their lives, mastering a weapon is a kind of grand "compensation" prize: *I'm not rich. I'm not politically powerful. The news media doesn't call me up and ask me what I think about things. I don't have scores of beautiful women after me. But by God I can kill anything that moves within 35 yards of me and have a good time doing it. I have that much power, anyway. I may never use it, but I know I've got the power if anyone ever tries to mess with me.* (189, his italics)

But strangely enough, just as the gun ads had already suggested, "the awful paradox of combat shooting was that the more powerful you got with a combat weapon, the more paranoid you became. At the very moment that men perceived that they could extend their boundaries to defeat enemies at five, ten, or twenty-five yards, those boundaries became extremely fragile." (190) The newly acquired power was accompanied by a renewed fear that the enemy was always out there: "Every moment of increasing physical and mental power was thus accompanied by increasing certainty that their power would be challenged in a lethal confrontation." (190) And because death now lurked everywhere, "everyone and anyone was potentially the enemy. Just as in New War fictions, the enemy existed wherever there were other people." (191) In this performative moment, "violent confrontation was the fundamental principle of existence, and it alone could make life meaningful. Only violent confrontations could provide the 'moment of truth' and confirmation as a warrior." (191)

Though most of the participants in these shooting sessions were ordinary citizens or policemen, others involved in New War mythology obviously were not. Some readers of *Soldier of Fortune* recruited in its pages for hit men; some readers went on to serve as mercenaries in Africa and Central America; and others were involved in supremacist activities (William Pierce, founder of the neo-Nazi National Alliance, once used *Soldier of Fortune*'s mailing lists to recruit members; though the magazine tried to prevent such usage, it could not control what it had helped bring about) and militias. On a general level, Gibson notes that men's participation in paramilitarized culture is often very differently inflected by social class and other factors, for which they may deserve some sympathy. At the same time, however, he argues that "their stories are more than personal tragedies; they are testimonies to the way in which paramilitary culture helped form personal identities [through] rapid oscillation between tremendous insecurity and extraordinary narcissism." (212) And that oscillation occurs within a narrative that does not question the warrior myth but all too easily locates the real culprit: "Only the government [is] at fault." (211–12)

Within this mythology, the gun finds its place at the very center of symmetrical layers of resonating meanings. I was told in a workshop on organizing my precinct for pro-life issues at the 1994 Christian Coalition that my most dependable voters would be members of the NRA, and Gibson finds NRA Executive Vice President J. Warren Cassiday mentioning religion in an even broader way: "You would get a far better understanding if you approached us as if you were approaching one of the great religions of the world." (253) A certain interpretation of the Second Amendment has become a fundamental part of the covenant between God and the American people, and threats to the right to own a gun constitute a threat to the very foundation of the American social contract.

iii.

This kind of warrior identity requires the symbolic guarantee of the True Woman if it is to function properly. What threatens that guarantee most is women's freedom to control their participation in reproduction, on the one hand, and to reject heterosexuality altogether, on the other. If society really has been, as Gilder, Timberg, and Gibson show us, at its most basic level divided into two different groups, warrior men and women/children, then both abortion and homosexuality constitute deeply symbolic threats to the men and women alike who have been promised a reality based on that view. The passions generated by these threats, along with the passions aroused by race, represent the most powerful obstacles to a genuine populist movement based on understanding the economic interests that constitute a far greater threat to masculinity than do gender confusions.

In shifting from the terms of warrior identity to the way a similar masculinity shows up in far-right conspiracy theories, a curious link between the public activities of warriors and the intimate domestic training with which this book began shows up in a now notorious tape available from Planned Parenthood. Reverend Matthew Trewhella of the U.S. Taxpayers Party, which brings the violent wing of the antiabortion movement together with the militia movement, speaks to the party's Wisconsin state convention, where Randall Terry, the founder of Operation Rescue, also spoke. Trewhella, who is a member of a group called the Missionaries to the Pre-Born, teaches his audience not only how to organize their members but how to raise their children:

> My son Jeremiah, I'm teaching him to be a free man. . . . I'd take my son, I'd play with his toes, I'd say toes, toes, toes . . . and I'd go up to his fingers and say fingers, fingers, fingers, and then I'd grab his trigger finger and I'd say *trigger* finger. I grab his trigger finger, and he's sixteen months old, and if you ask him "Jeremiah, where's your trigger finger?" — he'll go like this immediately. [Trewhella points to his own trigger finger.] And then I showed them how we need to quit playing these stupid little games . . . like Pin the Tail on the donkey instead of blindfolding them and sitting them down on the living room floor and saying, now put the weapon together.

He ends his talk with the admonition he had earlier given to his congregation: "So I told [them] I want you to do the most loving thing and I want you to buy each of your children an SKS rifle and 500 rounds of ammunition."[10] The audience applauds. In Trewhella's intimate training, the body is melded to the gun as it was in the New War games, in many ways constructing the relationship to the gun Gilder tried to make literal by claiming that it was part of man's essential nature.

The U.S. Taxpayers Party is an organization that brings radical libertarians, conspiracy theorists, constitutional literalists, and extremist antiabortion activists together within a theocratic frame. It was established in 1992 by Howard Phillips, the head of the U.S. Office of Economic Opportunity under Richard Nixon in 1973, who later founded the Conservative Caucus and along with Paul Weyrich, Richard Viguerie, and others helped mobilize the New Right. In 1979, Phillips helped create the Moral Majority with Weyrich and Jerry Falwell, but by the 1980s, the USTP had moved further to the right than mainstream conservatism, and its members became dissatisfied with the GOP of Reagan and Bush. Current members include the Reverend Michael Bray, who claims that the murder of abortion doctors is justified, and Randall Terry, who travels to meetings to offer his leadership institute and train activists. The party's platform claims that "the U.S. Constitution established a republic under God, not a democracy. . . . rights come from God, not the State!" essentially giving individuals the right to nullify laws with which they disagree.[11] In relation to that right, Terry asked a group at his Christian Leadership Institute, "Who in this room hasn't felt the bitter, hot breath of pagan, civic government?"[12] At the Wisconsin convention, Trewhella also called for the formation of armed militias, and a one-hundred-page guerrilla army manual on sale at the convention claimed that legalized abortion is a justification for taking up arms against the federal government.

The linkage between God, the Constitution, and masculinity provides a powerful foundation of emotion, and it finds a fascinating if bizarre home in the mind of Texe Marrs, a far-right extremist who heads the Living Truth Ministry and publishing house in Austin, Texas, and has his own radio talk show. Marrs's global conspiracy theories bring together every threat imaginable to make things perfectly clear for his readers and listeners. Though many people will see Marrs as a fanatic, his language sounds remarkably familiar, and it is a familiarity related to the structures of resonance with which the earlier chapters of this book were concerned. While mainstream conservatism tries to dissociate itself from people like Marrs, its exploitation of wedge issues too often unmistakably echoes his language and gives it legitimacy. Reasonable mainstream conservatives may have to ask themselves why Marrs's language *resonates* so strongly. For if we have not been reading Marrs, and most of us besides me have not, where, then, have we learned this language? Why does it sound so familiar?

Marrs attempts to establish an explanatory framework that produces total clarity that obviously cannot hold, and the places where that impossibility is most evident show up as what Jacqueline Rose calls "flashpoints of the social," nicely illustrated by the title of Marrs's monthly publication, *Flashpoint*. Marrs claims to be the author of over thirty books and to have taught political science, American government, and defense policy at the University of Texas at Austin and at two other universities (unidentified). I want to follow just one of his books: *Big Sister Is Watching You,* published by Living Truth Press in 1993. The blurb on the cover entices us in this way: "Hillary Clinton and the White House Feminists Who Now Control America and Tell the President What To Do"; the cover also features a stern-looking picture of Hillary Clinton, which is later compared to a photo of Hitler in a similar pose, as we are warned that the Christian church is now "about to be *religiously cleansed* by the femi-Nazis." (67) For Marrs, that cleansing process will attack the language of God in the interests of substituting the pronoun Her and "a feminine name or image," all part of an effort by the "shrewd and cunning leaders of WomanChurch" to make the old faith of Christianity "ready for the New Age of revived, national socialism." (67)

Recalling Gibson's description of the hatred aroused by the older female, the big sister who remembers the warrior when he was just a boy, Marrs begins a methodical assault not only on Hillary Clinton but on all the women in the first Clinton administration. The issue that most incenses Marrs is the monstrosity of gender confusion, and the most monstrous woman of all is the one who acts like a man: a cover blurb reads, "Move over, Big Brother . . . your meaner Big Sister is moving in!" She is not only the radical feminist but the lesbian criminal, the Fatal Woman Lynda Hart describes as the figure within the masculine imaginary that haunts representations of aggressive women. But there is nothing at all ghostly about Marrs's hatred of the monstrous lesbian.

"Hillary's Hellcats" consist of "a motley collection" of "lesbians, sex perverts, child molester advocates, Christian haters, and the most doctrinaire of communists." Attorney General Janet ("Johnny") Reno is "a hardened lesbian"; Donna Shalala is an "Amazon love sister," as well as the "most vicious Christian hater ever to hold a top cabinet post"; Laura Tyson, chairman of the Council of Economic Advisors, is "a big fan of the failed communist economies" of Ceaucescu and Stalin and says that Americans are not taxed enough; Roberta ("Bob") Achtenberg is a "lesbo crazy in charge of *all* federal housing policies"; (12) Ruth Bader Ginsburg is a femi-Nazi in favor of a unisex military and who wants to merge the Girl Scouts and Boy Scouts; Carol Browner is the "Land Grabber" and the "dean of Eco-Nonsense," her appointment part of a "sociofascist plot" to "steal people's land from them, claiming all the while that they're only doing it to preserve the 'diversity' of Mother Earth." (109) This is part of the "hideous, underlying Luciferian spiritual nature of the Hillbillary administration's environmental policies." (111) With curious logic, Marrs equates environmentalists' desire for state protection of the environment with an attempt to claim that the state is a part of nature, but the state then proves to be both pagan and Nazi.[13] And showing how populism is hijacked by this paranoia, he argues that the Clintonistas and the Rockefellers "will not be required to give up *their* property rights. . . . it is *we the people* who are being robbed of our land and stripped of our constitutional rights." (109)

Because these women are adherents of socialism and want to make socialism national, they are of course national socialists, "glorified femi-Nazis who consider themselves feminist leaders of a superior spiritual race." (28) And they threaten to remold culture in terms of the old feminine spirituality of the Goddess, whose origins were in the Garden of

Eden. There feminism and lesbianism had already contaminated even the origin of Creation because a domineering Eve brought "a docile and unmanly Adam into a conspiracy against God." (63) Eve's descendent is Big Sister,

> the ominous, end result of a universal yearning by unstable, mas-culinized, dominant-oriented feminists to establish control over men and women whom they consider to be their social and spiritual inferiors. It is an image of a society dominated by women who are rebelling against God. (63)

Replacing God by the Goddess and masculinity with femininity is monstrous enough, but this is made even more horrible by its connection to Satan: "The goddess is simply the devil in a feminist guise. She is *he,* and *he* is the serpent." (67) These monstrous women may in fact not even be women at all, because the True Woman can only be feminine in a narrow, "normal" sense, and the aggressive woman is *manly,* a mimic man, a serpent, the improper man who threatens real men. Here Marrs's fear of being feminized by a manly woman has fallen indistinguishably over into the fear of being feminized, sodomized, by an improper man. The indecidability of gender has produced monstrosity everywhere, with the manly man threatened from all sides. In this curious gender mixing, Hillary has become "Big Brother in Drag," the politically correct trans-vestite Big Brother, the leader of "today's raging psychopaths." (29) And as we now know, Big Sister encompasses Big Brother, and he remains phallic. He has not been "demasculinized, castrated, and transformed." He has instead "assumed a feminine mask. Behind the facade, the govern-mental behemoth . . . is still a *psychopath;* he [now also she] remains a seething dynamo of energy—a dark, brooding, evil force ready at any moment to explode." Marrs's text itself cannot keep these genders "straight."

He acknowledges that these male/female lesbian psychopaths can "pass" as normal, even though they are "angry women—women dedi-cated to totally changing and transforming society. Their goal is to rid the world of the traditional values, Christian morals, and male domination that they so furiously hate and loathe." (50) Even though they "can ap-pear normal and traditional, [internally they are] simmering with uncon-trollable urges and passions. The true female psychopath who is, for example, a lesbian, may well tend to keep the perverted facts of her per-verted sexual orientation hidden and in the closet." (51) And because such perverted women are the new superbeings of New Age globalism and community, any cultural use of those terms is now contaminated.

Just as the men in Gibson's study distrust the media, Marrs contends that the power of these abnormal women will be "advanced by a controlled media," who depict individualism as evil and selfish and who allow Big Sister to advance her schemes through "any and all means available, including political power and the apparatus of the government, including the punishment of thought and hate crimes." This Big Brother in drag will crush all opposition: "The future shall belong to the conscious superior race who know of and are dedicated to The Plan." (24) It has become obvious to Marrs that totalitarian power does not lie in the hands of either of the political parties, for the "elitists who have engineered the world conspiracy have no formal party label. . . . such infamous groups as Freemasonry, the Bilderbergers, the Council on Foreign Relations, and the Trilateral Commission are more than happy to admit loyal servants of any political party." (17)

While the anti-Semitic framework of such conspiracy theories has always been based on the image of a feminized Jew (dark, exotic, intellectual, small, emotional), the anti-Semitic man also paradoxically sees the weak Jew in control everywhere. Such omnipotence means not only that the anti-Semite's manliness is under threat by an all-powerful master, but far worse, in a repetition of the fear of being dominated by the weak brother, that he is now also threatened by a *feminized* omnipotent master. This familiar anti-Semitic framework becomes even more virulent as Marrs adds a new race of monstrous gender-mixers to the already omnipotent feminized Jews.[14] Such a threat becomes even clearer in Marrs's description of a photograph of Hillary Clinton and Alan Greenspan sitting beside each other at a State of the Union address, which proves that the Jewish financial conspiracy has now been intensified by its connection to a feminist conspiracy of manly women and unmanly men:

> Hillary represents the ultimate ascendance and preeminence of Woman. Greenspan represents Money, the ultimate asset, which guarantees, to those who possess it, *control and power* over the lives of those who do not.
>
> Hillary Clinton and Alan Greenspan together represent *Woman in Control,* the powerful and transformative idea that woman is at last taking her long sought-for position on the global political, religious,

and economic stage. Big Sister is born, and the world will never be the same. (31)

The Woman in Control, who is now also Big Money, controls not only reality but representation, requiring that history be rewritten, that homosexuality be made normal and heterosexuality aberrant, that patriotism be smashed by multiculturalism, and that the masses be taught to "despise white, male-dominated society as a throwback to the failed age of militarism and conflict." (23) The aim of this new world order commanded by Big Sister and superimposed over the framework of the Jewish conspiracy is to extinguish Christianity, which constitutes its "*gravest* threat."

The Woman in Control is also simultaneously a communist and a Nazi, for Hillary once gave money to the Institute for Policy Studies, to CISPES (Committee in Solidarity with the People of El Salvador), and to the National Lawyers Guild, "an official adjunct of the Communist Party," as well as to William Kunstler's Center for Constitutional Studies in order "to end American Government and bring about a global, Marxist paradise." (14) And not only is she willing to use the same tactics as Ceaucescu, Mussolini, Hitler, and Stalin, but she, like the other women of the administration, is "totalitarian in outlook":

> Not just politically correct, these women are *brutally correct*. They are the hard of the hard, the most militant of a militant and hostile generation. Spawned during the 60's in the age of the Beatles, gurus, LSD, and hippies, they are the misfits of American society. But now the misfits are in charge. The lunatics are running the insane asylum, and they're out to make us into the pathetic creatures they have become. They are the feminist vultures who flew over the cuckoo's nest. (14)

Marrs's fears have produced a laundry list of issues one hears on the part of traditionalist conservatism, even if rarely in such condensed and hysterical form. These women are

> trampling on our constitutional rights, employing ecological idiocy to grab people's land and property, and committing terrorist acts against horrified victims. . . . If Hitler and his henchmen had even a tiny fragment of the computerized, high technology spy, surveillance, and torture capabilities of today's CIA, IRS, FBI, ATF, and DEA, imagine what *additional* horrors they could have wreaked. These women have behind them the full apparatus of government to enforce their dictatorial demands and strange sexual appetites. (14–15)

It should come as no surprise that Marrs finds that this condensed mass of tyrannies came together in the attack on Waco, which clearly revealed "the chilling fate that awaits those who refuse to go along with the dictatorial blueprint of these coercive utopians." (15)

The male hysterical tone of Marrs's text reinforces George Mosse's argument that national identity historically depended on an analogy with normative masculine identity: "What we are seeing is an abrupt and complete break, or discontinuity, a separation, almost an earthquake-like cracking of the fabric of our national being." (Marrs 27) The fear of the freedom of women has extended threats to personal identity not only to the nation but to the globe: "These calculating and ruthless women are clever and diabolical enough to understand that only if the world can be transformed and molded into a *global dictatorship* can their control over us be complete." (25) But even this is too limited; they propose a socialist state that would replace the Real Constitution, which has already led us into a twilight zone "during which our constitution has been suspended and is no longer employed as our basic law. We are on a trek to an alien planet because our feminist leaders have launched Space Ship America into a new, *politically correct universe.*" (27)

But if we are to resist, what are we to do? Marrs's answers sound eerily familiar:

> I am convinced that there are only two things which deserve our trust — just two things that should inspire our actions: 1) God; and 2) The Constitution of the United States of America (*in that order*). To protect ourselves and our families, we must put God first in our lives and glorify his son, Jesus Christ. He, alone, is able to adequately and surely guide us toward victory. . . . As patriots, let us therefore commit ourselves to reviving and restoring the Constitution as left to posterity by our nation's founders. American freedom and liberty are worth fighting for, so let us renew our efforts and recharge our spirits for the long campaign which lies ahead. (17)

The seductiveness of Marrs's allegory comes from the way it produces passionate fear by means of a fantasy of totalitarian power within a framework of absolute simplicity and clarity. Big Sister is the flip side of Big Brother, "just as communism, with only a cosmetic makeover, becomes fascism; and political correctness, taken to extremes, becomes Nazism. If a person travels from any point on a circle of evil, he or she will eventually end up in the same place." (16) Everything is explainable if one applies this template to it; the unquestionable identity of the enemy condensed from so many different registers becomes a black hole of causality into which everything falls. This clear causality, however, also lets those who oppose this enemy know that no heroic expenditure of energy, no amount of rage in fighting it, will be too great.

iv.

Marrs's fear of the freedom of women links the condemnation of lesbians and the monstrosity of gender mixture to the deeply symbolic threat of abortion, which represents not only a matter of faith or an ethical decision, but the fact that control of women is fundamental to this version of masculine identity. George Gilder has already spelled out some of this in especially clear terms, an argument I repeat in part: "the usual assumption is that opposition to abortion on demand stems from a puritanical aversion to premarital sex, combined with a religious superstition that feticide is murder." But in fact, the real opposition concerns something else,

> the erosion of male sexuality. . . . Few males have come to psychological terms with the existing birth-control technology; few recognize the extent to which it shifts the balance of sexual power further in favor of women. A man quite simply cannot now father a baby unless his wife is fully and deliberately agreeable. . . . Male procreativity is now dependent, to a degree unprecedented in history, on the active pleasure of women. (107)

The woman who must now be taken into consideration in terms of procreation is not only the nonprocreative, aggressive dyke clarified for us by Marrs and the racialized woman in need of no man described by Gilder, but also the mother who can be characterized in terms of the most tabooed form of violence: the violence of a mother against her child. These violent, traumatic clashes of American identity come back to the intimate question of human identity itself and to the fear that it will be threatened if the clarity of belief is questioned. This leaves some people, not just men, sounding like this fourteen-year-old girl: "I live with the sense of God touching our family. I'd like to tell all the mixed-up teenagers that there is a God and only ONE God. If you aren't right with my God, then you will burn in Hell."[15]

These rigid binaries, which have become all the more brittle because the mourning of lost masculine identity has been blocked, are exacerbated in many ways by the background of contemporary media culture and its role in the new maladies of the soul that cross religious and secular boundaries, a point argued by Julia Kristeva.[16] She writes: "everyday experience points to a spectacular reduction of private life. These days, who still has a soul? . . . As for the renewed interest in religion, we have reason to wonder if it stems from a legitimate quest, or from a psychological poverty that requires that faith give it an artificial soul that might replace an amputated subjectivity." (7) We are "actor[s] or consumer[s] of the society of the spectacle who [have] run out of imagination." (10)

One might draw on that image of blocked imagination to show how the apocalyptic framework of traditionalist conservatism comes together with media culture, religious belief, and masculinity, all of which are dangerously intertwined around the issues of birth and abortion. Kristeva's psycholinguistic analysis suggests that unconscious fantasies of birth are a primary element in apocalyptic images and that these unconscious images are produced when things that a culture formerly tried to keep apart are mixed together; the most basic separation of traditionalist conservatism, of course, is the difference between the sexes. Drawing on the notion of the primal scene, or the image within the unconscious that Freud argued established an unconscious register for psychic identity, Kristeva suggests that the primal scene is not, as Freud argued, a fantasy of the intercourse of one's parents but the unconscious image of one's own birth. In an unsettlingly fluid way, that fantasy mixes up both one's own body and the body of one's mother with a sense of fear and violence: "giving birth [as] the height of bloodshed and life, scorching moment of hesitation (between inside and outside, ego and Other, life and death), horror and beauty, sexuality and the blunt negation of the sexual." (155) Such a terrifying image, Kristeva suggests, is located at the very "origin" of the ego for both men and women, and the ego tries to protect us from feeling its effects. However, when the boundaries of the ego are threatened in periods of cultural change and this dissolution cannot be held so securely in check, we experience a "doubtless very 'primal' narcissistic wound." (154) It is this wound whose dangers can perhaps only be avoided if it is both recognized and mourned, or worked through.

And it may be that this is most threatening for the male subject, for what is also a part of this unconscious fantasy is the horror of a maternal body that is both castrated and castrating, a much more frightening image than Freud's rather calm description of the boy's first glimpse of the little girl's lack. This fantasy of birth thus signifies not only castration, or the loss of a body part, but the destruction of the entire body itself, and it is associated with the maternal body, now felt to be actively aggressive and threatening. The emotional resonance and the fear set off by this fantasy in the unconscious invite an unsettling metaphorical question: was that his birth or his abortion?[17]

In relation to this unconscious anxiety, Jacques Lacan argued that the fantasies at the most basic level of the unconscious resemble the images of Hieronymus Bosch, providing "an atlas of all the aggressive images that torment mankind" and edging up to the fearfulness of birth, "the gates of the abyss through which they thrust the damned."[18] These kinds of images "crop up constantly in dreams, especially at the point when analysis appears to be turning its attention on the most fundamental, most archaic fixations." (12) Such images in the unconscious carry greater weight than do other unconscious images; Lacan refers to them as imagos. The specific imagos of the fragmented body "are the images of castration, mutilation, dismemberment, dislocation, evisceration, devouring, bursting open of the body." (11)

To extend the implications of these unconscious images of dismemberment, we might argue that Lacan has also described the horror and unease set off by the figure of the aborted fetus, whose unsettling, undecidable resonance is particularly unstable, whether one is pro-life or pro-choice. This is not only because it has to do with human life but also because it is connected to the figure whose identity guarantees masculine identity: the mother. And it is made even more emotionally powerful by the fact that it is related to the most tabooed violence of all, that of mothers in relation to children. As Barbara Johnson argues, "There is something about the connection between motherhood and death that refuses to remain comfortably and conventionally figurative."[19]

But though many feminist discussions of abortion suggest it is the uncertainty of a woman's identity that is reflected in the uncertain identity of the fetus, in fact, as we have seen, women's identity is secondary to the identity that has driven the fearful narratives of traditionalist conservatives. In an era in which feminists, gays, and lesbians are engaged in the irreversible project of dismantling traditional masculine identity, many men, even those sympathetic to those attempts, may find the experience of uncertain ego boundaries to be very traumatic, and it appears that it is man's increasingly uncertain status that is reflected in the uncertain status of the fetus.

The pro-life videotape *The Silent Scream* situates the circumstances of the fetus in a narrative that establishes an opposition between what is referred to as an intact, whole human being, the fetus, and the threatening aggression from the outside, repeating the apocalyptic cultural narrative that has resonated through this study. In somber, brooding dialogue, Dr. Bernard N. Nathanson leads us through a sonogram of an abortion in progress. As viewers we are situated to identify with the "unborn child," described as a "fully formed, absolutely identifiable human being" who is "moving quietly in its sanctuary." The generic conventions of the apocalyptic narrative then show us how this being begins to sense the aggression into the sanctuary that will lead to its apocalyptic ending.

Nathanson's "literal" description of the fragmented body parts of the aborted fetus eerily mirrors the imagos that Lacan noticed in the speech of analysands who were approaching the furthest reaches of fears about identity itself, or the ego. Nathanson's narrative describes the abortion in terms that repeat the kinds of phantasmatic, apocalyptic imagos Lacan described: the body is "torn apart, dismembered, disarticulated, crushed, and destroyed by the unfeeling steel instruments of the abortionist." The individual is deprived of its bodily unity, and what is left to be suctioned out are "shards, broken fragments, pieces of tissue." In a similar vein in another pro-life text, an observer at an abortion says that the doctor

> pulls out something, which he slaps on the instrument table. "Here," he says, "A leg." . . . He points to the instrument table, where there is a perfectly formed, slightly bent leg, about three inches long. It consists of a ripped thigh, a knee, a lower leg, a foot, and five toes. . . . My vision and my hearing though disengaged, continue, I note, to function with exceptional clarity. The rest of me is mercifully gone.[20]

This deservedly mournful, dazed observation, like pro-life belief in general, has to be respected. There is, however, another step to be taken here, and that is to look much more closely at how such deeply ethical concerns about human life are susceptible to being used as elements in the other story, about masculine anxiety. To do so, I turn to the story of a young pro-life activist named Gianna, briefly entering the world of pro-life believers in order to recognize the story's power and emotional resonance. At a national convention of Concerned Women for America in Washington, D.C., I attended an evening service in memory of all the fetuses aborted in America since *Roe v. Wade*. Thinking that I could keep my distance as an outsider and expecting to find the ceremony manipulative and repugnant, I quickly understood, as I watched Beverly LaHaye and other leaders of CWA walk out one by one to lay roses in an empty crib, how such rituals and their unambiguous, passionate language engage pro-life belief. Though tears and emotional responses are not uncommon at charismatic religious services, the large audience of CWA members and their families was emotionally shaken by this memorial, which unexpectedly moved me as well. The twelve-year-old girl sitting beside me was limp from the emotional impact of the ceremony and from crying. The effect of this service reminded me of the services we used to have for victims of the Contras, though the emotion there was more subdued, probably because of the different religious traditions, such as Quaker and mainline Protestant, with which the anti-Contra movement was affiliated. Whatever was going on at the CWA memorial looked like what, under different auspices, was called solidarity. The memorial could not be understood at all if it were only seen cynically or in terms of ideology imposed from above. It somehow had to be evaluated, at least for a moment, on its own terms, which were spiritual and emotional. The impact of this ceremony would define for that girl the humanity of the fetus, which would never again have to be articulated. That "fact" would be felt in terms of a belief that fully engaged her body, just as Matthew Trewhella's lesson had fully engaged the body of his son.

At that same convention, I heard a personal testimony by a young girl named Gianna, who is the focus of a biography written by Jessica Shaver and published by James Dobson's Focus on the Family in 1994. The term "biography" is a misnomer, however, as Gianna's biographer tells us, because she was never really born: "Whether Gianna's birth mother was pregnant 24 weeks or 26 or 29½ (the medical records conflict), the abortion was legal under Roe v. Wade. . . . Her doctor injected a saline solution into her uterus and expected her to deliver a dead fetus the next day. Instead she delivered a live baby. Gianna weighed two pounds."[21] At one speaking engagement, Gianna begins by denying that she was "born" as a "blob": "I am not a blob! I don't like to be called a blob. I wouldn't call you a blob! . . . I just want you to think about how many other babies go to the grave before they even get a chance to live. I like to run. I like to jump. I am a person! That's all I have to say." (76) Taken to a foster home after this traumatic delivery, Gianna suffered from cerebral palsy because of the damage to the maturing brain. Her doctors doubted she would crawl or sit up, much less stand or walk:

In most babies aborted that way, the corrosive effect of the salt strips away the outer layer of skin, revealing the raw subcutaneous layer. If the baby swallows the saline solution, it destroys the child's blood-clotting mechanism and produces multiple hemorrhagic or bruise marks. Incredibly, Gianna had no burns or bruises of any kind. (38)

Later adopted, she was eventually reunited with her birth mother, who had wanted to keep her but was forced to give her up to social services because she could not support her.

The book traces Gianna's life and her involvement in pro-life activism, which understandably engages her in a deeply personal way: "Why are the people in the audience so angry at me? she thought. I haven't done anything to them. I'm just giving the facts about the way I came into the world. They're treating me as if I did something bad by surviving an abortion!" (91) And in describing Gianna's reaction to pro-choice activists, the author writes, "You're the ones being brainwashed, thought Gianna. She had never felt so surrounded by evil as she did now. It was a force almost physical. She could practically visualize demons swirling about her, looking for points of weakness. . . . God and Satan are battling it out, she thought, and I'm right in the middle of it! She had a surge of confidence. God is protecting us. I can be a witness for the Lord." (98–99) Not only the passionate belief but an exhilarated sense of mission motivates the young people demonstrating with her in front of clinics: "The more you rescue, the more you get called Jesus freaks. . . . It's a perfect example of what it says in the Bible, that Christians will be hated." (102)

Gianna makes literal the question of absolute identity upon which not only warrior masculinity but also pro-life activism and the identity of the Pure Mother rest. As the other traditionalist women in this study have done, she provides the face, the figuration to define the fetus as a human being. Yet even though her story really does break my heart and even though I want to protect her, I am also forced to ask why she does not feel the same way about, for example, the people who will inevitably die because highway speed limits have been raised. Why does the human life under threat in those instances not arouse the same anguish for Gianna as the fetus does? Something else is clearly going on here that assigns the protection of this particular life much more passion than the protection of those others.

First of all, Gianna and the fetus can be drawn into a story, unlike those anonymous victims of highway accidents; she is given a face, just as the fetus and its tiny beating heart can now be personalized in a sonogram. Shaver quotes a statement by Right to Life spokeswoman Nancy Meyers: "Everyone gets tears in their eyes when Gianna stands there and says how glad she is to be alive. She's really an amazing person, very up — and it means something when this really cute, outgoing teenager says she's not a lump of tissue, that this is what abortion is all about — real people." She then adds her own comment: "Precious people." (135) Gianna's personalization of the fetus who survived is also heard by young people, one of whom sends her a letter describing the way he wins speech competitions with his talk about abortion: "They cry when I talk about the procedures and when I tell them . . . your story. It would serve as one of my illustrations and do more than any graph or chart ever would." (157)

But there is another element that differentiates the lives of the fetus and Gianna from the lives of those faceless drivers and passengers, and it may be the most important one. For her story circulates through the identity of man, and vice versa. Not only does she represent the personalized fetus, but her story depends on an identifiable character whose behavior can be controlled: the mother. Thus Gianna's story works on two levels at once, the symbolic one in which the narrative terms of human identity in a world that privileges men must be reinforced, and the actual political one, in which the impact of her story is inserted into the political activism of militant pro-life groups. She gives one of her sincere, personal talks, like the one I heard in Washington, D.C., at the April 1992 meeting of Human Life International (HLI) in Ottawa. HLI is an organization headed by Father Paul Marx, who also wrote the dedication to the biography. Founded in 1981, HLI is a worldwide network of militant antiabortion activism and activist training that exports the methods of the American pro-life campaigns like Operation Rescue throughout the world, with eighty-four branches in fifty-six countries. Besides the *Silent Scream* video, it also distributes brochures, booklets, rosaries, videocassettes, and fetal models all over the world, with much of its current activity focused on "re-Christianizing" Eastern Europe and the former Soviet Union. This involves restricting contraception, abortion, sex education, and the activities of the International Planned Parenthood Federation, as well as opposing population-control efforts of the United Nations. Highly controversial, Marx has been repudiated by many Catholic communities and pro-life organizations, and because of its extremism HLI was denied nongovernmental-organization status by the United Nations. Father Marx has been associated with many of the most extreme activists in the pro-life movement, such as Randall Terry and Paul Cameron, who advocates eliminating homosexuals in order to destroy AIDS.[22]

Marx describes his cause this way: "The enemies of life and family are always the same, feminists, Freemasons, Communists, secular humanists, and the ubiquitous International Planned Parenthood Federation."[23] The anti-Semitic subtext of such conspiracy theories then becomes much more overt: "The same segment of the Jewish community that accuses the Pope of insensitivity to the Jewish Holocaust not only condones but has more or less led the greatest holocaust of all time, the war on unborn babies." (quoted in DuBowski 10)[24] As Marx argued at the meeting Gianna attended, "Perhaps modern historians should apologize to Hitler for vilifying him as the worst demon the twentieth century has produced. The fact is, in terms of numbers of victims, cultural damage, and the sheer inhumanity of their methods and motives, the pro-abortionists of our current day take precedence." (177) This meeting was called the First International Gathering of Abortion Holocaust Survivors as part of the Eleventh World Conference on Love, Life, and Family. It drew scholars, priests, nuns, dignitaries, and lay people from fifty-eight countries.[25]

Gianna's moving biography must now be read in several ways. It cannot be read without acknowledging its deeply personal story, yet neither can it be read only as one girl's personal experience, for its staging is a major part of its message, and its staging is thoroughly implicated in the fear of the freedom of women we have been following in the various reconstructions of both motherhood and masculinity. Not only has Gianna's biography been published by Focus on the Family, but it is also used in the interests of Randall Terry, speaking here at one of his Christian Leadership Institute sessions, in language that is too familiar: "How are we going to rebuild if we don't have a blueprint . . . to rebuild America's politics, her judiciary, her schools, on the Law of God?" His own laundry list from the structure of clarity then takes over: "Land taxes are from the pit of Hell . . . and 'righteous slavery' would be 'better than prison' because the master would provide food and a separate house for the slave and the slave's family." Gianna's emotional story has thus been turned into an act on a stage constructed by Focus on the Family, by Beverly LaHaye, of Concerned Women for America (and a leading member of the Christian Coalition, itself a major influence in the Republican Party), and by Randall Terry and Father Marx. Even if they are not linked in some conscious conspiracy and even if we have to be very careful about assigning guilt by association, nevertheless messages like these are capable of resonating powerfully to a variety of different groups, that resonance exacerbated by claims to absolute clarity and truth. Traditional man is trying to prevent not simply the abortion of the individual fetus but his own abortion, and in the depths of his anxiety, he knows that all of his efforts, not simply his birth, depend on women. The greatest irony of all, and perhaps the one that makes him increasingly phobic and dangerous, is his recognition that it is up to traditionalist women to save him.

v.

After the Sturm und Drang of men's behaviors and fantasies, Gianna finally returns me to the much quieter issue with which this study began, the role of women in the politics I have been following and, in particular, the voice of the Oregon Citizens Alliance volunteer who left a message on my answering machine. Though that voice reminds me of my grandmother, my sisters, my mother, my cousins, my aunts, and even of myself, the content of her message is chilling and alien. Or maybe that's the most troubling part of it. It *should* be alien, but it isn't quite, and what frightens but mesmerizes me, all at the same time, is the mismatch between that content and the sound of her voice, its resonance.

I have to make myself draw back from her message, because her voice, like Gianna's or even Beverly LaHaye's or Kay Coles James's, seduces me to come closer, because it is already intimate, already inside me, in many ways. It is so familiar that only by consciously trying to make it repulsive and hateful can I disentangle myself. How can hate sound so *nice*? So I try to trivialize her, I feel sorry for her, I try to hate her for her involvement in this organization fueled by bigotry and men like Lon Mabon. And perhaps most fundamentally, I want to despise and loathe her for her weakness, for being a woman, for allowing herself to be used like this. In spite of all I know, I want her (and me) to be better than men, and I fall quickly and emotionally into misogyny and self-hatred, such anger always exceeding my anger at men, from whom I don't expect so much. But I guard myself far longer against anger at women, I make many more excuses for them, because when that anger explodes, it is always more amorphous, more uncontrolled, more tinged with betrayal. Her, my, failures throw me dizzingly into fury, into hatred of the female weakness that is much too close to what society says about women — and about me. But I am also afraid of her because I can't quite name her as either the woman I can trust intimately or the woman I can hate because she fails to live up to the special goodness I falsely demand. I love her and I hate her.

I can't keep her separate; she is simultaneously exactly like me and completely other. My reactions ultimately circle around the impossible place of the mother in both secular and religious contexts, as the mother's lack of agency is coupled with her tremendous power to symbolize the violent exclusiveness of the Father's law, while her voice seduces me into believing in personal immediacy, which I desperately want, especially when it is promised in a motherly voice. The mother's voice, at least as this culture teaches it to us, is like the nightingale's song, its promise of fullness symbolically overwhelming me with passion while the mother's actual place — the fact that masculine hatred of her has constructed the edifice of that symbolic power in the first place — leaves me both dizzy with desire for her and devastated by what she represents. But I am also sad because I have no idea who *she* is in all of this. The personal intimacy of her voice, my longing that makes me want her fullness even as I know that its intimacy has now been drawn fully into the public realm of the Pure Mother, blurs the language of power, as Derrida might have warned me: "Dream this umbilicus: it has you by the ear."[26]

Within this voice is the historical architecture of language, body, power, as its intimacy collapses politics into the flesh — hers, mine, ours. And as this motherly woman in all sincerity speaks in the interests of men, it is only with the utmost attentiveness that I can momentarily keep my balance and my critical distance. If those of us who want to understand contemporary conservatism could only decipher what we hear in this voice, we might also momentarily come much closer to understanding the passions of reactionary politics. And if there are conservatives who are appalled at being symbolically associated with these absolutist conservatives, perhaps they too need to understand a bit better the dangers of resonance, whose acoustical meaning — the intensification of sound produced by sympathetic vibrations — is especially important here. For in contemporary America, where passion and media blur all boundaries, responsibility has far less to do with intentions than it does with the recognition of the dangers of those sympathetic vibrations.

NOTES

Introduction

1 Jennifer Bradley, "At Bay," *New Republic* 22 January 1996: 20.

2 James Ridgeway and Susan Monaco, "It's the Economy, Stupid," *Village Voice* 25 June 1996: 22–24.

3 Jacqueline Rose, *Why War? Psychoanalysis, Politics, and the Return to Melanie Klein* (Cambridge, MA: Blackwell, 1993) 73.

4 Talk given at the 1995 Christian Coalition Road to Victory convention in Washington, D.C.

5 Allen Hunter, "Children in the Service of Conservatism: Parent-Child Relations in the New Right's Pro-Family Rhetoric," *Legal History Program: Working Papers,* series 2 (Madison: Institute for Legal Studies, 1988) 2–8.

6 David W. Murray, "Poor Suffering Bastards: An Anthropologist Looks at Illegitimacy," *Policy Review* 68 (spring 1994): 10. Not so coincidentally, the resulting culture wars have constructed the demon of "political correctness" as a scapegoat for denouncing critical modes of cultural analysis. In particular, those involve the critical strategies of defamiliarization, a term that refers to the version of critical thinking influenced by the intersection of historical materialism and aesthetic formalism early in this century. In that tradition, cultural images and forms were conceptualized as the carriers of history, making it possible to historicize forms that had come to be thought of as natural.

7 Peter Marshall in a talk given at the 1995 Christian Coalition Road to Victory conference in Washington, D.C.

8 Talk given at the 1995 Christian Coalition Road to Victory conference in Washington, D.C. Lapin, who founded Toward Tradition, is the founding rabbi of Pacific Jewish Center in Venice, California, and is on the board of fellows of the Jewish Policy Center in Washington, D.C. He appears regularly at Coalition conventions.

9 Michael O'Leary, *Arguing the Apocalypse: A Theory of Millennial Rhetoric* (New York: Oxford UP, 1994).

10 Elaine Pagels, *The Origin of Satan* (New York: Random, 1995) 181.

11 Talk given at the 1995 Christian Coalition Road to Victory conference in Washington, D.C. In his book *The New World Order* (Dallas: Word, 1991), Robertson has this to

say: "God's new world order [to be sharply distinguished from the satanic secular new world order] is coming much nearer than we believe. . . . Therefore, do not be anxious. God's work is right on schedule. The company of the sons of God is almost complete — perhaps this very decade may finish the task. God sometimes seems to be slow, but He is never late. In the fullness of time, He will announce His kingdom on earth. I do not believe that we have much longer to wait!" (247–48) See also the study of Robertson by Robert Boston, *The Most Dangerous Man in America? Pat Robertson and the Rise of the Christian Coalition* (Washington: Americans United for Separation of Church and State, 1996).

Jasper Griffin identifies another characteristic of the apocalyptic narrative, arguing that any version of the historical invention of the apocalyptic tradition and its canonization in the Old and New Testaments has been "a disaster for the world." In particular, he refers to the influence of the Book of Revelation, "the most important and influential of such works, [which] is written in the most violent spirit of anger and vengeance, and . . . also is exclusive, dwelling lovingly on the small number of the elect and the savageries in store for everybody else." Jasper Griffin, "New Heaven, New Earth," review of *Cosmos, Chaos, and the World to Come: The Ancient Roots of Apocalyptic Faith,* by Norman Cohn, *New York Review of Books* 41.21 (22 December 1994): 28.

12 As Ralph Reed says, the agenda of the Christian Coalition is to establish the most successful grassroots organization this country has ever seen. This means that they will not endorse candidates; instead candidates will have to endorse their agenda.

13 Talk given at the 1995 Christian Coalition convention in Washington, D.C.

14 The discussion of inerrancy in evangelical scholarship is far more nuanced than the absolutist versions of activists in this study. See, for example, such articles as Wendy Murray Zoba's "When Manuscripts Collide: Why We Need the Behind-the-Translation Work of Textual Critics," in *Christianity Today*'s special issue on interpretation (23 October 1995). Other articles include "Cruising the Electronic Bible" and "The Power of the Translated Word."

An earlier issue of the same magazine was devoted to a forum on a recently published book by Mark Noll, Wheaton College's McManis Professor of Christian Thought, entitled *The Scandal of the Evangelical Mind* (Grand Rapids: Eerdmans, 1994). Noll criticizes the anti-intellectualism of some evangelicals who resist scholarship on textuality and interpretation. Responses to his work were both supportive and angry, but this kind of dialogue suggests the richness of the evangelical tradition that is often invisible because the more rigid versions occupy such a prominent place in the discourse of conservative religious activists.

15 Julia Kristeva, "Place Names," *Desire in Language: A Semiotic Approach to Literature and Art,* ed. Leon S. Roudiez (New York: Columbia UP, 1980) 272.

1 Sacred Intimacy

1 LaHaye's book, like others of this genre, is formulaic, written in part by staff researchers and informed in part by the sensibility of the author. Books of this type, like William Bennett's *Book of Virtues,* often include postmodern, *Bartlett's Quotations* pastiches of citations taken out of historical context. LaHaye's quotations draw from

Blaise Pascal, Anne Frank, Charles Schultz, the Epicureans, the Stoics, Samuel Johnson, Henry Ford, Deborah Tannen, and Carol Gilligan, among others.

2   Beverly LaHaye, *The Desires of a Woman's Heart* (Wheaton, IL: Tyndale, 1993) 105. Both Left and Right have read Gramsci, whose discussions of ideology and hegemony owe much to the study of religious belief and the Catholic Church.

3   Richard White, *"It's Your Misfortune and None of My Own": A New History of the American West* (Norman: U of Oklahoma P, 1991).

4   Though a thorough study of the ambiguous effects of emotion in displacing the contradictions of politics would have to include New Age spirituality, it is beyond the scope of this book.

5   Sara Diamond, *Spiritual Warfare: The Politics of the Christian Right* (Boston: South End, 1989) 66.

6   As Michael Lind describes this southern coup, while the leadership of the defeated Democrats had been from the Northeast, the Midwest, and the Pacific Northwest, all but one of the new leaders were from the South, though many of them did not grow up in that region: Newt Gingrich is from Georgia (after having lived in many places because his was a military family), House Majority Leader Dick Armey and Whip Tom DeLay are both from Texas (Armey is originally from North Dakota), and Senate Majority Whip Trent Lott is from Mississippi. "The Southern Coup: The South, the GOP, and America," *New Republic* 19 June 1995: 20–29.

7   Stanley Aronowitz suggests that because the Left has itself relied too heavily on the state, it has been unable to understand the legitimate reasons for an attack on the welfare state. See his "Toward Radicalism: The Death and Rebirth of the American Left," *Social Text*, no. 44 (fall/winter 1995): 69–95.

8   Lind cites a campaign ad that helped defeat the antisegregationist New Dealer Frank Porter Graham in his run for reelection to the Senate after having been appointed by a progressive governor: "WAKE UP, WHITE PEOPLE. Do You Want Negroes Working Beside You, Your Wife and Daughters? Using Your Toilet Facilities? Frank Graham Favors Mingling of the Races." (26) The media consultant who helped defeat Graham was Jesse Helms.

9   LaHaye here quotes the writing of another Christian woman, Elisabeth Elliot, who is also frequently cited in books for Christian men. LaHaye cites other works by her: "Whose Am I?" *Moody Monthly* May 1980, and *The Shaping of a Christian Family* (Nashville: Thomas Nelson, 1992).

10 Though most writers capitalize the pronouns that refer to God, LaHaye here does not, presumably in the interests of personalizing the relationship.

11 Ralph Reed Jr., talk at Christian Coalition, September 1995. The anecdote is part of the lore of the Christian Coalition, often cited as proof of secular bigotry against religion.

12 Rebecca Merrill Groothuis, *The Culture War between Traditionalism and Feminism* (Grand Rapids: Baker, 1994).

13 As Kathleen Rowe reminded me, this is also the logic of the vows taken by nuns in the Catholic Church.

14 It would be a mistake to see the semiotic as irrational, such a reading being part of the historical binary opposition between rational and irrational that privileges head over heart, man over woman. Like the emotions and affect in general, the semiotic is

inherently neither rational nor irrational, neither masculine nor feminine, neither right nor left. Instead it simply constitutes a different level of signification than that of the symbolic order of language. Learning to read it involves learning to read feelings, sounds, touch, gestures, rhythms, and so on in terms of the staging of experience. A focus on the semiotic can show the importance a culture assigns to controlling women.

15   I am grateful to Suzanne Clark for her comments about the history of the metaphor of the heart in American literature and rhetoric.

16   The article is Elisabeth Elliott's "Whose Am I?" 129.

17   Julia Kristeva, "Women's Time," *Signs* 7.1 (autumn 1981): 31.

18   Connie Marshner, *Can Motherhood Survive? A Christian Looks at Social Parenting* (Brentwood, TN: Wolgemuth and Hyatt, 1990) 2.

19   Though the Christian Right's criticisms of the abortion-rights movement are locked in an absolutist frame, its analysis can be useful in pointing out that some institutions and practices related to the provision of abortion services are determined as much by the market economy as by concern for women's rights. For example, Carol Everett, who is now a pro-life speaker to audiences throughout the United States, Canada, and Australia, formerly operated what she calls an abortion franchise in Dallas, Texas. Her descriptions of the financial stakes and the commodification of abortion suggest that there is much to be gained for the pro-choice movement in remaining critical of the market economy's function in providing access to abortion services.

20   Diane Eyer, *Mother-Infant Bonding: A Scientific Fiction* (New Haven: Yale UP, 1992) 164.

21   Pat Robertson, *The New World Order* (Dallas: Word, 1991) 241.

22   George Gilder, *Men and Marriage* (Gretna, LA: Pelican, 1993) 112.

23   Diane Eyer makes that point in her study.

24   Thomas Byrne Edsall and Mary D. Edsall, "When the Official Subject Is Presidential Politics, Taxes, Welfare, Crime, Rights, or Values the Real Subject Is Race," *Atlantic Monthly* 267.5 (May 1991): 53–86. The Analysis Group study continues:

   [T]hese white Democratic defectors express a profound distaste for blacks, a sentiment that pervades almost everything they think about government and politics. Blacks constitute the explanation for their [white defectors'] vulnerability and for almost everything that has gone wrong in their lives; not being black is what constitutes being middle class; not living with blacks is what makes a neighborhood a decent place to live. . . . These sentiments have important implications for Democrats, as virtually all progressive symbols and themes have been redefined in racial and pejorative terms.

   The special status of blacks is perceived by almost all of these individuals as a serious obstacle to their personal advancement. (56)

25   See Teresa de Lauretis, "Desire in Narrative," *Alice Doesn't: Feminism, Semiotics, Cinema* (Bloomington: Indiana UP, 1987).

26   Marshner compares this situation to an earlier period, which she considers to have been unquestionably superior to the present: "They used to be [free to be mothers]. A few decades ago, motherhood was a national treasure." (12)

27   Mark Gerson, "Battler for the Republic: Irving Kristol's Terrible Swift Pen," *Policy Review* 62 (fall 1992): 57.

28 Linda Weber, *Mom, You're Incredible!* (Colorado Springs: Focus on the Family, 1994) 32.

29 The first quotation is taken from J. M. Greenstein, "Father Characteristics and Sex Typing," *Journal of Personality and Social Psychology* 3 (1966). In her documentation, Weber does not give page numbers, only the page range of the articles. The second is from E. M. Hetherington, "Developmental Study of the Effects of the Sex of the Dominant Parent on Sex-Role Preference Identification and Imitation in Children," *Journal of Personality and Social Psychology* 2 (1965): 188–94.

30 Kaja Silverman develops this argument in a discussion of the "dominant fiction" in the first chapter of *Male Subjectivity at the Margins* (New York: Routledge, 1992).

2 The Heart of the Matter

1 Lawrence Grossberg, *We Gotta Get Out of This Place: Popular Conservatism and Postmodern Culture* (New York: Routledge, 1992).

2 Talk given at the 1995 Christian Coalition convention in Washington, D.C.

3 The way this notion of American identity penetrates religion was evident at a workshop given by Ralph Reed at the 1995 Christian Coalition convention. The room had been used prior to Reed's talk by state caucuses as well as by the caucus from Canada, all of which met in separate small groups. As the crowd for Reed's talk began filtering in, the Canadians, about twenty or so, were off in a corner having their pictures taken with a Canadian flag, and they began to sing the Canadian national anthem. Nationalism trumped Christian bonding, however, as someone in the crowd filtering in leapt to the front of the room to conduct the Americans in the national anthem. It was sung loudly with the arrogance of a patriotism that uses love of country as a weapon, now with an American God added to the mix.

4 Archibald D. Hart, *The Sexual Man: Masculinity without Guilt* (Dallas: Word, 1994) provides a more urban version of this same kind of training.

5 Tim LaHaye and Beverly LaHaye, *The Act of Marriage: The Beauty of Sexual Love* (Grand Rapids: Zondervan, 1995) 7. The book was first published in 1976.

6 Archibald D. Hart's survey of his clients, all upstanding Christian men in Southern California, found that 82 percent reported that their religious views helped them achieve greater self-control and a greater respect for women, with 81 percent arguing that it gave them a greater understanding of the role sex plays in human life. Eighteen percent reported that their religious views were not helpful at all. As Hart says, "The impact of Christian faith on the formation of a healthy sexuality was more positive than negative." (207)

7 *Wait for Me*, videotape, Concerned Women for America, 1993.

8 In response to a question asked at the 1995 Christian Coalition convention about whether homosexual teachers should be in the classroom, Ralph Reed responded that they were "inadvisable."

9 *The Gay Agenda in Public Education*, videotape, Report, 1993. Trent Lott, elected Senate majority leader in 1996, appears on the tape, as does Lou Sheldon, head of the Traditional Values Coalition.

10 Elaine Pagels, *The Origin of Satan* (New York: Random, 1995) 49.

11   In Washington, D.C., in 1995, Ralph Reed advised Coalition members not to let their excitement and vision fade, because they were involved in a long-term process, a marathon, not a sprint, something to be treated not as a hobby but as a way of life. The most important focus for their activism, he argued, is not presidential politics but school boards, city and state governments, and public-policy organizations. The White House cannot govern without the school boards; better to have two thousand school boards and one thousand legislators than one president.

12   Shelly A. Uscinski, "Winning as a Religious Conservative," videotape, Christian Coalition School Board Training Seminars, 1995.

3   Kitchen Table Politics: The Folking of America

1   Beverly LaHaye, *Who But a Woman? Concerned Women Can Make a Difference* (Nashville: Thomas Nelson, 1984) 15.

2   The postmodern character of the Christian Coalition is illustrated in an article in the Coalition's magazine, *Christian American,* entitled "High Tech Activists: How Advanced Communications Are Changing the Way Pro-Family Advocates Work." The article features a photograph of Marjorie Dannenfelser on the phone and in front of her computer, as her two toddler sons stand near. She is able to care for them while operating a pro-life PAC from her home: "Technology like the fax, computer and voice mail have allowed me to create a rapidly expanding political action committee while keeping my family my first priority," she says. Also described is the Coalition's use of fax alerts and live video meetings with the grass roots via satellite, with 281 downlink sites, and the use made of those links by House Majority Whip Tom DeLay to coordinate grassroots pressure on Capitol Hill. The Coalition also has a show on satellite, entitled *Christian Coalition Live,* on the third Tuesday of each month to discuss pending legislation and answer questions from activists. The first half of the program is on NET, Paul Weyrich's conservative cable television network, billed as a Christian C-SPAN. Weyrich's Free Congress Foundation, which was also instrumental in forming the Heritage Foundation, funds two-thirds of NET's budget, with the rest coming from the sale of airtime to advertisers. Christians out of reach of those links can log onto CompuServe, where the Coalition has a Political Issues Forum for those with questions, and the Coalition's Internet home page (http://www.cc.org) makes it possible for activists to view the voting records of congressional members and send them e-mail.

In Colorado Springs, James Dobson, of Focus on the Family, has developed a sophisticated fax network to focus on Congress. Two years ago he created *Family Issues Alert,* a weekly two-page fax newsletter. Its subscriber list is organized by area code so that activists in critical local issues can be targeted.

Congressmen themselves are using digital technology to hold town meetings on NET, and Newt Gingrich has urged House members to become active on-line on the Internet. Carolyn Curtis, "High Tech Activists: How Advanced Communications Are Changing the Way Pro-Family Advocates Work." *Christian American* 6.8 (October 1995): 20–23.

3   Charles Rice, *Fifty Questions on the Natural Law: What It Is and Why We Need It* (San Francisco: Ignatius, 1993) 27–28.

4   Samuel A. Nigro, "Male/Female Differences in Natural Law," (St. Louis: Social Justice Review, 1993) 25–26. Copies were on sale at the Christian Coalition convention in Washington, D.C., September 1994. Natural law will bring together unlikely allies, here Catholics, evangelicals, and fundamentalists, even though one still finds books in Christian bookstores and at Christian Coalition conventions that claim that papists are not Christian.

    In the netherworld of far-right Christian groups, anti-Catholic rhetoric is common. Some of the wildest can be found in Texe Marrs's Living Truth Ministries newsletter, *Flashpoint,* published in Austin, Texas. Marrs's conspiracy theories will be discussed more fully in chapter 8. Pertinent to a discussion of Catholicism, however, are the investigative reports he offers for sale, one of which is an audiotape called "The Pope over Jerusalem," which promises to tell us "how the Pope is using recent accords of unity between Rome and world famous evangelists Billy Graham, Pat Robertson . . . to accomplish his end-time, Israel scenario. . . ." The tape also outlines "the surprising role to be played by Freemasonry in these mindboggling, last days events. Will the Pope's plans culminate in a mutually enriching, global Masonic dictatorship?" To seal the pope's tyranny, his top confidant and spiritual advisor is a *converted Jew* (italics in original). "Will this powerful Cardinal be chosen as the next Pope?" In this apocalyptic scenario, it is no surprise to find other themes familiar from the lore of supremacist and militia groups. The most predictable one is the demonization of the United Nations because of its supposed secret plans to override American sovereignty in the interests of One-World Government. Marrs refers to an element in this conspiratorial view of the United Nations, the mysterious black helicopters that are supposedly involved in secret U.N. activities throughout the country. Rumors of helicopter sightings throughout the rural west, midwest, and New England keep the fear of the U.N. alive: "Black Helicopters over America," "The Treaty from Hell: The United Nations Plan to Make 'Nature Worship' a State Religion." *Flashpoint: A Newsletter Ministry of Texe Marrs* May 1995.

5   Lynda Hart develops this argument in *Fatal Woman: Lesbian Sexuality and the Mark of Aggression* (Princeton: Princeton UP, 1994).

6   Other goals include the passage of laws prohibiting abortion, euthanasia, genetic engineering, and fetal tissue transplantation; restoring the quality of public-school education; balancing creation and evolution in the schools; presenting the religious heritage of the country without bias; and influencing public policy to "address the physical and moral dangers of 'alternative' lifestyles on our society." "Opportunities for Leadership in Concerned Women for America," *Leadership Manual,* Concerned Women for America, 1994, n.p.

7   Elizabeth Hickey, "Mrs. Family Values: Beverly LaHaye Leads Her Army of Concerned Women into the Conservative Fray," *Washington Times* 29 July 1992, 1E.

8   Letter from Beverly LaHaye in CWA leadership packet.

9   "Opportunities for Leadership in Concerned Women for America," *Leadership Manual,* Concerned Women for America, 1994, n.p. Other workshops included How the Church Can and Why It Must Participate in Elections; RU 486: The Menace of Chemical Abortion; What in the World Is Global Education?; People of Faith under Siege: The Real Gay Agenda; Defending the Right to Choose Life: A History of Attacks on

Crisis Pregnancy Centers; and Teens and Sex: Communicating the Abstinence Message Effectively, among others.

10   Though for tax reasons these voters' guides are not supposed to be overtly partisan, in fact, a familiar set of code words always results in the recommendation of one politician over another, almost always a Republican. The guides present a picture of both parties' candidates, a list of issues, and a tidy checklist on the candidates' positions. Examples of such issues are increased federal income taxes (opposes/supports), taxpayer funding of obscene art (opposes/supports), promoting homosexuality to school children, banning ownership of legal firearms, and so on. The phrasing of each issue has, of course, already determined which candidate should receive one's vote, and there is nothing to prevent the issue itself, if not the candidate, from being discussed in church that Sunday. Partisanship is obvious at CWA conventions; Republican politicians like Ronald Reagan, Dan Quayle, William Bennett, Jesse Helms, and Robert Dornan give keynote addresses at CWA. See also an article by Robert Boston, "Stacked Deck," *Church and State* 49.7 (July/August 1996): 4–10.

11   Beverly LaHaye, fundraising letter, May 1995.

12   Kay Coles James, *Never Forget* (Grand Rapids: Zondervan, 1992) 20.

13   Kay Coles James, "Changing the Culture of America," *Regent University Impact* 4.3 (August 1994): 4–5.

14   Star Parker, *Commentaries of a Black Christian Conservative Radical Republican Right-Wing Woman* (Los Angeles: NFTA, 1994).

15   Star Parker, *Commentaries of a Black Christian Conservative Radical Right-Wing Republican Woman* (Los Angeles: NFTA, 1994), n.p.

16   Angela Davis, *Women, Race, and Class* (New York: Vintage, 1983).

17   Star Parker, *A Culture of Dependency: The Morality of Welfare Reform* (Los Angeles: NFTA, 1994), n.p.

18   Tarso Ramos, "The Wise Use Radicals," *Western States Center News* 12 (fall 1995): 6. Ramos argues that Wise Use themes had been developed earlier by the neofascist Lyndon Larouche, whose followers are active in Wise Use movements both in the United States and abroad. The founder of the Wise Use movement, Ron Arnold, was allied with the American Freedom Coalition, part of Rev. Sun Myung Moon's Unification Church. Moon also owns the *Washington Times*. Others involved in Wise Use activism have been the John Birch Society, the networks of Paul Weyrich, and groups affiliated with the religious Right. See also David Helvarg's study of the Wise Use movement, *The War against the Greens* (San Francisco: Sierra Club, 1994), which traces some of its funding to South African mining companies, U.S. and Canadian timber companies, Japanese four-wheel-drive vehicle manufacturers, the Heritage Foundation, the American Farm Bureau Federation, and the NRA.

19   The policy suggestions presented in the magazine include, among others, the following:

1. Reform the excesses of current tort law to limit non-economic damages to a fair and reasonable amount.

2. Enact strong federal and state property rights protection laws.

3. Allow states to defer taxes on open spaces or other areas of natural resource value as long as the land remains undeveloped.

4. The federal estate is 704,915,500 acres which is too large to be effectively managed. The Bureau of Land Management controls some 268 million acres or 39.2% of the federal lands. Congress should consider abolishing this agency. Lands which are currently part of the National Wilderness Preservation System or are National Recreation Areas or other such designation could be transferred to states. Federal lands which are currently leased could be offered for purchase to current permit holders. Other BLM lands could be transferred to the states, or a commission could be established to sell it or transfer the land to the states.

5. Acquisition of new federal lands should be terminated. Land and Water Conservation Funds should first be dedicated to providing for takings claims against natural resources or environmental agencies at the federal level. Surplus funds could be used for incentive-based conservation programs, positive bounties or returned to the treasury to offset tax incentives based conservation programs. ("Policy Suggestions," *NWI Resource* 6.1 [spring 1995]: 44–45.)

20 Quoted in Steve L. Gardiner, *Rolling Back Civil Rights: The Oregon Citizens' Alliance at Religious War* (Portland, OR: Coalition for Human Dignity, 1992) 27. As Robertson writes in his column, "Ask Pat," in *Christian American,* when asked why concern for protecting the environment is not a major issue for conservatives,

> Conservative Christians do believe in protecting the environment, but many question whether the federal government is doing it the right way. According to a recent survey, less than one-third of Americans believe their tax dollars are being well spent when it comes to the environment. Now, I have nothing against animals. Many of you know of my love for horses. But if it came down to assuring the welfare of my family or the welfare of my horses, it's no contest—the horses are on their own. I think conservatives, who have a strong pro-life ethic have little patience with those who place the value of an owl or a snail darter over the well being of humans.
>
> Beyond that, Biblically God clearly has placed human beings over animals in the chain of command, and my view will change only when God changes his eternal law. (*Christian American* 5.8 [October 1995]: 16.)

21 Marion Goldman's study, "Continuity in Collapse: Departures from Shiloh," is published in *Journal for the Scientific Study of Religion* 34 (1994): 342–53. At the other end of the cultural scale was the Bhagwan Shree Rajneesh, who reacted to groups like Shiloh by concluding that Oregon was hospitable to new religious movements. Yet the cultural differences between the Rajneeshees, who numbered two thousand in 1984, and the rural people of eastern Oregon resulted in years of controversy, as the Rajneeshees renamed the town of Antelope and tried to take over public schools and county government. Their lifestyle was based on affirming the relation between luxury and spirituality, and the isolated Rajneeshpuram, located out in the middle of the eastern Oregon desert, was the site of boutiques, bookstores, wine shops, and fine restaurants as well as the Bhagwan's collection of ninety Rolls Royces. The belief system of this affluent commune of well-educated people was a fusion of the Western pleasures of materialism and the spiritual focus of Eastern thought; the Rajneesh International Meditation University also made available seventeen kinds of individual sessions, sixteen different sensitivity workshops, and fourteen therapy courses that lasted from two weeks to three months. As part of a belief that sex was part of the

search for transcendence, the Bhagwan also required his followers to engage in sexual experimentation; the Rajneeshpuram later developed open and detailed education about AIDS and sexually transmitted diseases. Though the community fell apart by 1985, its networks around the world are still intact. See Goldman's "What Oregon's New Religions Bring to the Mainstream," *Oregon Humanities* summer 1994: 31–34.

22   Steve L. Gardiner, "The One-World Conspiracy," *Dignity Report* 3.1 (winter 1995): 18–20. Gardiner also reports that David Barton, who speaks at every Christian Coalition convention as the resident authority on the Founding Fathers' intentions for a Christian America and whose organization, WallBuilders, publishes videos and books for use in churches and home schooling, spoke at the annual Bible retreat of Pete Peters, a pastor in the Christian Identity movement. Christian Identity is the supremacist movement that claims that Anglo-Saxons and Germanic peoples are the lost tribes of Israel, the legitimate heirs of Adam and Eve. The descendants of Cain, or, more literally, of the devil, are the Jews and their descendants, all people of color, or "mud people." As Gardiner says, "The hard-core racist right is actively reaching out to Christian right, Wise Use and gun rights activists, seeking both legitimacy and potential recruits from their more mainstream allies." (20)

Barton has become mainstream and has distanced himself from the far right. In addition to his book, *The Myth of Separation: What Is the Correct Relationship between Church and State?* (Aledo, TX: WallBuilders, 1993), he has also produced a widely distributed videotape, entitled *America's Godly Heritage* (Aledo, TX: WallBuilders, 1992). Considered to be the "historian" whose work justifies revisionary readings of American history, he picks out references to God and Christianity in the writings of the Founding Fathers, as well as in inscriptions on the walls of monuments and government buildings in Washington, D.C., including the Supreme Court, and finds there literal mandates for a Christian nation.

His work is used to teach American history, not only in religious schools and for home schooling, but even occasionally in public schools. Barton is described on the cover of *America's Godly Heritage* as the "founder of WallBuilders, an organization dedicated to the restoration and rebuilding of the values on which America was built and which, in recent years, have been seriously attacked and undermined. As so accurately stated by Benjamin Franklin, David believes that 'Whosoever shall introduce into public affairs the principles of . . . Christianity will change the face of the world.' . . . *America's Godly Heritage* is an excellent primer for those who want to know more about what was intended for America by the founders and what can be done to return America to its original guiding philosophy and is ideal to share with home gatherings, church groups, and Sunday school classes, or to use as a history supplement for children or schools."

23   I am especially grateful to Melissa Lippold for a copy of the videotaped interview and to Patsy Raney for help with this research.

24   *The Covert Crusade: The Christian Right and Politics in the West* (Portland, OR: Western States Center and Coalition for Human Dignity, 1993) 59.

25   Kathy Phelps, "GOP Must Stand for What Is Right, or It Stands for Nothing," *Register Guard* [Eugene, OR] 14 April 1994, 13A.

26 Walter Benjamin, *The Origin of German Tragic Drama,* trans. John Osborne (London: New Left, 1977).

27 This term is from Robert Reich, *The Work of Nations: Preparing Ourselves for 21st-Century Capitalism* (New York: Knopf, 1991).

28 *The Popcorn Report: Faith Popcorn on the Future of Your Company, Your World, Your Life* (New York: Doubleday, 1991).

29 Roger K. Lewis, "Gated Areas: Start of New Middle Ages," *Washington Post* 9 September 1995, E 1E.

30 Peggy Noonan, *What I Saw at the Revolution: A Political Life in the Reagan Era* (New York: Random, 1990).

31 Nancy Maclean, "White Women and Klan Violence in the 1920's: Agency, Complicity, and the Politics of Women's History," *Gender and History* 3.3 (1991): 295.

4   Tender Warriors

1   Steve L. Gardiner traces the affiliations of several of the African American clergy active with Promise Keepers: Wellington Boone, Joseph Garlington, E. V. Hill, and John Perkins. All have been involved in the Coalition on Revival (COR), whose beliefs are influenced by Christian Reconstructionism: "COR is a California-based organization that seeks to encourage the implementation of the Bible as law. It would, given its way, abolish most government functions including public schools, rewrite the Bill of Rights, and apply criminal sanctions for homosexuality and abortion." (6) Though, as Gardiner points out, Reconstructionism is hostile to the charismatic theology of Bill McCartney, nevertheless the Promise Keepers message of nondenominationalism and ecumenical outreach brings them together. Steve L. Gardiner, "Promises to Keep: The Christian Right Men's Movement," *Dignity Report* 3.4 (fall 1996): 1–9.
    Men of color generally do represent at least one-half or more of the speakers and singers. Gardiner argues that the appeal to racial reconciliation, while authentic, nevertheless is based on the *idea* of racism, rather than on a "struggle for real-world equality in economic and political terms. . . . In short, racism becomes a mere thought in the minds of white Promise Keepers, a thought which can be modified through prayer and 'reconciliation.'" (6)

2   Bob Horner, Ron Ralston, and David Sunde, *Applying the Seven Promises* (Colorado Springs: Focus on the Family, 1996) 8–9. The book is included in the kit entitled *The Next Step: From the Stadium to the Small Group,* multimedia package including videotape, audiotape, and booklet (Boulder: Promise Keepers, 1995).

3   Hans Johnson, "Broken Promises." *Church and State* 48.5 (May 1995): 9. See also Joe Conason, Alfred Ross, and Lee Cokorinos, "The Promise Keepers Are Coming: The Third Wave of the Religious Right," *The Nation* 263.10 (7 October 1996): 12–19.

4   Russ Bellant, "Mania in the Stadia: The Origins and Goals of Promise Keepers," *Front Lines Research* 1.5 (May 1995): 7–9.

5   Gardiner cites the pastor of St. Charles Bible Church of St. Charles, Minnesota, Rev. Dennis L. Finnan, a religious broadcaster troubled "that this seemingly wonderful movement, to unite men in the common bond of Jesus Christ, is being founded by

those who are at the least spiritually misguided and at the worst under Satanic delusions" (Gardiner 7).

6　Connections among these various groups are often close but indirect, not conspiratorial, even if often secret. For example, the Council for National Policy (CNP), founded in 1981, is an organization of over five hundred members that brings together many of the groups who work to influence public policy, many of them supporters of Promise Keepers. CNP functions as an umbrella group for strategy and met on the eve of the Republican Convention in San Diego in 1996 to help write the Party platform. Some of its members are Ralph Reed Jr., Pat Robertson, Rev. Donald Wildmon (American Family Association), Beverly LaHaye, Phyllis Schlafly (Eagle Forum), Larry Pratt (Gun Owners of America), Bill Bright (Campus Crusade for Christ), Howard Phillips (Conservative Caucus and the U.S. Taxpayers Party), Paul Pressler (Southern Baptist Convention), Richard DeVos (Amway), members of the Coors family, Oliver North, Gen. John K. Singlaub (former head of the World Anti-Communist League), Ed Meese (chairman of the CNP), Dick Armey (House majority leader), Rep. Tom DeLay, Sen. Lauch Faircloth, Sen. Jesse Helms, Senate majority whip Trent Lott, Sen. Don Nickles, Gary Bauer (Family Research Council), Ben Bull (American Center for Law and Justice), Dr. James Dobson (Focus on the Family), Bob Duggan (National Association of Evangelicals), Mike Farris (Home School Legal Defense Association), Ed Feulner (Heritage Foundation), Ron Godwin (*Washington Times*), Rebecca Hagelin (*Christian American*), Reed Irvine (Accuracy in Media), Bob Jones III (Bob Jones University), Dr. D. James Kennedy (Coral Ridge Presbyterian Church), Alan Keyes (talk show host and presidential candidate), Connie Marshner (activist), R. J. Rushdoony (Chalcedon Foundation), John Sununu (talk show host), Richard Viguerie (American Target Advertising), Paul Weyrich (Free Congress Foundation), John Whitehead (Rutherford Institute), Dr. Henry M. Morris (Institute for Creation Research), and many businessmen, including Howard Ahmanson Jr., Robert Bates (Guarantee Mutual Life Company Omaha), John Belk (Belk Stores), and Nelson Bunker Hunt (Hunt Energy Corporation). Edward Ericson Jr., "Behind Closed Doors at the CNP," *Church and State* 49.6 (June 1996): 7. See also Peter Eisler, "Conservatives Go Behind Closed Doors," *USA Today* 9 August 1996: 2A.

7　Randy Phillips, "Seize the Moment," *Seven Promises of a Promise Keeper* (Colorado Springs: Focus on the Family, 1994) 3, his italics. These are the seven promises:

1. A Promise Keeper is committed to honoring Jesus Christ through worship, prayer, and obedience to God's Word in the power of the Holy Spirit.

2. A Promise Keeper is committed to pursuing vital relationships with a few other men, understanding that he needs brothers to help him keep his promises.

3. A Promise Keeper is committed to practicing spiritual, moral, ethical, and sexual purity.

4. A Promise Keeper is committed to building strong marriages and families through love, protection, and biblical values.

5. A Promise Keeper is committed to supporting the mission of the church by honoring and praying for his pastor, and by actively giving his time and resources.

6. A Promise Keeper is committed to reaching beyond any racial and denominational barriers to demonstrate the power of biblical unity.

7. A Promise Keeper is committed to influencing his world, being obedient to the Great Commandment (see Mark 12:30–31) and the Great Commission (see Matt. 28:19–20) (8).

8   Wellington Boone, "Why Men Must Pray," *Seven Promises of a Promise Keeper* 26.

9   Edward Galbreath, "Manhood's Great Awakening," *Christianity Today* 39.2 (6 February 1995): 21–28.

10   Archibald D. Hart, *The Sexual Man: Masculinity without Guilt* (Dallas: Word, 1994) xiii.

11   Stu Weber, *Tender Warrior: God's Intention for a Man* (Sisters, OR: Multnomah, 1993) 13.

12   Harold Bell Wright was an American author who lived from 1872 to 1944. He wrote *The Shepherd of the Hills* (1907), *The Calling of Dan Matthews* (1909), and *When a Man's a Man* (1916). Wright's books were primarily about the open spaces of the Southwest and were "concerned with love and adventure and emphasized an incredibly wholesome morality and the superiority of the rugged natural man." The books were extremely successful in the popular market. (*The Oxford Companion to American Literature*, 5th ed., ed. James D. Hart [New York: Oxford UP, 1983].)

13   Weber quotes Joseph M. Stowell, "The Making of a Man," *Moody Monthly* May 1992: 4.

14   Max Horkheimer and Theodor W. Adorno trace the dangers of a representation that grounds an absolute meaning: "To the precise degree that the absolute is made to approximate the finite, the finite is absolutized." *Dialectic of Enlightenment*, trans. John Cumming (New York: Seabury, 1972) 177.

15   Israel is of special importance to fundamentalist and evangelical Christians because of the prophecy in the Book of Revelation that it will be the site of the final Battle of Armageddon, which signals the return of Christ.

16   From this point on, all the italics are those of the authors.

17   Howard G. Hendricks, "A Mandate for Mentoring," *Seven Promises of a Promise Keeper* 49, quoting Mornell.

18   Tony Evans, "Sexual Purity," *Seven Promises of a Promise Keeper* 73.

19   Weber includes another passage from C. S. Lewis's preface to *George McDonald: An Anthology:* "An almost perfect relationship with his father was the earthly root of all his wisdom. From his own father, he said, he first learned that fatherhood must be at the core of the universe. He was thus prepared in an unusual way to teach that religion in which the relation of father and son is of all relations the most central." (149)

20   Bill McCartney, "Seeking God's Favor," *Seven Promises of a Promise Keeper* 207.

21   Stu Weber, *Locking Arms: God's Design for Masculine Friendship* (Sisters, OR: Multnomah, 1995) 44. Blurbs on the first page are by Tom Osborne, head football coach at the University of Nebraska. Also noted is the fact that Osborne took his team to the Orange Bowl in 1994. Others who contribute statements are Coach Bobby Bowden of Florida State University (national champions in 1994) and Ken Ruettgers, left tackle for the Green Bay Packers. There is also praise from Dan Coates, senator from Indiana, as well as other Christian spokesmen.

22   John Hagee, *Bible Positions on Political Issues* (San Antonio: John Hagee and Global Evangelism Television, 1992) 75. He is described on the back cover as "a fourth-generation preacher in the tradition of his father and grandfathers before him," who not only shepherds the 13,000-member, nondenominational Cornerstone Church in San Antonio, Texas, but "is pastor to other pastors around the country through the Cornerstone Fellowship of Churches." He heads John Hagee Ministries Global Evangelism Television, Inc., and produces a television show, *Cornerstone,* broadcast around the country, as well as a live satellite broadcast of Sunday evening services from his Cornerstone Church in San Antonio, Texas. He has also written *Nine Bible Principles for Judging Prophecy, One Hundred and One Facts about Satanism in America, Should Christians Support Israel? Turn on the Light,* and *Beginning of the End.*

23   Jay Sekulow, "Time to Defend the Family," *Casenote: The American Center for Law and Justice* 2.6 (1995): 3.

24   Keith Fournier, "Faith and Culture: Defining and Defending the Family," in *Casenote: The American Center for Law and Justice* 2.6 (1995): 4.

25   Keith Fournier, *Religious Cleansing in the American Republic* (Washington: Life, Liberty, and Family, 1993) 51.

5   Postmodern Hunters and Gatherers

1   Christopher Badcock, in *Evolution and Human Behavior: An Introduction to Human Sociobiology* (Oxford: Basil Blackwell, 1991), characterizes sociobiology as a Freudian-Darwinian synthesis in which psychology and the social sciences are joined together under the umbrella of the general evolutionary theory of the biological sciences. With the discussion shifted into the realm of culture, the Freudian model of the mind is drawn on to explain the evolution of culture, with reproductive success the primary driving force.

2   Po Bronson, "George Gilder: Does He Really Think Scarcity Is a Minor Obstacle on the Road to Techno-Utopia?" *Wired* 4.3 (March 1996): 193.

3   Max Horkheimer and Theodor W. Adorno, *Dialectic of Enlightenment,* trans. John Cumming (New York: Seabury, 1972).

4   George Gilder, *Men and Marriage* (Gretna, LA: Pelican, 1993) 10.

5   In many ways, Gilder echoes Gramsci's critique of the concept of ideology because it could not account for religious belief; Gramsci's concept of hegemony was drawn in part from his study of Catholicism.

6   George Gilder, "End Welfare Reform As We Know It," *American Spectator* 28.6 (June 1995): 27. Subsequent references in the text will be identified by *AS.*

7   George L. Mosse, *Nationalism and Sexuality: Middle-Class Morality and Sexual Norms in Modern Europe* (Madison: U of Wisconsin P, 1985) 4–5.

8   Mosse uses the term "normalcy" here much as he uses "respectable": as a historical construct.

9   Suzanne Clark's work has shown how the sentimental and domestic discourses inhabited by women have existed in an uneasy relationship in which women worked both within and against them. See her *Sentimental Modernism: Women Writers and the Revolution of the Word* (Bloomington: Indiana UP, 1991).

10 John Cassidy, "Who Killed the Middle Class?" *New Yorker* 16 October 1995: 113–24.

11 The necessary fit here, within a binary system, between the sexual constitution and anticommunism is nicely explained by David Horowitz in the journal published by the American Enterprise Institute. Socialism, he argues, is "basically a religious phenomenon and it's an inability to come to terms with the fact that we are all unequal. We can't be made equal, there isn't going to be an end to conflict and war and all those things that make us human. It is a sexual religion and when it is a non-sexual religion, it is a form of idolatry." David Horowitz, "Socialism: Dead or Alive? A Roundtable Discussion," *American Enterprise* July/August 1995: 29.

In the same discussion, Horowitz describes the intellectual foundations of the university, as he sees it: "The culture of the university: its intellectual tradition is the tradition that produced Hitler and Stalin. If you think of the dominant thinkers in our academies — Marx, Nietzsche, Hegel, Heidegger, Gramsci, Walter Benjamin, Foucault, De Man — they're all totalitarians." (30) He also argues that "there has been a great intellectual degeneracy in the Left since the days when they just believed the source of all evil was private property. . . . Now that Marxism is gone, the Left owes far more of its intellectual roots to Mussolini than anyplace else. Today's socialism is based on the group. It's a reactionary, status-seeking ideology. Everybody is identified by their race, gender, class and sexual orientation. For Mussolini and Hitler it was the nation or an ethnic body. . . . These people begin by being alienated, hostile, angry, and at war with the system. Their intellectual doctrine is a war doctrine. They're very dangerous, and they're all over the place." (31)

12 David W. Murray, "Poor Suffering Bastards: An Anthropologist Looks at Illegitimacy," *Policy Review* 68 (spring 1994): 10.

13 Jacqueline Rose, *Why War? Psychoanalysis, Politics, and the Return to Melanie Klein* (Cambridge, MA: Blackwell, 1993). This point will be developed more fully in the last chapter.

14 Quoted in Angela Davis, *Women, Race, and Class* (New York: Vintage, 1983) 209.

15 A psychoanalytic case study by Joan Rivière that has been a central text in feminist theory, film theory, and theories of performance has never received the analysis it deserves in terms of the construction of whiteness. While the analysand constructed ways to challenge masculine privilege by means of strategies of masquerade, another fantasy accompanied her gender rebellion: she also dreamed of being raped by a black man and turning him over to the authorities. "Womanliness as a Masquerade," *International Journal of Psychoanalysis* 10 (1929): 303–13.

16 This rhetorical move, in which Gilder equates all quantitative economists and sociologists with all intellectuals and labels them all leftists, shows the logical frame in which he works. He does not argue according to evidence but according to the emotional impact of familiarity, whose impact is recorded when the audience recognizes their own "common sense" in his statements.

17 *The American Heritage Dictionary,* New College ed., s.v. "clear."

18 See Nancy Ammerman's *Baptist Battles: Social Change and Religious Conflict in the Southern Baptist Convention* (New Brunswick: Rutgers UP, 1990).

19 Samuel Francis, "Baptist Apology Signals Western Decline," *Washington Times,* natl. weekly ed., 3–9 July 1995: 30.

20   Joyce Bentson, letter, *Christianity Today* 39.3 (6 March 1995) 6.
21   Michele le Doeuff, *Hipparchia's Choice: An Essay Concerning Women, Philosophy, etc.*, trans. Trista Selous (Cambridge, MA: Blackwell, 1991) 313.

6   Riding the Entrepreneurial Frontier

1   Robert Zubrin, "A New Martian Frontier: Recapturing the Soul of America," *American Civilization: A Newspaper of Progress and Freedom* 1.2 (January 1995): 1.
2   I am grateful to Suzanne Clark, who reminded me of this.
3   Michael Rogin, *Ronald Reagan, the Movie and Other Episodes in Political Demonology* (Berkeley: U of California P, 1987) xiii.
4   The controversy over revisionist history that conflicts with popular history is familiar, repeated in the Smithsonian's treatment of the bombing of Hiroshima and Nagasaki, and in the debate over history standards in school reform. I am grateful to Jean Beck for her insights about Turner's thesis and the history of the West.
5   Garry Wills's dissection of the contradictions and inaccuracies in history professor Newt Gingrich's version of history illustrates the point Limerick makes about Turner's thesis. In some ways, it does not matter that Gingrich is wrong, because of the more influential fact that he is attuned to popular versions of American history. See Wills's "The Visionary," *New York Review of Books* 42.5 (23 March 1995): 4–8.
6   Richard White, "Frederick Jackson Turner and Buffalo Bill," in *The Frontier in American Culture,* ed. James Grossman (Berkeley: U of California P with Newberry Library, 1994) 45. The volume also includes Patricia Nelson Limerick's "The Adventure of the Frontier in the Twentieth Century."
      Grossman's introduction divides this cultural representation according to two epigrams: "The existence of an area of free land, its continuous recession, and the advance of American settlement westward, explain American development" (Turner); and "The bullet is the pioneer of civilization, for it has gone hand in hand with the axe that cleared the forest, and with the family Bible and school book" (Cody), n.p.
7   Jeffrey A. Eisenach and Albert Stephen Hanser, eds., *Readings in Renewing American Civilization* (New York: McGraw, 1993) v.
8   Newt Gingrich, "Introduction to Renewing American Civilization," *Readings in Renewing American Civilization* 1.
9   Stephen R. Covey and Keith Gulledge, "Personal Strength in American Culture," *Readings in Renewing American Civilization* 23. Covey, a member of the Mormon faith, has written a best-selling book, *Seven Habits of Highly Effective People* (New York: Simon, 1989), which is an example of the complexity of these issues. It is a helpful guide for organizing your life by situating work responsibilities in relation to your ethics and personal life; it does not simply give you advice about organizing your work life and expect you to squeeze everything else in last. I have given copies of it to my sons as well as to other friends, and none of us think of ourselves as religious. However, we are all ethical and responsible people caught in a thoroughly fragmented information society in which time has sped up in frightening ways. The value of ordering a postmodern life that is too fragmented and full of information is obvious, but this kind of ordering need not be absolutist. The issue, as always, is not whether or

not this sense of faith can provide a valuable meditative center to people's lives; after all, philosophy itself works on the model of providing some sense of meaning to fragmentation, as does art, which needs an organizing idea. The question is, rather, in whose hands and for what ends is the organization of meaning being exploited, and, most dangerously, who is excluded from its terms when it is made absolute?

10 George Gilder, "America's Entrepreneurial Spirit," *Readings in Renewing American Civilization* 59.

11 "Victim Victorious," *Village Voice* 7 March 1995: 31–33.

12 Arianna Huffington, "Twelve Steps to Cultural Renewal," *Readings in Renewing American Civilization* 218.

13 Huffington takes that further: "The Welfare State may insulate the individual from responsibility and choice, but it is the state of our *culture* that alienates him from so much more: his fellow man, his purpose, and his God.

"Adam Smith wrote *The Wealth of Nations*. But he also wrote another book, a much earlier book, entitled *The Theory of Moral Sentiments*. He would have been shocked by the suggestion that one could have the economic liberalism of *The Wealth of Nations* without the moral underpinning for society reflected in his other work." (221)

14 "We need to address head-on the crisis of meaning in our culture and, at the same time, reject the caricature of the American Dream as the two-car family with a time-share in the country. That is not a *dream,* it is an advertisement. And as a central idea, it is no more compelling than brand-name loyalty." (221)

15 "It is the critical step in all recovery programs. It is the slap in the face of secularism. It is, in a sense, the *first* step, the foundation to all understanding of our world and our place in it." (221)

16 "But we need to do more than snipe at television sitcoms or rap lyrics. We need to build the counterculture. We need to build our own city shining on a hill. In short, we need a new vision for our culture rather than a mere distaste for the one we see about us." (224)

17 Rush Limbaugh, "Why Liberals Fear Me," *Policy Review* 70 (fall 1994): 4. Subsequent citations are identified by *PR*.

18 Margaret Morse makes this argument in terms of popular culture in "The Ontology of Everyday Distraction: The Freeway, the Mall, Television," *Logics of Television: Essays in Cultural Criticism,* ed. Patricia Mellencamp (Bloomington: Indiana UP, 1990) 193–221.

19 Rush Limbaugh, *See, I Told You So* (New York: Pocket Star, 1994) xviii. Subsequent citations are identified by page number only.

20 Klaus Mann, *Mephisto,* trans. Robin Smyth (New York: Penguin, 1986). The book was made into a movie by the Hungarian director Istvan Szabo and a play by the French director and playwright Arianne Mnouchkine and the Théâtre du Soleil in Paris.

7 God's Intentions for the Multinational Corporation: Seeing Reality True

1 This activity has been traced in detail by Sara Diamond in *Spiritual Warfare: The Politics of the Christian Right* (Boston: South End, 1989) and *Roads to Dominion: Right-Wing Movements and Political Power in the United States* (New York: Guilford, 1995). See

also Sara Diamond, "Holy Warriors," NACLA: *Report on the Americas* (September/October 1988): 28–37.

2   See Sara Diamond, "Holy Warriors," NACLA: *Report on the Americas* (September/October 1988): 28–37. She describes the Global Mapping Project, which was one result of the Lausanne focus on global evangelizing. Ralph Winter founded the U.S. Center for World Missions, which he refers to as his "Missions Pentagon," in Pasadena, California, in 1975. At the Center, he developed a computer data bank to bring together field data from U.S. missions agencies, including the Wycliffe Bible Translators and World Vision, and to make available the latest statistics on "the language, culture, political attitudes and natural resources of ethnic groups from Papua New Guinea to the Amazon jungles." (31)

While mainstream missionary work by the liberal National Council of Churches dropped precipitously in the 1970s, the combination of social science and evangelical outreach in activities such as Winter's grew, often connected to counterinsurgency efforts. Diamond quotes *Christianity Today,* which reports that in 1975,

> between 10 and 25 percent of America's 35,000 Protestant and 7,000 foreign missionaries have given information to intelligence authorities. . . . The average would be higher among missionaries serving in rural areas—where reliable information is hard to come by—and in places where there is social and political unrest; lower among missionaries in urban areas, where information is readily obtainable. (32)

3   Fredric Jameson, "Postmodernism and the Market," *Mapping Ideology,* ed. Slavoj Žižek (New York: Verso, 1994) 281.

4   The Heritage Foundation would no doubt quarrel with AEI's description. It, too, claims to be the most widely cited think tank in the country. Heritage is often considered to be the most influential of conservative think tanks, having conducted the initiation sessions for newly elected Republican members of Congress in 1994. It was founded by Paul Weyrich, who is Eastern Orthodox. He then went on to found the Free Congress Foundation and the right-wing cable TV channel National Empowerment Television. Joseph Coors is often called the cofounder of Heritage, because of his contribution of funding. Richard Mellon Scaife has also contributed heavily to the foundation, as have other corporate donors, including some from South Korea and Taiwan, though information about those donors is rarely made available. Among its fellows have been the ubiquitous Dinesh D'Souza, Jack Kemp, and William Bennett.

Norman Solomon quotes two vice presidents of the foundation, Stuart Butler and Kim Holmes, from its 1995 annual report:

> Butler: Heritage now works very closely with the congressional leadership. . . . Heritage has been involved in crafting almost every piece of major legislation to move through Congress.
>
> Holmes: Without exaggeration, I think we've in effect become Congress's unofficial research arm. . . . We truly have become an extension of the congressional staff, but on our own terms and according to our own agenda.
>
> Butler: . . . There has also been an unprecedented demand on us to "crunch the numbers" for the new congressional leadership.

In many cases, Heritage has drafted the actual policy language of proposed legislation, and it carries out an ongoing propaganda campaign in the interests of corporations and in opposition to social justice issues. This takes the form of op-ed pieces, press releases, position papers, news conferences, and seminars, often aired on C-SPAN. Norman Solomon, "The Media's Favorite Think Tank: How the Heritage Foundation Turns Money into Media," *Extra! The Magazine of* FAIR 9.4 (July/August 1996): 9–12.

5   AEI's research arms include three divisions: economic policy studies, social and political studies, and defense and foreign policy studies. The following is a sample of the projects, which include research, seminars, and publications, included under those rubrics: Understanding Economic Inequality; Tax Reform, Social Security, and Entitlements Reform; Health, Safety, and Environmental Regulation; Economic Deregulation; Health Policy; International Trade; The Science Enterprise; White-Collar Crime; The Intellectual Foundations; American Politics and Political Institutions; Child and Family Welfare; Culture and Race; Religion, Capitalism, and Democracy; Fundamental Reform of the U.S. Defense Structure; Redefining American Foreign Policy; The New Atlantic Initiative; Asian Studies; Other Area Studies: Russia, Europe, and Latin America.

6   Michael Novak, *This Hemisphere of Liberty: A Philosophy of the Americas* (Washington: AEI, 1992) viii. Subsequent references will be abbreviated as *THL*.

7   Eric Hobsbawn, *The Age of Extremes: A History of the World, 1914–1991* (New York: Pantheon, 1994) 571. He adds this footnote: "The examples of successful export-led Third World industrialization usually quoted — Hong Kong, Singapore, Taiwan and South Korea — represent less than 2 per cent of the Third World population."

8   Michael Novak, *Toward a Theology of the Corporation* (1981; Washington: AEI, 1990) 44. Subsequent references will be abbreviated as *TTC*.

9   William Greider, *Who Will Tell the People: The Betrayal of American Democracy* (New York: Touchstone, 1992) 348. See especially chapter 15, "Citizen GE."

10   Jacqueline Rose makes this argument in relation to Thatcherism in chapter 2, "Margaret Thatcher and Ruth Ellis," in *Why War? Psychoanalysis, Politics, and the Return to Melanie Klein* (Cambridge, MA: Blackwell, 1993).

11   Novak is pluralistic in arguing, unlike some others of the religious Right, that ethical economic activity must include Christians, Jews, Muslims, atheists, and others.

12   Blaise Pascal, quoted by Slavoj Žižek, "How Did Marx Invent the Symptom?" *Mapping Ideology*, ed. Slavoj Žižek (New York: Verso, 1994) 318.

13   The ad was featured on the inside front cover of *Christianity Today* 26 April 1993. This is the rest of the text:

When it comes to the difference between The Founders Inn and the average run-of-the-mill hotel, there's more than meets the eye. Far beyond our beautiful appearance are all the unexpected extras you'll have to see to appreciate.

You won't find cookie-cutter guest rooms here. There are no ho-hum items on our restaurant menu. And there's no excuse not to exercise in our ultra-modern fitness center.

. . . Just a short drive away are the beaches and historic Williamsburg. But you don't have to leave the hotel to have fun. You can enjoy our own dinner theatre, or join us in the nearby CBN studios to watch a live production of "The 700 Club."

14   Regent University, *Graduate Catalog: 1994–96* (Virginia Beach: Regent University, 1994) 4.

8   Warriors and Babies

1   Quoted in Eric L. Santner, *Stranded Objects: Mourning, Memory, and Film in Postwar Germany* (Ithaca: Cornell UP, 1990) 158.

2   The rhetoric of war also framed the play war games of Newt Gingrich, whose leadership models are based on the German Wehrmacht's understandings of the need to win battles by controlling communication. Connie Bruck makes this argument in "The Politics of Perception," *New Yorker* 9 October 1995: 50–77.

3   Robert Timberg, *The Nightingale's Song* (New York: Simon and Schuster, 1995) 85.

4   Timberg describes a conversation between Bud Day and John McCain while they were in prison. It suggests how the terrain of real American identity was being formed: "Dr. Spock, Dave Dellinger, every wacko that had ever come down the pike and hated the country was on gook radio telling you how bad the United States was and how great Communism was. We would talk about the fact that there was no punishment that would adequately deal with these kinds of scuzz that are eating your country, taking all the benefits, and then tearing it apart from the inside." (122)

5   James William Gibson, *Warrior Dreams: Paramilitary Culture in Post-Vietnam America* (New York: Hill and Wang, 1994) 9.

6   Barbara Ehrenreich, foreword, *Male Fantasies Vol. 1: Women, Floods, Bodies, History*, by Klaus Theweleit (Minneapolis: U of Minnesota P, 1987) ix.

7   Brown had been a lieutenant in the army, a part of the Counterintelligence Corps, and a graduate student in political science at Boulder. He had also once tried to join the forces of Che Guevara, most likely as a counterinsurgent, then helped train Cuban exiles. As Gibson argues about SOF's readership, "more than half of the readers had at least some college education, and many were college graduates or held postgraduate degrees. About half were married. . . . And they liked guns, each spending over $1,000 a year on firearms and accessories." (148)

8   Forty-three people participated in this session, including eight members of a United States Marine Corps urban warfare battalion training to retake buildings from terrorists; two Marine machine gunners; three plainsclothes security agents and weapons instructors from the Department of Energy, who guarded nuclear weapons and radioactive materials shipped in unmarked trucks; a married couple who were members of the Los Angeles Police Department, one a member of a gang surveillance unit, the other a narcotics squad detective; a number of ordinary civilians (no survivalists), including a college student, two physicians, one of whom brought along his long-haired son, who was studying music at the University of California at San Diego; and a retired elementary school teacher and librarian from Wyoming. (175–76)

9   On the wall of the cinder-block classroom of Cooper's API, better known as Gunsite Ranch, was taped "A Reactionary Manifesto," which read, "Let us put women back on a pedestal, sex back in the bedroom, obscenity back in the outhouse, perversion back in the closet, murderers back on the gallows, education back in the schools, gold back in the money, America back on top." (174)

10 *U.S. Taxpayers Party Wisconsin Convention, May 27–28,* videotape, Public Policy Institute, Planned Parenthood Federation of America, 1994.

11 Sandi DuBowski and John Goetz, "Bushwhacked! The USTP and the Far Right," *Front Lines Research* 1.3 (November 1994): 1.

12 Jonathan Hutson, "Operation Rescue Founder Predicts Armed Conflict, Part II," *Front Lines Research* 1.5 (May 1995): 1.

13 Environmentalist concerns about nature are, in this paranoid view, indistinguishable from the monstrous state's totalitarianism. As a result, because the state attempts to protect nature, it also claims to *be* nature. Not only does it deify both itself and nature, it also elevates the community in collusion against the lone individual: "Philosophically, the deified state, organized by an elite, is nature. Theirs is a closed system of mutual, though stagnant, protection. What they see as the interconnectedness between animals (including humans), insects, birds, and all of the cosmos is a putrefying, closed system. In such a closed and decaying system, the *community* is exalted and made sacrosanct; whereas the *individual person* is debased and diminished." (110)

14 This new threat is even greater than the old conspiracy. Marrs cites Charles A. Provan, M.D., of the American Freedom Movement: "It used to be that we had to put up with the tuxedoed Council on Foreign Relations, Trilaterial Commission, New World Order, and Internationalists. Now we've got to put up with the red hot *Revolutionaries* in the driver's seat!" (78, his italics).

15 Cindy Weeks, "Lynn Minton Reports: Fresh Voices: Do You Believe in God? Readers Respond," *Parade Magazine* 11 June 1995: 10.

16 Julia Kristeva, *Tales of Love,* trans. Leon S. Roudiez (New York: Columbia UP, 1987) 5.

17 Kristeva suggests that part of this horror has to do with the fantasized death and decay associated with the feminine, "a panic hallucination of the inside's destruction . . . of an interiorization of death following the abolishment of limits and differences." Julia Kristeva, *Powers of Horror: An Essay on Abjection,* trans. Leon S. Roudiez (New York: Columbia UP, 1982) 159.

18 Jacques Lacan, "Aggressivity in Psychoanalysis," *Ecrits: A Selection,* trans. Alan Sheridan (New York: Norton, 1977) 11.

19 Barbara Johnson, "Apostrophe, Animation, and Abortion," *Diacritics* 16.1 (spring 1986): 38.

20 Randy Alcorn, *Pro-Life Answers to Pro-Choice Arguments* (Portland, OR: Multnomah, 1992) 148.

21 Jessica Shaver, *Gianna: Aborted and Lived to Tell about It* (Colorado Springs: Focus on the Family, 1995) 70, quoting the *Orange County Register.*

22 Sandi DuBowski, "Human Life International: Promoting Uncivilization," *Front Lines Research* 1.5 (May 1995): 10–11. *Front Lines Research* is the research publication of Planned Parenthood.

23 Quoted from Marx's *The Apostle of Life* in Karen Branan and Frederick Clarkson, "Extremism in Sheep's Clothing," *Front Lines Research* 1.1 (June 1994): 3.

24 Marx also writes this in his book, *Confessions of a Prolife Missionary:* "Notice how many Jews led the infamous 1971 abortion-planning meeting in Los Angeles, which I exposed . . . note the large number of abortionists (consult the Yellow Pages) and pro-abortion medical professors who are Jewish." (quoted in Branan and Clarkson 1)

25 Many antiabortion groups repudiate Marx and HLI, which is referred to by Msgr. George G. Higgins as a divisive force in both the pro-life movement and the Catholic Church. He describes HLI as engaging in "anti-Semitic imagery that has been clearly condemned by the church." Quoted in "FLR Update," *Front Lines Research* 1.5 (May 1995): 3.

26 Jacques Derrida, *The Ear of the Other: Otobiography, Transference, Translation* (New York: Schocken, 1985) 35.

SELECTED BIBLIOGRAPHY

Alcorn, Randy. *Pro-Life Answers to Pro-Choice Arguments*. Portland, OR: Multnomah, 1992.

Ammerman, Nancy. *Baptist Battles: Social Change and Religious Conflict in the Southern Baptist Convention*. New Brunswick: Rutgers UP, 1990.

——. "North American Protestant Fundamentalism." *Fundamentalisms Observed*. Vol. 2. Ed. Martin E. Marty and R. Scott Appleby. Chicago: U of Chicago P, 1991. 1–65.

Aronowitz, Stanley. "Toward Radicalism: The Death and Rebirth of the American Left." *Social Text,* no. 44 (fall/winter 1995): 69–95.

Badcock, Christopher. *Evolution and Human Behavior: An Introduction to Human Sociobiology*. Oxford: Basil Blackwell, 1991.

Barton, David. *America's Godly Heritage*. Videotape. Aledo, TX: WallBuilders, 1992.

——. *The Myth of Separation: What Is the Correct Relationship between Church and State?* Aledo, TX: WallBuilders, 1993.

Bellant, Russ. "Mania in the Stadia: The Origins and Goals of Promise Keepers." *Front Lines Research* 1.5 (May 1995): 7–9.

Bendroth, Margaret Lamberts. *Fundamentalism and Gender: 1875 to the Present*. New Haven: Yale UP, 1993.

Benjamin, Walter. *The Origin of German Tragic Drama*. Trans. John Osborne. London: New Left, 1977.

Bentson, Joyce. Letter. *Christianity Today* 39.3 (May 1995): 6.

Boone, Wellington. "Why Men Must Pray," *Seven Promises of a Promise Keeper* 25–31.

Boston, Robert. *The Most Dangerous Man in America? Pat Robertson and the Rise of the Christian Coalition*. Washington: Americans United for Separation of Church and State, 1996.

——. "Stacked Deck." *Church and State* 49.7 (July/August 1996): 4–10.

Bradley, Jennifer. "At Bay." *New Republic* 22 January 1996: 20.

Branan, Karen, and Frederick Clarkson. "Extremism in Sheep's Clothing." *Front Lines Research* 1.1 (June 1994): 1–7.

Break Down the Walls: Post Conference Highlight Video. Videotape. Denver: Promise Keepers, 1996.

Bright, Bill. *The Coming Revival: America's Call to Fast, Pray, and Seek God's Face.* Orlando: New Life, 1995.

Bronson, Po. "George Gilder: Does He Really Think Scarcity Is a Minor Obstacle on the Road to Techno-Utopia? (And Would He Please Stop Talking about Race and Gender?)." *Wired* 4.3 (1 March 1996): 122–30.

Bruck, Connie. "The Politics of Perception." *New Yorker* 9 October 1995: 50–77.

Cassidy, John. "Who Killed the Middle Class?" *New Yorker* 16 October 1995: 113–24.

Clark, Suzanne. *Sentimental Modernism: Women Writers and the Revolution of the Word.* Bloomington: Indiana UP, 1991.

Colson, Charles. *The Body: Being Light in Darkness.* Dallas: Word, 1992.

Conason, Joe, Alfred Ross, and Lee Cokorinos. "The Promise Keepers Are Coming: The Third Wave of the Religious Right." *The Nation* 263.10 (7 October 1996): 12–19.

Concerned Women for America. *History Video.* Purchased at Concerned Women for America national convention, Alexandria, VA, 1995.

——. "Opportunities for Leadership in Concerned Women for America," *Leadership Manual.* Concerned Women for America, 1994.

——. *Training Manual.* Concerned Women for America, 1994.

Contract with the American Family. Nashville: Moorings, 1995.

The Covert Crusade: The Christian Right and Politics in the West. Portland, OR: Western States Center and Coalition for Human Dignity, 1993.

Covey, Stephen R. *The Seven Habits of Highly Effective People.* New York: Simon and Schuster, 1989.

Covey, Stephen R., and Keith Gulledge. "Personal Strength in American Culture." *Readings in Renewing American Civilization.* 23–57.

Curtis, Carolyn. "High Tech Activists: How Advanced Communications Are Changing the Way Pro-Family Advocates Work." *Christian American* 6.8 (October 1995): 20–23.

Dale, Edwin L., Jeffrey A. Eisenach, Frank I. Luntz, Timothy J. Muris, and William Schneider Jr. *The People's Budget: A Common Sense Plan for Shrinking the Government in Washington.* Foreword by John Kasich. Washington: Regnery, 1995.

Davis, Angela. *Women, Race, and Class.* New York: Vintage, 1983.

De Lauretis, Teresa. *Alice Doesn't: Feminism, Semiotics, Cinema.* Bloomington: Indiana UP, 1987.

Derrida, Jacques. *The Ear of the Other: Otobiography, Transference, Translation.* New York: Schocken, 1985.

Diamond, Sara. "Holy Warriors." NACLA: *Report on the Americas* (September/October 1988): 28–37.

——. *Roads to Dominion: Right-Wing Movements and Political Power in the United States.* New York: Guilford, 1995.

——. *Spiritual Warfare: The Politics of the Christian Right.* Boston: South End, 1989.

du Bois, Page. *Centaurs and Amazons: The Pre-History of the Great Chain of Being.* Ann Arbor: U of Michigan P, 1982.

DuBowski, Sandi. "Human Life International: Promoting Uncivilization." *Front Lines Research* 1.5 (May 1995): 10–11.

DuBowski, Sandi, and John Goetz. "Bushwhacked! The USTP and the Far Right." *Front Lines Research* 1.3 (November 1994): 1–6.

Edsall, Thomas Byrne, and Mary D. Edsall. "When the Official Subject Is Presidential Politics, Taxes, Welfare, Crime, Rights, or Values the Real Subject Is Race." *Atlantic Monthly* 267.5 (May 1991): 53–86.

Ehrenreich, Barbara. Foreword. *Male Fantasies Vol. 1: Women, Floods, Bodies, History,* by Klaus Theweleit. Minneapolis: U of Minnesota P, 1987: ix–xxiii.

Eisenach, Jeffrey A., and Albert Stephen Hanser, eds. *Readings in Renewing American Civilization.* New York: McGraw, 1993.

Eisler, Peter. "Conservatives Go Behind Closed Doors." *USA Today* 9 August 1996, 2A.

Elizabeth Dole: Personal Testimony, Christian Coalition. Videotape. Christian Coalition, 1994.

Ericson, Edward, Jr. "Behind Closed Doors at the CNP." *Church and State* 49.6 (June 1996): 4–7.

Evans, Tony. "Sexual Purity." *Seven Promises of a Promise Keeper.* 73–81.

Eyer, Diane. *Mother-Infant Bonding: A Scientific Fiction.* New Haven: Yale UP, 1992.

Fournier, Keith. "Faith and Culture: Defining and Defending the Family." *Casenote: The American Center for Law and Justice* 2.6 (1995): 4.

———. *Religious Cleansing in the American Republic.* Washington: Life, Liberty, and Family, 1993.

Francis, Samuel. "Baptist Apology Signals Western Decline." *Washington Times,* natl. weekly ed. 3–9 July 1995, 30.

Galbreath, Edward. "Manhood's Great Awakening." *Christianity Today* 39.2 (6 February 1995): 21–28.

Gardiner, Steve L. "The One-World Conspiracy." *Dignity Report* 3.1 (winter 1995): 18–20.

———. "Promises to Keep: The Christian Right Men's Movement." *Dignity Report* 3.4 (fall 1996): 1–9.

———. *Rolling Back Civil Rights: The Oregon Citizens' Alliance at Religious War.* Portland, OR: Coalition for Human Dignity, 1992.

The Gay Agenda in Public Education. Videotape. Report, 1993.

George, Timothy. "What We Mean When We Say It's True." *Christianity Today* 39.12 (23 October 1995): 17–21.

Gerson, Mark. "Battler for the Republic: Irving Kristol's Terrible Swift Pen." *Policy Review* 62 (fall 1992): 50–57.

Gibson, James William. *Warrior Dreams: Paramilitary Culture in Post-Vietnam America.* New York: Hill and Wang, 1994.

Gilder, George. "America's Entrepreneurial Spirit." *Readings in Renewing American Civilization.* 59–79.

———. "End Welfare Reform As We Know It." *American Spectator* 28.6 (June 1995): 24–27.

———. *Men and Marriage.* Gretna, LA: Pelican, 1993.

Gingrich, Newt. "Introduction to Renewing American Civilization." *Readings in Renewing American Civilization.* 1–22.

Goldman, Marion. "Continuity in Collapse: Departures from Shiloh." *Journal for the Scientific Study of Religion* 34 (1994): 342–53.

———. "What Oregon's New Religions Bring to the Mainstream." *Oregon Humanities* summer 1994: 31–34.

Goldwin, Robert A., and William A. Schambra, eds. *How Capitalistic Is the Constitution?* Washington: AEI, 1982.

Greider, William. *Who Will Tell the People: The Betrayal of American Democracy.* New York: Touchstone, 1992.

Griffin, Jasper. "New Heaven, New Earth." Review of *Cosmos, Chaos, and the World to Come: The Ancient Roots of Apocalyptic Faith,* by Norman Cohn. *New York Review of Books* 41.21 (22 December 1994): 23–28.

Griffith, Stephen, and Bill Deckard. *What Makes a Man a Man? Twelve Promises That Will Change Your Life.* Colorado Springs: NavPress, 1993.

Groothuis, Rebecca Merrill. *The Culture War between Traditionalism and Feminism.* Grand Rapids: Baker, 1994.

Grossberg, Lawrence. *We Gotta Get Out of This Place: Popular Conservatism and Postmodern Culture.* New York: Routledge, 1992.

Grossman, James, ed. *The Frontier in American Culture.* Berkeley: U of California P with Newberry Library, 1994.

Hagee, John. *Bible Positions on Political Issues.* San Antonio: John Hagee and Global Evangelism Television, 1992.

Hardisty, Jean. "Kitchen Table Backlash: The Anti-Feminist Women's Movement." *Public Eye* 10.2 (summer 1996): 1–11.

Hart, Archibald D. *The Sexual Man: Masculinity without Guilt.* Dallas: Word, 1994.

Hart, Lynda. *Fatal Woman: Lesbian Sexuality and the Mark of Aggression.* Princeton: Princeton UP, 1994.

Helvarg, David. *The War against the Greens.* San Francisco: Sierra Club, 1994.

Hendricks, Howard G. "A Mandate for Mentoring." *Seven Promises of a Promise Keeper.* 47–55.

Hickey, Elizabeth. "Mrs. Family Values: Beverly LaHaye Leads Her Army of Concerned Women into the Conservative Fray." *Washington Times* 29 July 1992, sec. E: 1.

Hoberman, J. "Victim Victorious." *Village Voice* 7 March 1995: 31–33.

Hobsbawm, Eric. *The Age of Extremes: A History of the World, 1914–1991.* New York: Pantheon, 1994.

Horkheimer, Max, and Theodor W. Adorno. *Dialectic of Enlightenment.* Trans. John Cumming. New York: Seabury, 1972.

Horner, Bo, Ron Ralston, and David Sunde. *Applying the Seven Promises.* Colorado Springs: Focus on the Family, 1996.

Horowitz, David. "Socialism: Dead or Alive? A Roundtable Discussion." *American Enterprise* (July/August 1995): 28–35.

Huffington, Arianna. "Twelve Steps to Cultural Renewal." *Readings in Renewing American Civilization.* 217–26.

Human Life International. Information packet. Gaithersburg, MD: HLI 1994.

Hunter, Allen. "Children in the Service of Conservatism: Parent-Child Relations in the New Right's Pro-Family Rhetoric." *Legal History Program: Working Papers,* series 2. Madison: Institute for Legal Studies, 1988. 2–8.

Hutson, Jonathan. "Operation Rescue Founder Predicts Armed Conflict, Part II." *Front Lines Research* 1.5 (May 1995): 1–5.

Isaacs, Susan. "The Nature and Function of Fantasy." *International Journal of Psychoanalysis* 29.2 (1948): 73–97.

James, Kay Coles. "Changing the Culture of America." *Regent University Impact* 4.3 (August 1994): 4–5.

———. *Never Forget*. Grand Rapids: Zondervan, 1992.

Jameson, Fredric. "Postmodernism and the Market." *Mapping Ideology*. Ed. Slavoj Žižek. New York: Verso, 1994. 278–95.

Johnson, Barbara. "Apostrophe, Animation, and Abortion." *Diacritics* 16.1 (spring 1986): 24–39.

Johnson, Hans. "Broken Promises." *Church and State* 48.5 (May 1995): 9–12.

Kristeva, Julia. *Maladies of the Soul*. Trans. Ross Guberman. New York: Columbia UP, 1995.

———. "Place Names." *Desire in Language: A Semiotic Approach to Literature and Art*. Ed. Leon S. Roudiez. New York: Columbia UP, 1980. 271–94.

———. *Powers of Horror: An Essay on Abjection*. Trans. Leon S. Roudiez. New York: Columbia UP, 1982.

———. *Tales of Love*. Trans. Leon S. Roudiez. New York: Columbia UP, 1987.

———. "Women's Time." *Signs* 7.1 (autumn 1981): 13–35.

Lacan, Jacques. *Ecrits: A Selection*. Trans. Alan Sheridan. New York: Norton, 1977.

LaHaye, Beverly. *The Desires of a Woman's Heart*. Wheaton, IL: Tyndale, 1993.

———. Fundraising letter. May 1995.

———. *Who But a Woman? Concerned Women Can Make a Difference*. Nashville: Thomas Nelson, 1984.

LaHaye, Tim, and Beverly LaHaye. *The Act of Marriage: The Beauty of Sexual Love*. Grand Rapids: Zondervan, 1995.

Le Doeuff, Michele. *Hipparchia's Choice: An Essay Concerning Women, Philosophy, etc*. Trans. Trista Selous. Cambridge, MA: Blackwell, 1991.

Lewis, Roger K. "Grated Areas: Start of New Middle Ages." *Washington Post* 9 September 1995, 1E.

Limbaugh, Rush. *See, I Told You So*. New York: Pocket Star, 1994.

———. "Why Liberals Fear Me." *Policy Review* 70 (fall 1994): 4–11.

Limerick, Patricia Nelson. "The Adventure of the Frontier in the Twentieth Century." *The Frontier in American Culture*. Ed. James Grossman. Berkeley: U of California P with Newberry Library, 1994. 67–102.

Lind, Michael. "The Southern Coup: The South, the GOP, and America." *New Republic* 19 June 1995: 20–29.

Live Worship with Promise Keepers and the Maranatha! Promise Band. Videotape. Laguna Hills, CA: Maranatha! Music, 1996.

Maclean, Nancy. "White Women and Klan Violence in the 1920's: Agency, Complicity, and the Politics of Women's History." *Gender and History* 3.3 (1991): 285–303.

Mann, Klaus. *Mephisto*. Trans. Robin Smyth. New York: Penguin, 1986.

Marrs, Texe. *Big Sister Is Watching You*. Austin: Living Truth, 1993.

———. *Flashpoint: A Newsletter Ministry of Texe Marrs*. May 1995.

Marshner, Connie. *Can Motherhood Survive? A Christian Looks at Social Parenting*. Brentwood, TN: Wolgemuth and Hyatt, 1990.

Marx, Paul. *Eight Reasons You Should Consider Having One More Child*. Gaithersburg, MD: Human Life International.

McCartney, Bill. "Seeking God's Favor." *Seven Promises of a Promise Keeper.* 205–7.

Media and Spokesmanship with Rebecca Hagelin. Videotape. Christian Coalition Leadership School Video Training Series.

Minton, Lynn. "Lynn Minton Reports: Fresh Voices: Do You Believe in God? Readers Respond." *Parade Magazine* 11 June 1995: 10.

Morse, Margaret. "The Ontology of Everyday Distraction: The Freeway, the Mall, Television." *Logics of Television: Essays in Cultural Criticism.* Ed. Patricia Mellencamp. Bloomington: Bloomington UP, 1990. 193–221.

Mosse, George L. *Nationalism and Sexuality: Middle-Class Morality and Sexual Norms in Modern Europe.* Madison: U of Wisconsin P, 1985.

Murray, David W. "Poor Suffering Bastards: An Anthropologist Looks at Illegitimacy." *Policy Review* 68 (spring 1994): 9–15.

Neet, Loretta. Interview by Melissa Lippold. Videotape. 1993.

The Next Step: From the Stadium to the Small Group. Multimedia package including videotape, audiotape, and booklet. Boulder: Promise Keepers, 1995.

Toward American Renewal with Newt Gingrich. Videotape. Columbia, MD: Romano and Associates, 1995.

Nigro, Samuel A. "Male/Female Differences in Natural Law." St. Louis: Social Justice Review, 1993.

Noll, Mark. *The Scandal of the Evangelical Mind.* Grand Rapids: Eerdmans, 1994.

Noonan, Peggy. *What I Saw at the Revolution: A Political Life in the Reagan Era.* New York: Random, 1990.

Novak, Michael. *This Hemisphere of Liberty: A Philosophy of the Americas.* Washington: AEI, 1992.

———. *Toward a Theology of the Corporation.* 1981. Reprint, Washington: AEI, 1990.

O'Leary, Michael. *Arguing the Apocalypse: A Theory of Millennial Rhetoric.* New York: Oxford UP, 1994.

Pagels, Elaine. *The Origin of Satan.* New York: Random, 1995.

Parker, Star. *Commentaries of a Black Christian Conservative Radical Right-Wing Republican Woman.* Los Angeles: NFTA, 1994.

———. *A Culture of Dependency: The Morality of Welfare Reform.* Los Angeles: NFTA, 1994.

———. *The Killing of a Race: Abortion and the Black Community.* Los Angeles: NFTA, 1994.

———. *The State of Black America: Is It Too Late to Turn the Tide from Socialism?* Los Angeles: NFTA, 1994.

Peel, William Carr. *What God Does When Men Pray: A Small Group Discussion Guide.* Colorado Springs: NavPress, 1993.

Phelps, Kathy. "GOP Must Stand for What Is Right, or It Stands for Nothing." *Register Guard* [Eugene, OR] 14 April 1994, 13A.

Phillips, Kevin. *Arrogant Capital: Washington, Wall Street, and the Frustration of American Politics.* New York: Little, Brown, 1994.

Phillips, Randy. "Seize the Moment." *Seven Promises of a Promise Keeper.* 1–12.

"Policy Suggestions." *NWI Resource* 6.1 (spring 1995): 44–45.

Popcorn, Faith. *The Popcorn Report: Faith Popcorn on the Future of Your Company, Your World, Your Life.* New York: Doubleday, 1991.

Ramos, Tarso. "The Wise Use Radicals." *Western States Center News* 12 (fall 1995): 6–10.

Regent University. *Graduate Catalog: 1994–96*. Virginia Beach: Regent University, 1994.

Reich, Robert. *The Work of Nations: Preparing Ourselves for 21st-Century Capitalism*. New York: Knopf, 1991.

Rice, Charles. *Fifty Questions on the Natural Law: What It Is and Why We Need It*. San Francisco: Ignatius, 1993.

Ridgeway, James, and Susan Monaco. "It's the Economy, Stupid." *Village Voice* 25 June 1996: 22–24.

Rivière, Joan. "Womanliness as a Masquerade." *International Journal of Psychoanalysis* 10 (1929): 303–13.

Robertson, Pat. *The New World Order*. Dallas: Word, 1991.

———. "Ask Pat." *Christian American* 5.8 (October 1995): 16.

Rogin, Michael. *Ronald Reagan, the Movie: and Other Episodes in Political Demonology*. Berkeley: U of California P, 1987.

Rose, Jacqueline. *Why War? Psychoanalysis, Politics, and the Return to Melanie Klein*. Cambridge, MA: Blackwell, 1993.

Santner, Eric L. *Stranded Objects: Mourning, Memory, and Film in Postwar Germany*. Ithaca: Cornell UP, 1990.

Sekulow, Jay. "Time to Defend the Family." *Casenote: The American Center for Law and Justice* 2.6 (1995): 2–3.

Seven Promises of a Promise Keeper. Colorado Springs: Focus on the Family, 1994.

Shaver, Jessica. *Gianna: Aborted and Lived to Tell about It*. Colorado Springs: Focus on the Family, 1995.

The Silent Scream. Videotape. Cleveland: American Portrait Films International, 1984.

Silverman, Kaja. *Male Subjectivity at the Margins*. New York: Routledge, 1992.

Solomon, Norman. "The Media's Favorite Think Tank: How the Heritage Foundation Turns Money into Media." *Extra! The Magazine of FAIR* 9.4 (July/August 1996): 9–12.

———. "What Crack? What Contras?" *Texas Observer* 88.21 (25 October 1996): 21.

Star Parker: National TV Appearances. Videotape. Los Angeles: Coalition on Urban Affairs.

Tenth Annual Concerned Women for America Convention, 1993: Saturday Evening Banquet and Keynote Address. Videotape. GV308.

Theweleit, Klaus. *Male Fantasies Vol. 1: Women, Floods, Bodies, History*. Minneapolis: U of Minnesota P, 1987.

Timberg, Robert. *The Nightingale's Song*. New York: Simon and Schuster, 1995.

Uscinski, Shelly A. *Winning as a Religious Conservative*. Videotape. Christian Coalition School Board Training Seminars, 1995.

U.S. Taxpayers Party Wisconsin Convention, May 27–28. Videotape. Public Policy Institute, Planned Parenthood Federation of America, 1994.

Wait for Me. Videotape. Concerned Women for America, 1993.

Weber, Linda. *Mom, You're Incredible!* Colorado Springs: Focus on the Family, 1994.

Weber, Stu. *Locking Arms: God's Design for Masculine Friendship*. Sisters, OR: Multnomah, 1995.

———. *Tender Warrior: God's Intention for a Man*. Sisters, OR: Multnomah, 1993.

Weeks, Cindy. "Lynn Minton Reports: Fresh Voices: Do You Believe in God? Readers Respond." *Parade Magazine* 11 June 1995: 10.

White, Richard. "Frederick Jackson Turner and Buffalo Bill." *The Frontier in American*

Culture. Ed. James Grossman. Berkeley: U of California P with Newberry Library, 1994. 7–65.

——. *"It's Your Misfortune and None of My Own": A New History of the American West*. Norman: U of Oklahoma P, 1991.

Wills, Gary. "The Visionary." *New York Review of Books* 42.5 (23 March 1995): 4–8.

Wuthnow, Robert. *Producing the Sacred: An Essay on Public Religion*. Urbana: Illinois UP, 1994.

——. *The Restructuring of American Religion: Society and Faith since World War II*. Princeton: Princeton UP, 1988.

——. *The Struggle for America's Soul: Evangelicals, Liberals, and Secularism*. Grand Rapids: Eerdmans, 1989.

Žižek, Slavoj. "How Did Marx Invent the Symptom?" *Mapping Ideology*. Ed. Slavoj Žižek. New York: Verso, 1994. 296–331.

Zoba, Wendy Murray. "When Manuscripts Collide: Why We Need the Behind-the-Translation Work of Textual Critics." *Christianity Today* 23 October 1995: 30–31.

Zubrin, Robert. "A New Martian Frontier: Recapturing the Soul of America." *American Civilization: A Newspaper of Progress and Freedom* 1.2 (January 1995): 1.

INDEX

Abortion, 15, 24, 83–84, 255–56, 263, 276n19; and anxiety, 266–71; and birth fantasy, 263–65, 293n17; and control of mother, 265, 269; and property rights, 98–99; and racism, 90–91; and sexual constitution, 177

Absolutism: and African Americans, 88, 90–91; and choice, 179; and Christian men's movement, 113–14, 121, 126–28; and gender difference, 127–28, 143; and intimacy, 37–39; and language, 181–83, 211; and liberal attacks, 74–75; and morality, 36–37, 50; and motherhood, 49–50; and popular culture, 76; and racism, 181–82; and sociobiology, 154. *See also* Certainty; Clarity; Resonance

ACLJ. *See under* Regent University

Activism, 11–12; and aggressiveness, 79–80; and church community, 78–79; and familiarity, 96; and family, 86–87; and fear, 87–88; and government positions, 86–87; grassroots, 78, 82–83, 86–87, 93; and intimacy, 77–78; and motherhood, 35–36, 86; and personal appearance, 19, 27–28, 100–4, 153, 271; and prayer, 82–84; and Republican Party, 36; and retirees, 83; as sacred duty, 12; in schools, 73–76; social reform movements, 78–79

Act of Marriage: The Beauty of Sexual Love, The (LaHaye and LaHaye), 11, 56, 62–68

AFDC (Aid to Families with Dependent Children), 43, 89

Affect, 17–18, 58–59, 61–62, 204

Affirmative action, 170, 179. *See also* Work

African Americans, 12, 276n24; and absolutism, 88, 90–91; and capitalism, 89–91; and Christian men's movement, 111–12, 283n1; conservative, 24, 84–91; and gender relations, 172

Ailes, Roger, 209

Allegory, 105, 262

Allen, George, 84

Althusser, Louis, 229

America: as exceptional, 193–94; and family values, 57; as innocent, 193, 207; and multiculturalism, 194–95; as performative, 192, 197–98, 211; popular sense of, 19–20, 277n3; and property, 18; Transparent American Subject, 25, 61, 211. *See also* Frontier mythology; Plain folks Americanism

American Coalition for Traditional Values (ACTV), 23

American Dream, 106–7, 289n14

American Enterprise Institute (AEI), 14, 217, 221, 291n5

American Pistol Institute (API), 252–53, 292n9

American Spectator, 143, 144

Ammerman, Nancy, 21

Anti-intellectualism, 26, 32, 178–81, 274n14, 287n11, 287n16

Linda Kintz is Associate Professor of English at the University of Oregon.

Library of Congress Cataloging-in-Publication Data
Kintz, Linda
Between Jesus and the market : the emotions that matter
in right-wing America / Linda Kintz.
Includes bibliographical references and index.
ISBN 0-8223-1959-4 (cloth : alk. paper).
— ISBN 0-8223-1967-5 (paper : alk. paper)
1. Evangelicalism — Political aspects — United States — History —
20th century. 2. Conservatism — United States — History — 20th century.
I. Title.
BR1642.U5K56   1997
320.5'5'097309049 — dc21   96-49941 CIP